THE INNER LIFE

Students of occultism—even those who have been students for many years—sometimes seem to fail to realize the Masters as they truly are. It has been often found people thinking of them as some kind of angels or devas, or, at any rate, as so far removed from us by their greatness that it is scarcely possible for us to derive much help from them. Their greatness is indisputable...

THE INNER LIFE

Charles W. Leadbeater

New Age Books

ISBN: 978-81-7822-316-2

First Indian Edition: Delhi, 2008

Sixth Printing: 1996

© 1978 The Theosophical Publishing House

Published by
NEW AGE BOOKS
A-44 Naraina Phase-I
New Delhi-110 028 (INDIA)
Email: nab@vsnl.in
Website: www.newagebooksindia.com

Printed in India
at Shri Jainendra Press
A-45 Naraina Phase-I, New Delhi-110 028

PUBLISHER'S NOTE

When it was decided to reprint this classic work as an abridgment and bind it into one volume, it was recognized that it would be a difficult and delicate chore; yet it was considered necessary to be able to offer THE INNER LIFE to a new generation of seekers and students of the Ancient Wisdom.

Fortunately we were able to enlist the considerable knowledge of a longtime student of Theosophy, Shirley Nicholson, as editor. Although such editing has been kept to a minimum—there were passages which virtually belonged together that were separated when it was a two-volume work—so there are several places where positioning has been altered in the combining of both books into one. Otherwise very few changes have been made other than the Americanizing of the spelling or modernizing phrases which would not be understood as well by today's readers. Therefore the abridgment of the original two-volume work is minimal with the exception of two sections that would not be directly relevant to the lay reader for which this special abridged edition was prepared.

CONTENTS

Section Three

The Theosophical Attitude

Section Four

The Higher Planes

Section Five

The Ego and His Vehicles

Section Six

The After-Death Life

Section Seven

Astral Work

Section Eight

The Mental Body and the Power of Thought

Section Nine

Psychic Faculties

Section Ten

Devas and Nature-Spirits

Section Eleven

Reincarnation

Section Twelve

Karma

FOREWORD TO THE INDIAN EDITION

Our evening "Talks" at the Theosophical Headquarters at Adyar have become quite an institution, and a very considerable amount of information, due to new research, often arising from some question put by a student, is given in this friendly and intimate circle. Our good Vice-President, Sir S. Subramania Iyer, found so much help and illumination from these talks, that he earnestly wished to share his pleasure with his brethren in the outer world, and gave a sum of money to help in their publication. I cordially endorse his view of their value, and commend this volume and those which will follow it to the earnest study of all our members.

Annie Besant

PREFACE TO AMERICAN EDITION, VOLUME I

I wish that I could help my American readers to realise the conditions under which this book has been produced. The Theosophical Society as a whole does not by any means sufficiently understand or appreciate the work done at its Headquarters, and although for you in America it is away on the other side of the earth, I should like to help you to see it as it is. Readers of the *"Messenger"* must at least have some general idea of the appearance of the place, and must know something of the life which is lived here—a long life, a strenuous life, and a life lived under very peculiar conditions. Nowhere else in the world at this present moment is there such a center of influence—a center constantly visited by the Great Ones, and therefore bathed in their wonderful magnetism. The vibrations here are marvellously stimulating, and all of us who live here are therefore under a constant strain of a very peculiar kind, a strain which brings out whatever is in us. Strong vibrations from other planes are playing all the while upon our various vehicles, and those parts of us which can in any sense respond to them are thereby raised, strengthened and purified. But it must be remembered that there is another side to this. There may well be in each of us some vibrations the character of which is too far removed from the level of these great influences to fall into harmony with them, and where that is the case intensification will still take place, but the result may well be evil rather than good. To live at Adyar is the most glorious of all opportunities for those who are able to take advantage of it, but its effect on those who are constitutionally unable to harmonize with its vibrations may be dangerous rather than helpful. If a student can bear it he may advance rapidly; if he cannot bear it he is better away.

The workers here live mostly in the great central building, within the immediate aura of the shrine room and the President.* The students live chiefly half-a-mile away at various other houses, though all within the large estate which now belongs to the Society. Each during the day does his own work in his own way, but in the evening we all gather together upon the roof of the central building, in front of the President's rooms, formerly occupied by Madame Blavatsky herself, and there, under the marvellous night sky of India, so infinitely more brillant than anything that we know in what are miscalled temperate climes, we sit and listen to her teaching. All through the summer of last year, so much of which she spent in a tour through the United States, it fell to my lot to take charge of the meetings of the students here. In the course of that time I delivered many informal little addresses and answered hundreds of questions. All that I said was taken down in shorthand, and this book is the result of those notes. In a number of cases it happened that what was said on the roof at the meetings was afterwards expanded into a little article for *The Theosophist* or *The Adyar Bulletin*; in all such cases I reprint the article instead of the stenographic report, as it has had the advantage of certain corrections and additions. Necessarily a book of this sort is fragmentary in its nature; necessarily also it contains a certain amount of repetition; though this latter has been excised wherever possible. Many of the subjects treated also have been dealt with in my earlier books, but what is written here represents in all cases the result of the latest discoveries in connection with those subjects. The subjects have been classified as far as possible, and this volume represents the first series, containing five sections. The second volume, containing the nine remaining sections, is now in the printer's hands. A list of the subjects of which it will treat will be found at the end of this volume.

C. W. Leadbeater

Adyar, July, 1910.

*Mrs. Annie Besant

AUTHOR'S NOTE TO AMERICAN EDITION, VOLUME II

While Mrs. Besant was absent from Adyar on a tour through England and America last year, it fell to my lot to take charge of the daily meetings of the students here. In the course of that time I delivered many informal little addresses and answered hundreds of questions. All that I said was taken down in shorthand, and this book is the result of those notes. In a number of cases it happened that what was said on the roof at the meetings was afterwards expanded into a little article for *The Theosophist* or *The Adyar Bulletin;* in all such cases I reprint the article instead of the stenographic report, as it has had the advantage of certain corrections and additions. Necessarily a book of this sort is fragmentary in its nature; necessarily also it contains a certain amount of repetition; though this latter has been excised wherever possible. Many of the subjects treated have also been dealt with in my earlier books, but what is written here represents in all cases the result of the latest discoveries in connection with those subjects. The subjects have been classified as far as possible, and this volume is the second series, containing the remaning sections.

C. W. Leadbeater

ADYAR, *July,* 1911.

AN INTRODUCTION TO LEADBEATER'S WORLD VIEW

In today's climate of interest in the occult, a surge of new attention is being given to clairvoyant investigators like C. W. Leadbeater. Such gifted seers offer an expanded view of man and the universe which takes into account whole areas unknowable through physical means of investigation. The vistas they expose can provide clues for understanding otherwise inexplicable phenomena of current interest such as parapsychological events, prognostication, healing, etc.

As to the authenticity of clairvoyant faculties, Leadbeater himself felt even in his day "there is an overwhelming mass of irrefutable evidence in favor of the existence of this faculty." Twentieth century evidence is still more convincing. Parapsychologists collect and follow-up on spontaneous cases as well as conduct controlled laboratory studies. There are doctors who consult psychics in cases that are hard to diagnose. Even the police sometimes rely on psychics to solve puzzling crimes. But the most convincing evidence comes from the close correspondence between accounts regarding unseen worlds given by psychics and clairvoyants in both modern and ancient times. It seems they are responding to the same supersensory reality, though necessarily with their individual interpretation. As Leadbeater puts it:

> The clairvoyant is simply a man who develops, within himself, the power to respond to another octave out of the stupendous gamut of possible vibrations, and so enables himself to see more of the world around him than those of more limited perception.[1]

The talks which comprise this book, THE INNER LIFE, were given to students of Leadbeater and Annie Besant, his close associate and fellow clairvoyant. Leadbeater assumed his audience was thoroughly familiar with his enlarged world view. In this new edition it seems necessary to sketch out some of the main features of this view, in order to make the book more comprehensible.

This expanded world view did not originate with Leadbeater, though he filled in many details previously left blank. His scheme fits into a venerable tradition which has been with mankind since prehistoric times. History shows a kernel of truth appearing through the ages, sometimes taught openly and dominating a culture, as in ancient Greece, at other times taught in secret to the few who sought. The principles have been styled quite differently and various aspects have been emphasized at different times, but the fundamentals have remained unchanged throughout the centuries. This core of understanding is variously known today as the ancient wisdom, the occult philosophy, the esoteric tradition, theosophy. It is called "occult" because it deals with that which is hidden, not obvious. It deals with nature's processes and laws, with that which stands behind and beyond science. It connotes the study of the metaphysical principles that uphold the universe.

Traces of this philosophy can be found in such diverse sources as ancient Greece, Plato, Pythagoras, the Kabbalah, Zohar, Christian Gnosticism, Lao-tse, the Hindu and Buddhist traditions, Sufism, to mention only a few. The thread of truth running through such teachings was identified by H. P. Blavatsky in her remarkable work on occult philosophy, *The Secret Doctrine*. Leadbeater's investigations were conducted in the context of the ancient world view as developed in her teachings.

This philosophy rests on the premise that there is one changeless, homogeneous, divine substance principle from which the world arises. The visible, physical world emerges by degrees from its non-material divine source. This idea is highly plausible in the setting of modern physics. Einstein's theory of relativity shows time and space, not as distinct and separate, but as inseparable and interdependent. Nuclear physics—the science of subatomic particles—rests on the notion of wholly non-material electrical and magnetic fields. Speaking of quantum fields, or fields that can take the form of quanta or particles, Fritjof Capra says in *The Tao of Physics:*

> The quantum field is seen as the fundamental physicial entity; a continuous medium which is present everywhere in space. Particles are merely local condensations of the field; concentrations of energy which come and go, thereby losing their individual character and dissolving into the underlying field.[2]

Thus non-material fields and matter are seen as one; the material emerges from and disappears into its non-material origins.

But according to the occult philosophy the physical world is only a small part of the entire spectrum of matter. It is the most dense, most concrete of a series of worlds ranging from the extremely tenuous "superphysical" to the solid physical. This is an idea found in ancient Egyptian mysteries, Hinduism, and Buddhism, and it has parallels in the Greek notion of the Elements. Many clairvoyants like Leadbeater, who are sensitive to an increased range of stimuli, have given significant corroborative testimony to the existence of these finer worlds.

This notion is not so farfetched at a time when our television sets and radios, for example, give constant testimony to the existence of supersensory waves rushing about us. Instruments have revealed invisible light such as the ultra-violet, inaudible sound beyond the range of the human ear, x-rays, cosmic rays, microwaves, and many more. We know that the space around us is charged with a variety of energies we cannot detect with our senses.

The occult philosophy holds that there are several levels of supersensory material, structured in a significant, orderly way. According to Leadbeater's way of presenting this concept, the familiar physical world of solids, liquids, and gases extends itself into four rarer states of matter, collectively called the etheric plane or level. This subtle matter interpenetrates physical objects, including the bodies of living things in which its role is closely related to vitality and health.

Interpenetrating the physical and etheric worlds is an ever-moving, radiant sphere called the astral plane or world. Leadbeater, writing in the first decade of the twentieth century, says:

> ... in some of the experiments our scientific men must be actually disintegrating physical matter, and throwing it back on to the astral plane; in which case it would seem that they must presently be forced to admit the existence of astral matter, though they will naturally think of it as nothing but a further subdivision of physical matter.[3]

Today atoms are subdivided in ways undreamt of in Leadbeater's day. His statement suggests that perhaps the numerous short-lived particles that appear in the cloud chambers of modern physics are emerging from the astral plane.

Man has an aura or energy field at the astral level (called by Leadbeater the astral body) which is the vehicle for emotion and desires. Just as the life- or vital energy is the characteristic of the etheric, so feeling or emotion is the field phenomenon occurring at the astral level. The astral interpenetrates and interacts with the physical body by means of the etheric or vital, so that emotions and body work together closely. The next finer level, that of the concrete mind, is also closely linked with the astral level, both in a person's aura and in the plane of nature characteristic of it, called the lower mental or manasic plane. The whirling centers of energy called *chakras* exist at all these levels, helping to integrate forces from these planes. The chakras are centers of consiousness as well as foci of energy, and thus are also connected with spiritual awakening.

The upper levels of the mental plane are involved with deeper, abstract, philosophical thought. Leadbeater refers to this as the higher mental or manasic level. Beyond that lies a level called *buddhic* in many theosophical writings, the realms of intuitive insight, the most tenuous of all, is the source of the very sense of self in man, his spiritual essence in its purest embodiment.

Each of these levels exists as a unique state of rarefied matter throughout all of nature, as well as in individual vehicles in man, organized from the matter of that plane. Leadbeater refers to the matter of the astral and mental planes as "elemental essence". According to his presentation, each of the planes is subdivided into seven subplanes, ranging from finer to denser on that plane. These levels of existence are documented in Hindu philosophy and in Buddhism, where man's vehicles at different levels are referred to as *kosas* or sheaths. Lama Anagarika Govinda, the contemporary authority on Tibetan Buddhism, stresses the interpenetration of the different planes.

> These 'sheaths' therefore are not separate layers, which one after another crystallize around a solid nucleus, but rather in the nature of mutually penetrating forms of energy, from the finest 'all-radiant', all-pervading luminous consciousness down to the densest form of 'materialized consciousness', which appears before us as our visible, physical body. The correspondingly finer or subtler sheaths penetrate, and thus contain, the grosser.[4]

Each level has its unique characteristic and, like the notes in a chord, all are necessary for full expression. Arthur Osburn in *The Expansion of Awareness* refers to the planes as:

. . . other modes of energy organized in vibratory spheres to enable consciousness to function in definite and limited ways.[5]

Yet behind the varying modes and vehicles, man remains a single, unitary being. According to Raynor Johnson:

Viewed thus in its broadest outline, we can see Man as a synthesis of principles or vehicles of growing significance, and widening powers, as we approach toward his essence which is one with the ultimate reality.[6]

Man's inner being has three aspects, according to occultism, analogous to Paul's divisions of spirit, soul and body. Essentially man is a point of consciousness in the divine ground from which all emerges. This One Reality remains forever an undivided unity. Yet it emanates rays creating the immortal, indestructible *Atman*, as it is termed in Sanskrit. This ray is destined to become involved with denser and denser matter in order to obtain definiteness in the worlds of material expression. Clothed in a film of rarest matter it becomes the monad. Further encased in material from the higher mental realm, it becomes what Leadbeater calls the ego. His use of the word is far different from any modern usage. He means Atma-Buddhi-Manas, the spiritual triad or soul of man, which has a stable locus on the higher mental plane. This is the reincarnating entity which unfolds its powers by generating personalities over and over in the various cultures of man.

According to the occult philosophy, all of nature—including man—is evolving according to a grand design. The ancient Greeks held the idea of teleology, a purposed end that controls the course of events. Until recently this notion has been out of favor, largely due to interpretations of Darwin's theory of chance variation and survival of the fittest. However, many biologists today are finding this theory inadequate to account for evolution, which they are unable to reconcile with blind chance. Sir Alister Hardy and L. L. Whyte, among others, suggest that internal factors in organisms, that it—life itself—plays an important part in guiding evolution. Goal-directedness and purposiveness are obvious throughout the world of life. According to Arthur Koestler:

The part played by a lucky chance mutation is reduced to that of a trigger which releases the co-ordinated action of a system; and to maintain that evolution is the product of blind chance means to confuse the simple action of the trigger,

governed by the laws of statistics, with the complex purpo-
sive processes which it sets off.

Any directive process . . . implies a reference to the future.
The equifinality of developmental processes, the striving of
the blastula to grow into an embryo, regardless of the obstacles and hazards to which it is exposed, might lead the
unprejudiced observer to the conclusion that the pull of the
future is as real and sometimes more important than the
pressure of the past.[7]

E. Lester Smith and others have suggested some kind of non-
material matrix or force field that is guiding growth and development and evolution. Teilhard de Chardin, the Jesuit
paleontologist, put forth convincing arguments that the aim of
evolution is the enhancement of consciousness by its expression
in ever more refined forms. This agrees with the occult
philosophy.

In modern times, evolutionary changes in man's body are in-
significant. Julian Huxley was the first to suggest that the evolutionary thrust is not physical but psychosocial. Man is the primary agent of evolution as he passes on his achievements and
culture through language. According to the occult tradition, man
is still evolving in his ability to express his higher potentials which
reside in subtler, more spiritual levels.

This unfoldment is proceeding according to a long-range
scheme of evolution which has been outlined by Madame
Blavatsky. Man is destined to evolve through seven great stages,
called *root races*. This term does not coincide with the present
understanding of the word race. In the occult sense, a race is a
quality of consciousness rather than a physical type. So far, the
first five stages of consciousness, or "root races", have appeared.
The scheme of seven root races repeats itself seven times in great
cycles termed *rounds*, some of which occurred in the distant past
on superphysical planes. We are now in the fourth round. From
the occult point of view humanity is far older than anthropologi-
cal data suggest.

Mankind as a whole is in the fifth root race which began
development in prehistoric times in India, according to Madame
Blavatsky. Each root race accentuates a particular quality associated with one of the bodies of man. The fifth root race emphasizes the development of the concrete, rational mind. Root races
are subdivided into sub-races, each with its own secondary
emphasis of quality. At present the fifth sub-race is dominant in

America and western Europe, causing a double emphasis on the rational mind. Hence the phenomenal development of science and technology in the West. The sixth sub-race, which is now beginning to develop, will bring out the intuition and unitive insight. Foreshadowings of this can be found among some leading thinkers.

It is impossible to identify to which sub-race individuals in an ethnic group belong. As anthropologists point out, differences within the group are often greater than differences between groups. The qualities of each race and sub-race are necessary and of equal value, so that one cannot say earlier types are "inferior" to later types. The occult view of evolution is not merely based on a linear progression but on an expansion of consciousness in depth in which latent powers are actualized and brought under conscious control by the individual.

The occult philosophy holds that a man or woman as an ego or soul reincarnates many times in each of the races, developing the various qualities they provide. Reincarnation is an ancient idea in Eastern philosophies and today is held by over half the world's population. (In the West, even members of the scientific community are taking an interest. In recent years, Dr. Ian Stevenson has documented cases which seem explicable only through the concept of reincarnation.)[8] The occult philosophy holds that the essential meaning of a life is assimilated and incorporated into the soul between incarnations.

Eastern traditions teach that effects from the events and actions in one life can be carried over to other lives. Occultism holds that the universe is an inseparable web whose interconnections are dynamic. This view is corroborated by modern physics and studies in ecology. According to Buddhism and Hinduism, the dynamic balance of life is maintained by the law of karma, which means *action*. Capra defines karma as:

> . . . the active principle of the play, the total universe in action, where everything is dynamically connected with everything else. In the words of the *Gita*, 'Karma is the force of creation, wherefrom all things have their life.[9]

The balance produced by karma results in order and lawfulness which extends to the moral realm and human activity. The biblical expression, "As ye sow, so shall ye reap", captures the essence of this law at work. The result of our actions becomes manifest, not only in the events and circumstances of our lives, but in our characters. Speaking of the teaching of the Vedanta, Zimmer says:

> ... the karma-bearing fruit is the incidents and elements of our present biography, as well as the traits and dispositions of the personality producing and enduring them.[10]

Lama Govinda comments on the mechanism at work here:

> For character is nothing but the tendency of our will, formed by repeated actions. Every deed leaves a trace, a path formed by the process of walking, and whenever such a once-trodden path exists, there we find, when a similar situation arises, that we take to this path spontaneously. This is the law of action and reaction, which we call karma, the law of movement in the direction of the least resistance. . . . It is what is commonly known as the 'force of habit'. . . . When departing from one and entering into another life, it is the consciousness thus formed which constitutes the nucleus or germ of the new embodiment.[11]

In Leadbeater's terminology, this nucleus consists of "permanent atoms" which persist from one incarnation to another. An atom of matter from each of the lower planes becomes attached to a monad to serve as a repository of experience on that plane through all that individual's series of incarnations. The Buddhist notion of *skandhas* is similar to this idea.

Thus man himself is seen to be the author of his destiny, some of which he wrote in the distant past. But the results of his actions are not so much rewards and punishments as educative experiences for his growth. Futhermore, karma does not imply a fixed predestination. New attitudes and ways of responding to circumstances serve as new causes which can alter (but not obliterate) the outcome of previous actions. As a man becomes more in control of himself he can have greater conscious influence on the course of his life.

All religions teach of a way to quicken spiritual unfoldment. Spiritual practices such as yoga, meditation, prayer, mantras are designed to awaken latent powers. In this book, Leadbeater refers to many aspects of the inner life which are involved with spiritual growth. The talks from which the book was compiled were addressed to students on the path of spiritual unfoldment, seeking to develop themselves in order to be of greater service.

Leadbeater refers frequently to adepts, Masters, and other highly evolved beings. The existence of such beings is a natural consequence of the law of evolution of conscious life. In the East the existence of spiritually mature persons is taken for granted;

the guru-disciple tradition is based on this assumption. The West, too, has recognized initiates and adepts, particularly in ancient Egypt and in the days of the Greek mystery schools. Occultism as well as oriental philosophy posit grade on grade of evolved beings in an endless hierarchy. A few of these are known as great men of history, while most work silently and in seclusion. Various types of advanced beings are referred to as adepts, chohans, Dhyan Chohans, devas, and so on. They are distinct individual beings, yet they all inhere and are centers in the one divine, universal Life. Leadbeater particularly emphasizes a being far beyond the level of mankind whom he refers to as the Solar Logos. According to Leadbeater the life of the god-like being pervades, sustains, and guides the entire solar system.

Mr. Leadbeater was a man of utmost integrity, using his enlarged vision as objectively and carefully as possible. Most of his investigations were corroborated by other clairvoyants who worked with him. However, necessarily some of the cultural coloration and Victorian thought patterns of his day have crept into his interpretations. But any slight distortions or somewhat outmoded expressions are far outweighed by the grandeur of his view and his fascinating observations into nature's hidden realms.

Shirley Nicholson
November 6, 1977

References and Notes

1. C. W. Leadbeater, *Man Visible and Invisible*. Adyar, Madras, India: The Theosophical Publishing House, 1942. p. 26.
2. Fritjof Capra, *The Tao of Physics*. Boulder: Shambhala Publications, Inc., 1975. p. 210.
3. C. W. Leadbeater, *The Inner Life*, Vol. II. Wheaton: The Theosophical Press, 1942. p. 179.
4. Lama Anagarika Govinda, *Foundations of Tibetan Mysticism*. New York: Samuel Weiser, 1974. p. 148.
5. Arthur W. Osborn, *The Expansion of Awareness*. Adyar, Madras, India: The Theosophical Publishing House, 1961. p. 65.
6. Raynor C. Johnson, *The Imprisoned Splendour*. Wheaton: The Theosophical Publishing House, 1971, 1977. p. 262.
7. Arthur Koestler, *Nature*, 1965, 208, 1033.
8. Ian Stevenson, M.D., *Twenty Cases Suggestive of Reincarnation*, Charlottesville: University Press of Virginia, Rev. 2nd ed.
9. Capra, op. cit., p. 156.
10. Heinrich Zimmer, *Philosophies of India*. New York: Meridian Books, 1956. p. 442.
11. Govinda, op. cit., p. 243.

The Great Ones
and
The Way to Them

The Great Ones

Students of occultism—even those who have been students for many years—sometimes seem to fail to realize the Masters as they truly are. I have often found people thinking of them as some kind of angels or devas, or, at any rate, as so far removed from us by their greatness that it is scarcely possible for us to derive much help from them. Their greatness is indisputable, and from that point of view the gulf between them and ourselves may well seem incalculable in its extent; and yet from another point of view they are very close to us, so that their sympathy and help are very near and very real. That our thought on the subject may be clear, let us first of all try to define exactly what we mean by the term "Master."

We mean by it always one who is a member of the Great White Brotherhood—a member at such a level that he is able to take pupils. Now the Great White Brotherhood is an organization unlike any other in the world, and for that reason it has often been misunderstood. It has sometimes been described as the Himalayan or the Tibetan Brotherhood, and the idea has been conveyed of a body of Indian ascetics residing together in a monastery in some inaccessible mountain fastness. Perhaps this has risen largely from the knowledge of the facts that the two Brothers principally concerned in the foundation and work of the Theosophical Society happen at the moment to be living in Tibet, and to be wearing Indian bodies. To comprehend the facts of the case it may be better to approach its consideration from another point of view.

Most of our students are familiar with the thought of the four stages of the Path of Holiness, and are aware that a man who has passed through them and attained to the level of the Asekha has achieved the task set before humanity during this chain-period, and is consequently free from the necessity of reincarnation on this planet or on any other. Before him then open seven ways among which he must choose. Most of them take him away from this earth into wider spheres of activity, probably connected with the solar system as a whole, so that the great majority of those members of our humanity who had already reached this goal have passed entirely out of our ken.

The limited number who are still working directly for us may be divided into two classes—those who retain physical bodies, and those who do not. The latter are frequently spoken of under the name of Nirmanakayas. They hold themselves suspended as it were between this world and nirvana, and they devote the whole of their time and energy to the generation of spiritual force for the benefit of mankind. This force they pour into what may be described as a reservoir, upon which the Masters and their pupils can draw for the assistance of their work with humanity. The Nirmanakaya, because he remains to this extent in touch with the lower planes, has been called 'a candidate for woe,' but that is misleading. What is meant is that he has not the joy of the higher work, or of the nirvanic levels. He has chosen to remain upon lower planes in order to help those who still suffer. It is quite true that to come back from the higher life into this world is like going down from the fresh air and glorious sunlight into a dark and evil-smelling dungeon; but the man who does this to help some one out of that dungeon is not miserable and wretched while there, but full of the joy of helping, notwithstanding the greatness of the contrast and the terrible feeling of bondage and compression. Indeed, a man who refused such an opportunity of giving aid when it came to him would certainly feel far more woe afterwards, in the shape of remorse. When we have once really seen the spiritual misery of the world, and the condition of those who need such help, we can never again be careless or indifferent about it, as are those who have not seen.

Fortunately those of us who have seen and realized this have ever at our command a means whereby we can quite really and definitely help. Tiny though our efforts may be as compared with the splendid outpouring of force of the Nirmanakaya, we also can add our little drops to the great store of force in that reservoir. Every outpouring of affection or devotion produces a double result—one upon the being to whom it is sent, and another upon ourselves, who sent it forth. But if the devotion or affection be utterly without the slightest thought of self, it brings in its train a third result also. Ordinary affection or devotion, even of a high kind, moves in a closed curve, however large that curve may be, and the result of it comes back upon the sender. But the devotion or affection of the truly unselfish man moves in an open curve, and though some of its affects inevitably react upon the sender, the grandest and noblest part of its force ascends to the LOGOS Himself, and the response, the magnificent response of benediction which instantly pours forth from Him, falls into that reservoir for the helping of mankind. So that it is within the power of every one of us, even the weakest and the poorest, to help the world in this most beautiful manner. It is this adding to the reservoir of spiritual force which is really the truth that lies at the back of the Catholic idea of works of supererogation.

The still more limited number of adepts who retain physical bodies remain in even closer touch with us, in order to fill certain offices, and to do certain work necessary for our evolution; and it is to the latter that the names of the Great White Brotherhood and the Occult Hierarchy have sometimes been given. They are, then, a very small number of highly advanced men belonging not to any one nation, but to the world as a whole. On the physical plane they do not live together, though they are of course in continual communication on higher planes. Since they are beyond the necessity of rebirth, when one body wears out they can choose another whenever it may be most convenient for the work they wish to do, so that we need not attach any special importance to the nationality of the bodies which they happen to be wearing at any particular time. Just now, several of those bodies are Indian, one is Tibetan, one is Chinese, two at least are English, one is Italian, one Hungarian, and one Syrian, while one was born on the island of Cyprus. As I have said, the nationality of these bodies is not a matter of importance, but I mention these in order to show that it would be a mistake to think of the ruling Hierarchy as belonging exclusively to one race.

Reverence restrains us from saying much of the great Head of this Hierarcy, in whose hands is the fate of the continents, in whose name all initiations are given. He is one of the very few now remaining upon earth of the Lords of the Flame, the Children of the Fire-mist, the great beings who came down from Venus nearly eighteen million years ago to help and to lead the evolution of humanity on our chain. These Great Ones did not take bodies from our then entirely undeveloped humanity, but made for themselves bodies in appearance resembling ours by the force of their will, a kind of permanent materialization. At that period, and for long after it, no members of our humanity were sufficiently developed to fill any of the higher offices in this Hierarchy, and consequently we needed and received this help from without. Gradually, as humanity has evolved, it has become more and more able to provide for itself, and the great Lords of the Flame have been set free to go to the help of yet other evolutions. But one of them still holds this, the highest office of all—the position of the KING who guides and controls all evolution taking place upon this planet—not only that of humanity and of the animal, vegetable, mineral and elemental kingdoms below it, but also of the great non-human kingdoms of the nature-spirits of the devas, some of which rise so far above it.

Under him are various Heads of Departments, the broad outlines of whose work are more within our comprehension than his work. Though the details are far beyond us, we can form some slight idea of what must be the manifold responsibilities and activities of the Manu of a Root-race; and perhaps we can to some extent image to ourselves the duties of him who is Minister of Religion in this world-kingdom—who sends forth religion after religion, suiting each to the needs of a particular type of people and to the period of the world's history in which it is launched, sometimes deputizing one of his subordinates to found it, sometimes even incarnating himself for that purpose, as he may see fit. This Minister of Religion is often called in the East the Bodhisattva—one who is about to become a BUDDHA. The previous holder

of that high office was he whom we call the Lord Gautama
BUDDHA. The attainment of Buddhahood is not simply the gaining of enlightment; it is also the taking of a great and definite
initiation, and the man who has taken that step cannot again
incarnate upon earth, but hands over his work to his successor,
and usually passes away altogether from any connection with
earth.

The Lord Gautama, however, still remains to a certain extent
within touch of the world, in order that he may still be able to help
it. Once in each year he still shows himself to the brotherhood of
adepts, and pours down his blessing upon them, to be passed
through them to the world at large; and he may still be reached in
certain ways by those who know how. Mrs. Besant has told us, in
some of her recent writings, how he incarnated over and over
again as the great teacher of the earlier sub-races of the Aryan
race, how he was Hermes—the founder of the Egyptian
Mysteries—also the first and greatest Zoroaster, the original
founder of the worship of the sun and fire, and again he was
Orpheus, the founder of the Greek Mysteries. Those mentioned
of course were not his only births, for in the course of our
researches into the past we have seen him as founder of other
religions than these.

The statement made in some of the earlier Theosophical works
that he was reborn as Shankaracharya is an error for, from an
occult point of view, the two great teachers were on entirely
different lines. There was, however, a certain reason at the back
of the statement in the fact that some of the vehicles prepared by
one of them were also utilized by the other, as Madame Blavatsky
has explained in the third volume of *The Secret Doctrine*.

The deep reverence and the strong affection felt for the Lord
Gautama all over the East are due to two facts. One of these is that
he was the first of our humanity to attain to the stupendous height
of Buddhahood, and so he may be very truly described as the
first-fruits and the leader of our race. (All previous Buddhas had
belonged to other humanities, which had matured upon earlier
chains.) The second fact is that for the sake of hastening the
progress of humanity, he took upon himself certain additional
labors of the most stupendous character, the nature of which it is
impossible to comprehend. It is stated that when the time came at
which it was expected that humanity would be able to provide for
itself some one who was ready to fill this important office, no one

could be found who was fully capable of doing so. Few of our earthly race had then reached the higher stages of adeptship, and the foremost of these were two friends and brothers whose development was equal. These two were the mighty Egos now known to us as the Lord Gautama and the Lord Maitreya, and in his great love for mankind the former at once volunteered to make the tremendous additional exertion necessary to qualify him to do the work required, while his friend and brother decided to follow him as the next holder of that office thousands of years later.

In those far-off times it was the Lord Gautama who ruled the world of religion and education; but now he has yielded that high office to the Lord Maitreya, whom western people call the Christ—who took the body of the disciple Jesus during the last three years of its life on the physical plane. Anyone whose mind is broad enough to grasp this magnificent conception of the splendid reality of things will see instantly how it is worse than futile to set up in one's mind one religion as in opposition to another, to try to convert any person from one to another, or to compare depreciatingly the founder of one with the founder of another. In the last case indeed it is especially ridiculous, because the two founders are either two pupils of the same school, or two incarnations of the same person, and so are entirely in accord as to principles, though they may for the time be putting forward different aspects of the truth to suit the needs of those to whom they speak. The teaching is always fundamentally the same, though its presentation may vary widely. The Lord Maitreya had taken various births before he came into the office which he now holds, but even in these earlier days he seems always to have been a teacher or high-priest.

It is now generally known that the two Masters who have been most intimately concerned with the foundation and the work of the Theosophical Society have taken respectively the offices of temporal and spiritual leader of the new sixth root-race, which is to come into existence in seven hundred years' time. The Manu, or temporal leader, is practically an autocratic monarch who arranges everything connected with the physical-plane life of the new race, and endeavors in every way to make it as perfect an expression as possible of the idea which the LOGOS has set before him for realization. The spiritual teacher will be in charge of all the various aspects of religion in the new race, and also of the education of its children. It is clear that one of the main objects of the foundation of the Theosophical Society was that these two Masters might gather round them a number of men who would be intelligent and willing co-operators in this mighty work. Round them will be grouped others who are now their pupils, but will by that time have attained the level of adeptship.

We may then set before ourselves as a goal the privilege of being chosen to serve them in this wonderful work for the world which lies before them. There will be ample opportunity for the display of all possible varieties of talent, for the work will be of the most varied character. Some of us will no doubt be attracted to one side of it and some to the other, largely according to the predominance of our affection for one or other of its great Leaders. It has often been said that the characteristic of one is power, and of the other love and compassion, and this is perfectly true, though, if it is not rightly understood, it may very easily prove misleading. One of the Masters concerned has been a ruler in many incarnations, and was so even in the earlier part of this one, and unquestionably royal power shows forth in his every gesture and in the very look of his eyes, just as surely as the face of his brother adept beams ever with overflowing love and compassion. They are of different rays or types, having risen to their present level along different lines, and this fact cannot but show itself; yet we should err sadly if we thought of the first as in any degree less loving and compassionate than his brother, or of the second as lacking anything of the power possessed by the first. Other Masters also will be engaged in this work, and it may well be that some of us may have made our link through one of them.

It is probably that even the Masters who are by name best known to you are not so real, not so clear, not so well-defined to you as they are to those of us who have had the privilege of meeting them face to face and seeing them constantly in the course of our work. Yet you should endeavour by reading and thinking of them to gain this realization, so that the Masters shall become to you not vague ideals but living men—men exactly as we are, though enormously more advanced in every respect. They are men most emphatically, but men without failings, and so to us They seem like gods on account of the power, love and compassion radiating from them. It is most significant that, in spite of the awe necessarily produced by the sense of this tremendous power, in their presence one never feels in the least afraid or embarrassed, but always uplifted.

The man who stands before one of them cannot but feel the

deepest humility, because of the greatness of the contrast between himself and the Master. Yet with all this humility he yet feels a firm confidence in himself, for since the Master, who is also man, has achieved, that achievement is clearly possible even for him. In his presence everything seems possible and even easy, and one looks back with wonder on the troubles of yesterday, unable now to comprehend why they should have caused agitation or dismay. Now at least, the man feels, there can never again be trouble, since he has seen the right proportion of things. Now he will never again forget that, however dark the clouds may be, the sun is ever shining behind them. The vibrations of the Masters are so strong that only those qualities in you which harmonize with them are called out, so that you will feel the uttermost confidence and love, and the desire to be always in his presence. It is not that you forget that you have undesirable qualities in you, but you feel that now you can conquer them, and you do not in the least mind his knowing all about them, because you are so certain that he understands perfectly, and to understand all is to pardon all.

It may perhaps help us to realize the human side of our Masters if we remember that many of them in comparatively recent times have been known as historical characters. The Master K. H., for example, appeared in Europe as the philosopher Pythagoras. Before that he was the Egyptian priest Sarthon, and on yet another occasion chief-priest of a temple at Agade, in Asia Minor, where he was killed in a general massacre of the inhabitants by a host of invading barbarians who swooped down upon them from the hills. On that occasion he took immediately the body of a Greek fisherman, which had been drowned in his attempt to escape, and in that body the Master journeyed on to Persia, where he rendered great assistance to the last of the Zoroasters in the founding of the modern form of the Mazdayaznian religion. Later he was the flamen of the Temple of Jupiter in Rome, and later still Nagarjuna, the great Buddhist teacher. We have found him many times in our researches into the past lives of some members of our group, but almost always as a priest or teacher.

Again, in these researches into the remote past we have frequently found the disciple Jesus, who in Palestine had the privilege of yielding up His body to the Christ. As a result of that act He received the incarnation of Apollonius of Tyana, and in the eleventh century He appeared in India as the teacher

Ramanujacharya, who revived the devotional element in Hinduism, and raised it to so high a level.

No doubt some of you have heard a good deal about other Masters besides the two who principally take charge of Theosophical work. Another Master, for example, dictated for us *Light on the Path* and *The Idyll of the White Lotus*, while yet another has taken charge of a great deal of the work in Europe, and has written for us some of the most splendid works in the whole realm of literary activity. Then the one who was once the disciple Jesus stands ready especially to guide the various activities of the Christian Churches. Yet another looks especially after the work here in India.

Thus it may be seen that the evolution of the world is by no means left to itself, to get along as best it may, as people so often rashly suppose; on the contrary, it is being directed. For this Hierarchy of adepts is actually managing it, as far as it is possible to manage it while leaving its inhabitants their own free-will. The members of the Brotherhood, through their agents, are constantly trying to work with the important people of the world, putting advice and suggestions into their minds, endeavoring to move them onwards towards the great future of Universal Brotherhood when war shall have disappeared. But we must remember that the karma of all the people concerned has to be considered and respected. It would no doubt be easy to force the world along at a far more rapid rate, but that would not be for the real advantage of the people concerned. The Master K. H. once said in a letter which I received from him: "Of course I could easily tell you exactly what to do, and of course you would do it, but then the karma of the act would be mine and not yours, and you would gain only the karma of prompt obedience."

Men have to learn to be not merely intelligent servants; they have to learn to be co-workers, because they themselves will have the same work to do some day, and if they are to be fit for greater responsibilities in the future they must be willing to take up the smaller responsibilities now. Sometimes, it is true, a really great opportunity or responsibility of worldwide importance comes to one of us, but that may perhaps be once in many hundreds of lives. When it comes we shall take it or miss it, depending if we have or have not been in the habit of taking the smaller opportunities of daily life, so that we have got into the habit of doing the right thing, and shall do it automatically at the critical moment.

Our opportunities of doing good or harm are usually small in regard to the world as a whole; but when we have learned invariably and automatically to choose the right in these smaller matters, the Great Brotherhood will feel it safe to trust us in larger matters.

It is indeed well that we should try to understand these Great Ones, not as a mere matter of curiosity and interest, but in order that we may realize them as they are, and comprehend that they are men just as we are, varying among themselves just as we vary, although at so much higher a level. Wisdom, power and love are present in all of them equally, yet they are by no means all alike. They are individuals just as we are. They are at the top of the ladder of humanity, but let us not forget that we are somewhere on its lower rungs, and that one day we also shall reach their level and stand where they stand.

One important fact about them is their all-round development. If we examine ourselves we shall be sure to find that we are to some extent disproportionate in our development—one-sided in certain respects. Some of us are full of scientific faculty and intellectual development, but sadly lacking in devotion and compassion; others are full of whole-souled devotion, but defective on the intellectual side. A Master is perfect along both these lines, as may easily be seen when we think of the splendid intellect of Pythagoras along with the love and compassion of the Master K. H.

We must not misunderstand their wonderful knowledge. In order to atain the level of adeptship they must have cast off, among others, the fetter of avidya or ignorance, and it is often said that to cast off ignorance one must attain all-knowledge. Yet we know from personal acquaintance with them that this is not so in the mere literal sense; for example, there are Masters who do not know all languages, others who are not artists and musicians, and so on. I think that what is really meant by casting off the fetter of ignorance is the acquisition of a power by which they can at any moment command any knowledge upon any subject which they happen to require. They certainly have not all facts stored within their physical brains, but equally certainly they can very quickly obtain any knowledge of which they have need. As to the question of languages, for example, if a Master wishes to write a letter in a language which he does not know, he very frequently employs the brain of a pupil who is acquainted with that language, throwing the ideas into that pupil's brain, and then employing the words in which he sees them clothe themselves. If a man speaks to them in a language which they do not understand, they can instantly grasp on the mental plane the thought that lies behind the incomprehensible words.

It is often asked whether an ordinary man who met a Master on the physical plane would instantly recognize him as such. I do not see any reason why he should. He would certainly find the Adept impressive, noble, dignified, holy and serene. He could hardly fail to recognize that he was in the presence of a remarkable man; but to know certainly that that man was an adept it would be necessary to see his causal body, which of course the ordinary man could not do. In that causal body the development would show by its greatly increased size, and by a special arrangement of the colors, which would differ for each of the seven great types. But all this would be quite out of the reach of the ordinary man whom we are postulating.

Adepts have no definite external peculiarities by which they may be recognized, though there is a great calmness and benevolence common to them all; their faces are stamped always with a joyous serenity, the peace which passeth all understanding. Most of them are distinctly handsome men, because their physical bodies are perfect, for they live in an absolutely hygienic way, and above all they never worry about anything. In the case of most of us there is still a great deal of karma of various kinds to be worked out and among other things this modifies the appearance of our physical bodies. In their case all karma is long ago exhausted, and consequently the physical body is a perfect expression on the physical plane of the Augoeides, or glorified body, of the Ego. Not only therefore is the body of a Master usually splendidly handsome, but also any new body that he may take in a subsequent incarnation will be an almost exact reproduction of the old one, because there is nothing to modify it.

Another remarkable fact is that they are able to preserve their physical bodies very much longer than we can—owing no doubt to the perfect health and absence of worry which we have already mentioned. Almost all of the Masters whom we know appear as men in the prime of life, yet in many cases there is testimony to prove that their physical bodies must have long passed the ordinary age of man. I have heard Madame Blavatsky say that her Master as he appears now does not look a day older than when she first saw him in her childhood sixty years before. In one case only, that of a Master who has recently attained adeptship in the body which he is still wearing, there is a certain ruggedness in the face, which is doubtless the result of some remainder of past karma brought over into this incarnation, but I think we may feel sure that when he chooses to take another body that characteristic will not persist.

Probably they are more silent than most men; busy people have not much time for casual talk, and they are out of all proportion the busiest people in the world. Their pupil, Madame Blavatsky, was the most brilliant conversationalist that I have ever met, but she never made talk for the sake of making it. So with them; a Master never speaks without a definite object in view, and his object is always to encourage, to help or to warn. He speaks always gently and with the greatest kindness, though he often betrays a very keen sense of humor; yet the humor itself is always of the kindly order, and is used never to wound, but always to lighten the troubles of the way, or to soften some necessary rebuke. Certainly a man who has no sense of humor would not be likely to make much progress in occult matters.

The number of adepts who retain physical bodies in order to help the evolution of the world is but small—perhaps some fifty or sixty in all. But it must be remembered that the great majority of these do not take pupils, as they are engaged in quite other work. Madame Blavatsky employed the term *adept* very loosely, for in one place she actually speaks of adepts who have been initiated, and adepts who have not been initiated. In all later writings we have reserved the word "initiate" for those who have passed at least the first of the four great stages upon the Path of Holiness, and the word adept we have restricted to those who have attained the Asekha level, and so have finished the evolution required of them in this chain of worlds. The consciousness of the Asekha rests normally upon the nirvanic or atmic plane while his physical body is awake. But out of the number who have already attained adeptship only the very small proportion mentioned above retain physical bodies, and remain in touch with the earth in order to help it; and out of this a still smaller proportion are willing under certain conditions to accept men as pupils or apprentices; and it is to these last (the smallest number) only that we give the name of Masters. Yet few though they be, their office is of incalculable importance, since without their aid it would be impossible for man to enter the portals of initiation.

The Work of the Christ

You ask about the Great One whom we call the Christ, the Lord Maitreya, and about His work in the past and in the future. The subject is a wide one—one also about which it is somewhat difficult for us to speak with freedom, because of the restrictions with which we are bound. Possibly the suggestion may be of use to you that there is what we may call a "department of the inner government of the world" which is devoted to religious instruction—the founding and inspiring of religions, and so on. It is the Christ who is in charge of that department; sometimes He Himself appears on earth to found a great religion and sometimes He entrusts such work to one of His more advanced assistants. We must regard Him as exercising a kind of steady pressure from behind all the time, so that the power employed will flow as though automatically into every channel anywhere and of any sort which is open to its passage; so that He is working simultaneously through every religion, and utilizing all that is good in the way of devotion and self-sacrifice in each.

The fact that these religions may be wasting their strength in abusing one another upon the physical plane is of course lamentable, but it does not make much difference due to the fact that whatever is good in each of them is being simultaneously utilized from behind by the same great Power. This is true of course of all movements in the world; every ounce of the good in them is being used as a channel, while the evil in them is in each case just so much regrettable waste of force which might have been utilized if the people had been more sensible. The section in *The Secret Doctrine* entitled *The Mystery of Buddha* gives a good deal of information as to the relations between the Heads of this department of Religion, and it may give some useful hints as to the Christ also. This is a subject of paramount interest to the members of our Society, since one of our Masters has a specially close relation with that department.

The future work of the Christ was decided many thousands of years ago—some of it decided apparently in minute details, though it would seem that there is a good deal of flexibility with regard to other points. The utter certainty with which these Great Ones lay their plans many thousands of years ahead is one of the most wonderful features of this stupendous work that they do. Sometimes it is open to those of us who have been able to develop the faculties of the higher planes to be allowed a glimpse of their mighty schemes, to witness the lifting of a tiny corner of the veil which shrouds the future. Sometimes also we have glimpsed their plans in another way, for in looking back into the records of the distant past we have found them making prophecies, the fulfilment of which is even now passing before our eyes.

I know of nothing more stirring, more absorbingly interesting, than such a glimpse. The splendor, the colossal magnitude, of their plans takes away one's breath, yet even more impressive is the calm dignity, the utter certainty, of it all. Not individuals only, but even nations are the pieces in this game; but neither nation nor individual is compelled to play any given part. The opportunity to play that part is given to it or to him; if he or it will not take it there is invariably an under-study ready to step in and fill the gap. But, whoever may be the instrument, this one thing at least is utterly certain, that the intended end will be achieved; through whose agency this will be done matters very much to the agent but nothing at all to the total progress of the world. Nineteen hundred years ago Appollonius of Tyana was sent out by the Brotherhood upon a mission, one feature of which was that he was to found, in various countries, certain magnetic centers. Objects of the nature of talismans were given to him, which he was to bury at these chosen spots, in order that the force which they radiated might prepare these places to be the centers of great events in the future. Some of those centers have already been utilized, but some have not, and all these latter are to be employed in the immediate future in connection with the work of the future Christ. So that much of the detail of His work was already definitely planned nearly two thousand years ago, and arrangements even on the physical plane were being made to prepare for it. When once we realize this utter certainty, doubt and hesitation, anxiety and worry, all fade away and we gain a perfect peace and content, and the most absolute confidence in the Powers who are governing the world.

The Work of the Masters

The work of the Masters on their own planes is not easy for us to comprehend, though we can readily see that their activity must be tremendous. The number of adepts still retaining physical bodies is but small, and yet in their hands is the care of all the evolutions which are taking place on this globe. As far as humanity is concerned they seem to divide the world into parishes, but their parishes are continents, and an adept is appointed to look after each. The Theosophical Society appears to be rather of the nature of a mission sent out from Headquarters, so that those who take part in its activities are working not for any particular parish or any particular form of religion, but for humanity as a whole; and it is upon humanity as a whole, or at least upon the mass of humanity that the Masters chiefly act. They have a department which devotes itself to endeavoring to influence in the right direction the important people of the world—to affect kings and statesmen in the direction of peace, to impress more liberal ideas upon great preachers and teachers, to uplift the conceptions of artists, so that through them the whole world may be made a little happier and a little better.

But the working of such departments as these is mainly entrusted to their pupils, they themselves dealing rather with the egos in their causal bodies; they devote themselves to pouring spiritual influence upon them—raying out upon them as the sunlight radiates upon the flowers, and thereby evoking from them all that is noblest and best in them, and so promoting their growth. Many people are sometimes conscious of helpful influences of this description, but are quite unable to trace them to their source. The causal body of the average man has as yet almost no consciousness of anything external to itself on its own plane. It is very much in the condition of the chicken within the egg, which is entirely unconscious of the source of the heat which nevertheless stimulates its growth. When any person reaches the stage where he breaks through his shell, and becomes capable of some sort of response, the whole process takes on a different form, and is enormously quickened. Even the group-souls of animals on the lower part of the mental plane are greatly affected and assisted by such influence, for like sunlight the force floods the entire plane and affects to some extent everything which is within its radius. In pouring out this force the Masters frequently take advantage of special occasions and of places where there is some strong magnetic center. Where some holy man has lived and died, or where some relics of such a person create a suitable atmosphere, they take advantage of such conditions and cause their own force to radiate along the channels which are already prepared. When some vast assemblage of pilgrims comes together in a receptive attitude, again they take advantage of the occasion by pouring their forces out upon the people through the channels by means of which they have been taught to expect help and blessing.

It is owing to assistance of this nature given to us from above that humanity has progressed even to its present position. We are still in the fourth round, which should naturally be devoted to the development of desire and emotion, and yet we are already engaged in the unfolding of the intellect, which is to be the special characteristic of the fifth round. That this is so is due to the immense stimulus given to our evolution by the descent of the Lords of the Flame from Venus, and by the work of the adepts who have preserved for us that influence and steadily sacrificed themselves in order that we might make the better progress.

Those who understand anything of this work, and most especially those of us who have been privileged to see the Masters doing it, would never for a moment think of interrupting them in such altruistic labor as this by propounding any personal requests. The vast importance of the work which they are doing, and the enormous amount of it, make it obviously impossible that they should take up personal work with individuals. In the cases where such work has to be done it is always delegated to pupils or performed by means of elementals and nature-spirits. Therefore it becomes emphatically the duty of the student to fit himself to do some of this lower work, for the very good reason that if he does not do so, the work will for the present be left undone, since it would be obviously impossible for the Masters to turn aside from their far greater work for the whole world to attend to individual cases. The work of the invisible helpers on the astral plane would simply not be done unless there were pupils at the stage where that is the best work that they can do; for so soon as they pass beyond that stage and can do higher work, the higher work will certainly be given to them.

People sometimes ask why the Masters so often work through imperfect instruments; the answer is obviously because they have not time to do the work themselves, and they must therefore employ such instruments as they have, or the work will not be done at all. Take for example the writing of books for the helping of humanity. It is obvious that the Masters could do this very far better than any of their pupils can, and by doing it they could entirely avoid any possibility of erroneous or imperfect statements. But they have absolutely no time to devote to such work, and therefore if it were not done by pupils it would remain undone. Besides, if the Masters did it they would take away the opportunity of making good karma from those who can do it— certainly not as well as they, but yet after all well enough for the use of those who know so very much less.

We must remember that every Master has at his command only a certain amount of force which, enormous as it seems to us, is still a limited quantity, and it is his duty to employ this force to the best possible advantage for the helping of humanity. Therefore it would, if we may say so without irreverence, be absolutely wrong for him to waste that force upon anything lower than the very highest that it can reach, or to spend upon individual cases, however deserving, that which can be so much better employed for the welfare of all.

Masters and Pupils

It has already been said that out of the comparatively small number of adepts who retain their physical bodies and fill the offices connected with the administration of the world under the Great Hierarchy, there is a still smaller number who accept pupils, and to whom therefore we give the name of Masters. Let us see then what it means to be a pupil of one of these Masters, what is expected of one who aspires to this position and what is the work which he has to do.

First let us have it clearly in our minds that the Masters have absolutely dedicated themselves to the service of humanity, and that they are utterly absorbed in the work to the entire exclusion of every other consideration. In speaking to you on this subject before, I have mentioned that a Master has only a certain definite amount of force to expend, and that though the amount of that force seems to us almost incalcuable, he is nevertheless exceedingly careful to use every ounce of it to the best possible advantage. Obviously to take in hand and instruct a pupil will make some demand upon his time and upon this store of energy, and since he regards everything from the standpoint of its use in regard to the promotion of evolution he will not expend this time and energy upon any man unless he can see that it is a good investment.

He will take a man as a pupil, or perhaps we should rather say as an apprentice, when he sees that the amount of time and strength spent in training him will produce more result eventually than

any other way of expending the same amount—*but not otherwise.*
For example, a man might have many qualifications which would
make him useful as an assistant, but at the same time some one
great fault which would be a constant obstacle in his way, which
would nullify much of the good that he might otherwise do. No
Master would accept such a man as a pupil; but he might say to
him: "Go to work and conquer that special fault of yours, and
when you have succeeded, I will take you as my assistant, and will
train you further."

So many of our earnest students are full of the most benevolent
and altruistic feeling, and, knowing themselves to be in this way
very different from the majority of mankind, they sometimes say
to themselves, "I am so deeply anxious to work for humanity; why
will not the Master take me in hand and train me?"

Let us face the facts boldly. The Master will not train you
because you are still full of all sorts of minor imperfections. It is
quite true, as you no doubt feel within yourselves, that your
benevolence, your kindliness, your earnest wish to be helpful, are
far greater things on the credit side of the account than are all
these small faults on the debit side. But try to realize that there are
thousands of people in the world who are benevolent and well-
meaning, and that you differ from them only in the fact that you
happen to have a little more knowledge, and so you are able to
direct your benevolence into more definitely useful channels
than those others. If these were all the qualifications required for
discipleship, each Master might have thousands of pupils, and his
whole time would be taken up in endeavoring to bring into shape
those few thousands of people, with all their petty little faults on
the astral and physical planes, and in the meantime the Master's
splendid work with the egos on the higher levels would have to be
entirely neglected.

First of all then, to be a pupil of a Master means that one must
look upon life as the Master looks upon it, solely from the point of
view of what is best for the progress of the world. The pupil must
be prepared *absolutely* to forget himself, to sink his personality
entirely, and he must understand that this is *not* a mere poetical
figure or a fashion of speech, but that it means just exactly what it
says—that he must have no personal desires whatsoever, and
must be willing to order the whole of his life according to the work
that he has to do. How many of us are there who are whole-

heartedly willing to take even this first step towards accepted discipleship?

Think what it means to become a disciple. When any man offers himself for such a position the Master will at once say whether or not he considers him fit to enter upon the stage of the probationary pupil. If the candidate appears to be reasonably near the possession of the necessary qualifications the Master may take him upon probation, which means that he will remain for a period of some years under very close observation. Seven years is the average time of this probation, but it may be indefinitely lengthened if the candidate should prove unsatisfactory, or on the other hand it may be much shortened if it is seen that he has really taken himself in hand. I have known it to be extended to thirty years; I have known it to be reduced to five years, and even to three, and in one quite exceptional case it was only five months. During this period of probation the pupil is not in any sense in any kind of direct communication with the Master; he is little likely to hear or to see anything of him. Nor as a general rule are any special trials or difficulties put in his way; he is simply carefully watched in his attitude towards all the little daily troubles of life. For convenience of observation the Master makes what is called a "living image" of each such probationary pupil—that is to say, an exact duplicate of the man's astral and mental bodies. This image he keeps in a place where he can easily reach it, and he places it in magnetic rapport with the man himself, so that every modification of thought or of feeling in the man's own vehicles is faithfully reproduced in the image. These images are examined daily by the Master, who in this way obtains with the least possible trouble a perfectly accurate record of his prospective pupil's thoughts and feelings, and from this he is able to decide when he can take him into the far closer relationship of the second stage—that of the accepted pupil.

Remember that the Master is a channel for the distribution of the forces of the Logos, and not indeed a mere unconscious channel but a keenly intelligent cooperator; and he is this because he is himself consciously a part of the Logos. In just the same way at a lower level the accepted pupil is a channel of the forces of the Master, but he, too, must be not an unconscious channel but an intelligent co-operator, and in order to be this he must also become virtually part of the consciousness of the Master.

An accepted pupil is taken into his Master's consciousness to so great an extent that whatever he sees or hears is within the knowledge of his Master—not that the Master necessarily sees or hears it at the same moment (though that often happens) but that it lies within the Master's memory exactly as it does within the memory of the pupil. Whatever the pupil feels or thinks is within the astral and mental bodies of his Master. When we realize all that this means, we see very clearly why it would be utterly impossible for the Master to accept any pupil until the pupil's thoughts and feelings were such as the Master would wish to harbor within himself.

It unfortunately sometimes happens that there comes into the mind of the pupil some thought which is not fit to be harbored by the Master, and as soon as the Master feels that, he at once erects a barrier and shuts off from himself that vibration, but to do this diverts his attention for a moment from his other work, and takes a certain amount of energy. Once more we see clearly that it would be impossible for a Master to take into such a relation with himself one who often indulged in thoughts unfit for the Master's mind; to have to be continually, or even frequently, turned aside from his work in order to shut off undesirable thoughts or feelings would clearly be a quite intolerable tax upon the Master's time and strength.

It is not because of any lack of compassion or patience that a Master could not take such a man; it is simply that it would not be a good use either of his time or his energy, and to make the best possible use of both of them is his simple duty. If a man feels himself worthy to be accepted as a pupil, and wonders why this privilege has not already been extended to him, let him watch himself closely for even a single day, and ask himself whether during that day there has been in him any single thought or feeling which would have been unworthy of the Master. Remember that not only definitely evil or unkind thoughts are unworthy of him, but also trifling thoughts, critical thoughts, irritated thoughts—above all, thoughts of self. Who of us is sufficient for these things?

The effect which the Master seeks to produce by this wonderfully close association is the harmonizing and attuning of the pupil's vehicles—the same result which an Indian teacher tries to gain by keeping his disciples always in the neighborhood physically. Whatever may be the special kind of exercises of the special course of study prescribed, in all cases the principal effect upon the pupil is that produced not by either exercises or study, but by being constantly in the presence of the teacher. The various vehicles of the pupil are vibrating at their accustomed rates— probably each of them at various rates, due to the constant presence of passing emotions and wandering thoughts of all kinds. The first and most difficult task of the pupil is to reduce all this chaos to order—to eliminate the host of minor interests, and control the wandering thoughts, and this must be achieved by a steady pressure of the will exercised upon all his vehicles through a long period of years.

While he still lives in the world the difficulty of this undertaking is multiplied a hundredfold by the ceaseless pressure of disturbing waves of thought and emotion, which give him no moment of rest, no opportunity to collect his forces in order to make a real effort. This is why in India the man who wishes to live the higher life retires to the jungle—why, in all countries and in all ages, there have been men willing to adopt the contemplative life of the hermit. The hermit at least has breathing-space, has rest from the endless conflict, so that he can find time to think coherently. He has little to hinder him in his struggle, and the calm influences of nature are even to a certain extent helpful.

But the man who lives perpetually in the presence of one already upon the Path has a still greater advantage. Such a teacher has by the hypothesis already calmed his vehicles and accustomed them to vibrate at a few carefully selected rates instead of in a hundred promiscuous frenzies. These few rates of vibration are very strong and steady, and day and night, whether he is sleeping or waking, they are playing unceasingly upon the vehicles of the pupil, and gradually raising him to his teacher's key. Nothing but time and close association will produce this effect; and even then not with every one, but only with those capable of being attuned. Many teachers require to see a reasonable proportion of this result before they will impart their special methods of occult development; in other words, before teaching a pupil something which may easily do him much harm is wrongfully used, they wish to be certain by ocular demonstration that he is a man of the type to which this instruction is appropriate, and is sufficiently amenable to their influence to be held in the right way by it when the strain comes. A thousand times greater are the advantages gained by those whom the Master selects—who thus have the opportunity of such close and intimate contact with him.

This then is what is meant by being an accepted pupil of the Master—that the man becomes a kind of outpost of that Master's consciousness, so that the strength of the Great Ones may be poured out through him, and the world may be definitely the better for his presence in it. The pupil is so closely in touch with the Master's thought that he can at any time see what that thought is upon any given subject, and in that way he is often saved from error. The Master can at any moment send a thought through that pupil either in the form of a suggestion or a message. If, for example, the pupil is writing a letter or giving a lecture, the Master is subconsciously aware of that fact, and may at any moment throw into the mind of the pupil a sentence to be included in that letter or a useful illustration for that lecture. In earlier stages the pupil is often unconscious of this, and supposes these ideas to have arisen spontaneously in his own mind, but he very soon learns to recognize the thought of the Master. Indeed, it is eminently necessary that he should learn to recognize it, because there are many other entities on the astral and mental planes who are very ready in the most friendly way and with the best intentions to make similar suggestions, and it is assuredly well that the pupil should learn to distinguish from whom they come.

We must not, however, confuse such use by a Master of his pupil's body with the mediumship which we have so often characterized as objectionable. For example, there have been some occasions on which one or other of our Masters has spoken through Annie Besant, and it has been stated that on such occasions sometimes her very voice and manner and even her features have been changed. But it must be remembered that in all such cases she has retained the fullest consciousness and has known exactly who was speaking and why. That is a condition so different from what is ordinarily understood by mediumship that it would be quite unfair to call it by the same name. There can be no objection to such use of a pupil's body, but it is only in the case of a very few pupils that the Masters have ever done this.

When it happens, Mrs. Besant's consciousness is just as fully active in her physical brain as ever, but instead of directing her organs of speech herself she listens while the Master makes use of them. He formulates the sentences in his own brain and then transfers them to hers. While this is being done she can use her own brain-power, passively, to listen, to understand, and to admire; but I conceive that it would hardly be possible for her at absolutely the same moment to compose a sentence upon some quite different subject. I suppose that the highest form of spiritualistic control may more or less approximate this, but probably very rarely, and hardly ever completely.

The influence of a Master is so powerful that it may well shine through to almost any extent, and any one of the audience who is really impressible might be conscious of his presence to the extent of seeing his features or hearing his voice, instead of those of his pupil. It is not very probable that any actual physical change takes place, such as would be visible to non-sensitive spectators. In spiritualism I have indeed seen cases in which the medium's voice and manner, and even his very features, were actually physically entirely changed, but that always means a complete suppression of his ego by the entity speaking through him, and this would be quite foreign to the system of training adopted by our Masters.

There is yet a third stage of even more intimate union, when the pupil becomes what is called the "son" of the Master. This is accorded only after the Master has had considerable experience of the man as an accepted pupil, when he is quite certain that nothing can arise in the mind or astral body of the pupil which will ever need to be shut off. For that is perhaps the principal difference which can be readily explained on the physical plane between the position of the accepted disciple and of the "son"— that the accepted disciple, though truly a part of the Master's consciousness, can still be shut off when it seems desirable, whereas that "son" is drawn into a union so close and so sacred that even the power of the Master cannot undo what has been done to the extent of separating these consciousnesses even for a moment.

These then are the three stages of the relation of a pupil to his Master; first, *the probationary period*, during which he is not in any real sense a pupil at all; second, *the period of accepted discipleship*; third, *the period of "sonship."* It must be clearly understood that these relations have nothing whatever to do with initiations or steps on the Path, which belong to an entirely different category, and are tokens of the man's relation not to his Master but the the Great White Brotherhood and to its august Head. One may find an apt symbol of these respective relationships in the position in which an undergraduate stands with regard to the head of his college and to the university as a whole. The university as such requires the man to pass certain examinations, and the precise methods in which he prepares himself for this are, comparatively speaking, matters of indifference to it. It is the university, and not the head of the college, that arranges the examination and confers the various degrees; the work of the head of the college is simply to see that the candidate is duly prepared. In the process of such preparation he may, as a private gentleman, enter into whatever social or other relations he may think proper with his pupil; but all that is not the business of the university.

Just in the same way the Great White Brotherhood has nothing to do with the relations between the Master and his pupil; that is a matter solely for the private consideration of the Master himself. Whenever the Master considers that the pupil is fit for the first initiation, he gives notice of that fact and presents him for it, and the Brotherhood asks only whether he is ready for the initiation, and not what is the relationship between him and any Master. At the same time it is true that a candidate for initiation must be proposed and seconded by two of the higher members of the Brotherhood—that is to say, by two who have reached the level of adeptship; and it is certain that the Master would not propose a man for the tests of initiation unless he had with regard to him the certainty of his fitness, which could only come from such close identification with his consciousness as that of which I have already spoken.

When a student hears all this there naturally arises in his mind the question, "How can I become the pupil of a Master? What can I do that will attract his attention?" As a matter of fact it is quite unnecessary that we should try to attract his attention, for the Masters are ever watching for those whom they can help to be of use to them in the great work which they have to do, and we need not have the slightest fear that we shall be overlooked.

I remember very well an incident of the early days of my own connection with the Great Ones a quarter of a century ago. I met, on the physical plane, a man of great enthusiasm and of the most saintly character, one who believed thoroughly in the existence of the Masters, and devoted his life to the one object of qualifying himself for their service. He seemed to me a man in every way so entirely suitable for discipleship, so obviously better than myself in many ways, that I could not understand how it was that he was not already accepted; and so, being young in the work and ignorant, one day when a good opportunity offered itself I very humbly and as it were apologetically mentioned his name to the Master with the suggestion that he might perhaps prove a good instrument. A smile of kindly amusement broke out upon the Master's face, as he said:

"Ah, you need not fear that your friend is being overlooked; no one can ever be overlooked; but in this case there still remains a certain karma to be worked out, which makes it impossible at the moment to accept your suggestion. Soon your friend will pass away from the physical plane, and soon he will return to it again, and then the expiation will be complete and what you desire for him will have become possible."

And then, with the gentle kindness which is always so prominent a characteristic in him, he blended my consciousness with his in an even more intimate manner, and raised it to a plane far higher than I could then reach, and from that elevation he showed me how the Masters look out upon the world. The whole earth lay before us with all its millions of souls, undeveloped most of them, and therefore inconspicuous; but wherever amidst all that mighty multitude there was one who was approaching even at a great distance the point at which definite use could be made of him, he stood out among the rest just as the flame of a lighthouse stands out in the darkness of the night.

"Now you see," said the Master, "how utterly impossible it would be that any one should be overlooked who is even within measurable distance of the possibility of acceptance as a probationer."

We can do nothing on our side but steadily work at the improvement of our own character and endeavour in every possible way, by the study of theosophical works, by self-development, and by the unselfishness of our devotion to the interests of others, to fit ourselves for the honor which we desire, having within our minds the utter certainty that as soon as we are ready the acceptance will assuredly come. We can do nothing but fit ourselves, and know with certainty that as soon as we are ready we shall be accepted, because we know how great is the need of helpers. But until we can be utilized economically—that is to say, until the force spent upon us will bring forth, through our action, more result than it would if spent in any other way, it would be a violation of duty on the part of the Master to draw us into close relations with him.

We may be quite sure that there are in reality no exceptions to this rule, even though we may sometimes think that we have seen some. A man may become a probationary pupil of the Master while he has still some obvious faults, but we may be very sure that in such a case there are good qualities under the surface which far more than counterbalance the superficial evils. Another thing that must be remembered is that, like the rest of us, the Great Masters of Wisdom have a long line of lives behind them, and in those lives, like others, they have made certain karmic ties, and so sometimes it happens that a particular individual has a claim on them for some service rendered long ago in the remote past. In the lines of past lives which we have examined we sometimes come across instances of such a karmic link.

One well-known case is that of a certain member who, when a powerful noble in Egypt six thousand years ago, used his influence with the authorities of one of the great temples to introduce into it as a favored student a young man who displayed the keenest interest in occult matters. That young student took up occultism with the greatest eagerness and made the most astonishing progress in it, so that in every life thereafter he continued the studies begun in ancient Khem. Between then and now that young student has attained adeptship, and thus passed on far in advance of the friend who then introduced him to the temple. In the work which he has had to do in these later days he needed some one to put before the world certain truths which had to be published, because the time for such unfoldment was fully ripe. He looked round for an instrument whom he could use, and he found his old friend and helper of six thousand years ago in a position in which it was possible to employ him in this work. At once he remembered his ancient debt and repaid it by giving to his friend this wonderful privilege of being the channel of the truth to the world.

Such cases indeed are fairly numerous. We all know how at a period still far earlier one of the founders of the Theosophical Society saved the life of the other, who was at that time the eldest son of him who is now the Master and teacher of both, and thus established a karmic claim which has drawn those three into close relationship ever since. Again, on another occasion in the remote past Annie Besant saved the life of her present teacher when there was a conspiracy to assasinate him; and in yet another instance one who has but just passed the portals of initiation saved the life of the Bodhisattva, the great Lord Maitreya himself.

Now all these are unquestionably karmic links, and they constitute debts which will be fully repaid. It may have happened to any of us that in some past life we have come into touch with one who is now a Master, or done him some slight service, and if so, that may well prove to have been the commencement of an association which will ripen into discipleship on our side. It frequently happens that people are drawn together by a strong common interest in occultism, and in later lives, when some of these have outdistanced the others, those who were once friends and fellow-students often fall naturally into the relation of teacher and pupil.

No doubt a man may attract their attention in many ways; he may bring himself to the portals of the Path by association with those in advance of him, by the force of sheer hard thinking, by devotion, or by earnest endeavor in good works; but all these are after all merely so many divisions of the one Way, because they mean that he is making himself fit for one or other department of the work that is to be done. And so when by any of these methods he reaches a certain level, he inevitably attracts the attention of the Masters of the Wisdom and comes in some way into connection with them, though probably not upon the physical plane. The Master's usual plan is that he is brought into connection with one or other of their more prominent pupils, and this is very much the safest way, since it is impossible for any ordinary person to assure himself of the good faith of astral communications.

Unless a man has had very wide experience in connection with mediumship, he would find it very difficult to realize how many quite ordinary people there are upon the astral plane who are burning with the desire to pose as great world-teachers. They are generally quite honest in their intentions, and really think that they have teaching to give which will save the world. Now that they are dead they have fully realized the worthlessness of mere worldly objects, and they feel (quite rightly) that if they could only impress upon mankind in general the ideas which they have now acquired, the whole world would immediately become a very different place. They are also fully persuaded that they have only to publish their discoveries upon the physical plane in order at once to convince everybody of their inherent reasonableness, and so they select some impressionable lady and tell her that they have chosen her out of all the world to be the medium of a magnificent revelation.

Now it is rather flattering to the average person to be told that he or she is the sole medium in all the world for some mighty entity, the only channel for some exclusive and transcendent teaching; and even though the communicating entity should disclaim any special greatness (which he usually does not) this is put down to praiseworthy modesty on his part, and he is described as at least an archangel, even if not a still more direct manifestation of the Deity. What such a communicating entity forgets is that when he was alive on the physical plane other people were making similar communications through various mediums, and that then he never paid the slightest attention to them, nor was in any way affected by what they said, and so he does not realize that precisely as he, when immersed in the affairs of this world, declined to be moved by those very communications, so will all the world now go on contentedly with its own business and pay no attention to *him*.

Often such entities assume distinguished names from what may almost be called a pardonable motive, for they know human nature well enough to be aware that if John Smith or Thomas Brown comes back from the dead and enunciates a certain doctrine it will have very little chance of acceptance, no matter how excellent and how entirely true it may be; whereas the same words uttered by George Washington, Julius Casear or the Archangel Michael would be at least suspectfully considered and very probably blindly accepted.

Anyone functioning on the astral plane has a certain amount of insight into the thoughts and feelings of those with whom he is dealing, and therefore it is not wonderful that when such people come into contact with the Theosophists, and see their minds to be full of reverence for the Masters of Wisdom, they should sometimes impersonate those very Masters of Wisdom in order to command more ready acceptance for whatever ideas they wish to promulgate. Also it must not be forgotten that there are those who bear no good will to our Masters, and desire to do them any injury which lies within their power. They cannot of course harm them directly, and therefore they sometimes try to do so through the pupils whom they love. One of the easiest ways in which they can produce difficulties is by assuming the identity of the Master who is so strongly revered by their victim, and in many cases such an imitation is quite perfect, so far as the physical appearance is concerned, except that it always seems to me that they can never quite get the right expression into the eyes. One who has developed the sight of the higher planes cannot be thus deluded, as it is quite impossible for any of these entities to imitate the causal body of the Master.

Most assuredly we shall do well to heed diligently the wise precept in *The Voice of the Silence*, "Seek not the Guru in those mayavic regions." Accept no teaching from some self-appointed preceptor on the astral plane, but receive all communications and advice which comes from there precisely as you would receive similar advice or remarks made by a stranger on the physical plane. Take them for what they are worth, and accept the advice or reject it as your own conscience dictates, without paying attention to its alleged source. Seek rather for teaching which satisfies the intellect, and apply the test of intellect and conscience to any claims which are put forward.

Let it never be forgotten that ours are not the only lines. The two Masters who are most intimately associated with the work of the Theosophical Society represent two different rays or methods of teaching; but there are others besides these. All schools of the higher teaching give a preliminary training to purify the character, but the particular teachings given and practices recommended differ according to the type of the teacher. But all teachers who belong to the Great White Lodge insist upon the attainment of the highest only by means of the Path of Holiness, and the quenching of desire by conquering it and not by gratifying it.

The pupil will be employed by his Master in many different ways. Some are set to take up the lines of work indicated in the book *Invisible Helpers;* others are employed specifically in assisting the Masters personally in some piece of work which they happen to have undertaken; some are set astrally to deliver lectures to audiences of less developed souls, or to help and teach others who are free temporarily during sleep, or are permanently after-death denizens of the astral world. When a pupil falls asleep at night he usually reports himself to his Master, and he is then told if there is any definite piece of work which he can do. If there happens to be nothing special he will take up his usual nocturnal work, whatever that may be. Every invisible helper acquires a number of regular cases or patients who are put under his charge just exactly as are those of a doctor on the physical plane; and whenever there is no unusual work for him to do he simply goes on his ordinary rounds, visits these cases and does his best for them. So that he has always plenty of work of this kind to fill up his time when he is not especially needed, as for some sudden catastrophe which throws out a large number of souls simultaneously into the astral plane in a condition of terror. Most of such training in astral work as the pupil needs is usually given by one of the older pupils of the Master.

If it is necessary that the pupil should undertake any special system of psychic development on the physical plane, the Master will indicate it to him either directly or through one of his recognized pupils. What is prescribed in this way differs according to the character and need of the pupil, and it is usually best for us to wait until we are definitely told before attempting any practices of this kind. Even when we are told of them it is best that we should keep them to ourselves, and not discuss them with others, as it is more than probable that they would be unsuited to anyone else. Here in India among the hosts of minor teachers each man has his own methods, the difference depending partly on the different schools of philosophy to which they belong, and partly upon their different ways of looking at the same thing. But whatever their methods are, they usually keep them very secret in order to avoid the responsibility of their being wrongly used.

The harm that may be done by the indiscriminate publication of any of these half-physical systems has been very clearly exemplified in America, where a book by an Indian teacher guardedly mentioned certain practices, prefacing his teaching with a carefully expressed warning as to the necessity of preparation by the training of character. But nevertheless what he has written has caused a great deal of suffering, because people have uniformly disregarded his warning as to training and have recklessly tried to carry out the practices which he described. In a tour a few years ago in that country I met quite a number of people who through attempting to follow his directions had made themselves physical wrecks. Some had become insane, some were subject to fits, and others had fallen under the spell of various obsessing entities. In order that such practices as these may be attempted with safety it is absolutely necessary that they be undertaken (as they always are undertaken in India) in the actual presence of a teacher who watches the results and at once interferes when he sees that anything is going wrong. Indeed, in this country it is usual for the pupil to remain in physical proximity to his teacher, because here people understand what I mentioned some time ago—that the first and greatest work which a teacher has to do is to attune the aura of the pupil to his own—to annul the effect of the ordinary disturbed conditions which prevail in the world, to show him how to abandon all that and to live in a world of absolute calm. One of our own Masters said in one of the earlier letters, "Come out of your world into ours," and this of course refers not to a place but to a condition of mind.

Remember that everyone who meditates upon the Master makes a definite link with him, which shows itself to clairvoyant vision as a kind of line of light. The Master always subconsciously feels the impinging of such a line, and sends out along it in response a steady stream of magnetism which continues to play long after the meditation is over. The regular practice of such meditation and concentration is of the utmost help to the aspirant, and the regularity is one of the most important factors in producing the result. It should be undertaken daily at the same hour, and we should steadily persevere with it, even though no obvious effect may be produced. When no effect appears we must be especially careful to avoid depression, because depression makes it more difficult for a Master's influence to act upon us, and it also shows that we are thinking more of ourselves than of the Master.

The Path of Progress

When we state the great truth that all evolution came forth from the Divine, and that we ourselves are but sparks of the divine flame and one day to be reunited to it, people often ask us two not unnatural questions. First they say, "Why should the divine Being have sent us forth, since after all we are part of Him, and so were divine from the beginning? Why in fact did the LOGOS manifest Himself in matter at all, seeing that He was perfect and glorious and all-wise in the beginning? Secondly, if we emanate from the divine Spirit, why were we sent forth into wickedness, and how can man, coming forth from so pure a source, enter into such degradation as we constantly see around us?" Since these questions recur so often, it is worth while for us to consider how they may be answered.

Why the LOGOS manifested Himself is scarcely our business. It is enough for us to know that He has chosen to do so, that we are part of His scheme, and that it is therefore our duty to try to understand that scheme so far as we can, and to adapt ourselves to it. But if there be any who desire to speculate upon this mystery, perhaps no better suggestion can be found for them than that which was given by the Gnostic Doctors:

> God is Love, but Love itself cannot be perfect unless it has those upon whom it can be lavished and by whom it can be returned. Therefore He put forth of Himself into matter and He limited His glory, in order that through this natural and slow process of evolution we might come into being; and we in turn according to His will are to develop until we reach even His own level, and then the very Love of God itself will become more perfect, because it will then be lavished on those, His own children, who will fully understand and re-turn it, and so His great scheme will be realized and His Will will be done.

As to the further consideration why the emanation should have taken place in this particular way, that again is not our affair, for we are concerned only with the *facts* of evolution, not the reasons for it; yet there seems little difficulty in at least indicating the lines along which an answer may be found. It is quite true that man is an emanation from the substance of the Divine, but it must be remembered that the substance, when it issues forth, is undif-ferentiated, and from our point of view unconscious; that is, it has within it rather the potentiality of consciousness than anything to which we are in the habit of applying that term.

In its descent into matter it is simply gathering round it the matter of the different planes through which it passes, and it is not until, having reached the lowest point of its evolution in the mineral kingdom, it turns upwards and begins its return to the level whence it came, that it commences to develop what we call consciousness at all. It is for that reason that man began first of all to unfold his consciousness on the physical plane, and it is only after fully attaining that that he begins to be conscious upon the astral and mental planes in turn.

No doubt God might have made man perfect and obedient to the law by one act of His will, but is it not obvious that such a man would have been a mere automaton—that the will working in him would have been God's will, not his own? What the LOGOS desired was to call into existence, from His own substance, those who should be like unto Him in power and glory, absolutely free to choose and yet absolutely certain to choose the right and not the wrong, because in addition to perfect power they would have perfect knowledge and perfect love.

It is not easy to imagine any other way in which this result could be achieved but that which has been adopted—the plan of leaving man free and therefore capable of making mistakes. From those mistakes he learns and gains experience, and although in such a scheme as this it is inevitable that there should be evil, and therefore sorrow and suffering, yet when the part these play as factors in man's evolution is properly understood we shall see that the Chinese proverb is true which tells us that evil is but the dark shadow of good. Most emphatically it is true that, however black the clouds may look from below, those clouds are by their very nature transient, and above and behind them all the mighty sun, which will at last dissipate them, is always shining, so that the old saying is justified that *all* things, even the most unlikely-looking, are in reality working together for good.

This much at least all who have made any real progress *know* for themselves as an absolute certainty; while they cannot hope to prove it to those who have not as yet had the experience, at least they can bear testimony to it with no uncertain voice, and that testimony is surely not without its value for souls who are still struggling towards the light.

As to the second question, we may fairly point out that it assumes too much. It is not true to say that we are sent forth into wickedness and degradation. In fact, strictly speaking *we* are not sent forth at all. What happens is something quite different. The LOGOS pours forth into manifestation the stream of force which we may describe as part of Himself or of His vesture. This stream contains in potentiality the vast hosts of monads, each of which, when fully developed, may itself become a LOGOS. But for such development it is necessary that it should manifest itself through matter of various grades, that the individuality should very slowly and gradually be built up, and then that certain latent qualities should be brought out. This is the process of evolution, and all the great laws of the universe are arranged to facilitate this process. In its earlier stages the manifestation of the monad is entirely controlled by these laws, not having yet developed any sort of individuality or soul of its own.

But there comes a stage in which individuality is attained, and will is beginning to be developed. The plan of the Logos is to allow a man a certain amount of freedom (at first a very small amount) in the use of this dawning will, and naturally enough by the law of averages this primitive individual uses his will about as often wrongly as rightly, although he has almost always teachers belonging to earlier evolutions, who tell him the way in which he should walk. When he uses his will wrongly (that is to say, in a direction opposed to the current of evolution) the mechanical working of nature's laws brings suffering as the result of such action. Since this happens over and over again, the primitive ego at last learns by experience that he must obey the wiser teaching given to him, and as soon as the determination to do so has become actually a part of himself a wider field of freedom of action opens before him.

In this new field in turn he is sure to act wrongly sometimes as well as rightly, so that the same process is repeated again and again, always involving suffering where mistakes have been made. Whatever of "wickedness and degradation" may exist is always the result of the action of men who have used their free-will wrongly, and are in process of learning how to use it rightly. As soon as that lesson shall have been universally learned all these evil effects will pass away. It is therefore obvious that whatever of evil exists in the world is entirely the doing of its inhabitants, and is temporary in nature. However terrible and deeply rooted it may seem to us, it cannot possibly be permanent, for it is of the essence of things that it must pass away when its causes are removed. For its existence while it lasts we must blame, not the great First Cause, but ourselves, because we are failing to carry out His plan.

We often exhort people to follow the higher course rather than the lower, but I think that the truth is that a man always follows the highest about which he is really certain. The difficulty is that in so many cases the higher teaching seems vague and unreal to many people, and so although they profess to believe it, and really think that they do believe it, when it comes to the point of action they find it too vague to trust their lives to it.

For example, many people who think themselves religious are yet to be found seeking position and wealth. That attitude would be entirely reasonable if they were materialists and if they did not pretend to believe in anything higher; but when we find a religious man devoted to the pursuit of worldly objects there is clearly something wrong, something illogical. The fact is that he does not really believe in his religion; he is not thoroughly convinced of its truth, for if he were he could not be following after other things. He is following that about which he is really sure; he is quite certain, without the slightest mental reservation, about the desirability of money and power. He knows that he wants these things, and he thinks he knows that if he gets them they will make him happy. Therefore he devotes all his energy and time to their acquisition, and we must remember that in doing that he is at least developing will and perseverance.

Now if you can in any way manage to make him as sure of the value of the higher things as he is now about the value of pounds, shillings and pence, he will at once turn that will and that perseverance to the service of the higher development, and he will seek after realities with just the same intensity that he is now devoting to the pursuit of shadows. This is precisely what the study of theosophy will do for him. A man who thoroughly understands theosophy knows that he is here for a certain purpose, and that it is most emphatically his business to devote himself entirely to the working out of that purpose. He realizes thoroughly that there are things worth doing and aims worth pursuing, and he devotes himself to them with the same avidity which he previously displayed in following the acquisition of money or position.

But in order to do this it is not sufficient merely to be vaguely interested, merely to read a few books. The man must really believe it, must be thoroughly and utterly convinced of its truth. Now the only way in which this utter conviction can come to a man is by means of realizing some part of it, however small, for himself and at first-hand. Without going so far as that, of course, a man may be intellectually convinced of the truth of the doctrine, and may see that nothing else is logically possible; but there are very few of us who have the strength to act upon such a logical conviction about things entirely beyond our ken; for most of us it is really necessary that at least some small portion of the doctrine, some sample of it, as it were, should be definitely seen and known.

We who were the earlier students felt all this just as keenly as do the students of to-day, and when in those early days of twenty-five or twenty-seven years ago we asked Madame Blavatsky whether it was in any way possible that we could verify any of these things for ourselves she at once replied in the affirmative. She told us that if we chose to take the trouble to develop the requisite faculties we might unquestionably experience for ourselves the truth of a great deal of the teaching. She warned us that the way was long and arduous, and that no one could tell beforehand how long it would take for a man to tread it. But on the other hand she consoled us by saying that the end was absolutely certain, and that it was impossible that any man who started to reach it should fail to attain, though in many cases such attainment might lie, not in this life, but in some other in the future.

This was encouraging in one way, and yet somewhat daunting in another way; but at any rate a certain number of us took her at her word and threw ourselves heart and soul into the endeavour to live the life which was prescribed for us, and to do the work that lay before us. The degrees of our success were very varied, but of all of those who made this effort and persevered with it I think I may say that there was not one who did not obtain some result— enough at any rate to show him that what he had been told was true, and that if the progress which he made was smaller than he had hoped, the fault lay clearly with himself and not with the teachers.

There were those among us, however, who succeeded in verifying for ourselves a large number of the statements made by the Masters—first of all only in a small way, with regard to ourselves, our vehicles, our possibilities, and with regard to the astral life which immediately surrounds us. Then later on by long continued and more strenuous effort we developed the faculties of the mental body, and began for the first time really to understand what had been written for us about the life of the heaven-world. At first we had hopelessly misunderstood all this, because with the faculties then at our disposal we were actually incapable of comprehending it. By a strenuous further effort we reached the faculties of the causal body, and then the world of comparative realities began really to open before us.

We were able then to read the records of the past, and to see from them with absolute certainty how the great scheme of the

LOGOS is slowly unfolding itself and working itself out by means of successive births under the guidance of the great laws of evolution and cause and effect. We could see clearly then that we were unquestionably ourselves a part of this great scheme, and therefore it followed that it was alike our duty, our advantage, our privilege, to throw ourselves into the scheme and co-operate intelligently in its fulfillment. There was then no doubt for us about the fact of the great evolution and the future of humanity, for it was clear to us that we had risen through the lower kingdoms, and we could see many stages both below us and above us; all the various stages of human life arranged themselves for us as steps upon a ladder; we could see these steps stretching up and down from the point which we ourselves occupied, and there were beings upon every rung of that ladder, beings who were clearly engaged in climbing it.

The Masters who seemed to us to stand at its summit assured us that they were men like ourselves and that they had passed through the stage where we were now standing; between us and them there was no break in the continuity, for every step of the ladder was occupied, and we ourselves watched the progress of some of those higher than we from one of these steps to another. When through custom the wonderful light of the higher planes grew less dazzling to us, we were able to see that even beyond the stupendous level occupied by the Masters there arose still greater heights. Above them stood Manus, Christs, Buddhas, Lipika, great Devas, Dhyan Chohans, and many others of whom we can know nothing except that They exist, and that They, even at Their ineffable elevation, form part of the same mighty chain.

The whole of the past lies before us; we know the halting-places on the road, and the side-paths that branch off from it, and therefore we are justified in our confidence that where these great ones now stand we also shall one day stand. Seeing and understanding the inevitableness of our destiny, we also realize that it will be quite useless to endeavour to resist it. Progress is the law marked out for us. Only in progress is our happiness and our safety. As regards the progress that lies before us in this particular chain of worlds the great majority of us are by no means yet what is technically called "safe" or "saved." We reach that desirable position only when we have become members of the Great

Brotherhood which lasts from eternity to eternity, by passing the first of the great initiations, that of the Sotapatti or srotapanna, the man who enters upon the stream.

To have taken that step is to have achieved the most important result, to have passed the most critical point in the whole of human evolution. For in the course of that evolution three points stand out beyond all others. The first is the entrance upon humanity, the attainment of individuality, the gaining of a causal body, the becoming a definite and apparently separate ego. To gain this individuality was the aim of the animal evolution, and its development serves a very definite purpose. The object is to make a strong individual center, through which eventually the force of the LOGOS can be poured out. When this center is first formed it is only a baby ego, still but weak and uncertain; in order that it may become strong and definite it has to be fenced round by intense selfishness, and for many lives a strong wall of selfishness has to be maintained, in order that within it the center may grow more and more definite.

We may regard this selfishness as a kind of scaffolding, which is absolutely necessary for the erection of the building, but must be destroyed as soon as the building is completed, in order that it may be able to subserve the purpose for which it was erected. The scaffolding is not beautiful, and if it were left after the building is finished it would make it uninhabitable, and yet without it the building could not have been achieved. The object of the creation of the center is that through it the force of the LOGOS should radiate out upon the world, and such radiation would be quite impossible if the selfishness persisted, and yet without that self-ishness a strong center could never have been made. We see therefore that this most unlovely of qualities has its place in evolution. Now for us its work is over, and we ought to have got rid of it. But it is useless to be angry that what was a necessary virtue is still persisting. In point of fact the selfish man is an anachronism, a survival of prehistoric savagery. He is hopelessly behind the times.

How then is such a man to make himself unselfish, to bring himself abreast of the advancing current of evolution? The methods adopted by nature to secure this end are many and various, but they are all fundamentally one. For what is necessary is that the man shall realize the unity of all. And often he does this by gradually enlarging the self of which he thinks. Instead of thinking of himself as the unit he begins to regard the family as the unit for which he is working, and within its limits he gradually becomes unselfish. Presently he expands his ideas to include the tribe or clan to which he belongs, and he learns to be unselfish within its limits, while still absolutely selfish and even predatory to all who are outside it, whom he usually regards as natural enemies. Later on in his history he extends his ideas so as to include, in certain respects at least, the nation to which he belongs.

It is somewhere in the course of that stage of transition that the majority of humanity stand at the present moment. In almost all minor matters the ordinary man is still fighting for his family against the interests of all other families, but in a few wider matters he recognizes that his interests are identical with those of those other families, and so in those matters he develops what he calls patriotism and national feeling; but even in those matters he is still absolutely selfish as regards all those other families who happen to speak different languages and to be born in different climes. At some time in the future the average man will extend his ideas of self to include the whole of humanity, and then at last we may say that he has become by slow degrees unselfish.

While he is thus learning to take a wider view of his relation to others, he is also learning something with regard to himself. First he realizes that he is not his physical body, later that he is not his feelings, and further on still that he is not even his mind. This brings him eventually to the realization that he is the ego or soul, and still later on he realizes that even that ego is only apparently separate, and that there is in reality but one transcendant unity.

Thus the man treads the weary round of the seven hundred and seventy-seven incarnations, a time of slow and painful progress and of harrowing uncertainty, but at last after all those struggles the uncertainty ends with that plunge into the stream that makes the man safe forever, and so that is the second and still more important point in his evolution. But before he can take this step the man must have learned consciously to cooperate with nature, he must definitely have taken his own evolution in hand. The knowledge of the unity which makes him unselfish also makes him desire to be useful, for it gives him an incentive to study and to perfect himself—a reason for his actions and a criterion by which he can judge the feelings and thoughts within him, and also the value of all with which he comes into contact.

How then must he begin this work of perfecting himself? Obviously he must first pull up the weeds, that is to say he must eliminate one by one the undesirable qualities which he finds in himself; then he must seek the good qualities and cultivate them. He must definitely set himself to practice helpfulness, even although at first he may be very clumsy in the unaccustomed work. The formation of character is very slow and tedious for him, for there are many forces arrayed against his efforts, forces which he himself has made in the past. He has for many years been yielding himself to the sway of certain undesirable qualities, and so they have gained a great momentum.

Take the case of a vice such as irritability, for example. He has in the past been in the habit of yielding himself to outbursts of anger, and every such outburst makes it more difficult for him to control himself on the next occasion; so a strong habit has been set up, a vast amount of energy moving in that direction has been accumulated. This is stored up, not in the ego as an inherent quality, but in the permanent astral atom.* When he realizes the inadvisability of anger and sets himself against it he has to meet this store of force which he himself has generated during many past lives. Naturally he finds his task a difficult one, and he meets with many failures and discouragements; but the important thing for him to bear in mind is that however many times he may fail, victory is absolutely a scientific certainty, if only he will persevere.

However great the amount of force may be which he has stored up, it must be a finite amount, and every effort which he makes against it reduces it by just so much. But on his side there is a force which is infinite; if only his will is strong enough he can go on, if necessary through many lives, steadily renewing the force for good with which he combats the evil, and behind him in that effort is the infinite force of the LOGOS Himself, because that evolution is in accordance with His will. Until the man grasps the idea of unity he has no adequate motive for undertaking the hard

---

*Astral atom—a unit of astral matter which remains attached to the ego from one incarnation to the next. Editor.

and distasteful work of character-building, but when he has seen the necessity of this, the reason for trying is just as valid even though he has failed a thousand times as it was in the beginning. No number of failures can daunt the man who understands the scheme, just because he knows that however great the struggle may be the forces of infinity are on his side, and therefore in the end he cannot fail.

To be certain of remembering this purpose of his from life to life he should raise his consciousness to the ego; but during the stages when he is as yet incapable of this he will nevertheless impress that purpose upon the permanent atoms, and so it will be carried over with them from life to life. If the ego can be reached, the man will be born with the knowledge inherent in him; if he can only impress the permanent atoms, the knowledge will not actually be born with him as part of his stock-in-trade, but the moment that it comes before him in any form in his next incarnation he will immediately recognize its truth, seize upon it, and act accordingly. This steady practice of virtue and this persistent increase of knowledge will certainly lead him to the gate of the probationary path, and through that to the great initiation of which we have spoken.

After that initiation the third point is sure to follow—the gaining of the further shore of that stream, in the attainment of adeptship, when the man leaves the merely human evolution and enters upon that which is superhuman. We are told that after a man has entered upon the stream it takes him an average of seven incarnations to reach the fourth step, that of the arhat, the noble, the venerable, the perfect. That period is more often lengthened than shortened, and the lives are usually taken without an intervening stage in the heaven-world. Ordinarily it is only men of this stage who are able thus to dispense with or renounce the life of the heaven-world.

At the same time those who are so happy as to be chosen to take part in the noble task for which the great Masters are preparing us, that of working under the Manu in charge of the development of the sixth root-race, will certainly need many successive incarnations without any intervening periods of celestial rest. The possibility of this is however conditioned by the rule that a man must have experienced celestial consciousness before he can renounce the heaven-life; and furthermore it is not in the least merely a question of voluntarily renouncing a reward, but of being suffi-

ciently advanced to dispense for a time with that part of evolution
which for the majority comes most usually in the heaven-life.

When he stands upon the step of arhatship half his path from
the first initiation to adeptship may be said to have been trodden,
for he has then cast off five of the ten great fetters which hold
men back from nirvana. Before him lies the task of casting off the
remaining five, and for that also an average of seven incarnations
is allowed, but it must be understood that this average is in no
sense a rule, for many men take much longer than this, whereas
others with greater determination and perseverance move
through these initiations in very much less time. A case has been
known in which, by beginning very early in life, and by working
very hard, a man has been able to take all four of the great
initiations in one incarnation, but this is excessively rare, and not
one in ten thousand candidates could do it.

It will be remembered that to stand at the level of the arhat
involves the power fully to use the buddhic vehicle, and it will also
be remembered that when a man raises himself into his buddhic
body the causal body vanishes, and he is under no compulsion
whatever ever to re-form it. Clearly therefore the seven lives
which remain to him before he reaches the level of adeptship
need not involve a descent to the physical plane at all, and therefore they may not be what we ordinarily mean by incarnations.
Nevertheless in the great majority of cases they are taken upon
the physical plane, because the man has work to do upon that
plane for the Great Brotherhood.

The candidate spends these fourteen lives in passing through
the different stages of the Path of Holiness, and in acquiring all
the qualification which are described in detail in the concluding
chapters of *Invisible Helpers*. One who becomes a disciple of one
of our Masters takes always, not the path to selfish liberation—the
mere balancing of good and evil karma and the vanishing of all
desire, so that the man is no longer forced back into rebirth—but
the path of renunciation in which, having seen the scheme of the
LOGOS , the man throws himself into it and lives only to promote
the advancement of his fellow-men.

This has been called "The Path of Woe" because of the constant
self-sacrifice which it involves, but in truth this title is somewhat of
a misnomer, because although it is true that there is suffering, it is
always a suffering of the lower and not of the higher, and if the
man should avoid such suffering by supineness or idleness, and

leave undone the work which he might have done, there would assuredly be much greater suffering for him at a far higher level, in the shape of remorse. Such suffering as is inevitable in this path arises from the fact that the student is striving to do here and now in the fourth round what will be natural and easy in the seventh round. All our vehicles then will be much more developed, and even the very material of which they are built will be in an entirely different condition. Therefore to force our present undeveloped vehicles to do work which will be comparatively easy for those which in millions of years will be fully developed, involves a great deal of strain, and this strain is necessarily productive of a certain amount of suffering.

It is analogous to the suffering and privation which is cheerfully undergone by an athlete when he puts himself in training. If he wishes to compete in some great race or trial of strength, he must make his physical body do more than it would naturally do, and deny it many things which it greatly likes, the absence of which unquestionably causes it considerable discomfort, and perhaps even somewhat of positive suffering. Yet for the purpose which he has in view the athlete quite cheerfully undergoes this; indeed if, for the sake of avoiding these comparatively slight temporary discomforts, he should put aside the opportunity of taking part in the race or contest, it is quite likely that afterwards when he saw his comrades passing onward to victory he would feel a remorse for that self-indulgence, which would involve keener suffering on a higher plane. The analogy holds good in reference to the efforts necessary to progress along the path of renunciation; the man who fell aside from that path because of its difficulties and hardships would undoubtedly suffer far more in the long run from remorse when he saw those of his fellow-creatures going unhelped whom he might have aided, when he saw misery among them which he knew that he might have relieved if he had been less self-indulgent.

There is never any pain to the Self, but only to these lower vehicles, when they are being prematurely adapted. A good analogy may be taken from the growth of crabs and other crustaceans. These creatures have their bones outside for protection, in the form of a shell, while our bones are inside, in the form of a skeleton. A fatal objection to the crustacean scheme is that when the creature grows it has to burst the shell and then wait for another one to grow, which must be both a painful and inconvenient process. So in the process of our growth do we make ourselves shells of thought, as though we were mental crustaceans. Presently the shell becomes too small, and then we make a long series of efforts to crowd the new growth inside it and make it do somehow; but in the end this always proves impossible, and we have painfully to burst it. This however is inevitable, so chafe not at karma and at nature's changeless laws, for you made the shell yourself in the past, and now you yourself must break it. But if you did not go to the inconvenience of breaking it, you would suffer far more in the unsatisfied feeling that no progress had been made.

Many people are afraid of change, especially of a change of faith, and this arises not only from inherited prejudice, but also from actual fear of doubt—fear that if one once lets go one may be unable to find mental anchorage anywhere. Many a man is quite unable to make rational defense of his belief, or to answer the problems which inevitably arise in connection with it, and yet he is afraid to let it go. Sooner or later he will have to let go, though the widening out of his faith is sure to be accompanied by pain. Truly there would be no suffering for us if we never broke our shells, but then on the other hand there would be no progress.

The life of the disciple is full of joy—never doubt it for an instant. But it is not a life of ease. The work which he has to do is very hard, the struggle is a very real one. To compress into a few short lives the evolution of millions of years—the evolution for which the ordinary process of nature allows three rounds and a half—is not a mere holiday task. Annie Besant has written: "Disciples are the crucibles of nature, wherein compounds that are mischievous are dissociated and are recombined into compounds that promote the general good."

It is not *necessary* for any one to become such a crucible; perhaps it would be nearer the fact to say that to become one is a distinction eagerly sought after; nearer still to say that when once a man has *seen* the great sacrifice of the LOGOS there is no other possibility for him but to throw himself into it—to do his tiny best to share in it and to help it at whatever cost to his lower nature. And this is no child's play; it does indeed involve often a terrible strain. But an earnest student will be able to realize that a man may so love his work, and may be so full of joy in it, that outside of it there can be no pleasure worth considering, even though that work may tax almost beyond bearing every faculty and every vehicle—physical, astral or mental—which he possesses.

It must be remembered that when humanity in general has this work to do and this evolution to accomplish, it will be far better fitted for the effort than is the man who is trying now to take a shorter and steeper road. Many of his difficulties are due to the fact that he is attempting, with a set of fourth-round bodies, to achieve the result for the attainment of which nature will prepare her less adventurous children by supplying them in the course of the ages with the splendid vehicles of the seventh round. Of course even to gain those glorified vehicles these weaker souls will have to do the same work; but when it is spread over thousands of incarnations it naturally looks less formidable.

Yet beyond and above all his struggle the pupil has ever an abiding joy, a peace and serenity that nothing on earth can disturb. If he had not, he would indeed be a faithless servant of his Master, for he would be allowing the temporary strain on the vehicles to overbear his perception of the Self within; he would be identifying himself with the lower instead of with the higher.

There is therefore a certain element of the ridiculous in describing this Path as one of woe, when it is clearly evident that there would be much greater woe for the candidate if this Path were not taken. Indeed, to the man who is really doing his duty true sorrow is unknown: "Never doth any who worketh righteousness, O beloved, tread the path of woe." (*Bhagavad-Gita*, 40 vi.)

This is as regards the inner life of the disciple, but if one is to consider the treatment which he is likely to receive on the physical plane, the name of the path of woe is by no means inappropriate, at least if he has to do any sort of public work in which he tries to help the world. Ruysbroek, the Flemish mystic of the fourteenth century, writes of those who enter upon the Path: "Sometimes these unhappy ones are deprived of the good things of earth, of their friends and relations, and are deserted by all creatures; their holiness is mistrusted and despised, men put a bad construction on all the works of their life, and they are rejected and disdained by all those who surround them; and sometimes they are afflicted with divers diseases." Remember, too, how Madame Blavatsky writes: "Where do we find in history that 'Messenger' grand or humble, an Initiate or Neophyte, who, when he was made the bearer of some hitherto concealed truth or truths, was not crucified and rent to shreds by the 'dogs' of envy, malice and ignorance? Such is the terrible Occult law; and he who does not feel in himself the heart of a lion to scorn the savage barking, and the soul of a dove to forgive the poor ignorant fools, let him give up the Sacred Science." (*The Secret Doctrine*, iii. 90.)

The way in which the world usually treats a new truth is first to ridicule it, then to grow angry about it, and then to adopt it and pretend that it has always held that view. In the meantime the first exponent of the new truth has probably been put to death or died of a broken heart.

It is in the course of the training on this Path that the consciousness of the candidate passes through the three halls mentioned in *The Voice of the Silence*. This term is used there to indicate the three lower planes. The first, that of ignorance, is the physical plane, upon which we are born to live and die, and it is very truly described as a Hall of Ignorance, for all that we know in it is the merest outside of things. The second, the Hall of Learning, is the astral plane, which is very truly the place of probationary learning, for when the astral centers are opened we see so much more of everything than we do on the physical plane that at first it seems to us that we must indeed be seeing the whole, though further development soon shows us that this is not so.

But *The Voice of the Silence* warns us that beneath each flower in this region, however beautiful it may be, lies coiled the serpent of desire—that lower desire which the aspirant must stifle in order that he may develop in its place the higher desire which we call aspiration. In the case of affection, for example, the lower, the selfish, the grasping affection must be altogether transcended, but the high, pure, and unselfish affection can never be transcended, since that is a characteristic of the LOGOS Himself, and a necessary qualification for progress upon the Path. What men should cast aside is such love as thinks always "How much love can I gain? How much does so and so love me? Does he love me as he loves some one else?" The love which we need is that which forgets itself altogether, and seeks only the occasion to pour itself out at the feet of the loved one.

The astral plane is often called the world of illusion, yet it is at least one stage, and a very long stage, nearer to the truth of things than what we see on the physical plane. It often happens that men are easily deluded upon the astral plane, because they are as yet much in the position of babies there, new-born infants with no sense of distance and no developed capacity for locomotion. We must not forget that in the normal course of things people very slowly awaken to the realities of the astral plane, just as a baby awakens to the realities of the physical plane. But those of us who are deliberately and, as it were, prematurely entering upon the Path are developing such knowledge abnormally, and are consequently more liable to error.

Danger and injury might easily come in the course of our experiments but for the fact that all pupils who, under proper training, are endeavoring to open these faculties are assisted and guided by those who are already accustomed to the plane. That is the reason for the various tests which are always applied to one who wishes to become a worker on the higher planes; that is why also all sorts of horrible sights are shown to the neophyte, in order that he may understand them and become accustomed to them. If this were not done, and if he came across such a thing suddenly, he might receive a shock which would drive him back into his physical body, and this would not only prevent his doing any useful work, but might also be a positive danger to that body. Where the neophyte is deluded on the astral plane it is his own fault, and not that of the plane, because error is due only to his unfamiliarity with the surroundings.

The third hall is the mental plane—the Hall of Wisdom. As soon as a man is free from attachment to astral things he can pass beyond the probationary stage of his learning, and begin to acquire knowledge which is real and definite. Beyond that in turn lies the imperishable world of the buddhic plane, in which for the first time the man learns the true unity of all that to the lower vision seems to be separate.

It has been said, "Thou canst not travel on the Path before thou hast become that Path itself." As long as it is but a Path to us, and we are following it according to directions received, or because we have seen it and chosen it with the intellect only, we have not truly entered it at all. This is only a stage, leading on to the condition when you have become yourself the Law and the Path, and you fulfill its requirements, instinctively doing the right merely because it is the right, and because it is inconceivable that you could do anything else. Then only have you *become* the Path.

A man cannot climb if he does not try; though if he does not climb it is true that he will not fall far. The strong man often makes serious errors; but the very force which enables him to

make them also enables him to make great progress when he
turns his energies in the right direction. Rapid progress affects
the whole organism and is a great strain upon it, and this inevitably finds out whatever weak spots there are in the man. The plans
of the Hierarchy will be carried out whatever we may or may not
do, for we are but as pawns in the mighty game which is being
played; but if we are intelligent pawns, and are willing to cooperate, it gives much less trouble to the authorities, and incidentally to ourselves.

And what will be the end of it all? The attainment of perfection.
Yet even that is only relatively and not absolutely the end, for
when we have reached in fullest consciousness the LOGOS of our
system and have unified our consciousness with His, there still
remains the further Path which leads us to union with still higher
Powers. A great authority has told us that at the end of one of the
stages of evolution far beyond adeptship the perfect man will be a
decad, having a body upon each of the sub-planes of the lowest
cosmic plane, the triple LOGOS outside of time and space con-
stituting his Self, and thus completing the ten. But this consummation can only be reached when the man has power to create a
body for himself upon each of these planes.

We have been led to understand that of the total number of
egos which are engaged in this evolution about one-fifth will fully
succeed—that is to say will succeed in attaining the asekha level
before the end of the seventh round. Another fifth will by that
time, have gained the arhat level, and about an equal number will
be on the lower stages of the Path, while a number roughly stated
as the remaining two-fifths will have dropped out of this evolution altogether at the critical period at the middle of the fifth
round.

All those who have not fully attained the goal, and completed
their evolution, will have to resume it upon the next chain of
globes, and even those who are the failures of the fifth round will
be successes in the next chain. In the same way it is not improbable
that some of those who are adepts and Masters now may have
been among the failures of the previous chain—that is to say, that
they belonged to the humanity of that chain, but were somewhat
backward upon it, and so dropped out there, and came on in the
fore-front of this later evolution, exactly as a boy who failed to
pass an examination one year would be likely to be among the first
of his class when he tries the same examination again twelve
months later.

Remember that we are now only just past the middle of an evolutionary period, and that is why so very few people comparatively have as yet attained adeptship, just as very few boys in a class would be already fit to pass the final examination of the year after only six months of study. In precisely the same way very few animals are as yet attaining individuality, for the animal who attains individuality is as far in advance of his fellows as is the human being who attains adeptship in advance of the average man. Both are doing at the middle point of evolution what they are expected to be able to do only at the end of it. Those who achieve only at the normal time, at the end of the seventh round, will approach their goal so gradually that there will be little or no struggle.

Undoubtedly to attain in that way is very far easier for the candidate. But that method has the tremendous drawback that the man who attains by it will not have been able to give any help to others, but will on the contrary have required assistance himself. I remember from the days of my childhood a Christian hymn which gave this idea very beautifully. It described how a certain soul went to heaven and enjoyed its bliss, and wandered about there very happily for a time, but at last he noticed that the crown which he wore differed much in splendor from many of the others, and for a long time he wondered why this was so. At last he met the Christ Himself and mustered up courage to ask Him the reason of this peculiarity; and the answer given ran thus:

> I know thou has believed on Me,
> And Life through Me is thine;
> But where are all those glorious gems
> That in thy crown should shine?
>
> Thou seest yonder glorious throng
> With stars on every brow,
> For every soul they led to Me
> They wear a jewel now.

"They that are wise shall shine as the brightness of the firmament, but they that turn many to righteousness [are] as the stars for ever and ever."

When we are struggling onwards ourselves we can help others, and we should do all that we can in this direction, not because of the result to ourselves (though that is inevitable) but for the sake of helping the world. The man who drifts with the stream has to be carried along, but when he begins to swim himself he sets free the force that would otherwise have been spent in helping him. That can then be used for the helping of others, quite independently of what he himself may do in that line.

Adeptship sets the man free from the necessity of rebirth, and its achievement also involves the liberation of forces for the aid of others. The man who seeks liberation only for himself may balance his karma perfectly and may kill out desire, so that the law of karma will not longer compel him to rebirth. But though he thus avoids the action of the law of karma he does not escape from the law of evolution. It may be long before he comes under the influence of that law, because by the hypothesis a man who has already at this stage set himself free from all desire must be considerably in advance of the average. There will however inevitably come a time when the slow and steady advance of the law of evolution will overtake him, and then its resistless pressure will force him out of his selfish bliss into rebirth once more, and so he will find himself again upon the wheel from which he had hoped to escape.

It has often been asked how the secrets revealed at initiation are protected from those who are able to read thoughts. There is not the slightest danger that any of these secrets will ever be disclosed in this manner, for at the same time that the secret is told to the initiate the means by which he can guard it is also explained to him. If it could be possible that an initiate could ever be so false as to think of betraying what has been confided to him, even then there would be no danger, for he is in such close touch with the Brotherhood of which he is a part that they would at once know of his foul intention, and before he could speak the treacherous words he would have forgotten utterly that there was anything to betray. There is nothing that is in any way terrible about these secrets, except that the power which goes with them might well be terrible if wrongly used. Initiates always know one another, much in the same way as Freemasons do; and, just as with the latter, any initiate could hide his status from those below him, but not from those above him.

However sorely the Brotherhood may be in need of helpers no man can receive initiation until his character is developed to a stage when he is ready for it, and in exactly the same way if a man has raised himself to the level of initiation there is no power which can withhold it from him. It may very often happen, however, that a man is ready in every respect, save for a lack of some one quality; and that lack may hold him back for a very long time, which would probably mean that by the time he acquired the missing quality he would in all other respects be developed in advance of the requirements. So it must not be supposed that all initiates standing upon the same level are invariably equal in all respects. What the world calls a great man is not necessarily developed all round and fit for initiation. Anything in the nature of favoritism or neglect is utterly inconceivable. In this matter no man can give to another that which he has not earned, nor can any man withhold the due recognition of development won.

The Ancient Mysteries

What I can tell you with regard to the ancient mysteries is not derived from any special study of old manuscripts, or of the history of this subject. It happened to me in another life to be born in ancient Greece, and to become initiated there into some of the mysteries. Now a man who was initiated in this way in Greece gave a pledge not to reveal what he had seen, and this pledge is binding, even though it was given in a former incarnation; but those who stood behind those mysteries have since thought fit to give out to the world much of what was then taught only under the vow of secrecy, and so they have relieved us from our promise as far as those teachings go. Therefore I break no pledge when I tell you something about the instructions which were given in those ancient mysteries. Other subjects were taught, however, which I am not at liberty to name, because they have not yet been made public by the Great Ones.

In the first place, I should like to ask you to notice that all peoples and all religions have had their mysteries, including the Christian religion. I have often heard people say that in the Christian religion, at least, nothing was hidden: that everything was open for the study of the poor and the unlearned. Any one who says that does not know the history of the Christian Church. Now, indeed, everything the Church knows is given out, but that is only because it has forgotten the mysteries which it used to keep hidden. If you study the earliest history of the Church, you will find that old writers speak very distinctly of the mysteries, which were taught only to those who were full members of the Church.

There were many points on which nothing was said to those who were only "katechoumenoi," who had just entered the Church, but were still candidates for full membership.

Traces of this we can find still earlier, for you will remember that it is said in the Gospels that the Christ made known to His disciples many things which He gave to the multitude only in parables.

But one of the reasons of the failure of the Christian Church to control her more intellectual sons, as she should have done, is the fact that she has forgotten and lost the supernatural and philosophical mysteries which were the basis of her dogma. To see something of this hidden side of her teachings you have only to read the works of the great Gnostic writers. Then you will find that when we take this side as the inner doctrine for the scholars, and the present form of the Christian religion as the outer doctrine for the illiterate, we get in the two combined a perfect expression of the ancient Wisdom. But to take either of these teachings by itself, and to condemn the other as heresy, gives us only a one-sided view. So every religion has instruction for those who do not get beyond its outer form, but has always also higher instruction for those who penetrate to the inner.

However, when we speak of the ancient mysteries, we generally mean those which were connected with the great religion of ancient Greece. Only a few books exist on this subject. There is a book of Iamblichus, who was himself initiated into the mysteries, and there is a book written by a countryman of mine, Thomas Taylor, a Platonist, and also one by a Frenchman, Monsieur P. Foucart. Although they are very interesting, you will find that they give but little real information. Much that we think we know about the mysteries (I mean from an external point of view) comes to us through the writings of their exponents.

The Christian Church has had the habit—probably justifiable from her point of view—of destroying all books which stood for teachings other than her own, and we must not forget that almost all of our knowledge with regard to early Christian times comes to us through the hands of the monks of the middle ages. They were practically the only educated people of that time, and it was they who copied all the manuscripts. They had very pronounced opinions about what was useful and what was not; so very naturally only that part survived which agreed with their views, this being reported with emphasis, while anything of opposite character was discarded. Above all, the greater part of the knowledge which is accessible to the general world about the mysteries is found in the works of the Church Fathers, who were opposed to them. Without wishing to accuse the Fathers of having purposely misrepresented, we may certainly conclude that they tried to put forward their own view in the best and strongest light. Even at the present day if you wished to know the whole truth concerning the doctrine of some Protestant sect, you would not go to Catholic priests for information; nor, if you wanted good and just explanations concerning Catholicism, would you go to the Salvation Army to get them.

In regard to the mysteries we are in a similar situation, only much worse, because of the many and bitter disputes between the followers of the old religion and its mysteries and the Fathers of the Christian Church. Therefore we may accept only with considerable reserve and with great prudence what the Fathers say in regard to this subject. For example, you will find that they often maintain that the ancient mysteries contain much that is indecent and immoral.

Because I have carefully searched clairvoyantly through the mysteries of Greece, and in a former incarnation was myself an initiate of them, I can say with perfect certainty that there is not even a shadow of truth in those statements. There did exist certain mysteries with which were festivities and a form of Bacchus-worship, which degenerated later on into something very objectionable; but this was only in later times, and those mysteries belonged to quite another branch. They were not in the least related to the mysteries of Eleusis, but were only an imitation of them on a small scale, entirely exoteric.

I have, this evening, to treat a very extensive subject in a short time. I must try to give you a rough sketch of what those Greek mysteries were and what was taught to the initiates.

The fact will be known to you that two divisions are always mentioned: the lesser and the greater mysteries. Everybody knew that those existed, and the number of persons who were initiated was indeed quite a large proportion of the whole population. I think you may read in exoteric books of thirty thousand initiates gathering at one time, and this also shows that the fact that a man was initiated need not be kept secret, but that the outer world knew him as belonging to this numerous class. I mean that, although certain teachings given in the mysteries were always kept secret, the whole Greek and Roman world knew that the greater and lesser mysteries existed, and more or less who belonged to each of them.

But behind those two degrees, the existence of which was generally known, there were all the time the real secret mysteries; and the existence of the third degree, as one might call it, was unknown to the public. If one thinks of the conditions of that time one can readily understand the reason for this. Most of the Roman Emperors, for example, knew of the existence of the lesser and greater mysteries, and insisted upon being initiated. Now we know very well from history that many of the Roman Emperors were hardly of the character to be allowed to play a leading role in a religious body. But, all the same, it would have been very difficult for the leaders of the mysteries to refuse entrance to an Emperor of Rome. As was once said, one cannot argue with the master of thirty legions. The emperors would certainly have killed anyone who stood in the way of anything they wished. Thus it was desirable that the existence of the third degree should not be known, and nobody knew that there was such a degree before he was deemed, by those who could judge, worthy to be admitted to it.

The teachings of this third degree were never given to the public and never will be. But in the common mysteries, lesser and greater, are many things which can be told. In the first place, then, we were taught certain pithy sayings, or apophthegms, and if I quote you some of those you will understand the nature of the teaching. One of the best known was "Death is life, and life is death." This shows us that the higher life on the other side of death was well known. Another saying was, "He who seeks realities in this life shall also seek realities after death; and he who seeks unrealities in this life shall also seek unrealities after death." A great principle of their teaching was that the soul had descended from the higher spheres to the material. The principles of reincarnation were also contained in their instruction. You will remember that this did not appear in the external doctrine of the religions either of Greece or of Rome—that is to say, it was not taught publicly and in so many words—but you will find that this idea of the descent of the soul into matter is imparted in classic mythology. You will remember the myth of Proserpina, who was carried to the under-world while picking the flower of the narcissus.

Let us recall the myth of Narcissus. He was a youth of great beauty who fell in love with his own image reflected in the water, and was therefore changed into a flower and bound to earth. You need not have studied much theosophy to see what that means. We learn in *The Secret Doctrine* how the Ego looks down upon the waters of the astral plane and the lower world, how it reflects itself in the personality, how it identifies itself with the personality and, falling in love with its image, is bound to earth. So Proserpina, while picking the narcissus, is dragged away to the under-world, and afterwards passes half her life under the earth and half on the earth; that is, as you will see, half in a material body and half out of it.

In the same way, there are numbers of other myths of which it is very interesting to hear the theosophical explanation. For example, in this old mystery-teaching the minotaur was held to signify the lower nature in man—the personality which is half man and half animal. This was eventually slain by Theseus, who typifies the higher self or the individuality, which has been gradually growing and gathering strength until at last it can wield the sword of its Divine Father, the Spirit. Guided through the labyrinth of illusion which constitutes these lower planes by the thread of occult knowledge given him by Ariadne (who represents intuition) the higher self is enabled to slay the lower, and to escape safely from the web of illusion; yet there still remains for him the danger that, developing intellectual pride, he may neglect intuition, even as Theseus neglected Ariadne, and so fail for this time to realize his highest possibilities.

In ancient Greece the lesser mysteries were especially celebrated in a little place called Agrae, and the initiates were called "mystae." Perhaps you know that their official dress, the token of their dignity, was the skin of a fawn, which in the old symbology represented the astral body.

Its spotted appearance was thought to be emblematic of the many colors in an ordinary astral body. The reason why this was considered a fitting dress for those initiated into the lesser mysteries was because the principal teachings given in them concerned the astral plane. Those who were admitted learned what the astral life of man would be after death.

Much time was spent in making clear by example as well as by teaching what would be the effect in the astral world of a certain mode of life on earth. In the first place they taught by illustrations, on an extensive scale by representations in the temples, by a kind of play or drama in which was shown what, in the astral world, would be the condition of a man who had been, let us say, avaricious or full of sensual desires. In the old days of the mysteries, when the leaders were adepts or pupils of adepts, these representations were something like materializations. That is to say, the teacher, whoever he was, produced them by his own power out of astral or etheric matter, and created a real image for his pupils. But as time advanced, and later teachers were unable to bring about this phenomenon, they tried to represent these teachings in other ways—in some cases by what we should call acting. Members of the priesthood took the roles of different persons, while in other cases puppets were moved by machinery.

In addition to the teaching concerning the astral plane, instructions were also given in the same way as to the system of world-evolution. Among other things, pupils were taught how our solar system and its different parts came into existence. You can easily see how that could be represented, first by materialized nebulae and globes, and how, when this materialization was no longer possible, the arrangement of the different globes could be made clear by the use of what we now call an orrery—that is, a model of the solar system.

One of the most important things connected with the mysteries was that they explained the outer religion of the people in quite another way than that given to the general public. If you know anything about the religion of ancient Greece, you will understand that there were many things which badly needed some inner explanation, for certainly their religion does not appear to be very elevated or very reasonable when looked at from the ordinary standpoint. It seems to have been the object that all the stories which made up the outer teaching, many of which seem very extraordinary, should be learned by the people and retained in their minds—just a few simple, clear conceptions, and nothing more. But all earnestminded people joined the mysteries, and learned there the real meaning of the stories, which gave the whole thing quite another aspect.

Let me give you an idea of what I mean, by two or three very simple and short examples. I told you that, for the most part, the aim of those lesser mysteries was to inform the pupils about the effects on the astral plane of a certain mode of life here on earth. You probably know the myth of Tantalus. He was a man condemned to suffer in hell eternal thirst, while water surrounded him on all sides, but receded from his lips as soon as he tried to drink. The meaning of this is not difficult to see, when once we know what the astral life is. Every one who leaves this world of ours full of sensual desires of any kind—as, for example an alcoholic, or some one who has given himself up to sensual living in the ordinary meaning of the word—such a man finds himself on the astral plane in the position of Tantalus.

He has built up for himself this terrible desire which governs his whole being. You know how powerful the desire can be in the case of a drunkard; it conquers his feelings of honor, his love of his family, and all the better inclinations of his character. He will take money from his wife and children, will even take their clothes to sell them and obtain money to drink.

Remember that when a man dies he does not change at all. His desire is still as powerful as ever. But it is impossible to gratify it, because his physical body, through which only he could drink, is gone. There you have your Tantalus, as you see, full of that terrible desire, always finding that the gratification recedes as soon as he thinks he has it.

Recall also the story of Tityus, the man who was tied to a rock, his liver being gnawed by vultures, and growing again as fast as it was eaten. There you have an illustration of the effect of yielding to desire: an image of the man who is always tortured by remorse for sins committed on earth.

As perhaps a higher example of the same we can take the story of Sisyphus. You know how he was condemned always to roll a stone up a hill, and how, when he reached the top, the stone would always roll down again. That is the condition of an ambitious man after death, a man who has spent his life in making plans for selfish ends, for attaining glory or honor. In his case also death brings no change. He goes on making plans just as he did during life. He works out his plans, he executes them, as he thinks, till the point of culmination, and then he suddenly perceives that he has no longer a physical body, and that all was but a dream. Then he begins again and again, till he has learned at last that these desires are useless and that ambition must be killed. So Sisyphus goes on uselessly rolling the stone up the hill, till at last he learns not to roll it any more. To have learned that is to have conquered that desire, and he will come back in his next life without it; without the *desire*, but of course not without the weakness of character which made that desire possible.

So you see that conditions that seem terrible are but the effects in the other world of a wrong life here on earth. That is nature's method of turning wrong into good. Man does suffer, but what he suffers is only the effect of his own action and nothing else; it is not punishment inflicted upon him from outside, but entirely of his own making. And that is not all. The suffering he has to bear is the only means by which his qualities can be directed in the right way for his evolution and progress in another life. This was a point much emphasized in the teaching of the mysteries.

Now in regard to the greater mysteries. Those were celebrated principally in the great temple of Eleusis, not far from Athens. The initiates were named "epoptai," that is, "they whose eyes are opened." Their emblem was the golden fleece of Jason which is the symbol of the mind-body; for the yellow color in the human aura indicates the intelligence, as every clairvoyant knows. In this degree of initiation the teachings of the former degree were continued. In the first, as you remember, were taught the effects in the astral world of various ways of living. In the greater mysteries the pupil was shown what would be the effect in the heaven-world of a certain line of life, study and aspiration on earth. The whole history of the evolution of the world and of man, in its deeper aspect, was expounded in the greater mysteries. The same method of representation as in the other case was used here; although it was much more difficult to represent on the physical plane what belonged to the mental.

In each of these divisions of the mysteries, the lesser and the greater, there was an inner school which taught practical development to those who were seen to be ready for it. In the lesser mysteries theoretical knowledge about the astral plane was given, but the teachers carefully watched their pupils, and when they noticed one of whose character they felt sure, who showed that he was capable of psychic development, they invited him into the inner circle in which instruction was given as to the method of using the astral body and consciously functioning in it. When such a man passed on to the greater mysteries he received not only the ordinary teaching about the conditions of the mental plane, but also private instruction as to the development of the mental body as a vehicle.

Those who were thus received, not only into the recognized stages of the mysteries but into their inner schools, were also taught at the end of their course that all of this was in truth but exoteric—that all which they had learned, incalculable as had been its value, was really only a preparation for the true mysteries of initiation which would lead them to the feet of the Masters of Wisdom, and admit them to the Great Brotherhood which rules the world.

I may explain still further the meaning of some of those symbols which were used in connection with the mysteries. First, we will take what was called the *thyrsus*—that is, a staff with a pine-cone on its top. In India the same symbol is found, but instead of the staff a stick of bamboo with seven knots is used. In some modifications of the mysteries, a hollow iron rod, said to contain fire, was used instead of the thyrsus. Here again it is not difficult for the student of occultism to see the meaning. The staff or the stick with seven knots represents the spinal cord, with its seven centers, of which we read in the Hindu books. The hidden fire is the serpent-fire, kundalini, of which you may read in *The Secret Doctrine*. But the thyrsus was not only a symbol; it was also an object of practical use. It was a very strong magnetic instrument, used by initiates to free the astral body from the physical when they passed in full consciousness to this higher life. The priest who had magnetized it laid it against the spinal cord of the candidate and gave him in that way some of his own magnetism, to help him in that difficult life and in the efforts which lay before him. In connection with these mysteries, a certain set of objects called 'the toys of Bacchus' are spoken of. When you go over those lists of 'the toys of Bacchus' you will find them very remarkable.

While the child Bacchus (the LOGOS) plays with his toys he is seized by the Titans and torn to pieces. Later these pieces are put together and built into a whole. You will understand that this, however clumsy it may seem to us, is without doubt an allegory, which represents the descending of the One to become the many, and the re-union of the many in the One, through suffering and sacrifice. What, then, are the toys of the child Bacchus when he falls into matter and becomes the many? In the first place we find him playing with dice. Those dice are not common dice, but the five platonic solids; a set of five regular figures, the only regular polygons possible in geometry. They are given in a fixed series, and this series agrees with the different planes of the solar system. Each of them indicates, not the form of the atoms of the different planes, but the lines along which the power works which surrounds those atoms. These polygons are the tetrahedron, the cube, the octohedron, the dodecahedron, and the icosahedron. If we put the point at one end and the sphere at the other we get a set of seven figures, corresponding to the number of planes of our solar system.

You know that in some of the older schools of philosophy it was said: "No one can enter who does not know mathematics." What do you think is meant by that? Not what we now call mathematics, but the mathematics which embraced the knowledge of the higher planes, of their mutual relations and the way in which the whole is built by the will of God. Plato said, "God geometrizes," and it is perfectly true. Those forms are not conceptions of the human brain; they are truths of the higher planes. We have formed the habit of studying the books of Euclid, but we study them now for ourselves, and not as a guide to something higher. The old philosophers pondered upon them because they led to the understanding of the true science of life. We have lost sight of the true teaching, and grasp in many cases only the lifeless form.

Another toy with which Bacchus played was a top, the symbol of the whirling atom of which you will find a picture in *Occult Chemistry*. He also plays with a ball which represents the earth, that particular part of the planetary chain to which the thought of the LOGOS is specially directed at the moment. Also he plays with a mirror. The mirror has always been a symbol of astral light, in which the archetypal ideas are reflected and then materialized.* So you see that each of those toys indicates an essential part in the evolution of a solar system.

A few words may be said about the way in which people were prepared for the study of those mysteries by the different schools; for instance, the Pythagorean school, to which I belonged. In the Pythagorean schools, the pupils were divided into three classes. The first was called that of the *akoustikoi* or hearers. This means that they were learners, but it is also true that one of the rules was that they were to keep absolutely silent for two years.

I think this rule would be regarded as a serious drawback by many who join our Society at the present time, but in those olden times a great many people, not only men but women too, submit-

---

*Archetypal ideas are patterns on the higher mental plane that serve as blueprints for the formation of the manifested world. Editor

ted to this stipulation. The rule had also another meaning, but it is a fact that during two years the members of the first class were compelled to keep silence. The other meaning was that during all the time, however long, that a man stayed in this class of the *akoustikoi*, he might not give out any teaching, but continued to learn. I have wished that we had some such arrangement in the Theosophical Society, for it sometimes happens that members who do not yet know much themselves want to teach others, and the teaching is not always recognizable as theosophy.

The second class of Pythagoreans was called that of the *mathematikoi*. They passed their time in studying geometry, numbers and music. They brought these different subjects into relation to one another and worked out the relations between color and sound, which are very remarkable.

Let us take an example, which shows how our world is a coherent whole and how we can take facts from different parts which do not seem to have any connection whatever, and bring them into relation with each other. I just spoke about the five platonic polygons. Every one who knows anything about music knows that there is a fixed proportion between the length of the strings which produce certain tones. You know that you can tune a piano according to a certain system of fifths, and you can express the relation of the different tones to one another by the number of vibrations of each tone; so you can express a harmonious chord in mathematical numbers. This was first discovered simply by experiment; later the mathematicians found out what the proportions should be, and again by experiment they were found to be exact. But the peculiarity is that the set of numbers which produces a harmonious chord have the same relation to one another as that which exists between certain parts of these platonic solids. I believe that this point was worked out some time ago in an article in the *Theosophical Review* by one of the English cathedral organists.

It is very remarkable that our scale, so different from the old Greek scale, which consisted of five tones, can still be deduced from the proportion of those five platonic figures, which were studied some thousands of years ago in Greece. One is apt to think that there cannot be much relation between mathematics and music, but you see that they are both parts of one great whole.

The third class of the Pythagorean school was formed of the *physikoi*—those who studied physics, the inner connection between phenomena, world-building and metaphysics. They learned the truth about man and nature and, as far as they could learn it, about Him who made both.

There is still one point in the mysteries which we should not forget to consider—the life of the disciples. A life of perfect purity was strictly required. It is a remarkable coincidence that the life in the Pythagorean school is divided into five periods, almost similar to the five steps of the preparatory path of the Hindus, as described by me in *Invisible Helpers*, and by Mrs. Besant in *The Path of Discipleship*. Almost all the forms and symbols of the present Christian religion are derived from the Egyptian mysteries. All the symbolism, for example, that is related to the Latin cross, and to the descent and sacrifice of the Logos, is taken from the Egyptian mysteries. I have written about this in *The Christain Creed*.

Though the mysteries of Greece and Rome, of Egypt and Chaldaea, are long ago defunct, the world has never been left without avenues of approach to the inner shrine. Even in the gross darkness of the middle ages the Rosicrucians and some other secret societies were ready to teach the truth to those who were ready to learn; and now in these modern days of hurry and materialism the Theosophical Society still upholds the banner of true knowledge, and acts as a gateway by means of which those who are really in earnest may reach the feet of the Masters of the Wisdom.

You must also remember that many things given in those old days only under the seal of secrecy are now made public, and through our Society are given to the world. Many of the greatest and noblest characters of history have passed years in study and work to try to find what is now given us so easily and simply in a few books. Of us is perfectly true what is said in the Bible: "Many prophets and kings have desired to see those things which ye see, and have not seen them; and to hear those things which ye hear, and have not heard them." (*Luke*, 10:24.) Because this honor is reserved for us and this opportunity is given us, it seems to me that a great responsibility rests upon us, and that we should try to be worthy of the gift. It is good karma which allows this possibility to open before us. If we let it pass, we shall not deserve to have another offered us for thousands of years. If you knew, as I know, with what difficulties we had to contend in former days to learn all those things which are laid before us now, perhaps you would appreciate more the opportunity offered you. Let us try to make use of it to the utmost of our power, and show ourselves worthy of the privilege given us by theosophy.

SECTION TWO

Religion

The Logos

We have in the LOGOS of our solar system as near an approach to a personal (or rather, perhaps, individual) God as any reasonable man can desire, for of Him is true everything good that has ever been predicated of a personal deity. We cannot ascribe to Him partiality, injustice, jealousy, cruelty; those who desire these attributes in their deity must go elsewhere. But so far as His system is concerned He possesses omniscience, omnipresence, omnipotence; the love, the power, the wisdom, the glory, all are there in fullest measure. Yet He is a mighty Individual—a trinity in unity, and God in very truth, though removed by we know not how many stages from the Absolute, the Unknowable before which even solar systems are but as specks of cosmic dust. I do not think that we can image Him at all. The sun is His chief manifestation on the physical plane, and that may help us a little to realize some of His qualities, and to see how everything comes from Him. The sun may be considered as a sort of force-center in Him, corresponding to the heart of man, the outer manifestation of the principal center in His body.

Although the whole solar system is His physical body, yet His activities outside of it are enormously greater than those within it. I have myself preferred not even to try to make any image of Him, but simply to contemplate Him as pervading all things, so that even I myself am also He, so that all other men, too, are He, and in truth there is nothing but God. Yet at the same time, although this that we can see is a manifestation of Him, this solar system that seems so stupendous to us is to Him but a little thing, for, though He is all this, yet outside it and above it all He exists in a glory and a splendor of which we know nothing as yet. Thus though we agree with the pantheist that all is God, we yet go very much further than he does, because we realize that He has a far greater existence above and beyond His universe. "Having pervaded this whole universe with one fragment of Myself, I remain." (*Bhagavad Gita*, x. 41.)

I do not think that we can find any form of words that will at all express the method of our union with Him. We may in one sense be cells in his Body, but we are certainly very much more than that, for His life and power are manifested through us in a way which is out of all proportion to any such manifestation of our spiritual life as could be supposed to be given through the cells of our bodies. In His manifestation on the lowest cosmic plane we may take it that His first aspect is on the highest level, the second on that below it, and the third in the higher part of the nirvanic plane, so that when an adept gradually raises his consciousness plane by plane as he develops, he comes first to the third aspect and realizes his unity with that, moving on only after long intervals to full union with the second and the first.

I myself who speak to you have once seen Him in a form which is not the form of His system. This is something which utterly transcends all ordinary experience, which has nothing to do with any of the lower planes. The thing became possible for me only through a very daring experiment—the utter blending for a moment of two distinct rays or types, so that by means of this blending a level could for a moment be touched enormously higher than any to which either of the egos concerned could have attained alone. He exists far above His system; He sits upon it as on a lotus throne. He is the apotheosis of humanity, yet infinitely greater than humanity. We might think of the Augoeides carried up higher and higher, and to infinity. I do not know whether that form is permanent or whether it can be seen at a certain level only—who shall say? But this thing is a tremendous reality—that I know; and, once seen, such a manifestation can never be forgotten.

One little touch of higher experience I may mention, though it is one which is exceedingly difficult to describe adequately. When a man raises his consciousness to the highest subdivision of his causal body, and focuses it exclusively in the atomic matter of the mental plane, he has before him three possibilities of moving that consciousness, which correspond to some extent with the three dimensions of space. Obviously a way is open to him to move it downwards into the second subplane of the mental, or upward into the lowest subplane of the buddhic, if he has developed that sufficiently to be able to utilize it as vehicle.

A second line of movement open to him is the short cut which exists from the atomic subdivision of one plane to the corresponding atomic subdivisions of the planes above and below, so that without touching any intermediate sub-plane the consciousness may pass from that atomic mental downwards to the atomic astral or upwards to the atomic buddhic, again of course supposing the development of this latter to be already achieved. In order to image to oneself this short cut, one may think of the atomic subplanes as being side by side along a rod, the other sub-divisions of each plane hanging from the rod in loops, as though a piece of string were wound loosely round the rod. Obviously then to pass from one atomic sub-division to another one could move by the short cut straight along the rod, or down and up again through the hanging loop of string which symbolizes the lower sub-planes. But there is yet a third possibility—a possibility not so much yet of *movement* along another line at right angles to both of these others, but rather a possibility of looking up such a line— looking up as a man at the bottom of a well might look up at a star in the sky above him.

For there is a direct line of communication between the atomic sub-plane of the mental in this lowest cosmic plane and the corresponding atomic mental in the cosmic plane. We are infinitely far as yet from being able to climb upwards by that line, but once at least the experience came of being able to look up it for a moment. What is seen then it is hopeless to try to describe, for no human words can give the least idea of it; but at least this much emerges, with a certitude that can never be shaken, that what we have hitherto supposed to be our consciousness, our intellect, is simply not ours at all, but His; not even a reflection of His, but literally and truly a part of His consciousness, a part of His intellect. Incomprehensible, yet literally true! It is a commonplace of our meditation to say, "I am that Self; that Self am I," but to see it, to know it, to feel it, to realize it in this way, is something very different from that verbal recitation.

From Him comes forth all life in the successive outpourings which are described in our books—the first outpouring from His third aspect, which gives to previously existing atoms the power to aggregate themselves into the chemical elements—the action which is described in the Christian Scriptures as the spirit of God moving over the waters of space. When, at a later stage, the kingdoms of nature are definitely established, there comes the second outpouring, from His second aspect, which forms group-souls for the minerals, the plants, the animals, and this is the descent of the Christ principle into matter, which alone renders possible our very existence. But when we think of the human kingdom we remember that the ego itself is a manifestation of the third outpouring which comes from His first aspect, the eternal and all-loving Father.

Every fixed star is a sun like our own, and each one is a partial expression of a LOGOS.

Buddhism

In thinking of the Lord Buddha we must not forget that he is very much more than merely the founder of a religion. He is a great official of the Occult Hierarchy, the greatest of all save one, and the founder in previous incarnations of many religions before this one which now bears his title. For he was the Vyasa who has done so much for the Indian religion; he was Hermes, the great founder of the Egyptian mysteries; he was the original Zoroaster, from whom came the sun and fire worship; and he was also Orpheus, the great bard of the Greeks.

In this last of his many births, when he came as the Lord Gautama, it does not appear that he had originally any intention of founding a new religion. He appeared simply as a reformer of Hinduism—a faith which was already of hoary antiquity, and had therefore departed much from its original form, as all religions have. It had become hardened in many ways, and appears to have been very far less elastic even than it is now. Even now we all know, what an iron rigidity there is as to forms and ceremonies.

Imagine a condition in which all this was even far more rigid, in which the feeling was much more intense, in which all the ideas of life had been very much changed from what they were in the days of the original Aryan immigrants, when it was a religion full of joy, and holding out hope for everybody. A little before the time of the Buddha the general opinion seems to have been that practically no one but a brahman had any chance of salvation at all. Now as the number of the brahmans was always small, and even now is only something like thirteen millions out of the three hundred million inhabitants of India, it was clearly not a very hopeful religion for the majority of the people, since it indicated to them that they had to work on through very many lives, until they could earn admission into the small and exclusive brahman caste, before they could possibly escape from the wheel of birth and death.

Then came Lord Buddha, and by his teaching flung open wide the gates of the sweet law of justice, for he taught that men had departed entirely from the old form of religion. He repeatedly asserted that a man who, though born a brahman, did not live the life which a brahman should, was neither worthy of respect nor in the way of salvation, and that a man of any other caste who did live the true brahman life, should be treated as a brahman, and had in every way the same possibilities before him as though he had been born into the sacred caste.

Naturally enough in the face of teachings which placed all hope of final salvation so indefinitely far away in the future, the ordinary man of the world had become hopeless and consequently careless; on the other hand, the austerity of the brahman, who spent the whole of his life in ceremonies and in meditation, was not to their taste, and indeed was obviously impossible for them. But the Buddha preached to them what he called the middle way; he told them that although the life of austerity and of entire devotion to religion was not for them, there was no reason why, because of that, they should relapse into carelessness and evil living. He showed them that a higher life is possible for the man still in the world, and that, though they might not be able to devote themselves to metaphysics and to hairsplitting arguments, they could still obtain sufficient grasp of the great facts of evolution to form a satisfactory guide to them in their lives.

He declared that extremes in either direction are equally irrational; that on the one hand the life of the ordinary man of the world, wrapped up entirely in his business, pursuing dreams of wealth and power, is foolish and defective because it leaves out of account all that is really worthy of consideration; but that on the

other hand the extreme asceticism that teaches each man to turn
his back upon the world altogether, and to devote himself exclusively and selfishly to the endeavor to shut himself away from it
and escape from it, is also foolish. He held that the middle path of
truth and beauty is the best and safest, and that while certainly the
life devoted entirely to spirituality is the highest of all for those
who are ready for it, there is also a good and true and spiritual life
possible for the man who yet holds his place and does his work in
the world.

He based his doctrines solely on reason and commonsense; he
asked no man to believe anything blindly, but rather told him to
open his eyes and look around him. He declared that in spite of all
the sorrow and misery of the world, the great scheme of which
man is a part is a scheme of eternal justice, and that the law under
which we are living is a good law, and needs only that we should
understand it and adapt ourselves to it. He taught that all life is
suffering, but that man causes his own trouble for himself, because he yields himself perpetually to desire for that which he has
not, and he said that happiness and contentment can be gained
better by limiting desires than by increasing possessions.

To this end he tabulated his teaching in the most marvellous
manner, arranging everything under certain headings which
could be readily memorized. This constitutes, in reality, a carefully graded system of mnemonics. It is so simple in its broad
outline that any child can remember and understand its four
noble truths, its noble eightfold path, and the principles of life
which they suggest; yet it is carried out so elaborately that it
constitutes a system of philosophy which the wisest man may
study all his life through, and yet find in it ever more and more
light upon the problems of life.

He analyzed everything to an almost incredible extent, as may
be seen by a study of the twelve nidanas, or by his enumeration of
the steps which intervene between thought and action. Each of his
four noble truths is represented by a single word, and yet to any
who has ever heard the exposition of the system each of those
words inevitably calls up a great range of ideas. The same thing is
true of the words signifying the steps of the noble eightfold path,
and of the "great perfections" which are spoken of in *The Voice of
the Silence*. All of these perfections are simply wisdom, power and
love appearing in different forms. They are sometimes reckoned
as six, but more commonly as ten. The six are given as perfect

charity, perfect morality, perfect patience, perfect energy, perfect truth and perfect wisdom; and the other four which are sometimes added are perfect resignation, perfect resolution, perfect kindness and perfect abnegation.

The religion of Buddhism has practically disappeared from India, yet it has left behind it lasting results, and the country bears everywhere the strong impress of his teachings. Before his coming blood-sacrifices appear to have been universal; even now they still exist, but are comparatively rare, for he taught that such things were not pleasing to any noble diety, but that the Gods desired rather the sacrifice of a holy life.

In looking back upon the record of those times we see that he preached mostly in the open air, and nearly always sitting at the foot of a tree, with the listeners sitting on the ground about him, or standing leaning against the trees, men and women intermingling, and little children running about and playing upon the outskirts of the crowd. The great teacher had a most wonderful voice, gloriously full and sonorous, and a personality which instantly commanded the attention of all who heard him, and invariably won their hearts, even in the rare cases where they did not agree with what he said. The audiences were stirred up to great religious fervor; we find them constantly raising cries of "Sadhu, Sadhu," by way of applause, when anything was said which especially moved them, and at the same time raising their joined hands in an attitude of salutation.

Part at least of this influence was due to the tremendously strong vibrations of his aura, which was of very great size, so that the audience were actually sitting within it and being attuned to it while they listened to his discourse. Its magnetic effect was almost indescribable, and while his hearers were within its influence even the most stupid of them could understand to the full whatever he said, though often afterwards when they had passed away from that influence they found it difficult to comprehend it at all in the same way. To this marvellous influence also is due the phenomenon so often described in the Buddhist books—the attainment of the arhat level by such large numbers of his hearers. It is quite a common thing to read in the accounts given in the Buddhist scriptures that after a sermon of the Buddha hundreds of men, even thousands, reached the arhat level. Knowing what a very high degree of attainment this means, this seemed to us, when we read it, almost incredible, and we supposed it to be

simply a case of oriental exaggeration; but later and closer study
has shown us that the accounts are actually true. So remarkable a
result seemed to call for further investigation into its causes, and
we found that in order to understand all this it was necessary to
take into account not this one life only, but the work of many
previous incarnations.

We must remember that the Lord Gautama is the Buddha of
the fourth root-race, even though this last incarnation of his was
taken in the fifth. He had been born many times in various
Atlantean races, and always as a great teacher. In each of those
lives he had drawn around him many pupils, who had gradually
been raised to higher levels of thought and of life, and when he
came in India for this last culminating birth he arranged that all
those whom at many different times and in many different lands
he had influenced should be brought together into incarnation at
the same time. Thus his audiences were to a large extent composed of fully prepared and, as it were, highly specialized souls,
and when these came under the influence of the extraordinarily
powerful magnetism of a Buddha, they understood and followed
every word which he said, and the action upon them as egos was
of the most wonderfully stimulating nature. Therefore it was that
they so readily responded; therefore it was that so large a number
of them could be and were raised so rapidly to such dizzy heights.

In the third volume of *The Secret Doctrine* we shall find an
exceedingly interesting and suggestive section called *The Mystery
of Buddha*, which refers to the fact that the Buddha prepared his
own inner bodies of very high grades of matter, with the fullest
development of the spirillae. His buddhic, causal and mental
bodies are kept together for other Great Ones to use, because of
the exceeding difficulty of producing others equal to them. The
Christ used them along with the physical body of Jesus, while the
latter waited on higher planes in his own vehicles. Shankaracharya also used these "remains." Hence arose the incorrect
idea that he was a reincarnation of the Buddha.

Buddhism still claims a larger number of adherents than any
other religion in the world, and is a living influence in the lives of
millions of our fellow-men. It would be quite unfair to judge it by
what is written about it by European orientalists. When I was in
Ceylon and Burma I compared these accounts with the interpretation given to the doctrines by the living followers of this religion. Learned monks in these countries approach the subject with

an accuracy of knowledge at least equal to that of the most advanced orientalists, but their interpretation of the doctrines is very far less wooden and lifeless. By far the best book in English to give one a real idea of the religion as it is held by living men is *The Light of Asia*, by Sir Edwin Arnold; and another book, which makes a good second to it, is *The Soul of a People*, by H. Fielding Hall. Some critics have said that Sir Edwin Arnold has gone a little beyond the bare literal meaning of the words of the text, and is trying to read Christian ideas into them. I do not think this is so, and I have certainly found that he expresses far more closely the feeling and attitude of the Buddhists than any other writer.

Buddhism is now divided into two great Churches, the Northern and the Southern, and both of them have departed to some extent from the original teaching of the Buddha, though in different directions. The religion is so plain and straightforward, and so obviously commonsense that almost any person may readily adapt himself to it, without necessarily giving up the beliefs and practices of other faiths. As a consequence of this in the Northern Church we have a form of Buddhism with an immense amount of accretion. It seems to have absorbed into itself many ceremonies and beliefs of the aboriginal faith which it supplanted; so that in Tibet, for example, we find it including a whole hierarchy of minor deities, devas and demons which were entirely unknown to the original scheme of the Buddha. The Southern Church, on the other hand, instead of adding to the teaching of the Buddha, has lost something from it. It has intensified the material and the abstract sides of the philosophy.

It teaches that nothing but Karma passes over from life to life—that there is no permanent ego in man, but that in his next birth he is in effect a new man, who is the result of the karma of the previous life; and they quote various sayings of the Buddha in support of this. It is true that he often spoke very strongly against the persistence of the personality, and that he assured his hearers again and again that nothing whatever which they knew in connection with a man could pass over to another birth. But he nowhere denied the individuality; in fact many of his sayings absolutely affirm it. Take for example a text which occurs in the *Samannaphalasutta* of the *Digha-Nikaya*. When first mentioning the condition and training of the mind that are necessary for success in spiritual progress, the Buddha describes how he sees all the scenes in which he was in any way concerned passing in succession before his mind's eye. He illustrates it by saying:

> If a man goes out from his own village to another and
> thence to another, and from there comes back again to
> his own village, he may think thus: 'I indeed went from
> my own village to that other. There I stood thus; I sat
> in this manner; thus I spoke, and thus I remained
> silent. From that village again I went to another, and I
> did the same there. The same 'I am' returned from
> that village to my own village.' In the very same way, O
> King, the ascetic, when his mind is pure, knows his
> former births. He thinks: 'In such a place I had such a
> name. I was born in such a family, such was my caste,
> such was my food, and in such and such a way I
> experienced pleasure and pain, and my life extended
> through in some other place, and there also I had such
> and such conditions. Thence removed, the same 'I' am
> now born here.'

This question shows very clearly the doctrine of the Buddha
with regard to the reincarnating ego. He gives illustrations also in
the same Sutta of the manner in which an ascetic can know the
past births of others—how he can see them die in one place, and
after the sorrows and joys of hell and heaven the same men are
born again somewhere else. It is true that in the *Brahmajala Sutta*
he mentions all the various aspects of the soul, and says that they
do not *absolutely* exist, because their existence depends upon
"contact," that is to say upon relation. But in thus denying the
absolute reality of the soul he agrees with the other great Indian
teachers, for the existence not only of the soul but even of the
LOGOS Himself is true only relatively.

Untrained minds frequently misunderstand these ideas, but
the careful student of oriental thought will not fail to grasp
exactly what is meant, and to realize that the teaching of the
Buddha in this respect is exactly that now given by theosophy. It
is not difficult to see how various texts might be so emphasized or
distorted as to seem to contradict one another, and the Southern
Church has chosen to cling rather to the denial of the permanence of the personality than to the assertion of the continuity of
the individuality, just as in Christianity some people have acquired the habit of laying stress on particular texts, and ignoring
others which contradict them.

Another point as to which there is a very similar misunderstanding is the constantly repeated assertion that nirvana is equivalent to annihilation. Even Max Mueller, the great Oxford Sanskrit scholar, was under this delusion for many years, but later in his life with further and deeper study he came to understand that in this he had been mistaken. The description which the Lord Buddha himself gives to nirvana is so far above the comprehension of any man who is trained only in ordinary and worldly methods of thought that it is little wonder that it should have been misunderstood at first sight by the European orientalists; but no one who has lived in the East among the Buddhists can for a moment suppose that they regard annihilation as the end which they are striving to reach.

It is quite true that the attaining of nirvana does involve the utter annihilation of that lower side of man which is in truth all that we know of him at the present time. The personality, like everything connected with the lower vehicles, is impermanent and will disappear. If we endeavor to realize what man would be when deprived of all which is included under these terms we shall see that for us at our present stage it would be difficult to comprehend that anything remained, and yet the truth is that everything remains—that in the glorified spirit which then exists, all the essence of all the qualities which have been developed through the centuries of strife and stress in earthly incarnation will inhere to the fullest possible degree. The man has become more than man, since he is now on the threshold of Divinity; yet he is still himself, even though it be a so much wider self.

Many definitions have been given of nirvana, and naturally none of them can possibly be satisfactory; perhaps the best on the whole is that of peace in omniscience. Many years ago when I was preparing a simple introductory catechism of their religion for Buddhist children, the chief Abbot Sumangala himself gave me as the best definition of nirvana to put before them that it was a condition of peace and blessedness so high above our present state that it was impossible for us to understand it. Surely that is far removed from the idea of annihilation. Truly all that we now call the man has disappeared, but that is not because the individuality is annihilated, but because it is lost in divinity.

The Buddha himself once said: "Nirvana is not being, but also it is not non-being."

Another difference between the Northern Church of Buddhism and the Southern is that they adopt different versions of the scriptures. It is usually stated that the Northern Church adopts the Mahayana and the Southern the Hinayana, but whether even this much may be safely said depends upon the shade of meaning which we attach to a much-disputed word. *Yana* means vehicle, and it is agreed that it is to be applied to the dhamma or law, as the vessel which conveys us across the sea of life to nirvana, but there are at least five theories as to the exact sense in which it is to be taken.

1. That it refers simply to the language in which the law is written, the greater vehicle being by this hypothesis Sanskrit, and the lesser vehicle Pali—a theory which seems to me untenable. It is true that the Northern Church uses the Sanskrit translation, while the Southern scriptures are in Pali, the language which the Lord Buddha spoke when on earth. It is stated that the Pali scriptures which we now possess are not in the original form, but that all the originals existing (in Ceylon at least) were carefully destroyed by the Tamil invaders, so that the Pali scriptures which we now have are a retranslation made from a copy in Elu, then the vernacular language of Ceylon.

2. *Hina* may apparently be taken as signifying mean or easy, as well as small. One interpretation therefore considers that the Hinayana is the meaner or easier road to liberation—the irreducible minimum of knowledge and conduct required to attain it, while the *Maha*yana is the fuller and more philosophical doctrine, which includes much traditional knowledge about higher realms of nature. Needless to say, this interpretation comes from a Mahayana source.

3. That Buddhism, in its unfailing courtesy towards other religions, accepts them all as ways to liberation, though it regards the method taught by its founder as offering the shortest and surest route. According to this view Buddhism is the Mahayana, and the Hinayana includes Brahmanism, Zoroastrianism, Jainism, and any other religions which were existing at the time when the definition was formulated.

4. That the two doctrines are simply two stages of one doctrine—the Hinayana for the Sravakas or hearers, and the Mahayana for more advanced students.

5. That the word Yana is to be understood not exactly in its primary sense of 'vehicle,' but rather in its secondary sense, nearly equivalent to the English word 'career.' According to this in-

terpretation the Mahayana puts before the man the 'grand career' of becoming a Bodhisattva and devoting himself to the welfare of the world, while the Hinayana shows him only the smaller 'career' of so living as to attain nirvana for himself.

There has also been much discussion as to the exact meaning of the terms Adi-Buddha and Avalokiteshwara. I have made no special study of these things from the philosophical standpoint, but so far as I have been able to gather ideas from discussion of the matter with the living exponents of the religion, Adi-Buddha seems to be the culmination of one of the great lines of superhuman development—what might be called the abstract principle of all the Buddhas. Avalokiteshwara is a term belonging to the Northern Church, and seems to be the Buddhists' name for their conception of the LOGOS. European scholars have translated it: "The Lord who looks down from on high," but this seems to have in it a somewhat inaccurate implication, for it is clearly always the manifested LOGOS; sometimes the LOGOS of a solar system and sometimes higher than that, but always manifest. We must not forget that while the founders of the great religions see and know the things which They name, Their followers usually do not see; they have only the names, and they juggle with them as intellectual counters, and build up much which is incorrect and inconsistent.

The Buddhism of the Southern Church, which includes Ceylon, Burma, Siam and Cambodia, has on the whole kept its religion free from the accretions which have become so prominent in the Northern division of Japan, China and Tibet. In Burma no image appears in the temples except that of the Buddha, though of him there are in some cases hundreds of images, of different material, in different positions, presented by various worshippers. In Ceylon a certain concession seems to have been made to popular feeling, or perhaps to a foreign government during the time of the Tamil kings, for the images of certain Hindu deities are often to be seen in the temples, though they are always placed in a subordinate position and considered as a king of attendants upon the Buddha. We need not however blame the Tibetans very much for the fact that certain superstitions have crept into their Buddhism. The same thing happens in all countries, and with all religions, as time goes on. In Italy, for example, numbers of the peasants in the hills still follow what they call *the old religion*, and continue even in the present day the worship of Bacchus, under an Etruscan name which antedates even the time of the Roman Empire. The Catholic priests quite recognize the existence of this older faith, and set themselves against it, but without avail.

In Southern Buddhism there is remarkably little ceremony of any kind—practically nothing indeed that in any way corresponds to the Christian service. When the people pay their morning visit to the temple they usually call upon the monks to recite for them the three guides and the five precepts, which they then repeat after him, but even this can hardly be called a public service, for it is recited not once at a set time, but for each group of people as they happen to arrive. There is another ceremony called Paritta or Pirit (which means 'blessings') but this is not performed in the temple itself nor at any stated times, but it is considered a good work on the part of the laity to celebrate any special occasion by giving a Pirit ceremony—that is to say by erecting and elaborately decorating a temporary building in which the ceremony is held. It consists of the chanting of benedictory verses from the sacred scriptures, and is carried on for a certain number of days, usually a fortnight, by relays of monks who relieve one another every two hours.

Sometimes when a man falls ill one of these Pirit ceremonies is arranged for him, with the idea that it will promote his recovery. It is in reality a mesmeric ceremony, for the monks sit in a circle and hold in their hands a rope which runs round the circle, and they are instructed to recite their texts, keeping clearly in their minds all the time the will to bless. Naturally this rope becomes very strongly magnetized as the ceremony progresses, and strings run from it to a huge pot of water, which of course also becomes highly charged with magnetism. At the conclusion of the ceremony this water is distributed among the people, and the sick man often holds a thread which is connected with the rope.

The Southern Buddhists give a list of five psychic powers which may be gained by the man who is making progress on the Path. (1) The ability to pass through the air and through solid objects, and to visit the heaven-world while still alive. It is however possible that this may mean nothing more than ability to function freely in the astral body, because it is quite likely that in speaking of the heaven-world they do not really mean the mental plane, but only the higher levels on the astral. (2) Divinely clear hearing—which is evidently merely the astral faculty of clairaudience. (3) The ability to comprehend and sympathize with all that is in the minds of others—which appears to be thought-reading, or perhaps telepathy. (4) The Power to remember former births. (5) Divinely clear vision—that is to say, clairvoyance. To this is added in some lists the attainment of deliverance by wisdom. This must of course mean the attainment of freedom from the necessity of rebirth, but it does not seem to be of the same nature as the other powers, and perhaps should hardly appear in the same category.

Ananda is said to have been the favorite disciple of the Lord Buddha, just as John is spoken of as the beloved disciple of the Christ, and no doubt in both cases the special intimacy was the result of relationship in previous lives. Ananda was certainly not so chosen because he was the most advanced, for even after the death of the Buddha we hear that when the first great council was held in a cave within the living rock, and the condition of taking part in it was that none should enter who could not pass through the rock, Ananda found himself shut out from it because he had not yet attained this power. But it is said that his grief at this exclusion from a grand opportunity of serving his departed Master was so great that by a supreme effort of will he then and there developed the power which had been lacking, and passed in triumphantly to take his place among his brothers, though a little late.

This shows us that even those who are the most highly advanced of all humanity have still their special friendships, and that therefore to love one person more than another cannot be improper. It is true that such affection as you now feel for your nearest and dearest you will feel later on for the whole world, but at that time you will feel a thousand times more affection for those who are nearest to you. Your love will never be the same for all, although all will be included within it. It is impossible that we should feel towards another as we do towards our Master, for when he becomes a Logos we shall be part of his system, and even when far later on we ourselves become Logoi we shall still be part of him, for he will represent some far greater system. Although there will always be greater love for some than others, we shall help those whom we love less just as fully as those whom we love more. We shall always do our best for all, just as a doctor equally helps his patient whether he be a friend or not, for anything like dislike or hatred will have ceased aeons before.

At the time of the Lord Buddha many other spiritual teachers were sent forth to the world. We find for example Lao-tse, Confucius and Pythagoras, all working in their different spheres. Advantage was taken of the stupendous outpouring of spiritual force at the time to send forth teachers into many parts of the world.

Christianity

There is nothing in the principles of theosophy which is at all in opposition to the true primitive Christianity, though there may be statements which cannot be reconciled with some of the mistakes of modern popular theology. This modern theology attaches immense importance to texts; in fact it appears to me to be based upon one or two texts almost entirely. It takes these and gives to them a particular interpretation, often in direct opposition to the plain meaning of other texts from the same bible. Of course there are contradictions in the Christian scripture just as there must necessarily be in any book of that size, the various parts of which were written at such widely separated periods of the world's history, and by people so unequal in knowledge and in civilization.

It is impossible that all the statements made in it can be literally true, but we can go back behind them all, and try to find out what the original teacher did lay before His pupils. Since there are many contradictions and many interpretations it is obviously the duty of a thinking Christian to weigh carefully the different versions of his faith which exist in the world, and decide between them according to his own reason and commonsense.

Every Christian does, as a matter of fact, decide for himself now; he chooses to be a Roman Catholic, or a member of the Church of England, or a Methodist, or a Salvationist, though each of these sects professes to have the only genuine brand of Christianity, and justifies its claim by the quotation of texts. How then does the ordinary layman decide between their rival claims? Either he accepts blindly the faith which his father held, and does not examine the matter at all, or else he does examine it, and then he decides by the exercise of his own judgment.

If he is already doing that, it would be absurd and inconsistent for him to refuse to examine *all* texts, instead of basing his belief only upon one or two. If he does impartially examine all texts, he will certainly find many which support theosophical truth. He will find also that the creeds can be rationally interpreted only by theosophy. Of course in order to make an intelligent comparison between these different systems it will be necessary for him to make some enquiries into the history of his own religion, and to see how the Christian doctrine came to be what it now is.

He will find that in the early Christian Church there were three principal divisions or parties. There were first of all the Gnostic Doctors or teachers, wise and cultured men who held that the Christian Church had its system of philosophy of the same nature as the great Greek and Roman systems which existed at that time. They said that this system, while thoroughly comprehensive and very beautiful, was difficult to understand, and therefore they did not recommend its study to the ignorant. They spoke of it as the Gnosis or knowledge—the knowledge which was possessed by those who were full members of the church, but was not given out to the world at large, and not even told to the more ignorant members of the church while they were in that preliminary stage when they could not receive the sacraments.

Then there was the second division, a body of respectable middle-class people, who troubled themselves not at all about the philosophy, but simply were content to take the words of the Christ as their guide in life. They used as a sacred book a collection of His sayings, some leaves of which have recently been discovered by antiquarians.

Then there was, unfortunately, a great mass of ignorant and turbulent people who never had any grasp whatever of Christian doctrine, but became members of the church merely because of the prophecies, given by the Christ, of a good time to come. He was very much moved by the sufferings of the poor, and full of compassion and pity for them. He told them constantly, in His teachings, to take comfort, because the poor man who endures the struggle bravely and well will in the future have a better position and greater advancement than the rich man who misuses his opportunities. One can readily see how that doctrine preached to an exceedingly ignorant people might be taken in a one-sided manner. They would take the promises and not the conditions, and their idea of that good time might easily be that they in turn would be the oppressors and would take advantage of the rich man—something which of course the Christ never preached. So it came to pass that He attracted to himself a great crowd of men who for various reasons were against the existing government; and when these ignorant people in turn preached what they called Christianity to others, they naturally intensified and exaggerated their own misconceptions of it. This great mass of the common people, who called themselves "the poor men," speedily became a vast majority of the infant church, and gained so much power that they were eventually able to throw out the Gnostic Doctors as heretics; for the "poor men" resented the idea that any knowledge which they did not possess could be regarded as an essential part of Christianity.

There is yet another point of view from which the Christian may find theosophy of the greatest use to him. Many orthodox Christians attempt to apply ordinary commonsense and scientific methods to the examination of the religious teaching — the endeavor to understand religion instead of blindly believing it. For many ages the world has been told that ecclesiastical dogmas must be swallowed like pills, and that to attempt to reason about them is impious. There are many men in the world, and they are among the most intellectual of its citizens, who simply cannot accept doctrines thus blindly and uncomprehendingly. Before they can believe they must to some extent understand, and a statement does not become a living fact to them until they can relate it rationally to other facts, and regard it as part of a more or less comprehensive scheme of things.

It is ridiculous to say (as some of the orthodox do) that these people are inherently wicked and that their attitude is inspired by the devil. On the contrary they are precisely the men who truly appreciate God's great gift of reason, and are determined to employ it in the highest of all possible directions—for the elucidation of the truth about religion. The truth is that the critics are of the greatest possible service to religion; they are clearing up points in it which heretofore have been vague; they are stating with accuracy matters in connection with it which were previously very partially understood; they are trying to make a reasonable system out of what has until now been nothing but a mass of meaningless confusion.

If any of our members have orthodox friends who are disturbed by these efforts, who fear lest this liberalizing and rationalizing of their faith should refine it altogether out of existence, let them recommend to them the teachings of theosophy, for that is the very thing which they need. It will teach them to pause before throwing aside ancestral belief, and it will show them that when properly understood that belief has a real meaning and a real foundation, and that, while some of the vagaries of mediaeval ecclesiastical dogma may be incomprehensible and incredible, the original teaching of the Christ was a magnificent presentment of universal truth.

If they have somewhat outgrown the outer form of their religion, if they have broken through the chrysalis of blind faith, and mounted on the wings of reason and intuition to the freer, nobler mental life of more exalted levels, theosophy will show them that in all this there has been no loss, but a great and glorious gain. For it tells them that the glow of devotion which has meant so much to them in their spiritual life is more than justified, that the splendor and beauty and poetry of religious thought exist in fuller measure than they have ever hoped before—no longer as mere pleasant dreams from which the cold light of commonsense may at any time rudely awaken them, but as truths of nature which will bear investigation, which become only brighter and more perfect as they are more accurately understood. Certainly the Christian Bible ought not to be taken literally, for many of its statements are symbolical.

Sin

You ask what is the real meaning of sin. In the sense in which the word is ordinarily employed, at least by Christian preachers, I think sin may be defined as a figment of the theological imagination. It is popularly supposed to indicate a defiance of divine law—the performance of some action which the actor knows to be wrong. It is exceedingly doubtful whether this phenomenon ever occurs. In almost every conceivable case man breaks the law through ignorance or heedlessness, and not of deliberate intention. When once a man really knows and sees the divine intention he inevitably comes into harmony with it, for two reasons: at an earlier stage because he sees the utter futility of doing otherwise, and later because, seeing the glory and beauty of the design, he cannot but throw himself into its execution with all the powers of his heart and soul.

One of the most serious of the many misconceptions which we have inherited from the dark ages is that what is called "sin" is a perversity to be met with punishment and savage persecution, instead of what it really is, the result of a condition of ignorance that can only be dealt with by enlightenment and education. It may be objected that in daily life we constantly see people doing what they must know to be wrong, but this is a misstatement of the case. They are doing what they have been *told* is wrong, which is quite a different matter. If a man really *knows* that an action is wrong, and that it will inevitably be followed by evil consequences, he is careful to avoid it. A man really *knows* that fire will burn him; therefore he does not put his hand into it. It will be found that every one who does wrong justifies the wrong action to himself at the time of its commission, whatever he may think about it afterwards in cold blood. So I say that sin as ordinarily understood is a figment of the theological imagination; what really exists is an unfortunate condition of ignorance which often leads to infraction of the divine Law. This ignorance it is our duty to endeavor to dispel by the light of theosophy.

The Pope

A magnificent opportunity is waiting for the Pope who shall be ready and brave enough to take it. Instead of fulminating rescripts and bulls against theosophy and liberalism, he might himself propound the theosophical interpretation of Christianity. Remember that the Catholic Church possesses what is called the doctrine of development, and also that it has proclaimed the Pope to be the infallible exponent of divine doctrine, the viceregent of God upon earth. He would therefore be perfectly within his rights if, with regard to the theosophical interpretation, he should pronounce quite boldly:

> Certainly this which you bring forward is the true meaning of Christian doctrine. We have always known this, and we have plenty of manuscripts in the Vatican Library to prove it. We did not tell you this before, because all through the ages until now men have not been fit for such a revelation. They have been too crude, too rough, too undeveloped to understand a philosophical and mystical interpretation. The outer husk of the religion has been all that could usefully be offered to them. Now one stage more has been at-

tained and the world is ready for this further revelation. The second and inner meaning of our doctrine is therefore put before you, and while we must not condemn those who are still at the stage when they must cling to the outer husk, neither must they on their part be allowed to condemn those who are ready to take the further step and to receive a higher illumination.

But of course he must indeed be a strong as well as a wise man who should do this, for like all other great personages the Pope is surrounded by enormous masses of thought-forms, and he would find it a matter of extreme difficulty to break through these and make a new departure.

Ceremonial

The line of ceremonial is one along which many people come, but of course it must be understood that no religious ceremonial whatever is ever really essential, and the man who wishes to enter upon the Path of Holiness must realize this fully and must cast off belief in the necessity of ceremonies, as one of the fetters which hold him back from nirvana. This does not mean that ceremonies may not be sometimes quite effective in producing the results which are intended, but only that they are never really necessary for any one, and that the candidate for higher progress must learn to do utterly without them. The ceremonial line is an easy road for a certain type of people, and is really helpful and uplifting for them; but there is another type of men who always feel ceremonial as an obstacle between themselves and the deities which they wish to reach.

In Christianity this ceremonial line is the one appointed by its founder, through which his magic is to work. The consecration of the host, for example, is a means by which spiritual force is poured out over the people. There is often a vast amount of devotional feeling at the moment of the consecration, and the working of the magic is assisted by that, though it does not depend upon it. Those who are devotional unquestionably receive more because they bring with them an additional faculty of reception. On the other hand, there is always the probability that ignorant devotion will degenerate into superstition. In a recent enquiry into these matters from the occult point of view, made in Sicily, I found that there was certainly plenty of superstition, and much harmful interference in family matters on the part of the priests; but still on the whole the country was distinctly better than it would have been without it. We should remember also that in history we usually hear much of the worst effects of religious enthusiasm, whereas the good steady progress of many thousands under its influence makes but little impression.

Prayer

It is difficult to say anything on the question of prayer that would be universally applicable, because there are such very different kinds of prayer and they are addressed to beings who differ very widely in evolution. The founders of most great religions never in any way encouraged their followers to pray to them, and as a rule the latter have been far too enlightened to do anything of the kind. Whether a very strong thought directed towards them would reach them or not would depend upon the line of evolution which they have since followed—in fact upon whether they still remain within touch of this earth or not. If they were still so within reach, and if such a thought did reach them, it is probably that if they saw that it would be good for the thinker that any notice should be taken they would turn in his direction the attention of some of their pupils who are still upon earth. But it is quite inconceivable that a man who had any sort of conception of the magnificent far-reaching work done for evolution by the Great Ones on higher planes could dream of intruding his own petty concerns upon Their notice; he could not but know that any kind of help that he required would be far more fitly given to him by someone nearer to his own level. Even down here on this physical plane we are wiser than that, for we do not waste the time of the greatest scholars of our universities in helping babies over the difficulties of the alphabet.

As regards the saints of any of the churches the position is different, though even with them the ability to hear prayers will depend upon their position in evolution. The ordinary saint, who is simply a good and holy man, will of course take his heaven-life as usual, and will probably take a long one. His life on the astral plane would be likely to be but short, and it would be only during that that it would be possible for a prayer to reach him and attract his attention. If during that time it did so reach him, no doubt he would do anything that he could to satisfy the petitioner; but it is by no means certain that it would attract his attention, for he would naturally be fully occupied with his new surroundings.

When he entered upon his long rest in the heaven-world he would be entirely beyond any possibility of being disturbed by earthly things; yet even in such a case a prayer to him might not be without effect in connection with him. Such a man would almost certainly be pouring out a constant stream of loving thought towards humanity, and this thought would be a real and potent shower of blessing, tending generally towards the spiritual helping of those upon whom it fell; and there is no doubt that the man who was earnestly thinking of or praying to that saint would come into rapport with him, and would therefore draw down upon himself a great deal of that force, though entirely without the knowledge of the saint from whom it came. If the saint were sufficiently advanced to have entered upon a special series of births rapidly following one another the case would be different again. He would then be all the time within reach of earth, either living on the astral plane or in incarnation upon the physical, and if the prayer were strong enough to attract his attention at any time when he was for a moment out of his body, he would probably give any help in his power.

But fortunately for the many thousands who are constantly pouring forth their souls in prayer—in the blindest ignorance, of course, but still in perfect good faith—there is something else to depend upon which is independent of all these considerations. Shri Krishna tells us, in the *Bhagavad Gita*, how all true prayers come to him, to whomsoever they may have been ignorantly offered; there is a consciousness wide enough to comprehend all, which never fails in its response to any earnest effort in the direction of an increased spirituality. It works through many means; sometimes perhaps by directing the attention of a deva to the suppliant, sometimes through the agency of those human helpers who work upon the astral or mental planes for the good of humanity. Such a deva or helper so used would, if he showed himself, inevitably be taken by the petitioner for the saint to whom he had prayed, as there are many stories which illustrate this.

I myself, for example, have been taken under such circumstances for S. Philip Neri, and a junior helper who was with me on the occasion was supposed to be S. Stanislaus Kostka. Mrs.

Besant, too, has more than once been regarded as an angel by those whom she was assisting.

The Devil

The devil is non-existent. There are persons who imagine themselves to have made pacts with him, sometimes signed with their own blood. The result depends largely upon what sort of entity happened to impersonate him for the occasion. There are plenty of creatures of various sorts who would hugely enjoy such a joke at the expense of a man; but no such entity, whatever he may be, could possibly have any use for the "soul" of a man—nor would the "soul" of anybody foolish enough to make such a compact be likely to be of any use, either to the owner or anybody else. All these absurd superstitions are disproved by the fact that the man is the ego, and therefore cannot sell himself, and also that there are no buyers in such a transaction; so the whole thing is nothing but foolishness.

There are many entities who may be both willing and able to arrange twenty years of material prosperity for a person. They are generally willing to do it in return for some material consideration, such as the sacrifice of babies, goats or fowls. The ego has no share in these pacts, either in the rare individual cases, or in general fetish worship. These entities cannot possess the human ego, nor could they use it if it could come into their possession. A human body is sometimes convenient for them, and for the sake of being permitted to obsess it they will sometimes enter into an arrangement. The making of a compact of this nature gives the entity a strong hold upon the man; but as soon as he discovers the folly of his action, the proper course for the man to take is to resist such obsession to the utmost. Childish ceremonies, such as signing with his own blood, would of course make no difference whatever.

There is no hierarchy of evil. There are black magicians certainly, but the black magician is usually merely a single solitary entity. He is working for himself, as a separate entity, and for his own ends. You cannot have a hierarchy of people who distrust one another. In the White Brotherhood every member trusts the others; but you cannot have trust with the dark people, because their interests are built upon self.

You must, however, take care what you mean when you speak

of evil. The principle of destruction is often personified, but it is only that old forms are broken down to be used as material for building new and higher ones. Here in India there is Shiva, the Destroyer, but no one would think of him as evil; he is one of the highest manifestations of the deity. The principle of the destruc-tion of forms is necessary in order that life may progress. There is a Great One, a part of whose function it is to arrange when the great cataclysms shall take place—but he works for the good of the world. These things are not to be thought of as in any way evil. The notion of a supposed angel who revolted and was turned out of heaven is very much based upon John Milton. The conception is not at all the same in the Book of Job. In that story the devil is quite a different person from the gloomy hero in the Miltonic conception. Then the Buddhists have Mara—a personification of the karma of the past descending upon the man at once and taking many forms. There is an instant working-out of karma upon the attainment of enlightment.

The statement that all material things, all differences and limi-tations are evil is misleading. If by evil you mean what is ordinarily connoted by that word, and not some other and quite different notion of an abstract kind, then matter is not evil. Spirit and matter are equal. Matter is not in opposition to spirit. We find matter troublesome because of the bodies we have to use; but we are here in order to learn what without the physical life could not be conveyed to us. The physical plane experiences give a defi-niteness and precision to our consciousness and powers which we could never acquire on any plane unless we had spent the neces-sary time on this. But why do people bother about evil? There is plenty of good in the world, and it is better to think of that, for your thought strengthens that of which you think. To think and talk so much about black magicians unquestionably attracts their attention to you, and the results are often exceedingly undesir-able.

Hinduism

When ignorant missionaries dilate upon the three hundred and thirty million gods of the Hindus they are making a very gross misrepresentation of a religion which is far more scientific than their own. Hinduism, like every other religion, knows per-fectly well that there can be only one God, though there may be countless manifestations of Him. To call these "gods" is of course ridiculous. It is perhaps better to avoid the word "god" altogether, because of the exceedingly unpleasant ideas which have been associated with it by the Christians; but if it is to be used, at least it should never be applied to any being lower than the Logos of the solar system. All the good things attributed to the Christian God are true of the Logos; there is nothing in the system that is not He, and yet He is much more than His system. We could not possibly grasp the truth about the Absolute; anything which we are able to grasp must after all be small, since our minds are so small. The advice of the Lord Buddha to His people was always that they should not trouble themselves about such remote matters, since it was impossible to arrive at any conclusion, and nothing useful came from it.

The images of the Indian deities are usually highly magnetized, and when they are carried round the streets at the festivals their influence upon the people is unquestionably productive of much good. In many of the Hindu temples there are strong permanent influences at work, as is the case for example at Madura. Once when I visited that city some white ashes from the temple of Shiva were given to me, and also a bright crimson powder from the temple of Parvati, and I found that both of these were so powerfully magnetized as to retain their influence for some years and after much travelling.

India is essentially a country of rites and ceremonies. The religion is full of them, and a great many of them are said to have been prescribed by the Manu Himself, though it is quite obvious that many others have been added at a much later date. Some of them appear to be regulations such as would be quite necessary at the beginning of a new race, but now that it is thoroughly established it seems clear that they are useless. In many cases when one watches their performance one can see quite clearly what must originally have been intended, even though now the ceremony has become a mere empty shell, and no result follows upon it. Such things are not without their value for younger souls; indeed there are many who delight in them and obtain great benefit from them; but of course none of them can ever be really necessary, and all such bondage falls away altogether from the really developed man.

Originally, every householder was the priest of his own family, but as the civilization became more complex the rites and ceremonies grew more complex also, and therefore a class of specially instructed priests had to spring up, because no one who had anything else to do could possibly remember the wealth of unnecessary detail. In these days it would seem that most people perform them, or have them performed for them, much in the same spirit as they take medicine from a doctor, without understanding what it is, but with the faith that it will somehow do them good. There are, however, many people who cannot put heart and soul into a ceremony unless they do understand it, and these people usually end by breaking away from ceremonies altogether.

It is sad to see priests performing the old ceremonies and using the old forms which once were so effective, and yet producing no result worth mentioning. There seems to be no will in these days. They commence some of their recitations "Om, Bhur, Bhuvar, Swar"; but nothing whatever happens when they recite the words. In the old days the officiant who said this threw some will into it, and raised his own consciousness, as well as that of those present who were responsive, from one plane to the other as he spoke.

I remember seeing this strongly exemplified in the performance of a striking ceremony, when we were examining one of the earlier lives which occurred many thousands of years ago here in India. The people all entered an inner room and stood in absolute darkness. In the beginning of the ceremony the officiant slowly and solemnly uttered those words, and each produced its due effect upon the majority of those who stood around him. The word "Om" brought all the people in close harmony with him, and with the feelings which filled his mind. Then, at the utterance of the word "Bhur," to their senses the room was filled with ordinary light, and they were able to see all the physical objects in it; when, after an interval, the second word came, astral sight was temporarily opened for them; and the third word produced the same effect upon their mental sight, and brought round them all the bliss and power of the higher plane, and that condition persisted during the recitation of the various verses which followed.

Of course these effects were only temporary, and when the ceremony was over the higher consciousness faded away from those who had taken part in it, but nevertheless it remained for them a tremendous experience, and the effect of it was that on another similar occasion this higher consciousness was more readily and more fully aroused in them. But now nothing of this sort seems to be done anywhere. Now the priest arranges his fuel and utters a solemn invocation to Agni, and then—lights the fire with a match! In the old days that which is represented by Agni really did come, and the fire fell from heaven, to use an old expression. But all outer husks seem to remain.

There is a quite rational and scientific idea underlying the practice of pilgrimage. Great shrines are usually erected on the spot where some holy man has lived or where some great event has happened (such as an initiation) or else in connection with some relic of a great person. In any one of these cases a powerful magnetic center of influence has been created, which will persist for thousands of years. Any sensitive person who approaches the spot will feel this influence, and its effect upon him is unquestionably good. Where there is a strong vibration at a much higher level than any attained by ordinary humanity, its action upon any man who comes within its influence is to raise his own vibrations for the time towards unison with it.

The pilgrim who comes to such a spot and bathes himself in its magnetism, perhaps for several days together, is certainly the better for it, although different people will be affected in different degrees, according to their power of receptivity. Such a place of pilgrimage is the Bodhi tree at Buddha-gaya, the spot where the Lord Gautama attained His Buddhahood. This is true although the tree which is there now is not the original one. That fell some time in the middle ages, and the present tree is only an offshoot from it. But nevertheless the tremendously strong magnetism of the spot remains and is likely to do so for many a century yet to come.

Spiritualism

Never forget that the spiritualists are entirely with us on some most important points. They all hold (a) life after death as an actual vivid ever-present certainty, and (b) eternal progress and ultimate happiness for everyone, good and bad alike. Now these two items are of such tremendous, such paramount importance — they constitute so enormous an advance from the ordinary orthodox position—that I for one should be well content to join hands with them on such a platform, and postpone the discussion of the minor points upon which we differ until we have converted the world at large to that much of the truth. I always feel that there is plenty of room for both of us.

People who want to see phenomena, people who cannot believe anything without ocular demonstration, will obtain no satisfaction with us, while from the spiritualists they will get exactly what they want. On the other hand, people who want more philosophy than spiritualism usually provides will naturally gravitate in our direction. Those who admire the average trance-address certainly would not appreciate theosophy, while those who enjoy theosophical teaching would never be satisfied with the trance-address. We both cater for the liberal, the open-minded, but for quite different types of them; meantime, we surely need not quarrel.

In what Madame Blavatsky wrote on the subject she laid great stress on the utter uncertainty of the whole thing, and the preponderance of impersonations over real appearances. My own personal experience has been more favorable than that. I spent some years in experimenting with spiritualism, and I suppose there is hardly a phenomenon of which you may read in the books which I have not repeatedly seen. I have encountered many impersonations, but still in my experience a distinct majority of the apparitions have been genuine, and therefore I am bound to bear testimony to the fact. The messages which they give are often uninteresting, and their religious teaching is usually Christianity and water, but still it is liberal as far as it goes.

Not that some spiritualists are not bigoted—narrow and intolerant as any sectarian—when it comes to discussing (say) the question of reincarnation! Many students wonder that dead people should not all know and recognize the fact of reincarnation; but after all why should they? When a man dies he resorts to the company of those whom he has known on earth; he moves among exactly the same kind of people as during physical life. The average country grocer is no more likely after death than before it to come into contact with any one who can give him information about reincarnation. Most men are shut in from all new ideas by a host of prejudices; they carry these prejudices into the astral world with them, and are no more amenable to reason and commonsense there than here.

True, a man who is really open-minded can learn a great deal on the astral plane; he may speedily acquaint himself with the whole of the theosophical teaching, and there are dead men who do this. Therefore it often happens that scraps of theosophy are found among spirit communications. We must not forget that there is a higher spiritualism of which the public knows nothing, which never publishes any account of its results. The best circles of all are strictly private—restricted entirely to one family, or to a small number of friends. In such circles the same people meet over and over again, and no outsider is ever admitted to make any change in the magnetism; so the conditions set up are singularly perfect, and the results obtained are of the most surprising character. At public seances, to which any one may be admitted on payment, only quite undeveloped souls are attracted and appear, because of the promiscuous jumble of inharmonious magnetisms.

Symbology

Symbology is a very interesting study. To a certain type of mind everything expresses itself in symbols, and to some people they are of the greatest possible help. I myself do not happen to be of that type, and therefore I have not paid special attention to them or made any particular study of them. Some of them however are obvious, and readily comprehensible to any one who understands even a little of the principles of their interpretation. Think, for example, of those which appear on the earlier pages of *The Book of Dzyan*. On the first page is a white disc, signifying the condition of the unmanifested; on the second page a spot appears in the center of the white disc, signifying the first manifestation—the First Logos, or the Christ in the bosom of the Father; on the third page this spot has expanded into a bar, dividing the disc into two halves and so signifying the first great separation into spirit and matter—also the Second Logos, always spoken of as dual or androgynous; on the fourth page another bar has appeared at right angles to the first, giving us the forms of a circle divided into four equal parts or quarters, signifying the emergence of the Third Logos, though He is still in a condition of inactivity. On the next page the outer circle falls away, leaving us the equal-armed or Greek cross. This denotes the Third Logos ready for action, just about to descend into the matter of His cosmos.

The next stage of this activity is shown by various forms of the symbol. Sometimes the arms of the Greek cross widen out as they recede from the center, and then we get the form called the Maltese cross. Another line of symbology retains the straight arms of the Greek cross, but draws a flame shooting out from the end of each arm, to signify the burning light within. A further extension of this idea sets the cross whirling round its center, like a revolving wheel, and when that is done the flames are drawn as streaming backwards as the cross revolves, and in that way we get one of the most universal of all symbols, that of the svastika, which is to be found in every country in the world, and in connection with every religion.

The symbolic meaning of the ordinary Latin cross, as it is used in the Christian Church, has no connection whatever with this line of thought. Its meaning is entirely different, for it symbolizes the Second Logos, and His descent into matter, and it is also closely connected with the initiation rites of ancient Egypt. In the case of *The Book of Dzyan* the comprehension of the symbol is enormously assisted by the fact that the book itself is highly magnetized in a peculiar way, so that when the student who is privileged to see it takes one of the pages in his hand a remarkable effect is produced upon him. Before his mind's eye arises the picture of that which the page is intended to symbolize, and simultaneously he hears a sort of recitation of the stanza which describes it. It is very difficult to put this clearly into words, but the experience is a wonderful one.

I have myself seen and handled the copy which Madame Blavatsky describes—from the study of which she wrote *The Secret Doctrine*. That is of course not the original book, but the copy of it which is kept in the occult museum which is under the care of the Master K. H. The original document is at Shamballa, in the care of the Head of the Hierarchy, and is certainly the oldest book in the world. Indeed it has been said that part of it (the first six stanzas, I think) is even older than the world, for it is said to have been brought over from some previous chain. That most ancient part is regarded by some as not merely an account of the processes of the coming into existence of a system, but rather a kind of manual of directions for such an act of creation. Even the copy must be millions of years old.

Another well-known symbol is that of the "Great Bird," which is used to denote the Deity in the act of hovering over His universe, brooding over the waters of space, or darting onward along the line of His evolution. To repose between the wings of the Great

Bird means so to meditate as to realize union with the Logos, and it is said that the man who reaches that level may rest there for untold years.

The word Om is another presentation of the same idea; it is the sacred word of the fifth or Aryan root-race. The Atlantean sacred word was Tau, and it has been said that the sacred words given to the root-races in succession are all of them consecutive syllables of one great word, which is the true sacred Name.

Another obvious symbol, the heart, was prominent in the old Atlantean religion. In the innermost shrine of the great temple in the City of the Golden Gate there lay upon the altar a massive golden box in the shape of a heart, the secret opening of which was known only to the high-priest. This was called "The Heart of the World," and signified to them the innermost mysteries that. they knew. In it they kept their most sacred things, and much of their symbolism centered around it. They knew that every atom beats as a heart, and they considered that the sun had a similar movement, which they connected with the sun-spot period. Sometimes one comes across passages in their books which give the impression that they knew more than we do in matters of science, though they regarded it all rather from the poetic than from the scientific point of view. They thought, for example, that the earth breathes and moves, and it is certainly true that quite recently scientific men have discovered that there is a regular daily displacement of the earth's surface which may be thought of as corresponding in a certain way to breathing.

Another symbol is that of the lotus, and it is used to signify the solar system in its relation to its Logos. There is a real reason for this comparison in the actual facts of nature. The seven Planetary Logoi, although they are great individual entities, are at the same time aspects of the Solar Logos, force-centers as it were in His body. Now each of these great living centers or subsidiary Logoi has a sort of orderly periodic change or motion of his own, corresponding perhaps on some infinitely higher level to the regular beating of the human heart, or to the inspiration and expiration of the breath.

Some of these periodic changes are more rapid than others, so that a very complicated series of effects is produced, and it has been observed that the movements of the physical planets in their relation to one another furnish a clue to the operation of these great cosmic influences at any given moment. Each of these centers has His special location or major focus within the body of the sun, and has also a minor focus which is always exterior to the sun. The position of this minor focus is always indicated by a physical planet.

The exact relation can hardly be made clear to our three-dimensional phraseology; but we may perhaps put it that each center has a field of influence practically co-extensive with the solar system; that if a section of the field could be taken it would be found to be elliptical; and that one of the foci of each ellipse would always be in the sun, and the other would be the special planet ruled by the subsidiary Logos. It is probably that, in the gradual condensation of the original glowing nebula from which the system was formed, the location of the planets was determined by the formation of vortices at these minor foci, they being auxiliary points of distribution—ganglia as it were in the solar system. All the physical planets are included within the portion of the system which is common to all the ovoids; so that any one who tries mentally to construct the figure will see that these revolving ovoids must have their projecting segments, and he will therefore be prepared to understand the comparison of the system as a whole to a flower with many petals.

Another reason for this comparison of the system to a lotus is even more beautiful, but requires deeper thought. As we see them the planets appear as separate gloves; but there is in reality a connection between them which is out of reach of our brain-consciousness. Those who have studied the subject of the fourth dimension are familiar with the idea of an extension in a direction invisible to us, but it may not have occurred to them that it is applicable to the solar system as a whole.

We may obtain a suggestion of the facts by holding the hand palm upwards bent so as to form a kind of cup, but with the fingers separated, and then laying a sheet of paper upon the tips of the fingers. A two-dimensional being living on the plane of that sheet of paper could not possibly be conscious of the hand as a whole, but could perceive only the tiny circles at the points of contact between the fingers and the paper. To him these circles would be entirely unconnected, but we, using the sight of a higher dimension, can see that each of them has a downward expansion, and that in that way they are all parts of a hand. In exactly the same way the man using the sight of the fourth dimension may observe that the planets which are isolated in our three dimensions are all the time joined in another way which we cannot yet see; and from the point of view of that higher sight these globes are but the points of petals which are part of one great flower. And the glowing heart of that flower throws up a central pistil which appears to us as the sun.

It is not wise for the votary of modern science to ridicule or despise either the learning of old time or the strange and fanciful symbols in which it was expressed, for many of these ancient symbols are pregnant with meaning—often with meaning showing deeper knowledge than the outer world now possesses. The theosophical student at least will avoid the mistake of despising anything merely because he does not yet comprehend it— because he has not yet learned the language in which it is written.

Fire

On higher planes everything is what down here we should call luminous, and above a certain level everything may be said to be permeated by fire, yet not at all such fire as we know on the physical plane. What we call by that name down here cannot exist without something which either burns or glows, and it is only a kind of reflection or lower expression of a higher abstract thing which we cannot sense. Try to think of a fire which does not burn, but is in a liquid form, something like water. This was known to the followers of the first great Zoroaster, for they had this fire which burned no fuel on their altars, a sacred fire by means of which they symbolized divine life.

One way of reaching the Logos is along the line of fire, and the ancient Parsis knew this well, and raised themselves until they were one with the fire, so as to reach Him by way of it. The only way in which it can be done is through the assistance of certain classes of devas, but at this period of the world's history we are so grossly material that very few can stand the ordeal. The first Zoroaster had around him many who were able to take that way; and though under present conditions our lower vehicles would probably be destroyed if we should make such an attempt, in new races and on other planets we shall be able to take that way again. All this sounds strange and weird and incomprehensible, because it deals with conditions which are utterly unknown on the physical plane, but the student of occultism will find that in the course of his progress he has to face many things which cannot at all be expressed in words down here.

The Theosophical
Attitude

Common Sense

Above all things and under all circumstances the student of
occultism must hold fast to common sense. He will meet with
many new ideas, with many startling facts, and if he allows the
strangeness of things to overbalance him, harm instead of good
will result from the increase of his knowledge. Many other qualities are desirable for progress, but a well-balanced mind is an
actual necessity. The study of occultism may indeed be summed
up in this way: it is the study of much that is unrecognized by the
ordinary man—the acquisition therefore of a great multitude of
new facts, and then the adaptation of one's life to the new facts in
a reasonable and common-sense way. All occultism of which I
know anything is simply an apotheosis of common sense.

Brotherhood

The brotherhood of man is a fact in nature; those who deny it are
simply those who are blind to it, because they shut their eyes to
actualities which they do not wish to acknowledge. We need waste
little time over those who deny it; nature itself will refute their
heresy. More subtly dangerous are those who misunderstand it,
and their name is legion.

Remember not only what brotherhood means, but also what it does not mean. It emphatically does not mean equality, for twins and triplets are comparatively rare; under all but the most abnormal circumstances, brotherhood implies a difference in age, and consequently all sorts of other differences, in strength, in cleverness, in capacity.

Brotherhood implies community of interest, but not community of interests. If the family be rich all its members profit thereby; if the family be poor, all its members suffer accordingly. So there is a community of interest. But the individual interests of the brothers not only may be, but also for many years must be, absolutely different. What interests has the boy of fourteen in common with his brother of six? Each lives his own life among friends of his own age, and has far more in common with them than with his brother. What cares the elder brother of twenty-five, fighting his way in the world, for all the prizes and anxieties of school-life which fill the horizon of that second brother?

It is not to be expected, then, that because they are brothers men shall feel alike or be interested in the same things. It would not be desirable, even if it were possible, for their duties differ according to their ages, and the one thing which most promotes the evolution of the human family as a whole is that every man should strive earnestly to do his duty in that state of life to which it shall please God to call him, as the Church catechism puts it. This does not in the least imply that every man must always remain in the station in which his karma has placed him at birth; if he can honestly and harmlessly make such further karma as will raise him out of it he is at perfect liberty to do so. But at whatever stage he may be, he should do the duties of that stage. The child grows steadily; but while he is at a certain age, his duties are those appropriate to that age, and not those of some older brother. Each age has its duties—the younger to learn and to serve, and the older to direct and protect; but all alike to be loving and helpful, all alike to try to realize the idea of the great family of humanity. Each will best help his brothers, not by interfering with them, but by trying earnestly to do his own duty as a member of this family.

The brotherhood of our Theosophical Society ought to be a very real thing. It is important that we should recognize and realize a close fellowship, a feeling of real unity and drawing together. This will be achieved if members will forget their own personal feelings and think chiefly of the interests of others. The heart of the Theosophical Society is making for itself a body on the buddhic plane, a channel through which the Great Ones can work. The perfection of the channel as such depends upon the attitude of the earnest and devoted members. As yet it is very imperfect, because of the tendency of each member to think too much of himself as a unit, and too little of the good and well-being of the whole. The stones of the wall must be built each in its own place; one standing out of place here, or projecting there, causes roughness, and the wall as a whole is a less perfect wall. We form but a little part of a vast scheme, one wheel as it were of a machine. It is for us to make ourselves really fit for our little part; if we do that, though we may be quite unfit to take a leading position in the drama of the world, yet what little we do is well done and lasting, and will honorably fill its place in the greater whole.

You are all aware that in seven hundred years' time our two Masters will commence the founding of the sixth root-race, and that even already they are looking about for those who will be suitable assistants for them in that work. But there is something nearer than that to be done—and it is a work which will afford excellent practice in developing the qualities necessary for that larger work; and this is the development of the sixth sub-race of the Aryan culture, which is now just beginning to be formed in North America. Already signs are to be seen of the preparations for this work; different peoples are being welded together in one; and we too have our part to play in this. We all recognize how important it is that a child's early years should be surrounded by good influences, and it is just the same with the childhood of a race. If we can succeed in starting this young race along right lines much will be gained; and we can be of great help at this critical period of history, if we will.

Part of the scheme very shortly to be realized is the drawing together of the various branches of our fifth sub-race, the Teutonic people. Many of us belong to that—the English colonies, the Americans, the Scaninavians, the Dutch and the Germans; and many also in France and Italy, as for example the Normans, who are the descendants of the Norsemen, and also those in southern countries who are descendants of the Goths and Visigoths. What is desired in order to promote the work of the great plan is that all these should be drawn into much closer sympathy. This has already been achieved to a great extend in the case of England and America.

The time is rapidly approaching when a new religion shall be launched—a teaching which shall unify the other religions, and compared with them shall stand upon a broader basis and keep its purity longer. But before this can come about we must have gotten rid of the incubus of war, which at present is always hanging over our heads like a great specter, paralyzing the best intellects of all countries as regards social experiments, making it impossible for our statesmen to try new plans and methods on a large scale. Therefore one essential towards carrying out the scheme is a period of universal peace. Many efforts have already been made in various ways to bring about this result—but it seems that some other way will have to be tried.

How then can this best be attained? By making it to the interest of all these nations to insist upon universal peace. Remember that trade suffers during war. We of these various branches of the Teutonic people are the greatest trading nations of the world, and I hope that we may shortly realize that it is to our interest to bind ourselves together, and to stand for peace. Truly this is not a very high motive, for it is merely self-interest; but still when the rulers and great statesmen are moved to desire unity from the abstract love for humanity, this lower motive may help to bring their less developed fellow-countrymen into line with them, and cause them warmly to support any movement which they may set on foot for that object.

Each people has its own peculiarities, just as each individual has. If we wish to cooperate in the great work we must learn to allow for these, to be tolerant of them, and to regard them with a kindly interest, instead of sneering at them or letting them get on our nerves. What then can we do practically to help these great national affairs? This at least: that when in our presence unkind or sneering remarks are made about other nations, we can make a point of always putting forward considerations on the other side, and saying something kindly. We may not always be able to contradict the negative thing said, but at least we may supplement it with something that is good.

There are perhaps but few of us, but at least in the course of a year each of us probably meets at least a thousand others, and each of us may to that extent be a center for helping our own nation to see good in others, and thus, though it may be only in a small way, we may be able to smooth the path and make the way for union easier. Many are constantly in the habit of speaking with narrow prejudice against the peculiarities of other nations;

let us at least take care not to do this, but always bear in mind the importance of promoting friendly feeling. Do not let us despair when we think how little each one of us can do in the matter; let us rather remember that every little effort will be used by those who are working from behind. No doubt the scheme will be carried out whether or not we take the privilege which is offered to us of helping in it; but that is no reason why we should not do our best.

Nor is it only good people who are used in the promotion of the scheme. All sorts of forces are being used by the Great Brotherhood that stands behind to forward the necessary work. Yes, even the very selfishness and the failings of men. "Blindly the wicked work the righteous will of heaven," as Southey writes in Thalaba. And, "All things work together for good to them that love God." This was spoken as regards personal karma, but the same thing holds good in regard to greater and broader schemes. For example, the bigotry of the Christian Church, evil though it is, has not been altogether valueless, for it has helped to develop strength of faith, since the ignorant cannot believe strongly without being bigoted. Self-seeking in commercial pursuits is evil also, yet it has in it a certain power which can be turned to account by those who stand behind, for it develops strength of will and concentration, qualities which in a future life may be put to most valuable uses.

We each have an opportunity to help in this scheme, to cooperate on the side of good. If we do not take the opportunity offered to us, another will, and if not that other, then another, but in any case the work will be done.

Never for a moment must we fear that because of some defection the work will be allowed to suffer. We cannot but regret that our poor friends should lose their opportunities—that from ignorance and lack of clear-sightedness they are working so sadly against their own interests. Yet remember that their folly is but temporary; they will awaken to the truth some day—if not in this life, then in some other. Meantime inside all is well, and the Great Work is going forward.

The evolution of the world is, after all, like any other large undertaking. Think of the making of a railway, for instance. It does not matter to the railway company or to the future passengers which workman lays a certain rail or drives a certain bolt, so long as it is well and truly done; and the overseer will attend to that. It matters very much to the workman, for he who works receives the pay, while the other gets nothing. The overseer regrets it when a workman goes off in a fit of temper or of drunkenness and refuses to work for a day; but he thinks, "Never mind, he will come back tomorrow," and meantime he employs some one else. Many have left the work in just that way in an outburst of personality, but they will return. The question is not as to whether the work shall be done—the Masters will see to that in any case; it is only as to who will embrace the opportunity of doing it.

Many people who contend bitterly against the right are merely showing that they are not yet fit to pass this test; they have not yet reached the stage where they can forget themselves utterly in the work; their personalities are still rampant, and so they are capable of being shocked and thrown off their balance, if some new fact comes before them. It is sad, of course, but it is only temporary; they have lost a good opportunity for this life, because they are not yet strong enough for it; but there are many lives yet to come. Meantime others will take their places. Never forget that the one thing of importance is that the Masters' work should be done; let us at least be among those who are doing it now, even though there are many who cannot yet see clearly enough to help us.

If we would rise to our opportunity we must rub down our corners and get rid of our awkward personalities, and forget them in encouraging good feeling in every possible way. If we hear something said against somebody else let us at once try to put the other side, and this both with regard to nations and individuals. Counterbalance the evil by speaking the good—not to give a false impression, but to give the best possible aspect or interpretation of the facts. Our work is to make the machine run smoothly, and neutralize the friction. Our aim is to be a united whole as a Society, and to help towards harmony in the outside world. The scheme is great, the opportunity glorious; shall we take it?

Yet beware lest you should make the idea of preparing yourself for grand work in the future an excuse for neglecting the minor opportunities of every-day life. A good example of what I mean is offered by a letter which I recently received, in which the writer says that he finds himself in the position of having to teach a Theosophical Branch, and that he feels it a great responsibility, of which he cannot think himself worthy because his knowledge is at present so imperfect. Now in reply to this I shall say:

Do not be in the least troubled about your position toward your Branch. Assuredly it is a responsibility to teach, but on the other hand it is a very great privilege. Think of it rather in this way, that here are a number of hungry souls, and those who stand behind have been so kind to you as to give you the opportunity of being the channel through which these can be fed. You have the broad principles of the teaching clearly in mind, and your own common sense will keep you from going far wrong in details. I admire your extreme conscientiousness, but if you keep these main principles steadily before your pupils, you are very little likely to go wrong in your teaching.

We all have the responsibility of which you speak, and those of us who have to write the books and give the lectures feel it far more acutely than you can imagine. Indeed we have sometimes been told by friends that we ought to have attained adeptship before we wrote any books, so that it might be quite certain that there should be no mistakes in them. I can only say that we decided to share our imperfect knowledge with our brothers, even while we still have very much to acquire; and I think that the result has justified our decision. If we had waited until we attained adeptship, it is true that our books would have been perfect—and they are very far from being perfect now—but then you see you would all have had to wait a thousand years or so for them, which would have made a considerable difference to the work of the Theosophical Society in the present century. It seems to me that the problem that lies before you is an exactly similar one. You also might refrain from teaching until you knew everything; but what would become of your Branch in the meantime?

Helping the World

One of the first qualifications which are required for the treading of the Path is single-mindedness or one-pointedness. Even worldly men succeed because they are one-pointed, and we can learn from them the value of determination on our own line. Our goal is not so tangible as theirs, so we have more difficulty in keeping the one-pointed attitude of mind; but in India the importance of the unseen is more easily realized than in the West. It is good to seek the company of those who are more advanced, to whom the realities of the Path are constantly present; also to read and hear and think about our purpose frequently, and unwaveringly to practice the virtues by which alone the perfect knowledge can come to us.

This is an age of hurry and scurry; the tendency is for people to do a little of many things, but nothing thoroughly—to flutter from one thing to another. No man now devotes his life to a masterpiece, as was often done in the Middle Ages in Europe, in old days in India.

Occultism changes a man's life in many ways, but in none more than in this; it makes him absolutely one-pointed. Of course I do not mean that it causes him to neglect any duty that he used to do; on the contrary, the never-ceasing watch to fulfill every duty is its first prescription. But it gives him a keynote of life which is always sounding in his ears, which he never forgets for an instant—the keynote of helpfulness. Why? Because he learns what is the plan of the Logos, and tries to cooperate in it.

This involves many lines of action. To be able to help effectively he must make himself fit to help; hence he must undertake the most careful self-training, the elimination of evil qualities from himself, the development of good ones. Also he must maintain a constant watchfulness for opportunities to help.

One special method of helping the world lies ready to the hand of members of our Society—that of spreading Theosophic truth. We have no right and no desire to force our ideas on any one, but it is our duty and our privilege to give people the opportunity of knowing the real explanation of the problems of life. If, when the water of life is offered, a man will not drink, that is his own affair; but at least we should see that none perishes through ignorance of the existence of that water.

We have then this duty of spreading the truth, and nothing should be allowed to interfere with it. This is the work that as a Society we have to do, and we must remember that the duty is binding upon each of us. Our minds must be filled with it, we must be constantly thinking and planning for it, seizing every opportunity that offers. It is not for us to excuse ourselves because some other member seems to be doing nothing; that is his business, and we are in no way concerned in it; but if we ourselves neglect to do our very best, we are failing in our duty. It was not to illumine our own path that this glorious light came to us, but that we also in our turn might be light-bearers to our suffering brothers.

Criticism

If we wish to make any progress in occultism, we *must* learn to mind our own business and leave other people alone. They have their reasons and their lines of thought which we do not understand. To their own Master they stand or fall. Once more, we have our work to do, and we decline to be diverted from it. We *must* learn charity and tolerance, and repress the mad desire to be always finding fault with someone else.

It *is* a mad desire, and it dominates modern life—this spirit of criticism. Every one wants to interfere with somebody else's duty, instead of attending to his own; every one thinks he can do the other man's work better than it is being done. We see it in politics, in religion, in social life. For example the obvious duty of a government is to govern, and the duty of its people is to be good citizens and to make that work of government easy and effective. But in these days people are so eager to teach their governments how to govern that they forget all about their own primary duty of being good citizens. Men will not realize that if they will but do their duties, karma will look after the "rights" about which they are so clamorous.

How comes this spirit of criticism to be so general and so savage at this stage of the world's history? Like most other evils, it is the excess of a good and necessary quality. In the course of evolution we have arrived at the fifth sub-race of the fifth root-race. I mean that that race is the latest yet developed, that its spirit is dominant in the world just now, and that even those who do not belong to it are necessarily much influenced by that spirit.

Now each race has its own special lessons to learn, its own special quality to unfold. The quality of the fifth-race is what is sometimes called manas—the type of intellect that discriminates, that notes the *differences* between things. When it is perfectly developed, men will note these differences calmly, solely for the purpose of understanding them and judging which is best. But now, in this stage of half-development, most people look for differences from their own point of view *not* in order to *understand* them but in order to *oppose* them—often to violently persecute them. It is simply the point of view of the ignorant and unevolved man, who is full of intolerance and self-conceit, absolutely sure that he is right (perhaps he may be up to a certain point) and that everybody else therefore must be entirely

wrong—which does not follow. Remember that Oliver Crom-
well said to his council: "Brethren, I beseech you in the sacred
name of the Christ to think it possible that you may sometimes
mistake!"

We too must develop the critical faculty; but we should
criticize *ourselves*, not others.

There are always two sides to every question; generally more
than two. *Kritein* means to judge; therefore, criticism is useless
and can only do harm unless it is absolutely calm and judicial. It
is not a mad attack upon the opponent, but a quiet, unprejudiced weighing of reasons for and against a certain opinion or
a certain course of action. We may decide in one way, but we *must*
recognize that another man of equal intellect may emphasize
another aspect of the question, and therefore, decide quite
otherwise. And yet in so deciding he may be just as good, just as
wise, just as honest as we ourselves.

Yet how few recognize that; how few rabid Protestants really
believe Catholics to be good men; how few convinced redhot
radicals really believe that an old Tory squire may be just as good
and earnest a man as themselves, trying honestly to do what he
thinks his duty!

If a man reaches a decision different from our own we need not
pretend to agree with him, but we must give him credit for good
intentions. One of the worst features of modern life is its eager
readiness to believe evil—its habit of deliberately seeking out the
worst conceivable construction that can be put upon everything.
And this attitude is surely at its very worst when adopted towards
those who have helped us, to whom we owe thanks for knowledge
or inspiration received. Remember the words of the Master:
"Ingratitude is not one of our vices." It is always a mistake to rush
madly into criticism of those who know more than we; it is more
seemly to wait and think matters over, to wait and see what the
future brings forth. Apply the test of time and the result; "By
their fruits ye shall know them." Let us make a rule to think the
best of every man; let us do our work and leave others free to do
theirs.

Prejudice

Beware of the beginnings of suspicion: it will distort everything. I
have seen it come between friends and noticed how a little suspi-

cion soon grows into a giant misunderstanding. Every harmless word is distorted, and mistaken to be the expression of some unkind or improper motive, while all the time the speaker is utterly unconscious of the suspicion. It is the same when opinions differ about books or religion; a slight difference of opinion is fostered by dwelling upon all that tells on one's own side and against the other side, until the result is an absurdly distorted view. One finds it again with color prejudice, although those now wearing white bodies have worn brown ones and *vice versa*, and the habits of one have been or will be the habits of the other. Brotherhood means the getting rid of prejudices; knowledge of the fact of reincarnation ought to help us to overcome our limitations and uncharitableness.

We who are students of the higher life *must* rise above these prejudices. It is a difficult task, because they are ingrained—prejudices of race, of caste, of religion; but they *must* all be rooted out, because they prevent clear sight and true judgment. They are like colored glass—still more like cheap, imperfect glass; everything seen through them is distorted, often so much so as to look entirely different from what it really is. Before we can judge and discriminate we *must* see clearly.

It is always very easy to attribute some evil motive to others whom we have allowed ourselves to dislike, and to discover some evil explanation for their acts. This tendency forms a very serious impediment in the path of progress. We must tear away our own personalities, for only then shall we be at all able to see the other person as he is. A prejudice is a kind of growth upon the mental body, and of course when a man tries to look out through that particular part of the body he cannot see clearly. It is in reality a congested spot in the mental body, a point at which the matter is no longer living and flowing, but is stagnant and rotten. The way to cure it is to acquire more knowledge, to get the matter of the mental body into motion, and then one by one the prejudices will be washed away and dissolved.

This evil effect of prejudice was what Aryasangha meant when he said, in *The Voice of the Silence*, that the mind was the great slayer of the real. By that he was drawing attention to the fact that we do not see any object as it is. We see only the images that we are able to make of it, and everything is necessarily colored for us by these thoughtforms of our own creation. Notice how two persons with preconceived ideas, seeing the same set of circumstances, and agreeing as to the actual happenings, will yet make two totally different stories from them. Exactly this sort of thing is going on all the time with every ordinary man, and we do not realize how absurdly we distort things.

The duty of the theosophical student is to learn to see things as they are, and this means control, vigilance and a very great deal of hard work. In the West, for example, people are very much prejudiced along religious lines, for we are born into a certain religion and sedulously taught that all others are superstitions. Our ideas therefore are biased from the first, and even when we do learn to know a little about other religions and respect them it would be difficult for us to imagine ourselves born into them. Those who are Hindus can scarcely think of themselves as being born as Christians or Muhammadans, and just in the same way the Christian or Muhammadan has an equal difficulty in thinking of himself as a Hindu or a Buddhist, although it is practically certain that in some past life he has been in one or other of these religions.

The more ignorant people are, the greater is their distrust of that to which they are unaccustomed. The peasantry, for example, have an instinctive distrust of all foreigners, and there are many country places in England where, let us say, a Frenchman, unless in poverty and needing help, would certainly be regarded with suspicion. If he is hungry he will be fed, and treated with compassion; but let him come as a fellow-workman and all that he does will be criticized, laughed at, and suspected. Now of course all this comes from ignorance, and occurs because the peasantry are unaccustomed to meeting with foreigners.

The removal of such prejudice is one of the great advantages gained by an intelligent man when he travels. In the Theosophical Society men of different nations are being drawn much more closely together; Indians are learning to trust Europeans, and Europeans in turn are learning that Indians are much the same as themselves. I was working in Amsterdam during the Boer war, and though in Holland generally there was a strong feeling at the time against England, there was never the slightest trace of it among the Dutch Theosophical members. It is most interesting to attend one of the European Theosophical Conferences, and to see the really hearty good feeling which exists between men of different nations—how unfeignedly glad they are to see one another, and how they rejoice in one another's company. One sees at once that if such fellow-feeling as exists between the members of the Theosophical Society could only spread to a majority of their fellow-countrymen in the various nations, war would at once become a ridiculous impossibility.

As things are now we form opinions on very slight grounds; you meet a person for the first time, and something that he says, or some trivial gesture, arouses in you a little dislike of him, so that there is a slight wall between you and him. This may seem an unimportant matter, yet if you are not careful that slight bias against the person will grow into a barrier which will forever prevent you from understanding him. To a certain extent you see him through this thoughtform that you have made, and you cannot see him correctly, for it is like looking through a twisted and colored glass which distorts everything.

Sometimes, but not so often, a prejudice is in favor of the person, as in the case of a mother who can see no harm in what her child does, even though he may seriously harm others. Now whether they be against a person or in favor of him, both of these are equally prejudices, mental delusions which slay the real. The best way to see truly is to begin determinedly to look always for the good in every one, as our prejudices are generally on the other side, and we are sadly prone to see the evil where none exists. We differ from other people in color, in dress, in manners and customs, and in outer forms of religion, but all these are merely externals, and all that goes to make up the real man behind and beneath all this is much the same in us all. It is not after all so difficult to learn to look behind the outer shells in which people conceal themselves. Thereby they usually make the worst of themselves, for the main faults nearly always lie on the surface, and the real gold is often successfully concealed. One who aspires to make progress must overcome this blindness to the worth of others, this tendency to judge by surface characteristics.

Remember that no one who desires to stand on the side of good as against evil can ever be refused the opportunity, no matter how ignorant or bigoted he may be. The Masters always take the good and use it wherever it appears, even if there is in the same man much that is bad also; and their use of this force for good greatly helps the man who has generated it. For example, they will use the devotional force which is to be found even in a murderous fanatic, and thus they will allow him to do some good work and consequently to be helped.

We also should imitate the Great ones; we should always try to take the good in everything and everybody. Do not look for and accentuate the evil in any one, but select and emphasize the good. Go on doing your own work to the best of your ability, and do not trouble yourself about the work of another, or about how he is doing it. Even if other people make difficulties in your way, climb over them and do not worry; they are your karma, and after all these things from outside do not really matter. Do not make the mistake of thinking that others are trying to thwart your good purposes. All these people are much like yourself; think of it— would you deliberately choose to do a wicked thing like that?

Curiosity

Be so centered in your work that you have no time to find fault with others, or to pry into their affairs. If only each man would mind his own business the work would be infinitely happier.

This prying into other people's affairs works much of evil, and it is quite accurate to say that the person who does it is suffering from a disease. The man who is prying is not usually doing it for the purpose of helping, but simply to satisfy his curiosity about something which does not concern him, which is symptomatic of his disease. Another symptom is that the man cannot keep to himself the information which he has so nefariously acquired, but must everlastingly be pouring it out to others as foolish as himself. For it is wicked beyond all doubt, this gossip—one of the most wicked things in the world. Ninety-nine times out of a hundred what is said is an absolute fabrication, but it does an enormous amount of harm.

It is not only the damage done to another person's reputation; that is the least part of the evil. The gossip and his pestilential cronies perpetually make thoughtforms of some evil quality which they choose to attribute to their victim, and then proceed to hurl them upon him in an unceasing stream. The natural effect of this will be to awaken in him the evil quality of which they accuse him, if there is anything at all in his nature which will respond to their malicious efforts. In the one case out of a hundred in which there is some truth in their spiteful prattle, their thoughtforms intensify the evil, and so they pile up for themselves a store of the terrible karma which comes from leading a brother into wrong-doing. Theosophists especially should be careful to avoid these evils, because many of them are making some effort in the direction of developing psychic powers, and if they should use those for the purpose of prying into other people's affairs or for sending evil thoughts to them, their karma would be of the most terrible nature.

Never speak unless you know, and not even then unless you are absolutely certain that some definite good will come of it. Before you speak ask yourself about what you are going to say: "Is it true? Is it kind? Is it useful?" And unless you can answer these three questions in the affirmative, your duty is to remain silent. I am well aware that an absolute following of this rule would reduce the conversation of the world by about ninety per cent, but that would be an unspeakable advantage, and the world would advance much more rapidly.

When we understand the underlying unity of all we cannot be otherwise than helpful, we cannot stand aside from our brother's sorrow. Of course there may be many cases where physical aid is impossible, but at least we can always give the help of sympathy, compassion and love, and this is clearly our duty. For a man who realizes theosophy, harshness is impossible. Any member who acts roughly or coarsely is failing in his theosophy, and if he fails in patience he is failing in comprehension. To understand all is to forgive all, to love all. Every man has his own point of view, and the shortest road for one man is not by any means necessarily the best for another. Every man has a perfect right to take his own evolution in hand in his own way and to do, with regard to it, what he chooses so long as he does not cause suffering or inconvenience to any one else. It is emphatically not our business to try to put everybody right, but only to see that all is right on our side in our relation with others. Before we undertake an effort to force someone else into our path it will be best for us to carefully examine *his*, for it may be better for him. We ought to be always ready to help freely to the fullest extent of our power, but we ought never to interfere.

Know Thyself

The old Greek saying *Gnothi seauton*, know thyself, is a fine piece of advice, and self-knowledge is absolutely necessary to any candidate for progress. And yet we must beware lest our necessary self-examination should degenerate into morbid introspection, as it often does with some of the best of our students. Many people are constantly worrying themselves lest unawares they should be "sliding back," as they call it. If they understood the method of evolution a little better they would see that no one can slide back when the whole current is moving steadily forward.

As a torrent comes rushing down a slope, many little eddies are formed behind rocks, or perhaps where the water is whirling round and round, and therefore for the moment some of it is moving backward; but yet the whole body of water, eddies and all, is being swept on in the rush of the torrent, so that even that which is apparently moving backwards in relation to the rest of the stream is really being hurried forward along with the rest. Even the people who are doing nothing toward their evolution, and let everything go as it will, are all the while gradually evolving, because of the irresistible force of the Logos which is steadily pressing them onwards; but they are moving so slowly that it will take them millions of years of incarnation and trouble and uselessness to gain even a step.

The method in which this is managed is delightfully simple and ingenious. All the evil qualities in man are vibrations of the lower matter of the respective planes. In the astral body, for example, selfishness, anger, hatred, jealousy, sensuality, and all qualities of this kind are invariably expressed by vibrations of the lower type of astral matter, while love, devotion, sympathy, and emotions of that class are expressed only in matter of the three higher sub-planes. From this, two remarkable results flow. It must be borne in mind that each sub-plane of the astral vehicle has a special relation to the corresponding sub-plane in the mental body; or to put it more accurately, the four lower sub-planes of the astral correspond to the four kinds of matter in the mental body, while the three higher correspond to the causal vehicle.

Therefore it will be seen that only higher qualities can be built into the causal body, since the vibrations created by the lower can find in it no matter which is capable of responding to them. From there it emerges that while any good which the man develops within himself records itself permanently by a change in his causal body, the evil which he does and thinks and feels cannot possibly touch the real ego, but can only cause disturbance and trouble to the mental body, which is renewed for each fresh incarnation. Of course the result of this evil does store itself in the mental and astral permanent atoms, and so the man has to face it over and over again, but that is a very different matter from taking it into the ego and making it really a part of himself.

The second remarkable result produced is that a certain amount of force directed towards good produces an enormously greater effect in proportion than the same amount of force directed towards evil. If a man throws a certain amount of energy into some evil quality it has to express itself through the lower and heavier astral matter; and while any kind of astral matter is exceedingly subtle as compared with anything on the physical plane, yet as compared with the higher matter of its own plane it is just as gross as lead is on the physical plane when compared with the finest ether.

If therefore a man should exert exactly the same amount of force in the direction of good, it would have to move through the much finer matter of these higher sub-planes and would produce at least a hundred times as much effect, or if we compare the lowest with the highest, probably more than a thousand times. Remember that even in addition to what has been said as to the effect of force in different grades of matter, we have the other great fact that the Logos Himself is by His resistless power steadily pressing the whole system onwards and upwards, and that, however slow this cyclic progression may seem to us, it is a fact which cannot be neglected, for its effect is that a man who accurately balances his good and evil comes back, not to the same actual position, but to the same relative position, and therefore even he has made some slight advance, and is in a position just a little better than that which he has actually deserved and made for himself.

It will be clear from these considerations that, if any one is so foolish as to want to get really backwards against the stream, he will have to work hard and definitely towards evil; there is no fear of "sliding" back. That is one of the old delusions which remains from the times of the belief in the devil, who was so much stronger than God that everything in the world was working in his favor. Really the exact opposite is the case, and everything round a man is calculated to assist him, if he only understands it.

So many of our most conscientious people are just like the child who has a little garden of his own, and constantly pulls up his plants to see how the roots are growing—with the result of course that nothing grows at all. We must learn not to think of ourselves personally, nor of our personal progress, but enter the path of development, go on working for others to the best of our ability, and trust our progress to take care of itself. The more a scientist thinks about himself the less mental energy he has for the problems of science; the more a devotee thinks about himself the less devotion he has to lavish upon his object.

Some self-examination is necessary, but it is a fatal mistake to spend too much time in self-examination; it is like spending all one's time in oiling and tinkering at the machinery. We use what faculties we have, and in the use of them others will develop and true progress will be made. If you are learning a language, for example, it is a mistake to try to learn it from books quite perfectly before you make any attempt to speak it; you must plunge into it, and make mistakes in it, and in the effort you will learn, in due course, to speak without mistake. So in the course of time what is called renunciation will come naturally, and even easily. No doubt when men first attempt to live the higher life they do definitely renounce many things which are pleasures to others—which still have a strong attraction even for them; but soon the man finds that the attraction of such pleasures has ceased, and that he has neither time nor inclination for the lower enjoyments.

Learn above all things not to worry. Be happy, and make the best of everything. Try to raise yourself and help others. Contentment is not incompatible with aspirations. Optimism is justified by the certainty of the ultimate triumph of good, though if we take only the physical plane into account it is not easy to maintain that position. One's attitude in this matter depends chiefly upon the level at which one habitually keeps one's consciousness. If it is centered chiefly in the physical plane one sees little but misery, but when it becomes possible to center it at a higher level the joy behond always shines through. I know the Buddha said that life was misery, and it is quite true on the whole with regard to the manifested life down here, yet the Greeks and Egyptians managed to extract much joy even from this lower life by taking it from the philosophical point of view.

We never lose anything by making the best of things, but gain very much in happiness and in the power of making others happy. As our sympathy and our love grow we shall be able to receive within ourselves all the streams of emotion and of thought which come to us from others, and yet we shall remain within ourselves unaffected, calm and joyous, like the great ocean which receives the waters of many rivers and yet remains always in equilibrium.

The inner life of an aspirant ought not to be one on continual oscillation. Outer moods change constantly because they are affected by all sorts of outside influences. If you find yourself depressed, it may be due to any one of half-a-dozen reasons, none of them of any real importance. The physical body is a fertile source of such ills; a trifling indigestion, a slight congestion in the circulation, or a little over-fatigue may account for many conditions which *feel* quite serious. Even more frequently depression is caused by the presence of some astral entity who is himself depressed, and is hovering round you either in search of sympathy or in the hope of drawing from you the vitality which he lacks. We must simply learn to disregard depression altogether—to throw it off as a sin and a crime against our neightbors, which it really is; but, anyhow, whether we can succeed fully in dispersing its clouds or not we must learn simply to go on as though it were not there.

Your mind is your own mind, into which you should allow entrance only to such thoughts as you, the ego, choose. Your astral body is also your own, and you should not allow in it any sensations except those which are good for the higher self. So you must manage these vibrations of depression, and absolutely decline to give harborage to them. They must not be allowed to impinge upon you. If they do so impinge they must not be permitted to effect a lodgment. If, to some slight extent, in spite of your efforts, they do hang about you, then it is your duty to ignore them and to let no one else know that they even exist.

Sometimes people tell me they have had moments of splendid inspiration and exaltation, and glowing devotion and joy. They do not realize that these are precisely the moments when the higher self succeeds in impressing himself upon the lower, and that all that which they feel is *there all the time*, but the lower self is not always conscious of it. Realize by reason and by faith that it is always there, and it becomes as though we felt it, even in the time when the link is imperfect and down here we feel it not.

But many a man, while admitting the truth of this in the abstract, yet says that he cannot perpetually feel this happiness because of his own defects and constant failures. His attitude in fact is very much that adopted in the litany: "Have mercy upon us miserable sinners." Now we are all sinners in the sense that we all fall short of what we ought to do, and constantly do what we ought not to do, but there is no need to aggravate the offense by being *miserable* sinners. A miserable person is a public nuisance, because he is a center of infection, and is spreading misery and sorrow all round upon his unfortunate neighbors—a thing which no man has a right to do. Any man with just the same feelings, who contrives to keep himself reasonably happy even while making determined efforts to reform, is not injuring others in at all the same way.

People who think and speak of themselves as miserable worms are going exactly the right way to make themselves miserable worms, for what a man thinks, that he is. All such talk is usually hypocrisy, as you may easily see from the fact that the man who so readily calls himself a miserable worm in church would feel distinctly insulted if anybody else called him so in ordinary daily life. And whether it is hypocritical or not it is certainly nonsense. Anyone who understands at all the influence of thought will realize that a man who really thinks himself a miserable worm has already deprived himself of any power of rising out of that state, while the man who realizes strongly that he is a spark of the divine life will feel ever hopeful and joyous, because in essence the divine is always joy. It is a great mistake to waste time in repentance; what is past is past, and no amount of remorse can undo it. As one of our own Masters once said, "The only repentance that is worth anything whatever is the resolve not to do it again."

Asceticism

Some mistaken ideas seem prevalent among our members upon the subject of asceticism, and it may be worth while to consider what it really is, and how far it may be useful. The word is usually taken to signify a life of austerities and of mortification of the body, though this is somewhat of a departure from the original meaning of the Greek word *asketes*, which is simply one who exercises himself as an athlete does. But ecclesiasticism impounded the word and changed its sense, applying it to the practice of all sorts of self-denial for the purpose of spiritual progress, on the theory that the bodily nature with its passions and desires is the stronghold of the evil inherent in man since the fall of Adam, and that it must therefore be suppressed by fasting and penance. In the grander Oriental religions we sometimes encounter a similar idea, based on the conception of matter as essentially evil, and following from that the deduction that an approach to ideal good or an escape from the miseries of existence can be effected only by subduing or torturing the body.

The student of theosophy will at once see that in both these theories there is dire confusion of thought. There is no evil inherent in man except such as he has himself generated in previous births; nor is matter essentially evil, since it is just as much divine as is spirit, and without it all manifestation of the Deity would be impossible. The body and its desires are not in themselves evil or good, but it is true that before real progress can be made they must be brought under the control of the higher self within. To torture the body is foolish; to govern it is necessary. "The men who perform severe austerities . . . unintelligent, tormenting the aggregated elements forming the body, and Me also, seated in the inner body—know these demoniacal in their resolves." (*Bhagavad-Gita*, xvii. 5, 6.) And again, "The austerity done under a deluded understanding, with self-torture, . . . that is declared of darkness." (*Ibid*, xvii. 19.)

There appears to be a widespread delusion that to be really good one must always be uncomfortable—that discomfort as such is directly pleasing to the Logos. Nothing can be more grotesque than this idea, and in the above quoted texts from the *Bhagavad-Gita* we have a hint that it is perhaps worse than grotesque, for it is there said that they who torment the body are tormenting the Logos enshrined in it. With us in Europe this unfortunately common theory is one of the many legacies left us by Calvinism.

Our Masters, who are so far above us, are full of joy; full of sympathy but not of sorrow. We also must feel sympathy with others, but not identify ourselves with their sorrow. A man in great trouble can judge nothing clearly. To his vision all the world seems dark, and it appears as if no one should be happy. When he is in great joy, all the world appears bright, and it seems as if no one ought to be unhappy. Yet nothing is changed, not even he himself, but only his astral body. All the world is going on just the same, whether you are happy or unhappy. Do not identify yourself with your astral body, but try to get out of this web of illusion, these personal moods.

No doubt this ludicrous theory of the merit of discomfort comes partly from the knowledge that in order to make progress man must control his passions, and from the fact that such control is disagreeable to the unevolved person. But the discomfort is very far from being meritorious; on the contrary, it is a sign that the victory is not yet achieved. It arises from the fact that the lower nature is not yet dominated, and that a struggle is still taking place. When the control is perfect there will no longer be any desire for the lower, consequently no struggle and no discomfort. The man will live the right life and avoid the lower because it is perfectly natural for him to do so—no longer because he thinks he ought to make the effort, even though it may be difficult for him. So that the discomfort exists only at an intermediate stage, and not it, but its absence, is the sign of success.

Another reason for the gospel of the uncomfortable is a confusion of cause and effect. It is observed that the really advanced person is simple in his habits, and often careless about a large number of minor luxuries that are considered important and really necessary by the ordinary man. But such carelessness about luxury is the effect, not the cause, of his advancement. He does not trouble himself about these little matters because he has largely outgrown them and they no longer interest him—not in the least because he considers them as wrong; and one who, while still craving for them, imitates him in abstaining from them, does not thereby become advanced. At a certain stage a child plays with dolls and blocks; a few years later he has become a boy and his play is cricket and football; later again when he is a young man these in turn lose much of their interest, and he begins to play the game of love and life. But an infant who chooses to imitate his elders, who throws aside his dolls and blocks and attempts to play cricket, does not thereby transcend his infancy. As his natural growth takes place he puts away childish things; but he cannot force the growth merely by putting these away, and playing at being older.

There is no virtue whatever merely in becoming uncomfortable for discomfort's sake; but there are three cases in which voluntary discomfort may be a part of progress. The first is when it is undertaken for the sake of helping another, as when a man nurses a sick friend or labors hard to support his family. The second is when a man realizes that some habit to which he is addicted is a hindrance in his upward way—such a habit, say, as tobacco-smoking, alcohol-drinking, or meat-eating. If he is in earnest he gives up the habit instantly, but because the body is accustomed to that particular form of pollution it misses it, cries out for it, and causes the man a great deal of trouble. If he holds firm to his resolution his body will presently adapt itself to the new conditions, and when it has done so there will be no further discomfort. But in the intermediate stage, while the battle for mastery between the man and his body is still being fought, there may be a good deal of suffering, and this must be taken as the karma of having adopted the habit which he is now forsaking. When the suffering passes the karma is paid, the victory is won, and a step in evolution is achieved.

I am aware that there are rare cases (when people are physically very weak) in which it might be dangerous to relinquish a bad habit instantaneously. Drug addiction is an instance in point; one who is a victim to its horrors usually finds it necessary gradually to decrease the dose, because the strain of abrupt cessation might well be greater than the physical body could endure. It would seem that there are certain pitiable cases in which the same system of gradual decrease must be applied to the flesh-eating habit. Doctors tell us that while the digestion of meat takes place chiefly in the stomach, that of most forms of vegetable food belongs to the work of the intestines; and therefore a person in very weak health sometimes finds it advisable to give to these various organs a certain amount of time to adjust themselves to the necessary change, and to practice, as it were, the functions which they are now required to fulfill. The steady pressure of the will, however, will soon bring the body into subjection and adapt it to the new order of things.

The third case in which discomfort may have its use is when a man deliberately forces his body to do something which it dislikes, in order to make sure that it will obey him when necessary. But it must be distinctly understood that even then the merit is in the ready obedience of the body, and not in its suffering. In this way a man may gradually learn indifference to many of the minor ills of life, and so save himself much worry and irritation. In this training himself in will, and his body in obedience, he must be careful to attempt only such things as are advantageous. The Hatha Yogi develops willpower, assuredly, when one holds his arm above his head until it withers; but while he gains enormously in willpower he also loses the use of his arm. The willpower can be developed just as well by some effort the result of which will be permanently useful instead of permanently hampering—by the conquest, for example, of irritability or pride, impatience or sensuality. It would be well if all who feel a yearning for asceticism would take to heart the words of wisdom in the *Bhagavad-Gita:*

Purity, straightforwardness, continence and harm-
lessness are called the austerity of the body. Speech
causing no annoyance, truthful, pleasant and bene-
ficial . . . is called the austerity of speech. Mental
happiness, equilibrium, silence, self-control, purity of
nature—this is called the austerity of the mind. (xvii.
14, 15, 16.)

Note especially that in this last verse mental happiness is described as the first characteristic of the austerity of the mind—the
first sign of the perfect self-control necessary for one who wishes
to make real progress. It is emphatically our duty to be happy;
morbidity, gloom or depression mean always failure and weakness, because they mean selfishness. The man who allows himself
to brood over his own sorrows or wrongs is forgetting his duty to
his fellows. He permits himself to become a center of infection,
spreading gloom instead of joy among his brethren; what is this
but the grossest selfishness? If there be any one who feels a
yearning for asceticism, let him take up this mental austerity
advised in the scripture, and resolve that whatever may be his
private troubles or sufferings he will forget himself and them for
the sake of others, so that he may ever be pouring forth upon his
fellow-pilgrims the radiant happiness which comes from the fuller knowledge of the Theosophist, ever helping them towards the
realization that "Brahman is bliss."

Small Worries

Unnecessary worry appears to be the keynote of modern life. Not
only those who are making special efforts to progress are making
themselves unreasonably uncomfortable, but the same vice is
quite common even in ordinary life. The astral body of the
average man is a sad sight for a clairvoyant. The illustration in
Man Visible and Invisible of the astral body of a developed man
(Plate XXIII, opp. p. 86)* shows what an astral body ought to
be—merely a reflection of the colors of the mental, indicating that
the man allows himself to feel only what his reason dictates. But if
that be too much to expect at this stage of evolution, the picture
on (Plate X, opp. p. 54) gives us an assortment of colors which

*Quest Book edition cited.

represents an average astral body when comparatively at rest. In it there are many hues which show the presence of undesirable qualities—qualities which should be weeded out as soon as may be: but that side of the subject is treated in the book, and it is to another feature that I wish now to draw attention.

I have said that the illustration shows what an ordinary undeveloped astral body would look life if comparatively at rest; but one of the evils of what we have agreed to call civilization is that hardly any astral body ever is even comparatively at rest. Of course it is understood that the matter of an astral body must always be in perpetual vibration, and each of the colors that we see in the drawing marks a different rate of that vibration; but there should be a certain order in this, and a certain limit to it. The more developed man has five rates of vibration, but the ordinary man shows at least nine rates, with a mixture of varying shades in addition. That is clearly not so good as the other, but the case of the majority of people in the West is really far worse than that. To have even nine rates of simultaneous vibration is already bad enough, but in the astral body of many a man and woman one might easily observe fifty rates or even a hundred. The body should be divided into a few fairly definite areas, each swinging steadily at its normal rate, but instead of that, its surface is usually broken up into a multiplicity of little whirlpools and cross-currents, all battling one against the other in the maddest confusion.

All these are the result of little unnecessary emotions and worries, and the ordinary person of the West is simply a mass of these. He is troubled about this thing, he is annoyed about that, he is in fear about a third, and so on; his whole life is filled with petty little emotions, and all his strength is frittered away on them. A really great emotion, be it good or bad, sweeps over the whole of a man's astral body and for the time brings it all to one rate of vibration; but these small worries make little vortices or centers of local disturbance, each of which persists for a considerable time.

The astral body which thus vibrates fifty ways at once is a blot upon the landscape and a nuisance to its neighbors. It is not only a very ugly object—it is also a serious annoyance. It may be compared to a physical body suffering from some unusually aggravated form of palsy, with all its muscles jerking simultaneously in different directions. But to make the illustration even partially adequate we should have to assume that this palsy was contagious, or that every one who saw its unfortunate results felt an irresistible tendency to repoduce them. For this horrible chaos of catastrophic confusion produces an unpleasant and most disturbing effect upon all sensitive people who approach it; it infects their astral bodies and communicates to them a painful sensation of unrest and worry.

Only a few have yet unfolded the faculties which enable them to see this malefic influence in action; a larger number are vaguely conscious of discomfort when they approach one of these fussy persons; but probably the majority feel nothing definite at the time of meeting, though later in the day they will probably wonder why they are so inexplicably fatigued. The effect is there and the harm is done, whether it be immediately perceptible or not.

A person who is so foolish as to allow himself to get into this condition does much harm to many, but most of all to himself. Frequently the perpetual astral disturbance reacts through the etheric upon the dense physical vehicle, and all sorts of nervous diseases are produced. Numerous nervous problems are the direct result of unnecessary worry and emotion, and would soon disappear if the patient would but hold his vehicles still and possess his soul in peace.

But even in cases where a strong physical body is able successfully to resist this constant irritation from the astral, its effect upon its own plane is no less disastrous. These tiny centers of inflammation which thus cover the whole astral body are to it what boils are to the physical body—not only themselves causes of acute discomfort, sore spots upon which the least touch produces terrible pain, but also *weak* spots through which the life-blood of vitality drains away, and through which also blood-poisoning from without may take place. A person whose astral body is in this distracted condition can offer practically no resistance to any evil influence which he may encounter, while he is quite unable to profit by good influences. His strength flows out through these open sores, at the same time that all sorts of disease-causing influences find entrance by them. He is not using and controlling his astral body as a whole, but allowing it to break up into a number of separate centers and control *him*. His little worries and vexations establish themselves and confirm their empire over him until they become a legion of "devils" who possess him so that he cannot escape from them.

This is a painfully common condition; how is a man to avoid

falling into it, and if he is *already* in it, how is he to get out of it? The answer is the same to both questions; let him learn not to worry, not to fear, not to be annoyed. Let him reason with himself as to the utter unimportance of all these little personal matters which have loomed so large upon his horizon. Let him consider how they will appear when he looks back upon them from the next life, or even twenty years hence. Let him take to heart the words of wisdom, that of all the outward things that happen to a man "nothing matters much, and most things matter not at all." What he himself does or says or thinks *is* of importance to him, for that forms his future; what other people do or say or think matters to him nothing whatever. Let him abstract himself from all these little pin-pricks of daily life, and simply decline to be worried by them.

It will need some resolution at first, for it requires effort to conquer a well-established bad habit. He will find his mind muttering to him over and over again: "Mrs. Jones spoke evil of me; perhaps she is doing it now; perhaps other people may believe her; perhaps it may do me harm," and so on *ad infinitum*. But he must reply: "I don't care *what* Mrs. Jones has said, though I am sorry the poor woman should make such bad karma. I absolutely decline to think of it or of her. I have my work to do, and have no time to waste in thinking of foolish gossip."

Or it may be that forebodings of coming evil are constantly thrusting themselves into his brain: "Perhaps next year I may lose my position; perhaps I shall be starving; perhaps I shall be bankrupt; perhaps I may lose the affection of some friend." This also should be met firmly: "Perhaps all these things may happen, but also perhaps they may not, and it is useless to try to cross a bridge before one comes to it. I shall take all reasonable precautions, and when that is done I decline to think further of the matter. Worrying cannot affect whatever may be coming, but it can and certainly will make me unfit to meet it. Therefore I refuse to worry; I definitely turn my back on the whole subject."

Another common form of worry which leads to the most serious results is the folly of taking offense at something which somebody else says or does. Ordinarily common sense would lead a man to avoid this mistake, and yet those who do avoid it are few. It needs only that we should think dispassionately about the matter, and we shall see that what the other man has said or done cannot make any difference to us. If he has said something which has hurt our feelings, we may be sure that in nine cases out of ten he has not meant it to be offensive; why then should we allow ourselves to be disturbed about the matter? Even in the rare cases when a remark is intentionally rude or spiteful, where a man has said something purposely to wound another, it is still exceedingly foolish to allow oneself to feel hurt. If the man had an evil intention in what he said, he is much to be pitied, for we know that under the law of divine justice he will certainly suffer for his foolishness. What he has said need in no way affect us, for, if we think of it, no effect whatever has really been produced.

The irritating word does not in any way injure us, except insofar as we may choose to take it up and injure ourselves to be wounded in our feelings. What are the words of another, that we should let our serenity be disturbed by them? They are merely a vibration in the atmosphere; if it had not happened that we heard them, or heard of them, would they have affected us? If not, then it is obviously not the words that have injured us, but the fact that we heard them. So if we allow ourselves to care about what a man has said, it is *we* who are responsible for the disturbance created in our astral bodies, and not he.

The man has done and can do nothing that can harm us; if we feel hurt and injured and thereby make ourselves a great deal of trouble, we have only ourselves to thank for it. If a disturbance arises within our astral bodies in reference to what he has said, that is merely because we have not yet gained control over those bodies; we have not yet developed the calmness which enables us to look down *as souls* upon all this, and go on our way and attend to our own work without taking the slightest notice of foolish or spiteful remarks made by other men. This is the merest common-sense, yet not one in a hundred will act upon it.

The fact is that any one who wishes to become a student of occultism must not have any personal feelings that can be offended under any circumstances whatever. A man who has them is still thinking of himself; whereas our duty is to forget ourselves in order to remember the good of others. Nothing can offend you if you have resolved not to be offended—if you are thinking only how to help the other man, and not at all of yourself. ·

Another variant of the disease is less personal and therefore is so far less blameworthy, but hardly less prejudicial to progress. It is the habit of fussing over trifles in business or in household affairs. This always involves a lack of discrimination and of the sense of perspective. It is quite true that a household or a business must be orderly, that things must be done punctually and exactly; but the way to achieve this is to set up a high ideal and press steadily towards it—not to irritate every one by ceaseless, useless worry. The person who is so unfortunate as to be afflicted with a disposition of this kind should make a most determined fight against it, for until he conquers it he will be a force working always for friction and not for peace, and so will be of little real use in the world. His symptoms differ slightly from those of the more personal worrier; in his case there are fewer of the carbuncular vortices, but there is a perpetual tremor, an unrest of the whole astral body which is equally disquieting to others, equally subversive of happiness and advancement for the fusser himself.

The man *must* learn to be master of his mind and his feelings, and steadily reject every thought and emotion which his highest self does not approve. A chaos of petty emotions is unworthy of a rational being, and it is to the last degree undignified that man, who is a spark of the Divine, should allow himself to fall under the sway of his desire-elemental—a thing that is not even a mineral yet.

I have already said that this disastrous astral confusion is often prejudicial to physical health; but it is invariably worse than prejudicial to progress on the path—it is absolutely fatal to it. One of the first great lessons to be learned on that path is perfect self-control, and a long stage on the way to that is complete absence of worry. At first, from mere habit, the matter of the astral body will still be swept readily into unnecessary vortices, but every time that happens the man must firmly obliterate them, and restore the steady swing of the feelings which he, as an ego, really desires to have.

Let him fill himself so entirely with the divine love that it may be ever pouring from him in all directions in the shape of love for his fellow-men, and then there will be no room for unnecessary vibrations; he will have no time to worry over trifling personal matters if his whole life is spent in the service of the Logos, in trying to help forward the evolution of the world. To make any real progress or to do any real work a man must turn from the lower and reach towards the higher; he must come out of *our* world into Theirs—out of the restlessness into the peace which passeth understanding.

Destroying Desire

We are often told that we must kill desire; but it should be
remembered that this is a gradual process. The lower and coarser
desires which are meant by the Sanskrit word *kama* must certainly
be weeded out entirely before any sort of advancement can be
made, but in the English sense of the word we all of us still have
certain desires, and are likely to have them for a very long time to
come. We desire keenly, for example, to serve the Master; to
become his pupils; to help humanity. These also are desires, but
they should not be killed. What is necessary is to kill the lower and
reach up to the higher, that is to say, to purify our desires and to
transmute them into aspirations.

Later on another transmutation will take place. For example,
now we desire to make progress; but a time will come when we
shall be so sure of it that we shall cease to desire, because we know
that all the time it is going on as rapidly as is possible for us, and
because we mean that it shall so go on. Desire is then transmuted
into resolution. At this point there can be no more regret for
anything; you do your best and you know that in response to that
the best must come. Some people desire earnestly to gain this
quality or that; do not waste your power in desiring and wishing,
but *will* instead.

In the same way it is said that we should slay the "lunar form,"
that is to say the astral body. But that does not mean that the astral
body must be destroyed or that we must be without feelings and
emotions. If that could be so we should have no sympathy and no
understanding of others. What is intended is that we should keep
it completely under control, that we should have the faculty to
"slay the lunar form" *at will*. Purity is necessary, but it means not
only the abstinence from specified faults, but absolute selfless-
ness. Ambition, for example, is a very common form of desire,
but in it there is always a thought of self. The adept cannot be
ambitious. His will is one with the will of the Logos, and he wills
evolution. We are all parts of the Logos, and our wills are part of
his. It is only when we do not realize this that we set up desires in
our own separate lines. The regulations for our lives were very
well summed up by the Lord Buddha in one little verse of four
short lines:

Sabbapapassa akaranam
Kusalassa upasampada
Sachitta pariyo dapanam
Etam Buddhana sasanam.

Cease from all evil;
Learn to do well;
Cleanse your own heart;
This is the religion of the Buddhas.

The Center of My Circle

Of all the many obstacles that stand in the way of the aspirant who wishes to enter upon the Path, the most serious, because the most far-reaching and fundamental, is self-centeredness. Note that by this I do not mean the crude and ugly selfishness, which definitely seeks everything for itself even at the cost of others. I am, of course, supposing that *that* at least has been left behind long ago. But in those who have left it behind, there still lingers this other evil—so subtle and so deeply-rooted that they do not recognize it as an evil at all—indeed, they are not even aware of its existence. But let a man examine himself honestly and impartially, and he will find that all his thought is self-centered; he thinks often of other people and of other things, but always in their relation to himself; he weaves many imaginary dramas, but he himself occupies always a prominent role in them. He must always be in the center of his little stage, with the limelight playing upon him; if he is not in that position he at once feels hurt, annoyed, angry, and jealous of any other person who happens for the moment to be attracting the attention of those who ought to be worshipping at *his* shrine. To change so fundamental a quality is to change for him the root of all things, to make himself into an altogether different man. Most people cannot for a moment face the possibility of such a radical change because they do not even know that the condition exists.

Now, this attitude is absolutely fatal to any kind of progress. It must be utterly changed, and yet so few are making any attempt to change it. There is one way out of this vicious circle, and only one; and that is the way of love. That is the only thing in the life of the ordinary man which ever changes this condition for him, which seizes upon him with a strong hand and for the time being alters his whole attitude. For a time, at least, when he falls in love, as it is called, some other person occupies the center of his circle, and he thinks of everything in all the world in its relation to her, and not in its relation to himself. The divinity at whose shrine he offers this worship may in truth seem to the rest of the world to be but a very ordinary person, but for him she is temporarily the incarnation of grace and beauty; he sees in her the divinity which is in truth hers, because it lies latent in all of us, though normally we do not see it. It is true that in many cases after a time his enthusiasm fades and he transfers it to another object; but nevertheless for the time he has ceased to be self-centered, for the time he has had a wider outlook.

Now this, which the ordinary man thus does unconsciously, the student of occultism must do consciously. He must deliberately dethrone himself from the center of the circle of his life, and he must enthrone the Master there instead. He has been in the habit of thinking instinctively how everything will affect him, or what he can make of it, how he can turn it to his profit and pleasure. Instead of that he must now learn to think of *everything* as it affects the Master, and since the Master lives only to help the evolution of humanity, that means that he must regard every-thing from the standpoint of its helpfulness or hindrance to the cause of evolution. And though at first he will have to do this consciously and with a certain effort, he must persevere until he does it just as unconsciously, just as instinctively as heretofore he centered everything around himself. To use the words of a Mas-ter, he must forget himself utterly to remember only the good of others.

But even when he has dethroned himself and enthroned the work which he has to do, he must be exceedingly careful that he does not delude himself, that he does not return to the old self-centeredness in a subtler form. Many a good and earnest Theosophical worker have I known who committed this very mistake, who identified Theosophical work with himself, and felt that anyone who did not exactly agree with his ideas and his methods was an enemy of Theosophy. So often the worker thinks that his way is the only way, and that to differ from him in opinion is to be a traitor to the cause. But this means only that the self has crept skillfully back into its old place in the center of the circle, and that the work of dislodging it must be begun all over again. The only power which the disciple should desire is that which makes him seem as nothing in the eyes of men. When he is the center of his circle he may do good work, but it is always with the feeling that *he* is doing it; but when the Master is the center of his circle he will do the work simply in order that it may be done. The work is done for the sake of the work and not for the sake of the doer. And he must learn to look upon his own work precisely as though it were that of some one else, and upon the work of some one else precisely as though it were his own. The one thing that is important is that the work should be done. It matters little who does it. Therefore, he ought neither to be prejudiced in favor of his own work and unduly critical of that of another, nor be hypocritically depreciatory of his own work in order that others may praise it. To quote the words of Ruskin with regard to art, he ought to be able to say serenely: "Be it mine or yours, or whose else it may, this also is well."

Another danger there is, too, which is special to the Theosophical Society worker—the danger of congratulating himself too soon that he differs from the rest of the world. Theosophical teaching puts a new complexion upon everything, so naturally we feel that our attitude is quite different from that of most other people. There is no harm in thinking this obvious truth, but I have found that some of our members are apt to *pride themselves* upon the fact that they are able to recognize these things. It does not in the least follow that we, who find ourselves able to recognize them are, therefore, better than others. Other men have developed themselves along other lines, and along those lines they may be very far in advance of us, though along our line they lack something which we already have. Remember, the adept is the perfect man who is fully developed along *all* possible lines, and so while we have something to teach these others we also have much to learn from them, and it would be the height of folly to despise a man because he has not yet acquired theosophical knowledge, nor even perhaps the qualities which enable him to appreciate it. Therefore, in this sense also we must take care not to be the center of our own circle.

A good plan that you may adopt in order to keep yourself from slipping back into the center may be to remember, as a symbol of what ought to be your attitude, what I have before explained to you with regard to the occult view of the course and influence of the planets. You remember how I explained to you that each planet is a minor focus in an ellipse, the major focus of which is within the body of the sun. You are like that minor focus; you are going upon your own course and doing the work appointed to you, and yet all the time you are but a reflection of the major focus, and your consciousness is centered within the sun, for the Master of whom you are a part is a member of the Great Hierarchy which is ever doing the work of the Logos.

While a man is the center of his own circle he is perpetually making the mistake of thinking that he is the center of everybody else's. He constantly supposes that in everything which other people say or do they are somehow thinking of him, or aiming their remarks at him, and with many this becomes a kind of obsession, and they seem totally unable to realize that each of their neighbors is as a rule also entirely wrapped up in himself and not thinking of them at all. So the man makes for himself a great deal of totally unnecessary trouble and worry, all of which might be avoided if we would but see things in a sane and rational perspective. Again, it is because he is the center of his own circle that he is liable to depression, for that comes only to one who is thinking of himself. If the Master be the center of his circle, and all his energies are centered upon serving Him, he has no time for depression, nor has he the slightest inclination towards it. He is far too eagerly wishing for work that he can do. His attitude should be that indicated by Mrs. Besant in her *Autobiography*— that when a man sees a piece of work waiting to be done he should not say, as the ordinary man usually does: "Yes, it would be a good thing, and somebody ought to do it. But why should I?"—but rather he should say: "Somebody ought to do this. Why should it not be I?"

As he evolves, his circle will widen and in the end there will come a time when his circle will be infinite in extent, and then in a sense he himself will again be its center, because he has identified himself with the Logos, who is the center of all possible circles, since every point is equally the center of a circle whose radius is infinite.

Our Duty to Animals

While you are trying to do your best for all those around you, do not forget that you also have a duty towards forms of life lower than the human. In order that you may be able to do that, try to understand your lower brothers, try to understand the animals, just as you try to understand, on a higher level, the children with whom you have to deal. Just as you learn, if you want to help a child, to look at things from the child's point of view, so, if you want to help the animal evolution, try to see what is the animal's point of view. In all cases and with all forms of life our business is to love and to help, and to try to bring nearer the golden age when all shall understand one another and all shall cooperate in the glorious work that is to come.

There is no reason why our domestic animals should not be trained to help man, and to work in his service, so long as the work is not painful or excessive. But all the creatures around us should be trained in the way best for themselves; that is to say, we should always remember that their evolution is the object of the divine Will. So that while we should surely teach our animals all that we can, because that develops their intelligence, we must take care that we instill into them good qualities and not evil. We have various creatures brought among us. We have the dog, the cat, the horse and other originally wild animals given into our care—brought to us for affection and help. Why? That we may train them out of their ferocity, and into a higher and more intelligent state of life—that we may evoke in them devotion, affection and intellect.

But we must take good care that we help, not hinder; we must see that we do not increase in our animal the ferocious qualities which it is the business of his evolution to get rid of. For example, a man who trains a dog to hunt and kill is intensifying within him the very instincts which must be eliminated if the animal is to evolve, and in this way he is degrading a creature given into his charge instead of helping him on his way, even though at the same time he may be developing the animal's intelligence; and thus, though he may do a little good, he is at the same time doing a great deal of harm which far more than counterbalances it. The same thing is true of a man who trains his dog to be ferocious in order that he may be an efficient protector of his property.

A man who treats an animal harshly or cruelly may possibly be evolving his intellect, since the animal may learn to think more keenly in order to see how to avoid the cruelty. But along with whatever evolution may be gained in this way, there is also the development of the exceedingly undesirable qualities of fear and hatred. Thus when, later on, that animal wave of life evolves to the human level, we shall have a humanity starting terribly handicapped—starting with these awful qualities of fear and hatred ingrained in it, instead of a humanity all aspiring, devotional, loving and gentle, such as we might have had if the men to whom the animal part of that evolution was committed had done their duty.

We have also our duty towards other and even lower forms of life than that. There is the elemental essence, which is surrounding us everywhere; that elemental essence progresses by means of our thought, and of the action which we produce upon it by our thoughts, passions, emotions and feelings. We need not trouble ourselves especially about that, because if we carry out our higher ideals, if we try to see to it that all our thoughts and all our emotions shall be of the highest possible type, then that also will, at the same time and without further difficulty, be the discharging of our duty towards the elemental essence* which is influenced by our thought; it will be raised and not depressed; the higher qualities which we alone can reach will be set in motion, vivified and helped at its respective levels.

All through evolution the assistance of the higher is expected in the development of the lower, and it is not only by individualizing them that man has helped the members of the animal kingdom. In Atlantean days the very formation of their species was largely given over into his hands, and it is because he failed to do his duty properly that many things turned out rather differently from what was originally intended. His mistakes are largely responsible for the existence of carnivorous creatures which live only to destroy one another. Not that he was responsible for *all* carnivorous creatures; there were such among the gigantic reptiles of the Lemurian period, and man was not in any way directly engaged in their evolution; but it was in part his work to assist in the development from those reptile forms of the mammalia which play so prominent a part in the world now. Here was his opportunity to improve the breeds and to curb the undesirable qualities of the

---

*Elemental essence is the life that vivefies astral and mental matter. Ed.

creatures that came under his hands; and it is because he failed to do all that he might have done in this direction that he is to some extent responsible for much that has since gone wrong in the world. If he had done all his duty it is quite conceivable that we might have had no carnivorous mammals.

Mankind has for so long treated animals cruelly that the whole animal world has a general feeling of fear and enmity towards men. Men have generated, in this way, an awful karma which comes back upon them in terrible suffering, in various forms of disease and of insanity. Yet, even after all this bad behavior on the part of man, few animals will harm him if left alone. A serpent, for example, will not usually do any injury to a human being, unless he is first hurt or frightened; and the same thing is true of nearly all wild animals, except the very few who may regard man as food, and even they usually will not touch man if they can get anything else. Except when it is absolutely necessary in self-defense or in defense of another the destruction of any form of life ought always to be avoided, as it tends to retard nature's work. That is one of the reasons why all consistent Theosophists refuse to share the sin of slaughter by eating meat or fish, or by wearing such things as are obtained only by the slaughter of animals, like sealskin or the feathers of birds. Silk used to be obtained by the wholesale slaughter of silkworms, but I hear that there is now a new way of obtaining it without destroying the worms.

Sympathy

Never set yourself against the law of nature. Lately, man has gone astray from nature very much, and materialism has become widely spread. Many scientific men who know a great deal more about nature are very much less in sympathy with her than were their less instructed forefathers. In the useful, and indeed necessary, study of the exterior many have forgotten the interior; but men will pass through this intermediate stage of misunderstanding and come back into sympathy. The older people, who had a closer kinship with nature, carried on little of detailed examination, which would have seemed irreverent to them. Because we have become irreverent, have lost the living feeling, we pry remorselessly. We must take care not to lose the precision that we have gained by this intermediate stage, but must recover the sympathy. By sympathy one may find out a great deal which science alone can never discover. In the teaching of children, we need to make them feel that we understand them, even though in doing so we may sacrifice some scholastic advantages. The average child regards grownup people as foreign entities, strange arbitrary beings.

All this is true also in connection with our studies of nature. The nature-spirits are afraid of us, if we study them too scientifically; we must go with them into their life, and then they will be interested in the life of humanity also. In their blind way, flowers and other things feel joy and friendliness. Emerson said that it appeared to him that when he returned home, the trees in his garden felt glad to see or feel him again, and no doubt it was quite true. The trees and animals do know the people who love them. In India people speak of the "lucky hand" in planting, meaning that things will grow for some people, but not for others. One must be in sympathy with the purpose of the Logos. If we are actively helping in the progress of all, we are living in His will, which penetrates nature, and this is felt by nature at once; but if we put ourselves in opposition to evolution, nature shrinks back from us like a sensitive child.

Our Attitude Towards Children

What is your attitude towards your children? Remember that these are egos, sparks of the divine life. They have been entrusted to you, not that you may domineer over them and ill-treat them, and use them for your own profit and advantage, but that you may love them and help them in order that they may be expressions of that divine life. What an outpouring love then you ought to feel! How beyond all words your patience and compassion should be! How deeply you should feel the honor of being trusted to serve them in this way! Remember always that you are not the older and they the younger, but that as souls you are all about the same age, and therefore your attitude must not be that of a selfish and cruel dictator, but of a helpful friend. You do not regard your friend differently when he puts on a new coat; remember therefore that when you meet a child you are meeting a soul wearing a new coat, and you should try by perfect kindness and love to draw out the best that is in it, and to help it to fit on its new coat. Remember always that true good means good for all, and that good is *never* gained at the cost of suffering to others. That which is so gained is not really good at all.

The Fear of Death

The fear of death is a stern reality in the minds of many people. A far larger number suffer from it than one would suppose, and still more from the fear of what may happen to us after death. Naturally this is especially to be found among people who have ideas of hell.

But we know the law of karma, and realize that the states after death are simply a continuation of the life which we are now living, although on a higher plane and without a physical body; and when in addition we learn that what we commonly call life is only one day in the real and greater life, then all these things assume quite a different perspective. We know then that progress is absolutely certain. A man may stumble, he may set himself against the forces of progress, but he will be carried on by them in spite of himself, though when he resists there will be much of bruising and trouble for him. We see at once that this knowledge eliminates fear.

The so-called loss of a loved one by death is really only a temporary absence, and not even that as soon as a man develops the power to see on the higher planes. Those whom we think we have lost are with us still, even though with our physical eyes we cannot see them; and we should never forget that, although we may sometimes be under the delusion that we have lost them, they are not in the least under the delusion that they have lost *us*, because they can still see our astral bodies, and as soon as we leave the physical vehicle in sleep we are with them and can communicate with them exactly as when they were on the physical plane.

We need not worry ourselves about saving our souls; rather on the other hand, as a Theosophical writer once said, we may not be entirely beyond the hope that some day our souls may save us. There is no soul to be saved in the ordinary sense in which the words are used, because we ourselves are the souls; and furthermore there is nothing to be saved from except our own error and ignorance. The body is nothing but a vestment, and when it is worn out we cast it aside.

Cooperation

It is part of the scheme of the Logos that at a certain stage in its evolution humanity must begin to guide itself. Therefore all the future Buddhas, Manus and Adepts will be members of our own humanity, the Lords from Venus having gone on to other worlds. Therefore also the Logos actually counts upon us all, upon you and upon me. We may have ninety-nine faults and only one virtue, but if that one virtue is needed in the theosophical work (and what virtue is not needed?) we shall surely have the opportunity to use it.

We should then value our co-workers for what they can do, and not be constantly blaming them for what they cannot do. Many people have earned the right to do some particular kind of work, notwithstanding that their defects may be greater than their virtues. People often make a sad mistake in comparing their work with that of others, and wishing that they had the same opportunities. The truth is that each one has his own gifts and his own powers, and it is not expected of any man that he should do as much as some other man, but only that he should do his best—just his own best.

The Master once said that in reality there are only two classes of men—those who know and those who do not know. Those who know are they who have seen the light and have turned towards it, through whatever religion they have come, at however great a distance from the light they may as yet find themselves. Many of them may be suffering much in their struggle towards that light, but at least they have hope before them, and while we sympathize deeply with them and strive to help them we yet realize that they are by no means in the worst case. The people really to be pitied are those who are quite indifferent to all higher thought—those who do not struggle because they do not care, or think, or know that there is anything for which to strive. These are they in truth who constitute "the great orphan humanity."

A Day of Life

It is not wise to specialize beyond a certain point, because one can never really get to the end of any subject, and it tends more and more to narrow the mind and the outlook, to produce a one-sided and distorted development, and to cause one to view everything out of its due proportion. We are in the habit of thinking of a lifetime as a long period, but really it is only a day in the greater life. You cannot finish a really great piece of work in one day; it may need many days, and the work of one particular day may at the time show no appreciable result; but nevertheless every day's work is necessary to the completion of the great task, and if a man should idle day after day because the completion of the work seems so far off he would certainly not succeed in getting it done.

There are many to whom theosophy comes late in life, who feel themselves somewhat discouraged by the outlook, thinking they are too old now to take themselves in hand seriously or to do any valuable work, that the best that they can do now is to go quietly on to the end of this incarnation in the hope that they may have a better opportunity in the next.

This is a sad mistake, and that for various reasons. You do not know what kind of incarnation karma is preparing for you next time you return to earth. You do not know whether by any previous action you have deserved the opportunity of being born into theosophical surroundings. In any case the most likely way to secure such a birth is to make use of the opportunity which has come to you now, for, of all that we have learned about the working of this great law of cause and effect, this one fact stands out most clearly—that the result of taking an opportunity is invariably that another wider opportunity is given. If therefore you neglect the opportunity put before you by your encounter with theosophy now, it is possible that in the next incarnation the chance may not come to you again.

If a man sets to work earnestly and permeates his spirit as thoroughly as possible with theosophical ideas, that will build them well into the ego, and will give him so great an attraction towards them that he is certain, even though he may not remember them in detail, to seek for them instinctively, and to recognize them, in his next birth. Every man therefore should begin theosophical work just as soon as he hears of it, because whatever of it he contrives to achieve, however little it may be, will be just so much to the good, and he will begin tomorrow where he has left off this time. Also by trying to do what he can with such vehicles as he has, obstinate and unresponsive though they may prove through lack of pliability, he will assuredly do much to earn for himself more pliable vehicles for next time. So no effort is lost, and it is never too late in any given life to enter upon the long, long upward path, and to make a commencement in the glorious work of helping others.

With an eternal life before us it would be a mistake to worry because the present day is drawing near its evening, or in despair to neglect the preparations for the coming day. *Light on the Path* says: "Kill out desire of life." This is often misunderstood, but its meaning should be plain. You cannot lose your life; why then should you desire it? It cannot possibly be taken from you. At the same time the quotation means that you should kill out desire for particular bodily conditions.

Meditation

I think that our members sometimes err with regard to meditation, because they have not thoroughly understood the exact way in which it works. They sometimes think that because they do not feel happy and uplifted after a meditation it is therefore a failure and entirely useless, or they find themselves dull and heavy and incapable of meditation. There seems no reality in anything for them, no certainty about anything, and they feel that they are making no progress. They suppose that this must be somehow their own fault and they reproach themselves for it; but they often ask what they can do to improve matters and to restore the joy they used to feel.

That experience, in regard to meditation, is common to all seekers after the spiritual life; you will find that the Christian saints constantly speak of their sufferings at periods of what they call "spiritual dryness" when nothing seems any use. They feel as though they had lost sight of God altogether. Imagine that I am sitting looking through a wide-open window upon a beautiful hillside, but the sky is dull grey, heavy with a vast pall of cloud probably miles in thickness. I have not seen the sun for three days. I cannot feel his rays, but I know it is there, and I know that some day these clouds will roll away as others have done, and I shall see it again. What is necessary for the life of the world is that it should be *there*, not that I should see it; it is far pleasanter to see it and to feel the warmth of its rays, but it is not a necessity of life. I know just exactly how these people feel, and it is cold comfort to be told that our feelings do not matter, even though there is a very real sense in which it is true.

I think it is helpful to remember that our meditation has several objects—for example:

1. To ensure that, however deeply we may be immersed in the affairs of the world, we shall devote at least some time each day to the thought of a high ideal.

2. To draw us nearer to the Master and to the Logos, so that from Them strength may be poured upon us and through us to benefit the world.

3. To train our higher bodies, so that they may have constant practice in responding to the highest vibrations.

Now you will observe that all these objects are attained just the same whether we feel happy or not. A mistake that many people make is to suppose that a meditation which is unsatisfactory *to them* is therefore ineffectual. It is just like a little child performing daily her hour of practice upon the piano. Sometimes perhaps she partially enjoys it, but very often it is a weariness to her, and her only thought is to finish it as quickly as possible. She does not know, but we do, that every such hour is accustoming her fingers to the instrument, and is bringing nearer and nearer the time when she will derive from her music an enjoyment of which now she does not even dream. You will observe that this object is being attained just as much by the unpleasant and unsatisfactory hour of practice as by that which she enjoys. So in the work of our meditation sometimes we feel happy and uplifted, and sometimes not; but in both cases alike it has been acting for our higher bodies as do the exercises of physical culture or training for our physical body. It is pleasanter when you have what you call a "good" meditation; but the only difference between what seems a good one and a bad one lies in its effect upon the feelings, and not in the real work which it does towards our evolution.

The reason of the temporary dullness is not always in ourselves—or rather, it is not always attributable to anything that can reasonably be called our fault. Often it is purely physical, resulting from over-fatigue or a nervous strain; often it is due to surrounding astral or mental influences. Of course it is our karma to be subjected to these, and so in that more remote way we are responsible; but we must just do the best we can with them, and there is no need for us to be despondent, or to waste our time in reproaching ourselves.

Another reason also may be that at certain times the planetary influences are more favorable for meditation than at others. I know nothing of this myself, for I have never considered the planetary influences in these matters, but have always forced my way to what I desired; but I have heard a friend say that an astrologer told him that on certain occasions when Jupiter was in certain relationship to the moon this had the effect of expanding the etheric atmosphere and making meditation easier, or at least making it appear more successful. The astrologer gave him a list, which he consulted after taking notes of the conditions of his meditations daily for three or four weeks, when he found that the results exactly agreed with the influences which were said to be acting. Certain aspects with Saturn, on the other hand, were said to congest the etheric atmosphere, making the work of meditation difficult, and this also was verified in the same way.

The highest thought that we can have is that of the supreme Lord of all, but of course we must not suppose that our thought changes in the least the attitude of the Supreme towards us. We who are students ought to be far beyond the stage at which a man thinks that he can produce change in the Supreme—a thought which belongs only to the ignorant and unphilosophical. We ourselves however are certainly affected by opening ourselves to Him. If you open the window of your room to the sun, the condition of your room is much changed by the power of the sun, but the sun is in no way changed by your opening the window. Open the windows of your soul to God.

During meditation one may try to think of the Supreme Self in everything and everything in It. Try to understand how the Self is endeavoring to express itself through the form. One method of practice for this is to try to identify your consciousness with that of various creatures, such as a fly, an ant, or a tree. Try to see and feel things as they see and feel them, until as you pass inwards all consciousness of the tree or the insect falls away, and the life of the Logos appears. We are very much more than the tree or the ant; therefore there is no danger of our being unable to withdraw our consciousness when the experiment is finished. After all we do not imprison it in the form of the tree or the ant; we expand it to take in the life in every form. The man who does this for the first time is usually surprised when he realizes the limitations under which animals act. He had thought an animal acted in a certain way for what seemed quite obvious reasons, but when he really enters into the animal he finds that its motives and intentions are wholly different. The disciple has to go through this process also with lower classes of human beings, because without it he could not perfectly help them.

This enables us to get down to the bedrock of the Self, and clears away the darkness and loneliness which often comes over us at one stage of our progress. When we know quite certainly that we are part of a whole we do not so much mind where this particular fragment of it may be, or through what experiences it may be passing. Whatever loneliness we may feel, we know that we are never alone; the Master is always there waiting to help where help is possible. We must give up clinging to the particular forms, and we have no motive but to do the will of the Logos. We must never allow the feeling of loneliness to make us forget the Master or lose faith in Him, for no progress is possible unless we have the fullest confidence in the Master whom we choose to serve. If we have only a half-hearted questioning faith in Him we cannot progress. We need not make the choice of a Master unless we will; but having made it we *must* have faith in the Teacher and His message.

In controlling the mind, first turn the senses away from outward sounds and sights, and become insensitive to the waves of thought and emotion from others. That is comparatively easy, but the next stage is very difficult, for when this is done there come up from within disturbances which spring from the uncontrolled activity of the mind. The meditation of many beginners consists mostly of a continuous struggle to come back to the point. Here comes in the advice given in *The Voice of Silence*. "The mind is the slayer of the real; let the disciple slay the slayer." You must not of course destroy your mind, for you cannot get along without it, but you must dominate it; it is *yours*, not *you*. The best way to overcome its wandering is to use the will. It is often suggested that the pupil should help himself by making a shell round him; but after all shells are but crutches. Develop will, and you will be able to dispense with them. The astral body tries to impose itself upon you in the same way, and to make you believe that its desires are yours; but with that also we must deal in a precisely similar manner.

There is no limit to the degree to which will may be developed. There are decided limitations to the extent to which the strength of the physical body can be increased, but there seem to be no limitations in the case of the will. Fortunately we can train it in the ordinary small things of daily life every day and all day long, and we can have no better practice than this. It is much easier for a man to screw up his courage to face a dramatic martyrdom before a crowd of people than to go on doing the tiresome daily duty with tiresome people day after day and year after year. This latter needs much more willpower than the former. Be careful however that you do not make others suffer in your efforts to develop your own will. Sometimes people have shown willpower by leaving home and friends and going out to face all kinds of difficulties and privations in order to do theosophical work. That is quite right if a man is absolutely free to do it; but a man who left his wife and family for that purpose, or an only son who left parents that were dependent upon him, would evidently be neglecting his duty in a way which he does not have a right to do, even for the sake of the noblest motives.

As a result of determined meditation we begin to build into our bodies the higher kinds of matter. At this stage we often feel grand emotions, coming from the buddhic level and reflected in the astral body, and under their influence we may do fine work and show great self-sacrifice. But then is needed the development of the mental and causal bodies in order to steady and balance us; otherwise the grand emotions that have swayed us in the right direction may very readily become a little twisted and sway us along some other and less desirable lines. With feeling alone we never obtain perfect balance or steadiness. It is well that the high feelings should come, and the more powerfully they come the better, but that is not enough; wisdom and steadiness must also be acquired because we need directing power as well as motive force. The very meaning of buddhi is wisdom, and when that comes it swallows up all else.

Illumination may mean three quite different things. First, a man, by setting himself to think intensely and very carefully over a subject may arrive at some conclusion with respect to it. Second, he may hope to obtain some illumination from his higher self—to discover what the ego really thinks on its own plane about the matter in question. Third, a highly developed man may come into touch with Masters or devas. It is only in the first case that his conclusions would be likely to be vitiated by his own thought-forms. The higher self would be able to transcend these, and so would a Master or a deva.

All these would have no difficulty in presenting things as they really are; but we must remember that we have not only to absorb the information, but also to bring it down into the physical brain, and as soon as it reaches that brain it will begin to be colored by prejudices. What we can do in meditation depends upon what we are doing all day long. If we have built up prejudices in ordinary life we cannot escape from them during the time of meditation; but if we patiently endeavor to root out our prejudices and to learn that the ways of others are just as good as our own, we are at least on our way towards establishing a gentle and tolerant attitude which will assuredly extend itself to the special time of our meditation. It is easy for us to see the disadvantages of any new ideas or suggestions; these leap to the eyes. But look for the good also, which does not always so readily emerge.

For the development of the powers of the soul, thought-control is an essential prerequisite. When the thought is controlled and the will is strong a good deal may be achieved in various directions. Much help may be given both to the living and to the so-called dead, and those who are sick or sorrowful may be greatly helped and strengthened. It is well for each member to make it a daily practice to devote a certain time to the sending out of such thoughts to people who are personally known to him—in addition, I mean, to the ordinary meditation which he undertakes for the sake of his own development. The same thing can be done to some extent in group meditation; the thoughts of all may be concentrated for a few minutes upon some one who is known to be in trouble or suffering, and a determined effort made to send strength and consolation. The same power used in a different way will often cure physical diseases.

As to the development of astral sight and hearing, one hardly regards that as an end in itself, but rather as a means to an end. It seems best to utilize to the utmost all the powers that we already possess, and wait for these others to unfold themselves as the result of study and unselfish work. Such powers are undoubtedly a help, though they may be a danger if they come before the character is fully developed. For any one who wishes to hasten their enfoldment I should recommend the process which I describe in the last chapter of *The Other Side of Death*.

Where a house is large enough to permit it, it is a good idea to set apart a room especially for meditation. I see no harm in holding group-meetings in such a room if the group be earnest and harmonious, but *not* if there is to be anything of the nature of discussion or wrangling. You ask whether you should enter such a room when you feel worried. I advise you not to make a thought-form, "I am worried, therefore I must not enter," rather to take exactly the opposite line, "I am about to enter, therefore I am no longer worried." You will find that much more effective.

SECTION FOUR

The Higher
Planes

Nirvana

It has often been said that in the final consummation all individual souls merge into the Great Soul, and our students sometimes find it difficult to reconcile this with other statements which seem to imply that the individuality is maintained, in some form or other, even up to the very greatest heights. The fact is that no experience which we can have, and no ideas which we can formulate down here in our physical brain, will at all express the glorious realities of nirvana and the planes beyond it. We know so little of that transcendent glory, and what little we do know can never be put into adequate words. Perhaps, however, it is in a certain sense somewhat misleading to speak of individual souls as merging into the Great Soul. Every monad is fundamentally a spark of the divine triad; he cannot merge into that of which he is already a part. Surely a better explanation of what happens would be to say that as he evolves the spark develops into flame; he becomes more and more conscious of his unity with the divine, and so the Logos is able more and more to manifest Himself through him.

This much at least I can say, that up to the highest level of consciousness which any of our students has yet attained—up even to what is commonly called nirvana itself, there is no loss of individuality, of the power to think, to plan and to act. Long before that there is an entire loss of the sense of *separateness*, but that is a very different thing. Sir Edwin Arnold wrote of that beatific condition "the dewdrop slips into the shining sea." Those who have passed through that most marvelous of experiences know that, paradoxical as it may seem, the sensation is exactly the reverse, and that a far closer description would be that the ocean had somehow been poured the drop!

That consciousness, wide as the sea, with "its centre everywhere and its circumference nowhere," is a great and glorious *fact*; but when a man attains it, it seems to him that his consciousness was never his at all, but only the shining of the divine power and wisdom and love through him, and he is now at last beginning to realize that stupendous fact. The truth is that what is commonly understood by individuality is a delusion and has never existed, but all that is best and noblest in that conception is maintained up to adeptship and far beyond, even into the realm of the great Planetary Spirits, for They are assuredly individuals, though mighty beyond our feeble powers of conception.

Even though the attempt be foredoomed to failure, let me endeavor to give some slight idea of an experience which some of us once had in connection with this lofty plane. Before we ourselves, by our own efforts, were able to touch it, a Master, for certain purposes of His own, enfolded us in His higher aura, and enabled us through Him to know something of the glories of nirvana.

Try to imagine the whole universe filled with and consisting of an immense torrent of living light, and in it a vividness of life and an intensity of bliss beyond all description, a hundred thousand times beyond the greatest bliss of heaven. At first we feel nothing but bliss; we see nothing but the intensity of light; but gradually we begin to realize that even in this dazzling brightness there are brighter spots—nuclei, as it were—which are built of the light because there is nothing but the light, and yet through them somehow the light gleams out more brightly, and obtains a new quality which enables it to be perceptible upon other and lower planes, which without this would be altogether beneath the possibility of sensing its effulgence. And by degrees we begin to realize that these subsidiary suns are the great Ones, that these are

Planetary Spirits, Great Angels, Karmic Deities, Buddhas, Christs and Masters, and that through Them the light and the life are flowing down to the lower planes. Gradually, little by little, as we become more accustomed to the stupendous reality, we begin to see that, in a far lower sense, even we ourselves are a focus in that cosmic scheme, and that through us also, at our much lower level, the light and the life are flowing to those who are still further away—not from it, for we are all part of it and there is nothing else anywhere—but further from the realization of it, the comprehension of it, the experience of it.

If we can see and grasp even a little of the glory, we can to some extent reflect it to others who are less fortunate. That light shines for every one, and it is the only reality; yet men by their ignorance and by their foolish actions may so shut themselves away that they cannot see it, just as the sun floods the whole world with light and life, and yet men may hide themselves in caves and cellars where that light cannot be seen. Just as a mirror properly placed at the mouth of such a cave or cellar may enable those within to participate, at least to some extent, in the benefits of the light, so may we, when we see the light, reflect it to others who have so placed themselves that they cannot perceive it directly.

No words that we can use can really give even the least idea of such an experience as that, for all with which our minds are acquainted has long ago disappeared before that level is attained. There is of course at that level a sheath of some sort for the spirit, but it is impossible to describe it in any words. In one sense it seems as though it were an atom, and yet in another it seems to be the whole plane. Each man is a center of consciousness and therefore must have some position; that focus in the stream of the life of the Logos must, one would say, be in one place or another. Yet he feels as if he were the whole plane and could focus anywhere, and wherever for the moment the outpouring of this force stops, that is for him a sheath. The man still feels absolutely himself, even though he is so much more; and he is able to distinguish others. He is able to recognize with perfect certainty the Great Ones whom he knows, yet it is rather by instinctive feeling than by any resemblance to anything that he has seen before; but if he focusses his consciousness upon one of These he gets the effect of the form of the man as he knows it in the Augoeides, two planes below.

The Triple Spirit

The monads are clearly all centers of force in the Logos, and yet each possesses a very distinct individuality of his own. In the average man the monad is but little in touch with the ego and the lower personality, which are yet somehow expressions of him. He knows from the first what is his object in evolution and he grasps the general trend of it, but until that portion of him which expresses itself in the ego has reached a fairly high stage, he is scarcely conscious of the details of life down here, or at any rate takes little interest in them. He seems at that stage not to know other monads, but rests in indescribable bliss without any active consciousness of surroundings. As evolution progresses, however, he grasps matters on the lower plane much more fully, and finally takes them entirely into his own hands, and at that stage he knows both himself and others, and his voice within us becomes for us the Voice of the Silence. That voice differs for us at different stages. For us now in this lower consciousness it is the voice of the ego; when we identify ourselves with the ego it is the voice of the spirit; when we reach the spirit it is the voice of the monad, and when in the far-away future we identify ourselves wholly with the monad it will be the voice of the Logos; but in every case we have to subject the lower and rise above it, before the voice of the higher can be heard.

This monad resides permanently upon the second plane of nature—the monadic—and when he descends upon the third—the plane of nirvana—he manifests himself as the triple spirit. This triple spirit is a reflection or, more truly, an expression of the Logos as He manifests Himself in our set of planes. The first manifestation of the Logos on our highest plane is also triple. In the first of His three aspects He does not manifest Himself on any plane below the highest. In the second aspect He descends to the second plane and draws round Himself a garment of its matter, thus making quite a separate expression of Him. In the third aspect He descends to the upper portion of the third plane, and draws round Himself matter of that level, thus making a third manifestation. These three are the "three persons in one God," of which Christianity teaches, telling us in its Athanasian creed that we should worship "One God in Trinity and Trinity in Unity, neither confounding the persons nor dividing the substance"— that is to say, never confusing in our minds the work and function of the three separate manifestations, each on its own plane, yet never for a moment forgetting the eternal unity of the "substance," that which lives behind all alike on the highest plane, at the level where these three are one.

Now an exact repetition of this process takes place in the case of man, who is in very truth made in the image of God. The spirit is triple upon the third plane, and the first of its three manifestations does not descend below that level. The second manifestation descends one stage, on to the fourth plane, and clothes itself with its matter, and then we call it buddhi. Just as before, the third aspect descends two planes, and shrines itself in matter of the highest level of the mental plane, and we call that manas, and this trinity of atma-buddhi-manas, manifesting in the causal body, is what we call the ego.

Never forget that the ego is not the manas only, but the spiritual triad; at our present stage of evolution he rests in his causal body on the higher levels of the mental plane, but as he passes onwards his consciousness will be centered on the buddhic plane, and afterwards, when he attains adeptship, on the nirvanic. But it must not be supposed that when this further development takes place the manas is in any way lost. When the ego draws himself up into the buddhic plane, he draws up manas with him into that expression of manas which has all the time existed on the buddhic plane, but has not been fully vivified until now. In the same way when he draws himself up into the nirvanic plane, manas and buddhi exist within him just as fully as ever, so that now the triple spirit is in full manifestation on its own plane in all its three aspects. Therefore the spirit is truly seven-fold, for he is triple on his own plane, dual on the buddhic, and single on the mental, and the unity which is his synthesis makes seven. Though he draws back into the higher he retains the definiteness of the lower.

This is probably what Madame Blavatsky meant when she spoke of the auric egg, but she surrounded this idea with great mystery, and it seems likely that she was under some pledge not to write freely about it. She never clearly explained the triple spirit, but evidently endeavored to suggest the idea without clearly expressing it, for she laid great stress upon the fact that, just as the astral plane may be said to be a reflection of the buddhic, so may the physical be said to be a reflection of the nirvanic, and then she furthermore emphasized the fact that there are three bodies or vehicles of man on the physical plane—apparently going out of her way to make this agree, and for that purpose dividing the physical body of man into two parts, the dense and the etheric, and adding as a third principle the vitality which flows through them. Now as this vitality exists on all the planes, and might just as well be made into additional principles on the astral and mental planes as on the physical, it would seem that some reason is required for her rather peculiar arrangement, and perhaps this reason may be found in her desire to indicate the triple spirit without actually mentioning it. I think Mrs. Besant has said that when Madame Blavatsky spoke about the sacred auric egg she meant the four permanent atoms within an envelope of matter of the nirvanic plane.

Buddhic Consciousness

A selfish man could not function on the buddhic plane, for the very essence of that plane is sympathy and perfect comprehension, which excludes selfishness. A man cannot develop a buddhic body until he has conquered the lower planes. There is a close connection between the astral and the buddhic, the former being in some ways a reflection of the latter; but it must not therefore be supposed that a man can leap from the astral consciousness to the buddhic without developing the intervening vehicles.

Certainly on the highest levels of the buddhic plane a man becomes one with all others, but we must not therefore assume that he feels alike towards all. There is no reason to suppose that we shall ever feel absolutely alike towards everybody; why should we? Even the Lord Buddha had His favorite disciple Ananda; even the Christ regarded Saint John the Beloved in a different way from the rest. What *is* true is that presently we shall come to love every one as much as we now love our nearest and dearest, but by that time we shall have developed for those nearest and dearest a type of love of which we have no conception now. The buddhic consciousness includes that of many others, so that you may put yourself down into another man and feel exactly as he does, looking upon him from within instead of from without. In that relation you will feel no shrinking even from an evil man, because you will recognize him as a part of yourself—a weak part. You will desire to help him by pouring strength into that weak part of yourself. What is required is really to be in this attitude and to do it, not merely to talk about it or think vaguely of it; and it is not easy to acquire this power.

It is not necessary for every ego to go through every experience, for when you rise to the buddhic level you can gain the experience of others, even of those who have opposed progress. We shall feel by sympathy. We could withdraw if we did not want to feel another's suffering; but we should choose to feel it because we want to help. On the buddhic plane we enfold the man in our own consciousness, and though he knows nothing of such enfoldment it will to a certain extent lessen his sufferings. In all probability we have all had most of the experiences of the lower stages of human development. An adept would necessarily wish to remove or relieve suffering, but we may easily imagine a case in which he would see that the good which was being produced by the suffering so enormously outweighed the present pain that to interfere would not be kindness but cruelty to the sufferer. He would see the whole, not only the part. His sympathy would be deeper than ours, but he would not express it in action except when action was useful.

The Spheres

In any diagram which represents the various planes we usually draw them as lying one above the other like the shelves of a book-case. But then in explaining that diagram we are careful to say that this must not be taken literally, since all the planes interpenetrate and all of them are about us here all the time. That is perfectly true, and yet there is a sense in which the shelf-like arrangement is true also. We may perhaps draw an analogy from the condition of affairs which we find existing upon the surface of the physical earth. We may take the solid matter, for all practical purposes, as existing only under our feet, as the lowest stratum of physical matter, though of course countless millions of particles of solid matter are also floating in the air over our heads.

We may say that, roughly speaking, the liquid matter of the earth (chiefly water) lies upon the surface of the solid matter, though again a large amount of water interpenetrates the earth beneath us, and also millions of tons of water are raised above the surface of the earth in the form of clouds. Still, the great bulk of the liquid matter of the earth lies on the top of its solid matter in the form of the ocean, lakes and rivers. Then the gaseous matter of our earth (chiefly the atmosphere) lies upon the surface of the water and of the solid earth, and extends much further away into space than either the liquid or the solid.

All three conditions of matter exist here at the surface of the earth where we live, but the water in the form of clouds extends further above that surface than does ordinary dust, and again the air, though interpenetrating both the others, extends much further away still. This is by no means a bad analogy to explain the arrangement of the matter of the higher planes.

What we call our astral plane may also be considered as the astral body of the earth. It certainly exists all around us, and interpenetrates the solid earth beneath our feet, but it also extends far away above our heads, so that we may think of it as a huge ball of astral matter with the physical earth in the middle of it, much as the physical body of a man exists within the ovid form which is filled with astral matter, except that in the case of the earth the proportionate size of its astral body outside the physical is enormously greater than in the case of man. But just as in the case of the man the densest aggregation of astral matter is that which is within the periphery of the physical body, so in the case of the earth by far the greater part of its astral matter is gathered together within the limit of the physical sphere.

Nevertheless, the portion of the astral sphere which is exterior to the physical, extends nearly to the mean distance of the moon's orbit, so that the astral planes of the two worlds touch one another when the moon is perigee, but do not touch when the moon is in apogee. Incidentally, it follows that at certain times of the month astral communication with the moon is possible, and at certain other times it is not.

I knew of a case in which a dead man reached the moon, but could not then return. That was because the continuity of astral matter failed him—the tide of space had flowed in between, as it were, and he had to wait until communication was re-established by the approach of the satellite to its primary.

The mental plane of our earth bears about the same proportion to the astral as the latter does to the physical. It also is a huge globe, concentric with the other two, interpenetrating them both, but extending much further from the center than does the astral globe. It will be seen that the effect of this is that, while matter of all the planes exists together down here, there is a certain amount of truth in the illustration of the shelves, for beyond the limit of the physical atmosphere there is a considerable shell which consists only of astral and mental matter, and outside of that again another similar shell which consists of mental matter only.

When we reach the buddhic plane the extension becomes so great that the buddhic spheres of the different planets of our chain meet one another, and so there is but one buddhic vehicle for the whole chain, which means that in the buddhic level it is possible to pass from one of these planets to another. I presume that when investigations in a similar way are extended to the nirvanic plane it will be found that that matter extends so much further that other chains are included in it as well—perhaps the entire solar system.

All this is true as far as it goes, and yet it does not convey a really accurate idea of the true position of affairs, because of the fact that our minds can grasp only three dimensions, whereas in reality there are many more, and as we raise our consciousness from plane to plane, each step opens before us the possibility of comprehending one more of these dimensions. This makes it difficult to describe exactly the position of those who have passed away from the physical life to other planes. Some of such people tend to hover round their earthly homes, in order to keep in touch with their friends of the physical life and the places which they know; and the great majority of the denizens of the astral world spend most of their lives comparatively near to the surface of the physical earth; but as they withdraw into themselves, and their consciousness touches the higher types of matter, they find it easier and more natural than before to soar away from that surface into regions where there are fewer disturbing currents. I was once brought into touch with the case of a dead man who informed a friend of mine, during a series of spiritualistic seances, that he frequently found himself about five hundred miles above the surface of the earth. In this case the questioner was one who was well versed in occultism, and who would therefore know well how to conduct his enquiries and the investigations of his friend on the other side intelligently and his friend's assertions.

The average person passing into the heaven-life tends to float at a considerable distance above the surface of the earth, although on the other hand some of such men are drawn to our level. Still, broadly speaking, the inhabitants of the heaven-world may be thought of as living in a sphere, or ring, or zone round the earth. What Spiritualists call the summer-land extends many miles above our heads, and as people of the same race and the same religion tend to keep together after death just as they do during life, we have what may be described as a kind of network of summer-lands over the countries to which belong the people who have created them.

People find their own level on the astral plane, much in the same way as objects floating in the ocean do. This does not mean that they cannot rise and fall at will, but that if no special effort is made they come to their level and remain there. Astral matter gravitates towards the center of the earth just as physical matter does; both obey the same general laws. We may take it that the sixth sub-plane of the astral is partially coincident with the surface of the earth, while the lowest, or seventh, penetrates some distance into the interior.

The conditions of the interior of our earth are not easy to describe. Vast cavities, exist in it, and there are races inhabitating these cavities, but they are not of the same evolution as ourselves. One of these evolutions, which is at a level distinctly lower than any race now existing upon the surface of the earth, is to some extent described in the seventeenth life of Alcyone, in *The Lives of Alcyone*; the other is more nearly at our level, yet utterly different from anything that we know.

As the center of the earth is approached, matter is found to exist in a state not readily comprehensible to those who have not seen it; a state in which it is far denser than the densest metal known to us, and yet flows as readily as water. But yet there is something else within even that. Such matter is far too dense for any forms of life that we know, but nevertheless, it has connected with it an evolution of its own.

The tremendous pressures which exist here are utilized by the Third Logos for the manufacture of new elements; in fact, the central portions of the earth may with great truth be regarded as His laboratory, for temperatures and pressures are obtainable there of which we on the surface have no conception. It is there that, under His direction, troops of devas and nature-spirits of a particular type combine and separate, arrange and rearrange the ultimate physical atoms, working along their wonderful double spiral form. From this point also, incredible as it seems to us, there is a direct connection with the heart of the sun, so that elements made there appear in the center of the earth without passing through what we call the surface; but it is useless to speak of this until the higher dimensions of space are more generally understood. In investigating the interior of the earth we did not find a central shaft running from pole to pole, though there are certain forces which play through concentric layers. As in the case of the physical, the densest astral matter is far too dense for the ordinary forms of astral life; but that also has other forms of its own which are quite unknown to students of the surface.

There is unquestionably a force of etheric pressure just as there is of atmospheric pressure, and it can be utilized by man as soon as he can discover some material which is ether-proof. The same pressure exists in the astral world. The most ordinary example of this is what happens when a man leaves his body in sleep or in death.

When the astral body is withdrawn from the physical, we must not suppose that that physical body is left without an astral counterpart. The pressure of the surrounding astral matter—and that really means the action of the force of gravitation on the astral plane—immediately forces other astral matter into that astrally empty space, just as, if we create a vortex and draw out the air from a room, other air flows in instantly from the surrounding atmosphere. But that astral matter will correspond with curious accuracy to the physical matter which it interpenetrates. Every variety of physical matter attracts astral matter of corresponding density, so that solid physical matter is interpenetrated by what we may call "solid" astral matter—that is, matter of the lowest astral sub-plane; whereas physical liquid is interpenetrated by matter of the next astral sub-plane—astral liquid; while physical gas in turn attracts its particular correspondence—matter of the third astral sub-plane from the bottom, which might be called astral gas.

Take the case of a glass of water; the tumbler (being solid matter) is interpenetrated by astral matter of the lowest sub-plane; the water in the tumbler (being liquid matter) is interpenetrated by astral matter of the second sub-plane, counting from the bottom upwards; while the air which surrounds both (being gaseous matter) is interpenetrated by astral matter of the third sub-plane, counting from the bottom upwards.

We must also realize that just as all these things—the tumbler, the water, and the air,—are interpenetrated by etheric matter, so are their astral correspondences further interpenetrated by the variety of astral matter which corresponds to the different types of etheric matter. So when a man withdraws his astral body from the physical there is an inrush of all three varieties of astral matter, because man's physical body is composed of solid, liquid and gaseous constituents. Of course there is etheric matter in the physical body as well, so there must also be astral matter of the higher sub-planes to correspond to that.

The temporary astral counterpart formed during the absence of the real astral body is thus an exact copy of it so far as arrangement is concerned, but it has no real connection with the physical body, and could never be used as a vehicle. It is constructed of any astral matter of the required kind that happens to be handy; it is merely a fortuitous concourse of atoms, and when the true astral body returns it pushes out this other astral matter without the slightest opposition. This is one reason for the extreme care which ought to be exercised as to the surroundings in which we sleep, for if those surroundings are evil, astral matter of the most objectionable type may fill our physical bodies while we are away from them, leaving behind it an influence which cannot but react horribly upon the real man when he returns. But the instant inrush when the body is abandoned shows the existence of astral pressure.

In the same way, when the man has finally left his physical body at death, what he leaves is no longer a vehicle, but a corpse—not in any true sense a body at all, but simply a collection of disintegrating material in the shape of a body. Just as we can no longer call that truly a body, so we cannot call the astral matter which interpenetrates it truly a counterpart in the ordinary sense of the word. Take an imperfect yet perhaps helpful analogy. When the cylinder of an engine is full of steam, we may regard the steam as the moving force within the cylinder, which makes the engine move. But when the engine is cold and at rest, the cylinder is not necessarily empty; it may be filled with air; yet the air is not its appropriate moving force, though it occupies the same position as did the steam.

Astral matter is never *really* solid at all—only relatively solid.

You know that the mediaeval alchemists always symbolized astral matter by water, and one of the reasons for that was its fluidity and penetrability. It is true that the counterpart of any solid physical object is always matter of the lowest astral sub-plane, which for convenience we often call astral solid matter; but we must not therefore endow it with the qualities with which we are familiar in solids on this plane. The particles in that densest kind of astral matter are further apart relative to their size than even gaseous particles; so that it would be easier for two of the densest astral bodies to pass through each other than it would be for the lightest physical gas to diffuse itself in the air.

On the astral plane one has not the sense of jumping over a precipice, but simply of floating over it. If you are standing upon the ground, part of your astral body interpenetrates the ground under your feet; but through your astral body you would not be conscious of this fact by anything corresponding to a sense of hardness, or by any difference in your power of motion. Remember that upon the astral plane there is no sense of touch that corresponds to ours upon the physical. One never touches the surface of anything, so as to feel it hard or soft, rough or smooth, hot or cold; but on coming into contact with the interpenetrating substance one would be conscious of a different rate of vibration, which might of course be pleasant or unpleasant, stimulating or depressing. When on awakening in the morning we remember anything corresponding to our ordinary sense of touch, it is only that in bringing the remembrance through, the physical brain adopted the means of expression to which we are accustomed.

Though the light of all planes comes from the sun, yet the effect which it produces on the astral plane is entirely different from that on the physical. In astral life there is a diffused luminosity, not obviously coming from any special direction. All astral matter is in itself luminous, and an astral body is not like a painted sphere, but rather a sphere of living fire. It is also transparent, and there are no shadows. It is never dark in the astral world. The passing of a physical cloud between us and the sun makes no difference whatever to the astral plane, nor of course does the shadow of the earth which we call night.

The invisible helper would not pass through a mountain, if he thought of it as an obstacle; to learn that it is not an obstacle is precisely the object of one part of what is called "the test of earth." There cannot be an accident on the astral plane in our sense of the word, because the astral body, being fluidic, cannot be destroyed or permanently injured, as the physical body can. An explosion on the astral plane might be temporarily as disastrous as an explosion of gunpower on the physical, but the astral fragments would quickly collect themselves again.

People on the astral plane can and do pass through one another constantly, and through fixed astral objects. Remember that on the astral plane matter is so much more fluidic and so much less densely aggregated. There never can be anything like what we mean by a collision, and under ordinary circumstances two bodies which interpenetrate are not even appreciably affected. If, however, the interpenetration lasts for some time, as it does, for example, when two persons sit side by side through a service in a church or a performance in a theater, a considerable effect may be produced.

There are many currents which tend to carry about persons who are lacking in will, and even those who have will but do not know how to use it. During physical life the matter of our astral bodies is constantly in motion, while after death, unless the will is exercised for the purpose of preventing it, it is arranged in concentric shells with a crust of the coarsest matter on the outside. If a man wishes to be of service on the astral, this shelling must be prevented, for those whose astral bodies have been thus rearranged are confined to one level. If the rearrangement has already occurred, the first thing that is done when a person is taken in hand is to break up that condition and set him free on the whole of the astral plane. For those who are acting as invisible helpers on the astral plane there are no separate levels; it is all one.

Atmospheric and climatic conditions make practically no difference to work on the astral and mental planes. But being in a big city does make a great difference, on account of the masses of thought forms. Some psychics require a temperature of about eighty degrees in order to do their best work, while others do not work well except at a lower temperature.

If necessary, occult work can be done anywhere, but some places afford greater facilities than others. For example, California has a very dry climate with much electricity in the air, which is favorable for the development of clairvoyance. Here in Adyar there is no resistance to our thought forms on account of the environment, because we are all thinking more or less along the same lines. But we must remember that there may always be resistance on the part of the person to whom we are sending thoughts, for some persons have for a whole lifetime built round themselves such shells of selfishness that one cannot penetrate them even when one wishes to do them good.

The Ego
and
His Vehicles

The Ego and the Personality

There are still many of our members who do not fully understand the problem of the higher and the lower self. This is not surprising, for we are repeatedly told that there is only one consciousness, and yet we often clearly feel two. It is not remarkable that students should be uncertain as to the real relation between these two, and should wonder whether the ego is entirely dissociated from his physical body and has an existence of his own among his fellows on his own plane.

This problem of the lower and higher self is an old one, and it is undoubtedly difficult to realize that there is, after all, only one consciousness, and that the apparent difference is caused only by the limitations of the various vehicles. The whole consciousness works on its own higher mental plane, but in the case of the ordinary man, only partially and vaguely as yet. So far as it is active it is always on the side of good, because it desires that which is favorable to its evolution as a soul. It puts a portion of itself down into lower matter, and that portion becomes so much more keenly and vividly conscious in that matter that it thinks and acts as though it were a separate being, forgetting its connection with that less developed yet far wider self-consciousness above. So sometimes it seems as though the fragment worked against the whole; but the man who is instructed declines to be deluded, and reaches back through the keen alert consciousness of the fragment to the true consciousness behind, which is as yet so little developed.

Undoubtedly the ego is only very partially expressed by his physical body, yet we should not be accurate in speaking of him as dissociated from that body. If we imagine the ego as a solid body and the physical plane as a surface, the solid body if laid upon that surface could manifest itself on that surface only as a plane figure, which would obviously be an exceedingly partial expression. We can see also that if the various sides of the solid were laid upon the surface successively we might obtain expressions which differed considerably, though all of them would be imperfect, because in all cases the solid would have an extension in an entirely different direction, which could by no means be expressed in the two dimensions of the superficies. We shall obtain a nearly accurate symbolism of the facts as far as the ordinary man is concerned if we suppose the solid to be conscious only so far as it is in contact with the surface, although the results gained through the manifestation of such consciousness would inhere in the solid as a whole, and would be present in any later expression of it, even though that might differ considerably from previous expressions.

It is only in the case of those already somewhat advanced that we can speak of the ego as having a conscious existence among his fellows on his own plane. From the moment that he breaks off from his group-soul and commences his separate existence, he is a conscious entity; but the consciousness is of an exceedingly vague nature. The only impression on the physical brain which the ego occasionally makes on some persons is at the moment of awakening in the morning. There is a state intermediate between sleeping and waking in which a man is blissfully conscious that he exists, and yet is not conscious of any surrounding objects, not capable of any movement. Indeed, he sometimes knows that any movement would break the spell of happiness and bring him down into the ordinary waking world, and so he endeavors to remain still as long as possible.

That condition—a consciousness of existence and of intense bliss—closely resembles that of the ego of the average man upon the higher mental plane. He is wholly centered there only for a short time which intervenes between the end of one life in the heaven-world and the commencement of his next descent into incarnation; and during that short period there comes to him the flash of retrospect and prospect—a glimpse of what his last life has done for him, and of what his next life is intended to do. For many ages these glimpses are his only moments of full awakening, and it is his desire for a more perfect manifestation, his desire to feel himself more thoroughly alive and active, which drives him into the effort of incarnation. It is not desire for life in the ordinary sense of the word, but rather for that complete consciousness which involves the power to respond to all possible vibrations from the surroundings on every plane, so that he may attain the perfection of sympathy.

When the ego is still undeveloped the forces of the higher mental plane pass through him practically without affecting him, as he cannot respond to more than a very few of these extremely fine vibrations. It needs powerful and comparatively coarse vibrations to affect him at first, and these do not exist upon his own plane, and for that reason he has to put himself down to lower levels in order to find them. Therefore full consciousness comes to him at first only in the lowest and densest of his vehicles, his attention being focussed for a long time down in the physical plane; so that, although that plane is so much lower than his own and offers so much less scope for activity, in those early stages he feels himself much more alive when he is working there. As the consciousness increases and widens its scope he gradually begins to work more and more in matter one stage higher—that is, in astral matter.

At a much later stage, when he has attained to clear working in astral matter, he begins to be able also to express himself through the matter of his mental body and the end of his present effort is achieved when he works as fully and clearly in the matter of the causal body on the higher mental plane as he does now on the physical plane.

These stages of full development of consciousness must not be confounded with the mere learning to use to some extent the respective vehicles. A man is using his astral body whenever he expresses an emotion; he is using his mental body whenever he thinks. But that is very far from his being able to utilize either of them as independent vehicles through which consciousness can be fully expressed. When a man is fully conscious in his astral body, he has already made a considerable amount of progress;

when he has bridged over the chasm between the astral consciousness and the physical, day and night no longer exist for him,
since he leads a life unbroken in its continuity. For him death also
has ceased to exist, since he carries that unbroken consciousness
not only through night and day, but also through the portals of
death itself and up to the end of his life upon the astral plane.

One step of further development lies open to him—the consciousness of the heaven-world; and then his life and memory are
continuous during the whole of each descent into incarnation.
Yet one step more raises the full consciousness to the level of the
ego on the higher mental plane, and after that he has always with
him the memory of all his lives, and he is capable of consciously
directing the various lower manifestations of himself at all points
of his progress.

It must not be supposed that the development of any of these
stages of consciousness is ever sudden. The actual rending of the
veil between two stages is usually a fairly rapid process, sometimes
even instantaneous. A man who has normally no memory of what
happens on the astral plane may unintentionally, by some accident or illness, or intentionally by certain definite practices,
bridge over the interval and make the connection, so that from
that time onward his astral consciousness will be continuous, and
his memory of what happens while the physical body is asleep will
therefore be perfect. But long before such an effort or accident is
possible for him the full consciousness must have been working in
the astral body, even though in the physical life he knew nothing
of it.

In exactly the same way a man must have been for a long time
thoroughly practiced in the use of his mental body as a vehicle
before he can hope to break the barrier between that and the
astral, so that he can have the pleasure of continuous recollection.
By analogy this leads us to see that the ego must have been fully
conscious and active on his own plane for a long time before any
knowledge of that existence can come through to us in our physical life.

There are many in whom the ego has already to some extent
awakened from the condition of mere bliss which was described
above, and is at least partially conscious of his own surroundings,
and therefore of other egos. From that time on he leads a life and
has interests and activities on his own plane; but even then we
must remember that he puts down into the personality only a very
small part of himself, and that that part constantly becomes

entangled in interests which, because they are so partial, are often along different lines from the general activities of the ego himself, who consequently does not pay any particular attention to the lower life of the personality, unless something rather unusual happens to it.

When this stage is reached he usually comes under the influence of a Master; indeed often his first clear consciousness of anything outside himself is his touch with that Master. The tremendous power of the Master's influence magnetizes him, draws his vibrations into harmony with its own, and multiplies manyfold the rate of his development. It rays upon him like sunshine upon a flower, and he evolves rapidly under its influence. This is why, while the earlier stages of progress are so slow as to be almost imperceptible, when the Master turns His attention upon the man, develops him and arouses his own will to take part in the work, the speed of his advancement increases in geometrical progression.

Of that stream of divine influence poured upon the ego by the Master, the amount which can be passed on to the personality depends upon the connection between it and the ego, which is very different in different cases. There is almost infinite variety in human life. The spiritual force rays upon the ego, and some little of it certainly comes through into the personality, because though the ego has put forth a part of himself he does not cut himself off entirely from it, notwithstanding the fact that in the case of all ordinary people the ego and the personality are very different things.

The ego in ordinary men has not much grasp of the personality, nor a clear conception of his purpose in sending it forth; and, again, the small piece which meets us in the personality grows to have ways and opinions of its own. The personality is developing by the experience which it gains, and this is passed on to the ego; but along with this real development he usually gathers a good deal which is hardly worthy of that name. He acquires knowledge, but also prejudices, which are not really knowledge at all. He does not become quite free from these prejudices—not only of knowledge (or rather its absence) but of feeling and action as well—until the man reaches adeptship. He gradually discovers these things to be prejudices, and progresses through them; but he has always a great deal of limitation from which the ego is entirely free.

As to the amount of the spiritual force which is passed to the personality, one can only decide in a particular case by using clairvoyance. But something of it must flow through always, because the lower is attached to the higher, just as the hand is attached to the body by the arm. It is certain that the personality must get something, but he can have only what he has made himself able to receive. It is also a question of qualities. The Master often plays upon qualities in the ego which are much obscured in the personality, and in that case of course very little comes down. As only those experiences of the personality can be handed on to the spiritual or permanent ego which are compatible with his nature and interests, so only those impulses to which he is able to respond can express themselves at that level of the personality. Remember, though, that the former tends to exclude the bad and the latter the good—or rather we should call them the material and the spiritual, for nothing is bad.

One may sometimes see by the clairvoyance many of these influences at work. On a certain day, for example, we may see a characteristic of the personality much intensified, with no outward reason. The cause is often to be found in what is taking place at some higher level—the stimulation of that quality in the ego. Sometimes a man finds himself overflowing with affection or devotion, and quite unable on the physical plane to understand why. The cause is usually, again, the stimulation of the ego, or it may be that the ego is taking some special interest in the personality for the time being.

In meditation we sometimes draw such attention on the part of the ego, though it is well to keep in mind that we must try to reach up to join that higher activity, rather than to interrupt it to draw down its attention to the lower. Remember, physical meditation is not for the ego, but for the training of the various vehicles to be a channel for the ego. The higher influence is certainly invited by right meditation, which is *always* effective, even though on the physical plane things may seem to be very dull and quite without zest. If the ego is at all developed he will meditate also upon his own level; but it does not follow that his meditation will synchronize with that of the personality. . . .The yoga of a fairly well-developed ego is to try to raise his consciousness first into the buddhic plane and then through its various stages. He does this without reference to what the personality happens to be doing at the time. Such an ego would probably also send down a little of himself at the personal meditation, though his own meditations are very different.

The reaching upwards of the ego himself often means his

neglect to send energy down to the personality, and this, of course, leaves the latter feeling rather dull and in the shade. The extent, then, to which the personality is influenced by the effort of the Master depends upon two things principally—the strength of the connection at the time between the ego and the personality; and the particular work which the Master is doing upon the ego, that is, the particular qualities upon which He is playing.

Meditation and the study of spiritual subjects in this earthly life make a very great difference in the life of the ego. The ordinary person who has not taken up spiritual matters seriously has only a thread of connection between the higher and the lower self. The personality in his case seems to be all, and the ego, though he undoubtedly exists on his own plane, is not at all likely to be doing anything actively there. He is very much like a chicken which is growing inside an egg. But in the case of some of us who have been making efforts in the right direction, we may hope that the ego is becoming quite vividly conscious. He has broken through his shell, and is living a life of great activity and power. As we go on, we shall become able to unify our personal consciousness with the life of the ego, as far as that is possible, and then we shall have only the one consciousness; even down here we shall have the consciousness of the ego that will know all that is going on. But with many people at the present day there is often considerable opposition between the personality and the ego.

There are other things to be taken into account. It is by no means always accurate to judge the ego by his manifestation in the personality. An ego of intensely practical type may make much more show on the physical plane than another of far higher development, if the energy of the latter happens to be concentrated almost exclusively upon the causal or buddhic levels. Therefore people who see only on the physical plane are frequently entirely wrong in their estimation of the relative position of others.

If you have to deal with a fairly advanced ego, you will sometimes find him rather inconsiderate of his body. You see whatever is put down into the personality is so much taken from *him!* I have again and again seen cases in which the ego was to some extent impatient and withdrew into himself somewhat; but on the other hand in cases such as these there is always a flow between the ego and the personality, which is not possible with the ordinary man. In the ordinary man the part is put down and left, though not of course quite cut off; but at this more advanced stage there is a constant communication between the two along the channel. Therefore, the ego can withdraw a great deal of himself whenever he chooses, and leave a very poor representation of the real man behind. So the relation between the lower and the higher self varies much in different people and at different stages of development.

As to the work of the ego, he may be learning things on his own plane; or he may be helping other egos—there are many kinds of work for which he may need an accession of strength. And then he may forget for a time to pay his personality proper attention, just as even a good man may occasionally, under some special pressure of business, forget his horse or his dog. Sometimes when that happens the personality reminds him of its existence by blundering into some foolishness which causes serious suffering. You may have noticed that sometimes, after you have completed a special piece of work that has needed the cooperation of the ego to a large extent—as, for example, lecturing to a large audience—he takes away the energy and leaves the personality with only enough to feel rather dispirited. For a time he admitted that there was some importance in the work, and therefore poured down a little more of himself, but afterwards he leaves the poor personality feeling rather depressed.

Of course, depression comes much more often from other reasons, such as the presence of an astral entity in a low-spirited condition, or of some non-human beings. And joy also is not always due to the influence of the ego, for the fact is that the man does not think much about his own feelings when he is in a fit condition to receive an influx of power. Joy may be produced by the proximity of harmonious nature-spirits, or in a variety of other ways. The channel between the ego and personality is by no means always open. Sometimes it appears to be almost choked up—a condition of affairs which is quite a possibility in view of its narrowness in most cases. Then the force may break through again on some occasion, such as that of a conversion. But for many of us there is a constant flow in some measure. Meditation, conscientiously done, opens the channel and keeps it open. Always remember, though, that it is better to try to go up to the ego than to bring it down to the personality.

Every ego has a certain knowledge of his own. He obtains a glimpse, between lives, of his past and future; in the undeveloped man this awakens the ego for a moment, after which he falls asleep again. During physical life the ordinary ego is to some extent capable of brooding watchfulness and a little effort, but is still in a sleepy condition. With a developed man the ego is fully awake. The ego, in course of time, discovers that there are a good many things which he can do, and when this happens he may rise into a condition in which he has a definite life on his own plane, though in many cases it is even then but dreamy. It is the ego's purpose to learn to be fully active on all planes, even the physical.

Suppose you have an ego whose principal method of manifesting himself is by affection. That quality is what he wants exhibited by his personality, and if you down here try to feel strong affection and make a specialty of that, the ego will promptly throw more of himself down into the personality, because he finds in it exactly what he desires. Be careful to provide what he needs, and he will quickly take advantage of it. Egos on their own plane can help other egos, when they are sufficiently developed to do so. The ego of the ordinary person has rather a vegetable consciousness or life, and seems to be only just aware of other egos. The personality will not know what the ego does, unless they have been unified. The ego may know the Master while the personality does not. The study of inner things, and living the life, wakes up the ego. Purely unselfish devotion belongs to the higher planes and concerns him.

I do not think the experiences of the personality can be transmitted to the ego, but the essence of them may. He cares little for the details, but he wants the essence of it. Any of those thoughts that we consider evil are impossible for the ego. For precise definition he must come down into the physical body. He devotes himself more especially during the heaven-life to the assimilation of the experiences of the personality, but he is doing it all the time. When you take up the study of theosophy, and live the life, you begin to call the attention of the ego by sending up vibrations to which he can respond. The ordinary man has in his life little that appeals to the ego.

Highly unselfish affection and devotion belong to the highest astral sub-plane, and these reflect themselves in the corresponding matter of the mental plane, so that they touch the causal, not the lower mental. Thus only unselfish thoughts affect the ego. All the lower thoughts affect the permanent atoms, but not the ego; and corresponding to them you would find gaps in the causal body, not bad colors. Selfishness below shows in it as absence of affection or sympathy, and when the good quality develops the gap will be filled up. In the causal body you can see whether a man can possibly fail in this or that quality. Try to develop the qualities the ego wants, and he will come down to help.

As is said in *Light on the Path*, watch for the ego, and let him fight through you, and yet at the same time never forget that you are the ego. Therefore identify yourself with him and make the lower give way to you, the higher. Yet do not be too greatly disheartened if you should fall even many times, for even failure is to a certain extent a success, since we learn by it and so are wiser to meet the next problem. We cannot always succeed now at every point, though we surely shall do so ultimately. But never forget that it is not expected of us that we shall always succeed, but only that we shall do our best.

Counterparts

When the ego descends into incarnation, he draws round himself a mass of astral matter, not yet formed into a definite astral body; this takes, in the first place, the shape of that ovoid which is the nearest expression that we can realize of the true shape of the causal body. But when the further step downward and outward into physical incarnation is taken, and a little physical body is formed in the midst of that astral matter, the body immediately begins to exert a violent attraction over it, so that the great majority of the astral matter (which previously may be thought of as fairly evenly distributed over the large oval) now becomes concentrated into the periphery of that physical body.

As the physical body grows, the astral matter follows its every change, and thus we find man presenting the spectacle of an astral body, ninety-nine per cent of which is compressed within the periphery of his physical body, only about the remaining one per cent filling the rest of the ovoid form. In the plates in *Man, Visible and Invisible* we have sketched in the outline of the physical body merely in pencil, so that it shows but slightly, because my especial desire in that book was to emphasize the colors of the ovoid, and the way in which they illustrate the development of man by the transfer of vibrations from the lower bodies to the higher; but in reality that astral counterpart of the physical body is very dense and definite, and quite clearly distinguishable from the surrounding ovoid.

Note, therefore, that the astral matter takes the exact form of the physical matter merely because of the attraction which the latter has for the former. But we must further realize that although we may speak of the lowest sub-plane of the astral as corresponding to solid physical matter, it is yet very different in texture, for all astral matter bears to its corresponding physical matter something the same sort of relation that the liquid bears to the solid. Therefore the particles of the astral body, whether in the finest or coarsest parts of it, are constantly in motion among themselves, just as are particles of flowing water; and it will consequently be seen that it is quite impossible for the astral body to possess specialized organs in the same sense as does the physical body.

No doubt there is an exact counterpart in astral matter of the rods and cones which make up the retina of the physical eye; but the particles which at one moment are occupying that particular position in an astral body may, a second or two later, be moving through the hand or the foot. One does not, therefore, see upon the astral plane by means of the astral counterpart of the physical eyes, nor does one hear with the astral counterpart of the physical ears; indeed, it is perhaps not exactly correct to apply the terms "seeing" and "hearing" to astral methods of cognizance, since these terms are commonly held to imply specialized sense-organs, whereas the fact is that every particle in the astral body is capable of receiving and transmitting vibrations from one of its own type, but its own type only. Thus when one obtains a glimpse of astral consciousness, one is surprised to find oneself able to see on all sides simultaneously, instead of only in front as one does on the physical plane. The exact correspondence of the astral body to the physical therefore is merely a matter of external form, and does not at all involve any similarity of function in the various organs.

But the attraction continued all through life sets up a kind of habit or momentum in the astral matter, which causes it to retain the same form even while it is withdrawn temporarily from the attraction of the physical body at night and permanently after death; so that even through the long astral life the lineaments of the physical body which were put aside at death will still be preserved almost unchanged. Almost—because we must not forget that thought has a powerful influence upon astral matter and can readily mold it, so that a man who habitually thinks of himself after death as younger than he actually was at the time of that death will gradually come to present a somewhat younger appearance.

A questioner asks, "If the arm of a man, the branch of a tree, or the leg of a chair were cut off, would in each case the astral counterpart also be removed, and can we, by breaking an astral counterpart, produce a fracture in a physical object? That is to say, if with the hand of my astral body I break the astral counterpart of a chair, will the physical chair also be broken?"

The three cases given are not quite analogous. Both the tree and the man have the life within them which makes the astral body in each case a coherent whole. It is strongly attracted by the particles of the physical body, and therefore adapts itself to its shape, but if part of that physical body be removed, the coherence of the living astral matter is stronger than the attraction towards that severed portion of the physical. Consequently the astral counterpart of the arm or branch will not be carried away with the severed physical fragment. Since it has acquired the habit of keeping that particular form, it will continue for a short time to retain the original shape, but will soon withdraw within the limits of the maimed form.

In the case of an inanimate body, such as a chair or a basin, there would not be the same kind of individual life to maintain cohesion. Consequently when the physical object was broken the astral counterpart would also be divided; but it would not be possible to break an astral counterpart, and in that way to affect the physical object. In other words the act of fraction must begin on the physical plane.

One could of course move a purely astral object by means of an astral hand if one wished, but not the astral counterpart of a physical object. In order to perform this latter feat it would be necessary to materialize a hand and move the physical object, when the astral counterpart would of course accompany it. The astral counterpart is there because the physical object is there, just as the scent of a rose fills the room because the rose is there. To suggest that by moving the astral counterpart one could also move the physical object is like suggesting that by moving the smell one could move the physical rose which causes the smell.

The astral body changes its particles as does the physical, but fortunately the clumsy and tiresome process of cooking, eating and digesting food is not a necessity on the astral plane. The particles which fall away are replaced by others from the surrounding atmosphere. The purely physical cravings of hunger and thirst no longer exist there; but the desire of the glutton to gratify the sensation of taste, and the desire of the drunkard for the exhilaration which follows, for him, the absorption of alcohol—these are both astral, and therefore they still persist, and cause great suffering because of the absence of the physical body through which alone they could be satisfied.

So far as we are at present aware the astral body does not appear to be susceptible to fatigue. The ordinary man while possessing a physical body naturally never has the opportunity of working for any length of time consecutively upon the astral plane, for his nights of astral work alternate with days of physical work. I knew, however, of one case of a man who, having the right to take a rapid reincarnation, had to wait upon the astral plane twenty-five years for the special conditions which he required. He spent the whole of this time in working for the help of others, without any intermission except the occasional attendance at classes held by pupils of our Masters; and he assured me that he had never felt the slightest sense of fatigue—that in fact he had forgotten what it meant to be tired.

We all know that excessive or long-continued emotion tires us very quickly in ordinary life, and since emotion is an expression of the astral, that may perhaps lead some to suppose that fatigue of the astral body is possible. I think, however, that it will be found that what is subject to fatigue is merely the physical organism through which everything in us which manifests on this plane must pass. What we call mental fatigue is a parallel case. There is no such thing as fatigue in the *mind*; what we call by that name is only fatigue of the physical brain through which that mind has to express itself.

A spectator who has not been able to raise his sight above the astral level will of course see only astral matter when he looks at the aura of his fellow-men. He will see that this astral matter not only surrounds the physical body but also interpenetrates it, and that within the periphery of that body it is much more densely aggregated than in that part of the aura which lies outside. This is due to the attraction of the large amount of dense astral matter which is gathered together there as the counterpart of the cells of the physical body.

When during sleep the astral body is drawn from the physical this arrangement still persists, and then any one looking at the astral body with clairvoyant vision would still see, just as before, a form resembling the physical body surrounded by an aura. That form would now be composed only of astral matter, but still the great difference in density between it and its surrounding mist would be quite sufficient to make it clearly distinguishable, even though it is itself only a form of denser mist.

There is a considerable difference in appearance between the evolved and the unevolved man. Even in the case of the latter the features and shape of the inner form are recognizable always, though blurred and indistinct; but the surrounding egg scarcely deserves the name, for it is in fact a mere shapeless wreath of mist, having neither regularity nor permanence of outline.

In the more developed man the change is very marked, both in the aura and the form within it. This latter is much more distinct and definite—a closer reproduction of the man's physical appearance; while instead of the floating mist-wreath we see a sharply defined ovoid form preserving its shape unaffected amidst all the varied currents which are always swirling round it on the astral plane. Though the arrangement of the astral body is largely changed after death, such alteration does not in any way affect the recognizability of the form within the egg, though the natural changes which take place tend on the whole to make the form grow somewhat fainter and more spiritual in appearance as time passes on.

Colors in the Astral Body

Any comparatively permanent color in the astral body means a persistent vibration, which in the course of time produces its effect upon the mental body, and also upon the causal body, so that the higher qualities developed by the life on the lower planes are gradually built into the permanent causal body, and so become qualities of the soul itself. The colors may be mingled to any extent; for example, affection (rose) mingled with religious devotion (blue) will give a lovely violet. It is only the *good* thought or feeling which can produce an effect in the causal body, and so be permanently stored up as part of the man. Other kinds of thought and feeling remain in the lower vehicles and are comparatively impermanent. The size of a thought-form shows the strength of the emotion.

The Causal Body

The causal body could not be fully contained in any number of physical bodies, any more than any number of lines can make a square, or any numbers of squares can make a cube. The ego puts himself down into his various bodies with the hope of gaining two results—to make the causal body learn to respond to more vibrations, and also to increase its size. Most people are barely conscious in the causal body. With such egos their strings cannot be played upon directly, but are affected from below by way of overtones. The causal body is composed of matter from the three highest sub-planes of the mental plane. Most men at present can only work on the matter of the third sub-plane of the mental, the lowest part of their causal bodies, indeed only the lower matter even of *that* is usually in operation. When they are on the Path, the second sub-plane opens up. The adept uses the whole causal body while his consciousness is on the physical plane. A rough and ready way of deciding at what stage a man stands is to look at the causal body, which also shows how he arrived there. Men develop unequally—we are all undeveloped in some way. An animal has a minimum-sized causal body as soon as he is individualized; then it has to be developed as to size and color.

The Desire-Elemental

Much of the matter of the astral body is vivified by elemental essence* which is cut off for a time from the general mass of astral matter and becomes a man's expression on that plane. This is a living, though not an intelligent essence. But it has a kind of instinct which Mr. Sinnett calls "dawning intelligence," which guides it into getting what it wants. Blindly and without reason, but instinctively, it seeks its ends, and shows great ingenuity in obtaining its desires and in furthering its evolution.

Evolution for it is a descent into matter; its aim is to become a mineral monad. Therefore, its object in life is to get as near to the physical plane as it can, to come into contact with as many of the vibrations as coarse a type as possible. It knows nothing of *you*; it could not know or imagine anything of you; but it does realize that it is apart from the general stock, and that it is good to be

*Elemental essence—the life of astral or mental matter which is in an earlier stage of manifestation even than minerals. It is descending into matter to ensoul minerals, and later vegetable and animal life. —Ed.

apart. It is not a devil, and you must not get the idea that it is to be hated.

It is part of the Divine Life, just as you are; but its interests are diametrically opposed to yours. *It* wants to evolve downwards; *you* want to evolve upwards. It desires to preserve its separate life, and it feels that it can do so only by means of its connection with you. It is conscious of a something which is your lower mind, and realizes that if it can englobe this mind, and persuade you that its interests and yours are one, you will increasingly supply it with the sensations it desires. When it gets the matter sufficiently entangled to suit its purpose, you cannot then withdraw it, the result being that some of this matter of the lower mind is then lost to you altogether in the life after death.

So, you see, here is the desire-elemental seeking its own ends; not knowing that it is injuring you by trying to entangle your lower mind. The more it can do this the better for it, for the more mental matter it can entangle the longer will be its astral life—that life still enduring even after you have passed into the heaven-world. In Theosophical phraseology it has been known as the shade. *Your* business is not to allow yourself to be deceived; *it* understands nothing of your evolution, and is not responsible for it; it simply tries to turn you to its own purpose. If it knew of our existence, we should appear to it to be evil beings and tempters, trying to prevent the evolution which it knows to be right for it. If we steadfastly refuse to allow our astral body to vibrate at the rate peculiar to the coarser matter, that coarser matter will gradually be discharged from the body, which will become finer in texture, and the desire-elemental will be of a less active kind. Do let us realize this: that this elemental is not ourselves. It is never *you* who desire these lower things, but this creature.

It is not so much that we have to make a great fight against it, but we should shake ourselves free, saying: "This is not I; I do not want this lower thing." You are responsible for its likes and wants, for in your last life you made it what it is. Not that this particular collection of astral matter and elemental essence existed then; it did not, for it was newly gathered together at your birth this time. But it is an exact reproduction of the matter in your astral body at the end of your last astral life. Nevertheless it is not you; and you must ever bear this in mind all through life, and even more during the life after death, for then it has still greater power to deceive you.

But you may think that by thus refusing to allow it to influence you, you are checking its evolution. Not at all. You are doing better for the elemental if you control the lower passions, and take a firm stand of your own. It is true you do not develop its lowest parts, but you may drop the lower and evolve the higher. An animal can supply the lower kinds of vibrations even better than you can, whereas none but man can evolve the higher type of essence.

After the death of the physical body the ordinary man, who has never heard all this, finds himself when he wakes up on the other side in a totally unexpected condition of affairs, and is generally more or less disturbed thereby. Finally, he accepts these conditions which he does not understand, thinking them necessary and inevitable. Some no doubt are, but some are not, and with knowledge the latter could be transcended.

The elemental is afraid, because it knows that the death of the physical body means that the term of its separated life is limited; it knows that the man's astral death will more or less quickly follow, and then it will lose its means of vivid and intense sensations. Consequently it adopts the best plan it can think of for the preservation of the man's astral body. It evidently knows enough of astral physics to realize that the coarsest matter can hold together longest, and best stand friction. So it arranges the matter in rings, the coarsest on the outside. And in so doing it is right, from its point of view. The rearrangement which the desire-elemental produces after death is over the surface of the counterpart of the physical body, not over the surface of the egg which surrounds it. The elemental has, by this arrangement of the matter of your body, shut you up, as it were, in a box of astral matter, which enables you to see and hear things of the lowest and coarsest plane only.* If you object to being shut up in this way, it endeavors to make you believe that unless you do thus firmly root yourself into the lower matter you will float off, and lose yourself in a nebulous vagueness. The elemental tries to inspire a feeling of terror in the man who is jolting him out of this arrangement, in order to deter him from doing so.

But if, on the other hand, you were to set your will to oppose it, then at once there would be a difference. The particles of the

---

*See section "Localization of States" for further discussion of this. Ed.

astral body would be kept all intermingled, as in life; and you would, in consequence, be free to experience all the sub-planes.

The final struggle with it takes place at the conclusion of the astral life, for then the ego endeavors to draw back into himself all that he put down into incarnation at the beginning of the life which has just closed—to recover, as it were, the principal which he has invested, plus the interest of the experience which has been gained and the qualities which have been developed during that life. But when he attempts to do this he is met with determined opposition from this desire-elemental, which he himself has created and fed.

Though it can hardly be described as intelligent, it has a strong instinct of self-preservation, which leads it to resist with all the force at its command the extinction which threatens it. In the case of all ordinary mortals it attains a certain measure of success in its efforts, for much of the mental faculty has during life been governed by the lower desires and prostituted to their service, or in other words the lower mind has been so seriously entangled by desire that it is impossible for it to be entirely freed. The result of the struggle is therefore that some portion of the mental matter and even of causal matter is retained in the astral body after the ego has completely broken away from it. When a man has during life completely conquered his lower desires and succeeded in absolutely freeing the lower mind from desire, there is practically no struggle, and the ego reclaims in full both principal and interest; but there is unfortunately an opposite extreme when he is able to reclaim neither.

So our business, both during life and after death, is to control this desire-elemental, and not let *it* control us. Realize that you are a god in the making. All the power and force of the universe are on your side. The result is certain. Range yourself on the side of the Law, and all will be simplified.

Absolute control of passions is eminently desirable, but is obtained by few. While functioning on the astral plane, you have to keep your temper. You see many dreadful things, and if you have not all feelings thoroughly under control you may easily do something for which you will be sorry. Down here people often commit casual brutality and think nothing of it; a callous schoolmaster, for example, beats a child without realizing his wickedness; but on the astral plane the heinousness of such an act is at once obvious, and even the awful horrors of the karma which it entails may often be seen. On the astral you see the full effects of even an unkind word. Tremendous and violent passions may often attract low kinds of beings, who enter into the thought forms and enjoy the vibrations. Such animated thought forms may last for years, and even produce poltergeist phenomena.

Lost Souls

It is an unspeakable relief to be set free by the common sense of theosophical teaching from the awful nightmare of the doctrine of eternal damnation which is still held by the more ignorant among the Christians, who do not understand the real meaning of certain phrases attributed in their gospels to their Founder. But some of our students, filled with glad enthusiasm by the glorious discovery that every unit must finally attain perfection, find their joy somewhat dampened by gruesome hints that, after all, there are conditions under which a soul may be lost, and they begin to wonder whether the reign of divine law is really universal, or whether there is not some method by which man can contrive to escape from the dominion of the Logos and destroy himself. Let such doubters take comfort; the Will of the Logos is infinitely stronger than any human will, and not even the utmost exertion of perverse ingenuity can possibly prevail against Him.

It is true that He allows man to use his free-will, but only within certain well-defined limits; if the man uses his will well, those limits are quickly widened, while more and more power over his own destiny is given to him; but if he uses that will for evil, he thereby increases his limitations, so that while his power for good is practically unbounded, because it has in it the potentiality of infinite growth, his power for evil is rigidly restricted. And this not because of any inequality in the incidence of the law, but because in the one case he exerts his will in the same direction as that of the Logos, and so is swimming with the evolutionary tide, while in the other he is struggling against it.

The term "lost souls" is not well chosen, for it is almost certain to be misunderstood, and taken to imply much more than it really means. In everyday parlance, the word "soul" is used with exasperating vagueness, but on the whole it is generally supposed to denote the subtler and more permanent part of man, so that to the man in the street 'to lose one's soul' means to lose oneself, to be lost altogether. That is precisely what can never happen; therefore the expression is misleading, and a clear statement of the facts may be of use to students. Of such facts there seem to be three classes; let us consider them one by one.

1. Those who will drop out of this evolution in the middle of the fifth round. This dropping out is precisely the aeonian (*not* eternal) condemnation of which the Christ spoke as a very real danger for some of His unawakened hearers—the condemnation meaning merely the decision that they are incapable as yet of the higher progress, but not implying blame except in cases where opportunities have been neglected. Theosophy teaches us that men are all brothers, but not that they are all equal. There are immense differences between them; they have entered the human evolution at various periods, so that some are much older souls than others, and they stand at very different levels on the ladder of development. The older souls naturally learn much more rapidly than the younger, and so the distance between them steadily increases, and eventually a point is reached where the conditions necessary for the one type are entirely unsuitable for the other.

We may obtain a useful working analogy by thinking of the children in a class at school. The teacher of the class has a year's work before him, to prepare his boys for a certain examination. He parcels out the work—so much for the first month, so much for the second, and so on, beginning of course with what is easiest and gradually leading up to what is more difficult. But the boys are of various ages and capacities; some learn rapidly and are in advance of the average, while some lag behind. New boys, too, are constantly coming into his class, some of them barely up to its level. When half the year has run its course, he resolutely closes the list for admissions, and declines to receive any more new boys.

That took place for us at the middle point of the fourth round, after which the door was shut for passage from the animal kingdom into the human, save for a few exceptional cases, which belong, as it were, to the future; just as you have a few men attaining adeptship, who are not belated remnants of the previous chain, but people in advance of the rest of humanity. In the same way there are a few animals at the stage of individualization, which the majority is expected to reach at the end of the seventh round. On the next planet an arrangement will be made by which these exceptions will have the opportunity of taking primitive human bodies.

A little later the teacher can clearly foresee that some of his boys will certainly pass the examination, that the chance of others is doubtful, and that there are yet others who are sure to fail. It would be quite reasonable if he should say to these last:

> We have now reached a stage when the further work of this class is useless for you. You cannot possibly by any effort attain the necessary standard in time for the examination; the more advanced teaching which must now be given to the others would be entirely unsuited for you, and as you could not understand it you would be not only wasting your own time but would be a hindrance to the rest of the class. It will therefore be better for you at once to transfer yourselves to the next class below this, perfect yourselves there in the pre-liminary lessons which you have not yet thoroughly learned, and come back to this level with next year's class, when you will be sure to pass with credit.

That is exactly what will be done in the middle of the fifth round. Those who cannot, by any effort, reach the prescribed goal in the time which remains will be put back into a lower class, and if the class-room doors are not yet open they will wait in peace and happiness until the appointed time. They may be described as lost *to us*, lost to this particular little wave of evolution to which we belong; they are no longer "men of our year" as we say at college. But they will very certainly be "men of the next year"— even leading men in it, because of the work that they have already done and the experience that they have already had.

Most of these people fail because they are too young for the class, although they were too old to be put in the first place into the class below. They have had the advantage of going through the first half of the year's work, and they will therefore take it up again next time readily and easily, and will be able to help their more backward fellow-pupils who have not had their advantages. For those who are too young for the work there is no blame in failure.

But there is another large class who might succeed by deter-mined effort, but fail for want of that effort. These exactly cor-respond to the boy who drops behind his class not because he is too young, but because he is too lazy to do his work. His fate is the same as that of the others, but it is obvious that while they were blameless because they did their best, he is blameworthy precisely because he did not do his; so he will carry with him a legacy of karma from which they are free. It is to men of that class that the Christ's exhortations were addressed—men who had the opportunity and ability to succeed, but were not making the necessary effort.

It is of these that Madame Blavatsky speaks in such vigorous terms as "useless drones who refuse to become co-workers with Nature, and who perish by millions during the manyantaric life-cycle." (*Secret Doctrine*, iii, 526.) But note that this "perishing" is merely from this "manvantaric life-cycle", and that it means for them delay only, and not total extinction. Delay is the worst that can happen to people in the ordinary course of evolution. Such a delay is undoubtedly most serious, but, bad though it be, it is the best that can be done under the circumstances. If either through youth, or through laziness and perversity, these people have failed, it is clear that they need more training, and this training they must have. Obviously that is best for them, even though it means many lives—lives, many of which may be dreary, and may even contain much suffering. Still, they must go through to the end, because that is the only way by which they can attain the level which the more advanced races have already reached through similar long-continued evolution.

It was with the object of saving as many people as possible from that additional suffering that the Christ said to His disciples: "Go ye into all the world and preach the gospel to every creature; he that believeth and is baptized shall be saved, but he that believeth not shall be damned." For baptism and its corresponding rites in other religions are the sign of the dedication of the life to the service of the Brotherhood, and the man who is able to grasp the truth, and consequently sets his face in the right direction, will certainly be among the "saved" or "safe," who escape the condemnation in the fifth round; while those who do not take the trouble to see the truth and follow it will assuredly fall under that condemnation. But remember always that the "damnation" means only rejection from this "aeon" or chain of worlds, a throwing back into the next of the successive life-waves. "Lost souls," if you will; lost to us, perhaps, but not to the Logos; so they would be better described as temporarily laid aside. Of course it must not be supposed that the "belief" which saves them is the knowledge of theosophy; it does not matter in the least what their religion is, so long as they are aiming at the spiritual life, so long as they have definitely ranged themselves on the side of good as against evil, and are working unselfishly onward and upward.

2. Cases in which the personality has been so much emphasized that the ego is almost shut out from it. Of these there are two varieties—those who live only in their passions, and those who live only in their minds; and as both types are by no means uncommon it is worth while to try to understand exactly what happens to them.

We often speak of the ego as putting himself down into the matter of the lower planes, yet many students fail to realize that this is not a mere figure of speech, but has a very definite and very material side to it. The ego dwells in a causal body, and when he takes upon himself in addition a mental and an astral body, the operation involves the actual entangling of a portion of the matter of his causal body with matter of those lower astral and mental types. We may regard this "putting down" as a kind of investment made by the ego. As in all investments, so in this; he hopes to get back more than he puts out, but there is a risk of disappointment—a possibility that he may lose something of what he invests, or under very exceptional circumstances there may even be a total loss which leaves him, not indeed absolutely bankrupt, but without available capital.

Let us consider the elaboration of this analogy. The ego possesses in his causal body matter of three levels—the first, second, and third sub-planes of the mental; but for the enormous majority of mankind there is as yet no activity beyond the lowest of these three types, and even that is usually very partial. It is therefore only some of this lowest type of causal matter that can be put down to lower levels, and only a small fraction even of that part can be entangled with mental and astral matter.

The ego's control over what is put down is very weak and imperfect, because he is still half asleep. But as his physical body grows up his astral and mental bodies are also developed, and the causal matter entangled with them is awakened by the vigorous vibrations which reach it through them. This fraction of a fraction which is fully entangled gives life and vigor and a sense of individuality to these vehicles, and they in turn react strongly upon it and arouse it to a keen realization of life. This keen realization of life is exactly what it needs, the very object for which it is put down; and it is the longing for this keen realization which is spoken of as *trishna* (the thirst for manifested life, the desire to feel oneself really vividly alive), the force which draws the ego down again into reincarnation.

But just because this small fraction has had these experiences, and is therefore so much more awake than the rest of the ego, it may often be so far intensified as to think itself the whole, and forget for the time its relation to "its Father which is in heaven." It may temporarily identify itself with the matter through which it should be working, and may resist the influence of that other portion which has been put down, but is not entangled—that which forms the link with the great mass of the ego on his own plane.

In order to understand this fully we must think of that portion of the ego which is awakened on the third sub-plane of the mental (remembering always how small a fraction even that is of the whole) as itself divided into three parts: (*a*) that which remains on its own plane) (*b*) that which is put down, but remains unentangled in lower matter; and (*c*) that which is thoroughly entangled with lower matter and receives vibrations from it. These are arranged in a descending scale, for just as (*a*) is a very small part of the real ego, so (*b*) is but a small part of (*a*), and (*c*) in turn a small part of (*b*). The second acts as a link between the first and third; we may symbolize (*a*) as the body, (*b*) as the arm stretched out, and (*c*) as the hand which grasps, or perhaps rather the tips of the fingers which are dipped into matter.

We have here a very delicately balanced arrangement, which may be affected in various ways. The intention is that the hand (*c*) should grasp firmly and guide the matter with which it is entangled, being fully directed all the time by the body (*a*) through the arm (*b*). Under favorable circumstances additional strength, and even additional matter, may be poured from (*a*) through (*b*) into (*c*), so that the control may become more and more perfect. (*c*) may grow in size as well as strength, and the more it does so the better, so long as the communication through (*b*) is kept open freely and (*a*) retains control. For the very entanglement of the causal matter which constitutes (*c*) awakens it to a keen activity and an accuracy of response to fine shades of vibration which it could gain in no other way, and this, when transmitted through (*b*) to (*a*), means the development of the ego.

Unfortunately the course of events does not always follow the ideal plan of working indicated above. When the control of (*a*) is feeble, it sometimes happens that (c) becomes so thoroughly enmeshed in lower matter that it actually identifies itself with this matter and forgets for the time its high estate, and thinks of itself as the whole ego. If the matter of the lower mental plane, we shall then have down here on the physical plane a man who is wholly materialistic. He may be keenly intellectual perhaps, but not spiritual; he may very likely be intolerant of spirituality and quite unable to comprehend or appreciate it. He may probably call himself practical, matter-of-fact, unsentimental, while in reality he is hard as the nether millstone, and because of that hardness his life is a failure, and he is making no progress.

If the matter in which he is so fatally entangled be astral, he will be (on the physical plane) one who thinks only of his own gratification, who is absolutely ruthless when in pursuit of some object which he strongly desires, a man utterly unprincipled and of brutal selfishness. Such a man lives in his passions, just as the man enmeshed in mental matter lives in his mind. Cases such as these have been spoken of in our literature as "lost souls," though not irretrievably lost. Madame Blavatsky says of them:

> There is, however, still hope for a person who has lost his Higher Soul through his vices, while he is yet in the body. He may still be redeemed and made to turn on his material nature. For either an intense feeling of repentance, or one single earnest appeal to the Ego that has fled, or best of all, an active effort to amend one's ways, may bring the Higher Ego back again. The thread of connection is not altogether broken. (*Secret Doctrine*, iii. 527.)

These are cases in which (c) has asserted itself against (b), and pressed it back towards (a); the arm has become attenuated and almost paralyzed, its strength and substance being withdrawn into the body, while the hand has set up for itself, and makes on its own account jerky and spasmodic movements which are not controlled by the brain. If the separation could become perfect it would correspond to an amputation at the wrist, but this very rarely takes place during physical existence, though only so much of communication remains as is necessary to keep the personality alive.

As Madame Blavatsky says, such a case is not entirely hopeless, for even at the last moment fresh life may be poured through that paralyzed arm if a sufficiently strong effort be made, and thus the ego may be enabled to recover some proportion of (c), as he has already recovered most of (b). Nevertheless, such a life has been wasted, for even if the man just contrives to escape serious loss, at any rate nothing has been gained, and much time has been frittered away.

It may well be thought incredible that such men as I have described could in any case escape serious loss; but, fortunately for our possibilities of progress, the laws under which we live are such that to achieve a really serious loss is no easy matter. The reason for that may perhaps be made clear by the following considerations.

All the activities that we call evil, whether they are working as selfish thoughts on the mental plane or as selfish emotions on the astral plane, invariably show themselves as vibrations of the coarser matter of those planes, belonging to their lower levels. On the other hand, every good and unselfish thought or emotion sets in vibration some of the higher types of matter on its plane; and because that finer matter is far more easily moved, any given amount of force spent in good thought or feeling produces perhaps a hundred times as much result as precisely the same amount of force sent out into the coarser matter. If this were not so, it is obvious that the ordinary man could never make any progress at all.

We shall probably do the quite undeveloped man of the world no injustice if we assume that ninety per cent of his thought and feeling is self-centered, even if not actually selfish; if ten per cent of it is spiritual and unselfish, he must already be rising somewhat above the average. Clearly if these proportions produced corresponding results, the vast majority of humanity would take nine steps backwards for every one forwards, and we should have a retrogression so rapid that a few incarnations would deposit us in the animal kingdom out of which we evolved. Happily for us the effect of ten per cent of force directed to good ends enormously outweighs that ninety per cent devoted to selfish purposes, and so on the whole such a man makes an appreciable advance from life to life. A man who has even one per cent of good to show makes a slight advance, so it will be readily understood that a man whose account balances exactly, so that there is neither advance nor retrogression, must have been living a distinctly evil life; while to obtain an actual descent in evolution a person must be an unusually consistent villain.

Thanks to this beneficent law the world is steadily but slowly evolving, even though we see round us all the while so much that is undesirable; and even such men as I have described may not after all fall very far. What they have lost is rather time and opportunity than actual position in evolution; but to lose time and opportunity means always additional suffering.

To see what they have lost and what they have failed to do, let us revert for a moment to the analogy of investment. The ego expects to recover that which he puts out to interest in lower matter—the block that we have called (c)—and he expects it to be improved both in quality and quantity. Its quality is better because it has become much more awake, and capable of instant and accurate response to a far more varied gamut of vibrations than before—a capacity which (c) when reabsorbed necessarily communicated to (a), though of course the store of energy which made such a powerful wave in (c) creates only a ripple when distributed throughout the substance of (a).

It should be noted here that although the vehicles, containing as they do the grosser as well as the finer types of the matter of their respective planes, can respond to and express evil thoughts and emotions, and although their excitement under such vibrations can produce perturbation in the entangled causal matter (c), it is quite impossible for that matter (c) to reproduce those vibrations or to communicate them to (a) or (b). Matter of the three higher mental levels can no more vibrate at the rate of the lowest plane than the string of a violin tuned to a certain pitch can be made to produce a note lower than that pitch.

(C) should be increased in quantity as well as quality because the causal body, like all other vehicles, is constantly changing its matter, and when special exercise is given to a certain part of it, that part grows in size and becomes stronger, precisely as a physical muscle does when it is used. Every earth-life is an opportunity carefully calculated for such development in quality and quantity as is most needed by the ego; a failure to use that opportunity means the trouble and delays of another similar incarnation, its sufferings probably aggravated by the additional bad karma incurred.

Against the increment which the ego has a right to expect from each incarnation we must offset a certain amount of loss which in the earlier stages is scarcely avoidable. In order to be effective the entanglement with lower matter must be very intimate, and it is found that when that is so, it is scarcely ever possible to recover every particle, especially from the connection with the astral vehicle. When the time comes for separation from that it is almost always a shade in which the ego remains partially entangled and not a mere shell of disintegrating astral matter that is left behind on the astral plane; and that very distinction means that something of the causal material is lost. Except in the case of an unusually bad life, however, this amount should be much smaller than that gained by growth, and so there should be on the whole a profit on the transaction. With such men as I have described—men living entirely in their passions or their minds—there would be no gain either in quality or quantity, since the vibrations would not be such as could be stored in the causal body; and on the other hand, as the entanglement had been so strong, there would certainly be considerable loss when the separation took place.

We must not allow the analogy of the arm and hand to mislead us in thinking of (*b*) and (*c*) as permanent appanages of the ego. During a life-period they may be considered as separate, but at the end of each life-period they withdraw into (*a*), and the result of their experience is distributed, as it were, through the whole of its substance; so that when the time comes for the ego to put part of himself out into incarnation once more, he does not stretch out again the old (*b*) and (*c*), for they have been absorbed in him and become part of him, just as a cupful of water emptied into a bucket becomes part of the water in the bucket and cannot be separated from it.

Any coloring matter which was present in the cup is distributed (though in paler tint) through the whole bucketful of water; and that coloring matter may be taken as symbolizing the qualities developed by experience. Just as it would be impossible to take out again from the bucket exactly the same cupful of water, so the ego cannot again put out the same (*b*) and (*c*). The plan is one to which he was accustomed before he became a separate ego at all, for it is identical with that pursued by the group-soul, except that the latter puts down many tentacles simultaneously, while the ego puts forth only one at a time. Therefore the personality in each new incarnation is a different one, though the ego behind it remains the same.

3. Cases in which the personality captures the part of the ego which is put down, and actually breaks away are, happily, excessively rare, but they have happened, and they represent the most

appalling catastrophe that can occur to the ego concerned. This time (c), instead of repelling (b) and driving it gradually back into (a), by degrees absorbs (b) and detaches it from (a). This can only be accomplished by determined persistence in deliberate evil— black magic, in short. Reverting to our former analogies, this is equivalent to amputation at the shoulder, or to the loss by the ego of nearly all his available capital. Fortunately for him he cannot lose everything, because (b) and (c) together are only a small proportion of (a), and behind (a) is the great undeveloped portion of the ego on the first and second mental sub-planes. Mercifully a man, however incredibly foolish or wicked, cannot completely wreck himself, for he cannot bring that higher part of the causal body into activity until he has reached a level at which such evil is unthinkable.

Now that the central point of our immersion in matter is passed in the scheme of evolution, the whole force of the universe is pressing upwards towards unity, and the man who is willing to make all his life an intelligent cooperation with nature gains as part of his reward an ever-increasing perception of the reality of this unity. But on the other hand it is obvious that men may set themselves in opposition to nature and, instead of working unselfishly for the good of all, may debase every faculty they possess for purely selfish ends; and of them also, as of the others, the old saying is true, "Verily I say unto you, they have their reward." They spend their lives in striving for separateness, and for a long time they attain it. But it is said that their fate of experiencing the sensation of being utterly alone in space is the most awful fate that can ever befall the sons of men.

This extraordinary development of selfishness is the characteristic of the black magician, and it is among their ranks only that men can be found who are in danger of this terrible fate. Many and loathsome are their varieties, but they may all be classed in one or other of two great divisions. They both use such occult arts as they possess for purely selfish purposes, but these purposes differ.

In the commoner and less formidable type the object pursued is the gratification of sensual desire of some sort, and naturally the result of a life devoted to nothing but that is to center the man's energy in the desire-body; so that if the man who works on these lines has succeeded in killing out from himself every unselfish or affectionate feeling, every spark of higher impulse, naturally nothing is left but a remorseless, ruthless monster of lust, who finds himself after death neither able nor desirous to rise above the lowest sub-division of the astral plane. The whole of such mind as he has is absolutely in the grip of desire, and when the struggle takes place the ego can recover none of it, and finds himself seriously weakened in consequence.

By his carelessness in permitting this the ego has for the time cut himself off from the current of evolution, from the mighty wave of the life of the Logos, and so, until he can return to incarnation, he stands (what appears to him to be) outside that life in the condition of avichi, the waveless. Even when he does return to incarnation it cannot be among those whom he has known before, for he has not enough available capital left to provide ensoulment for a mind and body at his previous level. He must now be content to occupy vehicles of a far less evolved type; so that he has thrown himself far back in evolution and must climb over again many rungs of the ladder. It has been said that he may even throw himself so far back that he may be unable to find upon the world in its present condition any type of human body low enough for the manifestation which he now requires, so that he may even be incapacitated from taking any further part in this scheme of evolution, and may therefore have to wait in a kind of condition of suspended animation for the commencement of another.

Meanwhile what of the amputated personality? It is no longer a permanent evolving entity, but it remains full of vigorous and wholly evil life, entirely without remorse or responsibility. As the fate before it is disintegration amidst the unpleasant surroundings of what is called the "eighth sphere", it naturally tries to maintain some sort of existence on the physical plane as long as possible. Vampirism of some kind is its sole means of prolonging its baneful existence, and when that fails it has been known to seize upon any available body, driving out the lawful owner. The body chosen might very probably be that of a child, both because it might be expected to last longer and because an ego which had not yet really taken hold of its body could be more easily dispossessed. In spite of its frenzied efforts its power seems soon to fail, and I believe there is no instance on record of its successfully stealing a second body after its first theft is worn out. The creature is a demon of the most terrible type—a monster for which there is no permanent place in the scheme of evolution to which we belong.

Its natural tendency therefore is to drift *out* of this evolution, and to be drawn by the irresistible force of law into that astral cesspool which in earlier Theosophical writings was called the eighth sphere, because what passes into it stands outside the ring of seven worlds, and cannot return into their evolution. There, surrounded by loathsome relics of all of the concentrated vileness of the ages that are past, burning ever with desire, yet without possibility of satisfaction, this monstrosity slowly decays, its mental and causal matter being thus at last set free—never indeed to rejoin the ego from which it has torn itself, but to be distributed among the other matter of the plane to enter gradually into fresh combinations, and so put to better uses. It is consoling to know that such entities are so rare as to be practically unknown, and that they have the power to seize only those who have in their nature pronounced defects of kindred type.

But there is another type of the black magician, in outward appearance more respectable, yet really even more dangerous, because more powerful. This is the man who instead of giving himself up altogether to sensuality of one kind or another, sets before himself the goal of a more refined but not less unscrupulous selfishness. His object is the acquisition of an occult power higher and wider indeed, but to be used always for his own gratification and advancement, to further his own ambition or satisfy his own revenge.

In order to gain this he adopts the most rigid asceticism as regards mere fleshly desires, and starves out the grosser particles of his astral body as perseveringly as does the pupil of the Great White Brotherhood. But though it is only a less material kind of desire with which he will allow his mind to become entangled, the center of his energy is none the less entirely in his personality, and when at the end of the astral life the time of the separation comes, the ego is able to recover no whit of his investment. For the man therefore the result is much the same as in the former case, except that he will remain in touch with the personality much longer, and will to some extent share its experiences so far as it is possible for an ego to share them.

The fate of that personality, however, is very different. The comparatively tenuous astral integument is not strong enough to hold him for any length of time on the astral plane, and yet he has entirely lost touch with the heaven-world which should have been his habitat. For the whole effort of the man's life has been to kill out such thoughts as naturally find their result at that level. His one endeavor has been to oppose natural evolution, to separate himself from the great whole and to war against it; and as far as the personality goes he has succeeded. It is cut off from the light and life of the solar system; all that is left to it is the sense of absolute isolation, of being alone in the universe.

We see therefore that in this rarer case the lost personality practically shares the fate of the ego from which is in process of detaching itself. But in the case of the ego such an experience is only temporary, although it may last for what we should call a very long time. The end of it for him will be reincarnation and a fresh opportunity. For the personality, however, that end of it is disintegration—the invariable end of that which has cut itself off from its source; but through what stages of horror the lost personality passes before that is reached, who shall say. Yet, be it remembered that neither of these states is eternal—that neither of them can in any case be reached except by deliberate life-long persistence in evil.

I have heard from Mrs. Besant of yet another even more remote possibility, of which I have never myself seen an instance. Just as (c) may absorb (b) and revolt against(a), set up on its own account and break away, it is just within the limits of practicability that the deadly disease of separateness and selfishness may infest (a) also. It too may be absorbed into the monstrous growth of evil and may be torn away from the undeveloped portion of the ego, so that the causal body itself may be hardened and carried away, instead of only the personality.

If this be so, it constitutes yet a fourth group, and would correspond not to an amputation, but to an entire destruction of the body. Such an ego could not reincarnate in the human race; ego though it be, it will fall into the depths of animal life, and would need at least a whole chain-period to regain the status which it had lost. But this, though theoretically possible, is scarcely conceivable. Yet it will be noted that even *then* the undeveloped part of the ego remains as the vehicle of the monad.

We learn that millions of backward egos, unable as yet to bear the strain of the higher evolution, will fall out in the middle of the fifth round and come along on the crest of the following wave; that those who live selfishly, whether in the intellect or the passions, do so at their own proper peril, and at the serious risk of much sorrow and loss; that those who are so foolish as to dabble in black magic may bring upon themselves horrors before which imagination shrinks appalled; but that the term "lost soul" is, after all, a misnomer; since every man is a spark of the divine fire, and therefore can never under any circumstances be lost or extinguished. The will of the Logos is man's evolution. In our blindness we may for a time resist Him, but to Him time is naught, and if we cannot see today He waits patiently till tomorrow, but always in the end His will is done.

The Focus of Consciousness

The consciousness in man can only be focussed in one vehicle at a time, though he may be simultaneously conscious through the others in a vaguer way. If you will hold up a finger in front of your face you will find that you can so focus your eyes as to see the finger perfectly. At the same time you will see the wall and furniture behind the finger, but not perfectly, because they are out of focus. In a moment you can change the focus of your eyes, so that you will see the wall and the furniture perfectly; in that case you will still see the finger, but will see it only dimly, because it in turn is now out of focus.

Precisely in the same way if a man who has developed astral and mental consciousness focusses himself in the physical brain as in ordinary life, he will see perfectly the physical bodies of his friends, and will at the same time see their astral and mental bodies, but only somewhat dimly. In far less than a moment he can change that focus so that he will see the astral quite fully and perfectly. In that case he will still see the mental and physical bodies, but not in full detail. The same thing is true of the mental sight and of the sight of higher planes.

You ask how it is possible for an entity functioning on the astral plane to be aware of a physical accident or to hear a physical cry. It would not be the physical cry that he would hear; physical sounds assuredly produce an effect upon the astral plane, though I do not think that we should be quite correct in calling that effect sound. Any cry which had in it strong feeling or emotion would produce a strong effect upon the astral plane, and would convey exactly the same idea there as here. In the case of an accident the rush of emotion caused by the pain or the fright would flame out like a great light, and could not fail to attract the attention of a seer if he were anywhere near. A case in which this very thing occurred is related in *Invisible Helpers*—a case in which a boy fell over a cliff; and was supported and comforted by Cyril until physical help could be brought.

Force-Centers

In each of our vehicles there are certain force-centers which in Sanskrit are called chakras—a word which signifies a wheel or revolving disc. These are points of connection at which force flows from one vehicle to another. They may easily be seen in the etheric double, where they show themselves as saucer-like depressions or vortices in its surface. They are often spoken of as corresponding to certain physical organs; but it must be remembered that the etheric force-center is not in the interior of the body, but on the surface of the etheric double, which projects a quarter of an inch beyond the outline of the denser matter.

The centers which are usually employed in occult development are seven, and they are situated in the following parts of the body: (1) the base of the spine; (2) the navel; (3) the spleen; (4) the heart; (5) the throat; (6) the space between the eyebrows; and (7) the top of the head. There are other force-centers in the body besides these, but they are not employed by students of the white magic. It may be remembered that Madame Blavatsky speaks of three others which she calls the lower centers: there are schools which use these, but the dangers connected with them are so serious that we should consider their awakening as the greatest of misfortunes.

These seven are often described as corresponding to the seven colors and to the notes of the musical scale; and in the Indian books certain letters of the alphabet and certain forms of vitality are mentioned as attached to each of them. They are also poetically described as resembling flowers, and to each of them a certain number of petals is assigned.

It must be remembered that they are vortices of etheric matter, and that they are all in rapid rotation. Into each of these open mouths, at right angles to the plane of the whirling disc or saucer, rushes a force from the astral world (which we will call the primary force)—one of the forces of the Logos. That force is sevenfold in its nature, and all its forms operate in all the centers, though in each of them one of the forms is always greatly predominant.

This inrush of force brings the divine life into the physical body, and without it that body could not exist. These centers through which the force can enter are therefore actually necessary to the existence of the vehicle, and so are in operation in every one, but they may be whirling with very different degrees of activity. Their particles may be in comparatively sluggish motion, just forming the necessary vortex for the force and no more, or they may be glowing and pulsating with living light so that an enormously greater amount of force passes through them, with the result that various additional faculties and possibilities are opened to the ego as he functions on that plane.

Now those forces which rush into the center from without set up at right angles to themselves (that is to say, in the surface of the etheric double) secondary forces in undulatory circular motion, just as a bar-magnet thrust into an induction coil produces a current of electricity which flows round the coil at right angles to the axis or direction of the magnet. The primary force itself having entered the vortex, radiates from it again at right angles, but in straight lines, as though the center of the vortex were the hub of a wheel, and the radiations of the primary force its spokes. The number of these "spokes" differs in the different force-centers, and determines the number of "petals" which each of them exhibits.

Each of these secondary forces, which sweep round the saucer-like depression, has its own characteristic wave-length, just as has light of a certain color; but instead of moving in a straight line as light does, it moves along in certain relatively large undulations of various sizes, each of which is some multiple of the smaller wave-lengths within it, though the exact proportions have not as yet been calculated. The number of undulations is determined by the number of spokes in the wheel, and the secondary force weaves itself under and over the radiating currents of the primary just as basket-work might be woven round the spokes of a carriage-wheel. The wave-lengths are infinitesimal, and probably some thousands of them are included within one of the undulations. As the forces rush round in the vortex, these undulations of different sizes, crossing one another in this basket-work pattern, produce an appearance which is not inaptly described in the Hindu books as resembling the petals of a flower; or it is still more like certain saucers or shallow vases of wavy iridescent glass which I have seen in Venice. All of these undulations or petals have that shimmering iridescent effect, like mother-of-pearl, yet each of them has usually its own predominant color.

In the ordinary men, in whom these centers are just active enough to be channels for sufficient force to keep his body alive, these colors glow with a comparatively dull light; but in those in whom the centers have been aroused and are in full activity they are of blinding brilliancy, and the centers themselves, which have gradually grown from a diameter of about two inches to the size of an ordinary saucer, are blazing and coruscating like miniature suns.

The first center, at the base of the spine, has a primary force which radiates out in four spokes, and therefore arranges its undulations so as to give the effect of its being divided into quadrants, with hollows between them. This makes it seem as though marked with the sign of the cross, and for that reason the cross is often used to symbolize this center, and sometimes a flaming cross is taken to indicate the serpent-fire which resides in it. When aroused into full activity this center is fiery orange-red in color, corresponding closely with the type of vitality which is sent down to it from the splenic center. Indeed, it will be noticed that in the case of every one of these centers a similar correspondence with the color of its vitality may be seen.

The second center, at the navel or solar plexus, receives a primary force with ten radiations, so it vibrates in such a manner as to divide itself into ten undulations or petals. It is very closely associated with feelings and emotions of various kinds. Its predominant color is a curious blending of various shades of red, though there is also a great deal of green in it.

The third center, at the spleen, is devoted to the specialization, subdivision and dispersion of the vitality which comes to us from the sun. That vitality is poured out again from it in six horizontal streams, the seventh variety being drawn into the hub of the wheel. This center therefore has six petals or undulations, and is specially radiant, glowing and sun-like.

The fourth center, at the heart, is also of a glowing golden color, and each of its quadrants is divided into three parts, which gives it twelve undulations, because its primary force makes for it twelve spokes.

The fifth center, at the throat, has sixteen spokes, and therefore sixteen apparent divisions. There is a good deal of blue in it, but its general effect is silvery and gleaming, with a kind of suggestion as of moonlight upon rippling water.

The sixth center, between the eyebrows, has the appearance of being divided into halves, the one predominantly rose-colored, though with a great deal of yellow about it, and the other predominantly a kind of purplish-blue, again closely agreeing with the colors of the special types of vitality that vivify it. Perhaps it is for this reason that this center is mentioned in Indian books as having only two petals, though if we are to count undulations of the same character as those of the previous centers we shall find that each half is subdivided into forty-eight of these, making ninety-six in all, because its primary force has that number of radiations.

The seventh, the center at the top of the head, is when stirred into full activity perhaps the most resplendent of all, full of indescribable chromatic effects and vibrating with almost inconceivable rapidity. It is described in Indian books as thousand-petalled, and really this is not very far from the truth, the number of the radiations of its primary force in the outer circle being nine hundred and sixty. In addition to this it has a feature which is possessed by none of the other centers—a sort of subsidiary whirlpool of gleaming white flushed with gold in its heart—a minor activity which has twelve undulations of its own.

I have heard it suggested that each of the different petals of these force-centers represents a moral quality, and that the development of that quality brings the center into activity. I have not yet met with any facts which confirm this, nor am I able to see exactly how it can be, because the appearance is produced by certain quite definite and easily recognizable forces, and the petals in any particular center are either active or not active according as these forces have or have not been aroused, and their development seems to me to have no more connection with morality than has the development of the biceps. I have certainly met with persons in whom some of the centers were in full activity, though the moral development was by no means exceptionally high, whereas in other persons of high spirituality and the noblest possible morality the centers were not yet vitalized at all, so that there does not seem to me to be any connection between the two developments.

Besides the keeping alive of the physical vehicle, these force-centers have another function, which comes into play only when they are awakened into full activity. Each of these etheric centers corresponds to an astral center though as the astral center is a vortex in four dimensions it has an extension in a direction quite different from the etheric, and consequently is by no means always co-terminous with it, though some part is always coincident. The etheric vortex is always on the surface of the etheric body, but the astral center is frequently quite in the interior of that vehicle.

The function of each of these etheric centers when fully aroused is to bring down into physical consciousness whatever may be the quality inherent in the astral center which corresponds to it; so, before cataloguing the results to be obtained by arousing the etheric centers into activity, it may be well to consider what is done by each of the astral centers, although these latter are already in full activity in all cultured people of the later races. What effect, then, has the quickening of each of these astral centers produced in the astral body?

The first of these centers, that at the base of the spine, is the home of that mysterious force called the serpent-fire or, in *The Voice of the Silence*, the World's Mother. I will say more about this force later; for the moment let us consider its effects on the astral centers. This force exists on all planes, and by its activity the rest of the centers are aroused. We must think of the astral body as having been originally an almost inert mass, with nothing but the vaguest consciousness, with no definite power of doing anything, and no clear knowledge of the world which surrounded it. The first thing that happened, then, was the awakening of that force in the man at the astral level. When awakened it moved on to the second center, corresponding to the navel, and vivified it, thereby awakening in the astral body the power of feeling—a sensitiveness to all sorts of influences, though without as yet anything like the definite comprehension that comes from seeing or hearing.

Then it moved on to the third, that corresponding to the physical spleen, and through it vitalized the whole astral body, enabling the person to travel consciously, on the astral plane, though with only a vague conception as yet of what he encountered on his journeys.

The fourth center, when awakened, endowed the man with the power to comprehend and sympathize with the vibrations of other astral entities, so that he could instinctively understand their feelings.

The awakening of the fifth, that corresponding to the throat, gave him the power of hearing on the astral plane—that is to say, it caused the development of that sense which in the astral world produces on our consciousness the effect which on the physical plane we call hearing.

The development of the sixth, that corresponding to the center between the eyebrows, in a similar manner produced astral sight—the power to perceive definitely the shape and nature of astral objects, instead of vaguely sensing their presence.

The arousing of the seventh, that corresponding to the top of the head, rounded off and completed for him the astral life, and endowed him with the perfection of its faculties.

With regard to this center a certain difference seems to exist according to the type to which men belong. For many of us the astral vortices corresponding to the sixth and seventh of these centers both converge upon the pituitary body, and for those people the pituitary body is practically the only direct link between the physical and the higher planes. Another type of person, however, while still attaching the sixth center to the pituitary body, bend or slant the seventh until its vortex coincides with the atrophied organ called the pineal gland, which is by people of that type vivified and made into a line of communication directly passing through the intermediate astral plane in the ordinary way. It was for this type that Madame Blavatsky was writing when she laid such emphasis upon the awakening of that organ.

Thus these centers to some extent take the place of sense-organs for the astral body, and yet without proper qualification that expression would be decidedly a misleading one. It must never be forgotten that though, in order to make ourselves intelligible, we constantly have to speak of astral seeing or astral hearing, all that we really mean by those expressions is the faculty of responding to such vibrations as convey to the man's consciousness, when he is functioning in his astral body, information of the same character as that conveyed to him by his eyes and ears while he is in the physical body.

But in the entirely different astral conditions specialized organs are not necessary for the attainment of this result. There is matter in every part of the astral body which is capable of such response, and consequently the man functioning in that vehicle sees equally well the objects behind him, above him, and beneath him, without needing to turn his head. The centers, therefore, cannot be described as organs in the ordinary sense of the word, since it is not through them that the man sees or hears, as he does here through the eyes and ears. Yet it is upon their vivification that the power of exercising these astral senses depends, each of them as it is developed giving to the whole astral body the power of response to a new set of vibrations.

As all the particles of the astral body are constantly flowing and swirling about like those of boiling water, all of them in turn pass through each of the centers or vortices, so that each center in its turn evokes in all the particles of the body the power of receptivity to a certain set of vibrations, and so all the astral senses are active equally in all parts of the body. But even when these astral senses are fully awakened it by no means follows that the man will be able to bring through his physical body any consciousness of their action.

While all this astral awakening was taking place, then, the man in his physical consciousness knew nothing whatever of it. The only way in which the dense body can be brought to share all these advantages is by repeating that process of awakening with the etheric centers. That is to be achieved precisely in the same way as it was done upon the astral plane—that is to say, by the arousing of the serpent-fire, which exists clothed in etheric matter on the physical plane, and sleeps in the corresponding etheric center, that at the base of the spine.

In this case the arousing is done by a determined and long-continued effort of the will, and to bring that first center into full activity is precisely to awaken the serpent-fire. When once that is aroused, it is by its tremendous force that the other centers are vivified. Its effect on the other etheric centers is to bring into the physical consciousness the powers which were aroused by the development of their corresponding astral centers.

When the second of the etheric centers, that at the navel, comes into activity the man begins in the physical body to be conscious of all kinds of astral influences, vaguely feeling that some of them are friendly and others hostile, or that some places are pleasant and others unpleasant, without in the least knowing why.

When the third center, that at the spleen, is awakened, the man is enabled to remember his vague astral journeys, though sometimes only very partially. The effect of a slight and accidental stimulation of this center is often to produce half-remembrance of a blissful sensation of flying through the air.

Stimulation of the fourth, that at the heart, makes the man instinctively aware of the joys and sorrows of others, and sometimes even causes him to reproduce in himself by sympathy their physical aches and pains.

The arousing of the fifth, that at the throat, enables him to hear voices, which sometimes make all kinds of suggestions to him. Also sometimes he hears music, or other less pleasant sounds. When it is fully working it makes the man clairaudient as far as the etheric and astral planes are concerned.

When the sixth, between the eye-brows, becomes vivified, the man begins to see things, to have various sorts of waking visions, sometimes of places, sometimes of people. In its earlier development, when it is only just beginning to be awakened, it often means nothing more than half-seeing landscapes and clouds of color. The full arousing of this brings about clairvoyance.

The center between the eyebrows is connected with sight in yet another way. It is through it that the power of magnification of minute physical objects is exercised. A tiny flexible tube of etheric matter is projected from the center of it, resembling a microscopic snake with an eye at the end of it. This is the special organ used in that form of clairvoyance, and the eye at the end of it can be expanded or contracted, the effect being to change the power of magnification according to the size of the object which is being examined. This is what is meant in ancient books when mention is made of the capacity to make oneself large or small at will. To examine an atom one develops an organ of vision commensurate in size with the atom. This little snake projecting from the center of the forehead at the etheric level was symbolized upon the head-dress of the Pharaoh of Egypt, who as the chief priest of his country was supposed to possess this among other occult powers.

When the seventh center is awakened the man is able by passing through it to leave his body in full consciousness, and also to return to it without the usual break, so that his consciousness will be continuous through night and day. When the fire has been passed through all these centers in a certain order (which varies for different types of people) the consciousness becomes continuous up to the entry into the heaven-world at the end of the life on the astral plane, no difference being made by either the temporary separation from the physical body during sleep or the permanent division at death.

Before this is done, however, the man may have many glimpses of the astral world, for especially strong vibrations may at any time galvanize one or other of the centers into temporary activity, without arousing the serpent-fire at all; or it may happen that the fire may be partially roused, and in this way also partial clairvoyance may be produced for the time. For this fire exists in seven layers or seven degrees of force, and it often happens that a man who exerts his will in the effort to arouse it may succeed in affecting one layer only, and so when he thinks that he has done the work he may find it ineffective, and may have to do it all over again many times, digging gradually deeper and deeper, until not only the surface is stirred but the very heart of the fire is in full activity.

The Serpent-Fire

As we know it, this serpent-fire (called in Sanskrit kundalini) is the manifestation on the physical plane of one of the great world-forces—one of the powers of the Logos. You know that what we call electricity is a manifestation of one of His forces, and that that force may produce energies, such as heat, light and motion. Another of His forces is vitality—what is sometimes called prana, but this is not interchangeable with any of those other forms which we have just mentioned. We may say then that prana and electricity are, as it were, the lower ends of two of His streams of force.

This serpent-fire may be taken as the lower end of another of His streams, the physical plane manifestation of another of the manifold aspects of His power. Like prana, it exists on all planes of which we know anything; but it is the expression of it in etheric matter with which we have to do. It is not convertible into either prana or electricity, and does not seem to be affected in any way by either. I have seen as much as a million and a quarter volts of electricity put into a human body, so that when the man held out his arm towards the wall huge flames rushed out from his fingers, yet he felt nothing unusual, nor was he in the least burnt unless he accidentally touched some external object; but even this enormous display of power had no effect whatever upon the serpent-fire.

In *The Voice of the Silence* this force is called "the Fiery Power" and "the World's Mother." There is much reason for all these strange names, for it is in very truth like liquid fire as it rushes through the body, and the course through which it ought to move is a spiral one like the coils of a serpent. It is called the World's Mother because through it our various vehicles may be vivified, so that the higher worlds may open before us in succession.

In the body of man its home, as we have said, is at the base of the spine, and for the ordinary person it lies there unawakened, and its very presence unsuspected, during the whole of his life; and it is indeed far better to allow it thus to remain dormant until the man has made definite moral development, until his will is strong enough to control it and his thoughts pure enough to enable him to face its awakening without injury. No one should experiment with it without definite instruction from a teacher who thoroughly understands the subject, for the dangers connected with it are very real and terribly serious. Some of them are purely physical. Its uncontrolled movement often produces intense physical pain, and it may readily tear tissues and even destroy physical life. This, however, is the least of the evils of which it is capable, for it may do permanent injury to vehicles higher than the physical.

One very common effect of rousing it prematurely is that it rushes downwards in the body instead of upwards, and thus excites the most undesirable passions—excites them and intensifies their effects to such a degree that it becomes absolutely impossible for the man to resist them, because a force has been brought into play in whose presence he is as helpless as a swimmer before the jaws of a shark. Such men become satyrs, monsters of depravity, because they are in the grasp of a force which is out of all proportion to the ordinary human power of resistance. They may probably gain certain supernormal powers, but these will be such as will bring them into touch with a lower order of evolution with which humanity is intended to hold no commerce, and to escape from its awful thraldom may take them more than one incarnation. I am not in any way exaggerating the horror of this thing, as a person to whom it was all a matter of hearsay might unwittingly do. I have myself been consulted by people upon whom this awful fate has already come, and I have seen with my own eyes what happened to them. There is a school of black magic which purposely uses this power in this way, in order that through it may be vivified those lower force-centers which are never used by the followers of the Good Law.

Even apart from this greatest of its dangers, its premature unfoldment has many other unpleasant possibilities. It intensifies everything in man's nature, and it reaches the lower and evil qualities more readily than the good. In the mental body, for example, ambition is very readily aroused, and soon swells to an incredibly inordinate degree. It would be likely to bring with it a great intensification of the power of intellect, but at the same time it would produce abnormal and satanic pride, such as is quite inconceivable to the ordinary man. It is not wise for a man to think that he is prepared to cope with any force that may arise within his body; this is no ordinary force, but something resistless. Assuredly no uninstructed man should ever try to awaken it, and if such a one finds that it has been aroused by accident he should at once consult some one who fully understands these matters.

It may be noticed that I have specially and intentionally refrained from explaining how this arousing is to be done, or mentioning the order in which the force (when aroused) should be passed through these various centers, for that should by no means be attempted except at the express suggestion of a Master, who will watch over His pupil during the various stages of the experiment.

I most solemnly warn all students against making any effort whatever in the direction of awakening these tremendous forces, except under such qualified tuition, for I have myself seen many cases of the terrible effects which follow from ignorant and ill-advised meddling with these very serious matters. The force is a tremendous reality, one of the great basic facts of nature, and most emphatically it is not a thing to be played with, or to be lightly taken in hand, for to experiment with it without understanding it is far more dangerous than it would be for a child to play with nitroglycerine. As is very truly said in the *Hathayoga-pradipika*: "It gives liberation to yogis and bondage to fools." (iii. 107.)

In matters such as these, students so often seem to think that some special exception to the laws of nature will be made in their case, that some special intervention of providence will save them from the consequences of their folly. Assuredly nothing of that sort will happen, and the man who wantonly provokes an explosion is quite likely to become its first victim. It would save much trouble and disappointment if students could be induced to understand that in all matters connected with occultism we mean just exactly and literally what we say, and that it is applicable in every case without exception. For there is no such thing as favoritism in the working of the great laws of the universe.

Everybody wants to try all possible experiments; everybody is convinced that he is quite ready for the highest possible teaching and for any sort of development, and no one is willing to work patiently along at the improvement of character, and to devote his time and his energies to doing something useful for the work of the Society, waiting for all these other things until a Master shall announce that he is ready for them. The old aphorism still remains true: "Seek ye first the kingdom of God and His righteousness, and all these things shall be added unto you."

There are some cases in which the fire wakes spontaneously, so that a dull glow is felt; it may even begin to move of itself, though this is rare. In this latter case it would be likely to cause great pain, as, since the passages are not prepared for it, it would have to clear its way by actually burning up a great deal of etheric dross —a process that cannot but engender suffering. When it thus awakes of itself or is accidentally aroused, it usually tries to rush up the interior of the spine, instead of following the spiral course into which the occultist is trained to guide it. If it be possible, the will should be set in motion to arrest its onward rush, but if that proves to be impossible (as is most likely) no alarm need be felt. It will probably rush out through the head and escape into the surrounding atmosphere, and it is likely that no harm will result beyond a slight weakening. Nothing worse than a temporary loss of consciousness need be apprehended. The really appalling dangers are connected not with its upward rush, but with the possibility of its turning downwards and inwards.

Its principal function in connection with occult development is that by being sent through the force-centers in the etheric body, as above described, it vivifies these centers and makes them available as gates of connection between the physical and astral bodies. It is said in *The Voice of the Silence* that when the serpent-fire reaches the center between the eyebrows and fully vivifies it, it confers the power of hearing the voice of the Master—which means in this case the voice of the ego or higher self. The reason for this statement is that when the pituitary body is brought into working order it forms a perfect link with the astral vehicle, so that through it all communications from within can be received.

All the higher force-centers have presently to be awakened, and each must be made responsive to all kinds of astral influences from the various astral sub-planes. This development will come to all in due course, but most people cannot gain it during the present incarnation, if it is the first in which they have begun to take these matters seriously in hand. Some Indians might succeed in doing so, as their bodies are by heredity more adaptable than most others; but it is really for the majority the work of a later round altogether. The conquest of the serpent-fire has to be repeated in each incarnation, since the vehicles are new each time, but after it has been once thoroughly achieved these repetitions will be an easy matter. It must be remembered that its action varies with different types of people; some, for example, would see the higher self rather than hear its voice. Again, this connection with the higher has many stages; for the personality it means the influence of the ego, but for the ego himself it means the power of the monad, and for the monad in turn it means to become a conscious expression of the Logos.

It may be of use if I mention my own experience in this matter. In the earlier part of my residence in India twenty-five years ago I made no effort to rouse the fire—indeed not knowing very much about it, and having the opinion that, in order to do anything with it, it was necessary to be born with a psychically gifted body, which I did not possess. But one day one of the Masters made a suggestion to me with regard to a certain kind of meditation which would evoke this force. Naturally I at once put the suggestion into practice, and in course of time was successful. I have no doubt, however, that He watched the experiment, and would have checked me if it had become dangerous. I am told that there are Indian ascetics who teach this to their pupils, of course keeping them under careful supervision during the process. But I do not myself know of any such, nor should I have confidence in them unless they were specially recommended by some one whom I knew to be possessed of real knowledge.

People often ask me what I advise them to do with regard to the arousing of this force. I advise them to do exactly what I myself did. I recommend them to throw themselves into theosophical work and wait until they receive a definite command from some Master who will undertake to superintend their psychic development, continuing in the meantime all the ordinary exercises of meditation that are known to them. They should not care in the least whether such development comes in this incarnation or in the next, but should regard the matter from the point of view of the ego and not of the personality, feeling absolutely certain that the Masters are always watching for those whom they can help, that it is entirely impossible for any one to be overlooked, and that they will unquestionably give their directions when they think that the right time has come.

I have never heard that there is any sort of age limit with regard to the development, and I do not see that age should make any difference, so long as one has perfect health; but the health is a necessity, for only a strong body can endure the strain, which is much more serious than any one who has not made the attempt can possibly imagine.

I have said that the astral and etheric centers are in very close correspondence; but between them, and interpenetrating them in a manner not readily describable, is a sheath composed of a single layer of physical atoms much compressed and permeated by a special form of vital force. The divine life which normally descends from the astral body to the physical is so attuned as to pass through this with perfect ease, but it is an absolute barrier to all other forces. This web is the natural protection provided by nature to prevent a premature opening up of communication between the planes—a development which could lead to nothing but injury.

It is this which under normal conditions prevents clear recollection of what has happened during sleep, and it is this also which causes the momentary unconsciousness which always occurs at death. But for this merciful provision the ordinary man, who knows nothing about all these things and is entirely unprepared to meet them, could at any moment be brought by any astral entity under the influences of forces beyond his strength to cope with. He would be liable to constant obsession by any being on the astral plane who desired to seize upon his vehicles.

It will therefore be readily understood that any injury to this web is a serious disaster. There are several ways in which injury may come, and it behooves us to use our best endeavors to guard against it. This injury comes either by accident or by continued malpractice. Any great shock to the astral body, such for example as a sudden terrible fright, may rend apart this delicate organism and, as it is commonly expressed, drive the man mad. (Of course there are other ways in which fear may cause insanity, but this is one.) A tremendous outburst of anger may also produce the same effect. Indeed it may follow upon any exceedingly strong emotion of a violent character which produces a kind of explosion in the astral body.

The malpractices which may more gradually injure this protective web are of two classes—the use of alcohol or narcotic drugs and the deliberate endeavor to throw open the doors which nature has kept closed, by means of such a process as is described in spiritualistic parlance as sitting for development. Certain drugs and drinks—notably alcohol and all the narcotics, including tobacco—contain matter which on breaking up volatilizes, and some of it passes from the physical plane to the astral. (Even tea and coffee contain this matter, but in quantities so infinitesimal that it is usually only after long-continued abuse of them that the effect manifests itself.)

When this takes place in the body of man these constituents rush out through the force-centers in the opposite direction to that for which they are intended, and in doing this repeatedly they seriously injure and finally destroy the delicate web. This deterioration or destruction may be brought about in two different ways, according to the type of the person concerned and to the proportion of the constituents in his etheric and astral bodies. First, the rush of volatilizing matter actually burns away the web, and therefore leaves the door open to all sorts of irregular forces and evil influences.

The second result is that these volatile constituents, in flowing through, somehow harden the atom so that its pulsation is to a large extent checked and crippled, and it is no longer capable of being vitalized by the particular type of force which welds it into a web. The result of this is a kind of ossification of the web, so that instead of having too much coming through from one plane to the other, we have very little of any kind coming through.

We may see the effects of both these types of deterioration in the case of alcoholism. Some of those who are affected in the former way fall into delirium tremens, obsession or insanity; but those are after all comparatively rare. Far more common is the second type of deterioration—the case in which we have a kind of general deadening down of the man's qualities, resulting in gross materialism and brutality, in the loss of all finer feelings and of the power to control himself. He no longer feels any sense of responsibility; he may love his wife and children when sober, but when the fit of drunkenness comes upon him he will use the money which should have bought bread for them to satisfy his own cravings, the affection and the responsibility having apparently entirely disappeared.

The second type of effect is very commonly to be seen among those who are slaves of the tobacco habit; again and again we find that they persist in their self-indulgence even when they know perfectly well that it causes misery to their neighbors. We shall recognize the deterioration at once when we think that this is the only practice in which a gentleman will persist when he is aware that it causes acute annoyance to others. Clearly in this case the finer feelings have already been seriously blunted.

All impressions which pass from one plane to the other are intended to come only through the uppermost sub-plane, as I have said; but when this deadening process sets in, it presently infects not only other matter of the first sub-plane, but matter of even the second and third sub-planes, so that the only communication between the astral and the etheric is when some force acting on the lower sub-planes (upon which only unpleasant and evil influences are to be found) happens to be strong enough to compel a response by the violence of its vibration.

Nevertheless, though nature takes such precautions to guard these centers, she by no means intends that they shall always be kept rigidly closed. There is a proper way in which they may be opened. Perhaps it would be more correct to say that the intention is not that the doors should be opened any wider than their present position, but that the man should so develop himself as that he can bring a great deal more through the recognized channel.

The consciousness of the ordinary man cannot yet use pure first sub-plane matter either in the physical body or in the astral, and therefore there is normally no possibility for him of conscious communication at will between the two planes. The proper way to obtain that is to purify both the vehicles until the rarest matter in both is fully vivified, so that all communications between the two may be able to pass by that road. In that case the web retains to the fullest degree its position and activity, and yet is no longer a barrier to the perfect communication, while it still continues to fulfill its purpose of preventing the close contact between lower sub-planes which would permit all sorts of undesirable influences to pass through.

That is why we are always adjured to wait for the unfolding of psychic powers until they come in the natural course of events as a consequence of the development of character, as we see from the study of these force-centers that they surely will. That is the natural evolution; that is the only really safe way, for by it the student obtains all the benefits and avoids all the dangers. That is the Path which our Masters have trodden in the past; therefore that is the Path for us today.

Obsession and Insanity

We must distinguish carefully between obsession and insanity. The latter is a break in the connection between the ego and his vehicles, while the former is the ousting of the ego by some other entity. Only a weak ego would permit obsession—an ego, I mean, who had not much hold upon his vehicles. As a rule children are not more easily obsessed than adults, because though the hold of the ego upon its bodies is less strong in childhood, it is also true that the adult is far more likely to have in him qualities which attract undesirable entities and make obsession easy. In the case of a little child, any entity trying to obsess the body would have first to face the elemental or astral and etheric entity who is in charge of the building of it, and he is not at all likely to succeed in ousting that. After the age of seven, when that elemental has been withdrawn, obsession might take place if the ego was very weak; but it is fortunately rare.

Obsession may be permanent or temporary, and it is undertaken for various reasons. Often some dead person is filled with burning desire to come again into touch with the physical plane, generally for the satisfaction of the lowest and grossest desires, and in his desperate yearning he seizes upon any vehicle which he can steal. Sometimes, on the other hand, obsession is a definite and calculated act of revenge—not always upon the person obsessed. I knew a case in which a man who hated another deliberately went to work to obtain control of and obsess his enemy's favorite daughter; I also know of another instance even worse than that. Sometimes the obsessing entity is not human at all, but only a nature-spirit who desires experience of human life. In any and all cases obsession should be determinedly resisted by the victim.

Insanity is an entirely different matter. Let us try to look at it from the occult point of view. Every cell in the physical brain and every particle of its matter has its corresponding and interpenetrating astral matter; and behind (or rather within) that, it has also the still finer mental matter. Of course the brain is a mass in three dimensions, but for the purposes of our examination let us suppose that it could be spread out upon a surface so that it should be only one particle thick. Then further suppose that the astral and mental matter belonging to it could also be laid out in layers in a similar manner, the astral layer a little above the physical, and the mental a little above the astral.

Then we should have three layers of matter of different degrees of density, all corresponding one to the other. Now suppose that each physical particle is joined to the corresponding astral particle by a little tube, and each astral particle is joined to its corresponding mental particle in the same way, and even (higher up still) each mental particle to something which corresponds to it in the causal body. So long as all these tubes were perfectly in alignment there would be clear communication between the ego and his brain; but if any one of the sets of tubes were bent, closed, or knocked partially aside, it is obvious that the communication might be wholly or partially interrupted.

From the occult standpoint, therefore, we divide the insane into four great classes, each of course having many sub-divisions:

1.—those who are insane merely from a defect of the dense physical brain—from its insufficient size, perhaps, or from some accident like a heavy blow, or some growth which causes pressure upon it or from gradual softening of the tissue.

2.—those whose defect is in the etheric part of the brain, so that its particles no longer correspond perfectly with the denser physical particles, and so cannot properly bring through the vibrations from the higher vehicles.

3.—those in whom the astral body is defective instead of the etheric—in whom its tubes are bent, as it were, so that there is a want of accurate adjustment between its particles and those of the vehicles either above or below it.

4.—those in whom the mind-body itself is in some way out of order, and consequently is unable to bring through the instructions or wishes of the ego.

It makes a very great difference to which of these classes an insane person belongs. Those of the first and second types are quite sensible when out of the body during sleep, and also after death, so that the ego loses only the expression of himself during waking life. Those of the third type do not recover until they reach the heaven-world, and the fourth class not until they return into the causal body; so that for this last class the incarnation is a failure. But fortunately more than ninety per cent of the insane belong to the first and second classes.

Three questions are asked upon the unsavory subject of obsession; I will proceed to answer them. The first is: *What is the best way to get rid of an excarnate human being who persists in occupying one's body?*

I should simply and absolutely decline to be so obsessed. The best and kindest plan would be to have an explanation from the dead person, to enquire what he wants and why he makes such persistent attempts. Quite probably, he may be some ignorant soul who does not at all comprehend his new surroundings, and is striving madly to get into touch again with the only kind of life that he understands. In that case if matters are explained to him, he may be brought to a happier frame of mind and induced to cease his ill-directed efforts. Or the poor creature may have something on his mind—some duty unfulfilled or some wrong unrighted; if this be so, and the matter can be arranged to his satisfaction, he may then be at peace.

If, however, he proves not to be amenable to reason, if in spite of all argument and explanation he refuses to abandon his reprehensible line of action, it will be necessary gently but firmly to resist him. Every man has an inalienable right to the use of his own vehicle, and encroachments of this nature should not be permitted. If the lawful possessor of the body will confidently assert himself and use his own will-power no obsession can take place.

When such things occur, it is almost always because the victim has in the first place yielded himself to the invading influence, and his first step therefore is to reverse that act of submission, to determine strongly to take matters into his own hands again and to resume control over his property. It is this reassertion of himself that is the fundamental requirement, and though much help may be given by wise friends, nothing which they can do will take the place of the development of will-power on the part of the victim, or obviate the necessity for it. The exact method of procedure will naturally vary according to the details of the case.

The second question runs thus: *I have long been troubled by entities who constantly suggest evil ideas and make use of coarse and violent language. They are always urging me to take strong drink, and goading me on to the consumption of large quantities of meat. I have prayed earnestly, but with little avail, and am driven to my wits' end. What can I do?*

You have indeed suffered greatly; but now you must make up your mind to suffer no more. You must take courage and make a firm stand. The power of these entities over you is only in your fear of them. Your own will is stronger than all theirs combined if you will only know that it is; if you turn upon them with vigor and determination they must yield before you. You have an inalienable right to the undisturbed use of your own vehicles, and you should insist on being left in peace. You would not tolerate an intrusion of filthy and disgusting beings into your house on the physical plane; why should you submit to it because the entities happen to be astral? If an indolent tramp forces himself into a man's house, ᴜne owner does not kneel down and pray—he kicks the tramp out; and that is precisely what you must do with these astral tramps.

You will no doubt say to yourself that when I give you this advice I do not know the terrible power of the particular demons who are afflicting you. That is exactly what they would like you to believe—what they will try to make you believe; but do not be so foolish as to listen to them. I know the type perfectly, and mean, despicable, bullying villains they are; they will torment a weak woman for months together, but will fly in cowardly terror the moment you turn upon them in righteous anger! Of course, they will bluster and show fight, because you have let them have their own way for so long that they will not tamely submit to expulsion; but face them with iron determination, set your will against them like an immovable rock, and down they will go. Say to them: "I am a spark of the divine fire, and by the power of the God within me I order you to depart!" Never let yourself think for an instant of the possibility of failure or of yielding; God is within you, and God cannot fail.

The fact of their demanding meat shows what low and coarse entities they are; you should avoid all flesh-food and alcohol, because these things minister to such evil beings and make it more difficult for you to resist them.

The third question is: *If it is possible for a man to become obsessed while he has temporarily lost control of his body during a fit of anger, is it not also possible for obsession to take place when one is out of the body during sleep?*

I would submit that the circumstances are entirely different. Sleep is a natural condition, and thoᴜgh the ego leaves the body, he always maintains a close connection with it, so that under ordinary circumstances he would quickly be recalled to it by any attempt that might be made upon it. There are individual cases in which the ego is not so easily recalled, and a sort of temporary obsession is possible which may cause somnambulism, but these cases are abnormal and comparatively rare. A fit of extreme anger on the other hand is unnatural—an infraction of the natural laws under which we live. In this case it is the astral which has escaped from control; the desire-elemental has rebelled against his master and has broken away from the hold of the ego exercised through the mental body, which alone keeps him safe as part of an astral mechanism. The rightful owner being dispossessed, the astral body is in the condition of a vessel whose helm has been abandoned; anyone who happens to be at hand can seize the wheel, and it may be a difficult matter to recover it.

Sleep

I am asked what is the real cause of sleep, but I have not the detailed physiological knowledge which is needed to answer this question fully. But I have always understood that the necessity of sleep is due to the fact that the bodies grow tired of one another. The astral vehicle, which so far as we know is practically incapable of fatigue upon its own plane, since it can work incessantly for twenty years without showing signs of it, very soon becomes tired of the heavy labor of moving the particles of the physical brain, and needs a considerable period of separation from it to enable it to gather strength to resume the irksome task.

The physical body, on its side, also becomes worn out, because while it is in a waking condition it is always spending force a little faster than it can draw it in. With every thought or feeling, and with every muscular exertion, certain slight chemical changes appear to take place. The ordinary machinery of a healthy body is all the while working to counteract this change and to restore the condition previously existing, but in this it never quite succeeds. So that with every thought or action there is a slight, almost imperceptible loss, and the cumulative effect eventually leaves the physical body too exhausted to be capable of further thought or work. In some cases even a few moments of sleep will give the recuperative powers an opportunity to reassert themselves and regain the ground that they have lost, thus restoring the balance sufficiently to enable the machine to go on working.

Students often ask what is the best time for sleep. Unquestionably the rule of nature is that the day is for work and the night is for rest, and no infringement of nature's laws can ever be a good thing. One of the serious evils of our modern unnatural life is that noon is no longer, as it should be, the center of the day. If a man lived by himself and could regulate his own affairs he could, no doubt, return at once to that obviously natural condition; but, surrounded as we are by a mighty so-called civilization which is in many ways distorted and unnatural, we are unable to follow our individual predilections in this matter, and must to some extent adapt ourselves to the general custom.

It is impossible to lay down rules as to the amount of sleep which is necessary for man, because there is so much difference in constitutions; but when it is possible that sleep should be taken between 8 P.M. and 5 A.M. Some men need the whole of that time, while others may find themselves perfectly healthy on a smaller allowance. Such details of life each man must decide for himself according to his circumstances.

People often ask whether there is any way in which they can control their dreams. The dreamer cannot usually change the course of his dream while it is going on; but the dream-life can indirectly be controlled to a very considerable extent. If a man's thought be pure and high while waking, his dreams will be pure and good also, and a specially important point is that his last thought as he sinks to sleep should be a noble and elevating one, since that strikes the keynote which largely determines the nature of the dreams which follow. An impure thought draws round the thinker impure influences, attracts to him all the gross and loathsome creatures who come near him. These will, in turn, react upon his mind and his astral body, and disturb his rest by awakening all kinds of earthly desires. If, on the other hand, a man enters the portals of sleep with his mind fixed upon high and holy things, he thereby draws round him the elementals created by like efforts in others; his rest is peaceful, his mind open to impressions from above and closed to those from below, for he has set it working in the right direction.

The dreaming of ordinary events does not interfere with astral work, because that dreaming is all taking place in the physical brain, while the real man is away attending to other business. Of course if the man, when out in his astral body, devotes himself to thinking over the events of his physical life, he will be unable during the time of such thought to do any other work, but that is a totally different thing from a mere ordinary dream of the physical brain, though when the man wakes in the morning it is frequently difficult for him to distinguish between the two sets of recollections. It really does not matter what the physical brain does so long as it keeps itself free from impure thoughts, but it is undesirable that the man himself should waste his time in introspection when he might be working on the astral plane.

Somnambulism

You ask what is the cause of sleep-walking. I have never had the opportunity of observing a case of somnambulism, so I am unable to speak from direct knowledge; but from reading accounts of such cases I should imagine that the phenomena may be produced by several widely different causes. There are instances in which it appears that the ego is able to act more directly upon his physical body during the absence of the intermediate mental and astral vehicles—instances in which a man during his sleep is able to write poetry or to paint pictures which would go far beyond his powers when awake.

There are other cases in which it is obvious that the dim consciousness inherent in the physical body is working uncontrolled by the man himself, so that it performs quite meaningless acts, or carries out to some extent the idea which was dominant in the mind before falling asleep. To this class belong the stories of servants who have risen in the middle of the night to light the fire, of ostlers who have harnessed horses in their sleep, and so on.

Again, there are cases in which some outside intelligence, whether incarnate or discarnate, has seized upon the body of a sleeping man and used it for his own ends. This would be most likely to happen with a person who is what is called mediumistic—that is to say, whose subtle bodies are more loosely joined together than usual, and therefore more readily separable; but oddly enough there seems to be a type of somnambulism which is due to a directly opposite condition, when the bodies fit more tightly than usual, so that when the man would naturally visit some neighboring spot in his astral body, he takes the physical body along with him as well, because he is not wholly dissociated from it. Somnambulism is probably also connected with the whole complex problem of the various layers of consciousness in man, which under perfectly normal circumstances are unable to manifest themselves.

The Physical Body

Physical immortality is not a possibility, for that which has a beginning must also have an end, and birth, growth, decay and death are the rules of the physical universe. No reasonable being could desire to retain the same body continuously; it is precisely as though a small child should wish to wear the same suit of clothes during the whole of his life. As man evolves, his successive vehicles will become purer and nobler, and better fitted to meet the needs of his increasing capacity, so that even if a man could keep the same body he would check his growth by doing so, just as the child's growth would be checked by always wearing something of iron rigidity which was much too tight for him.

At the same time it is our duty to take the best possible care of our bodies and to improve them as much as we can. Never ill-treat the physical body. Take care of it as you would of a valuable horse, giving it enough rest and food, and keeping it scrupulously clean. It can do only a certain amount of work; for example, a very strong body might walk a hundred miles without resting, but it could not walk a thousand. In meditation put it into a comfortable position and then forget about it. You cannot forget it, if it is uncomfortable, as it would constantly call you back.

What should you eat? Well, so long as you avoid alcohol and meat-eating it probably does not matter very much. Certain vegetables are coarser than others, and therefore when there is a choice it is as well to abstain from them. Among those I should class onions, mushrooms and cabbages. Rice is very pure food, but wheat, barley and oats give more nutriment in the same amount. I consider eggs undesirable, though I should unhesitatingly take them if no other food was to be had.

There is no question that vegetarianism is better in every way than the devouring of flesh. It furnishes more real nutriment, diminishes the liability to disease, gives greater strength, and does not stimulate the lower nature. The vegetarian diet makes it far easier for a man to develop his higher qualities. It is known that our Masters make a single physical body last much longer than an ordinary man can do, by living always in accordance with hygienic laws and by absolute freedom from worry. In that respect we should all try to copy them as nearly as we can, but to endeavor to retain the same body indefinitely has always been a mark of those who follow the selfish path.

There are various undesirable means by which such men have prolonged physical life—sometimes by vampirism, merely depleting the vitality of others, and sometimes by the complete transference to themselves of a succession of other human lives. But it is hardly necessary to warn theosophists against proceedings of this nature. It is obvious that a person adopting such a plan would be one who is *not* evolving; and even if he succeeded he would only be as it were patching and enlarging an old coat, but with all his efforts it would remain an old coat still.

Tobacco and Alcohol

The evil effect of the tobacco habit is obvious in the physical, the astral and the mental bodies. It permeates the man physically with exceedingly impure particles, causing emanations so material that they are frequently perceptible to the sense of smell. Astrally, it not only introduces impurity, but it also tends to deaden many of the vibrations, and it is for this reason that it is frequently found to "soothe the nerves," as it is called. But, of course, for occult progress we do not want the vibrations deadened nor the astral body weighed down with foul and poisonous particles. We need the capacity of answering instantly to all possible vibrations, and yet at the same time we must have perfect control, so that these desires shall be as horses guided by the intelligent mind to draw us where we will, not to run away with us wildly, and carry us into situations where our higher nature knows that it ought never to be found. Therefore, for any person who is really anxious to develop his vehicles, tobacco is undoubtedly a bad thing.

Also it has a singularly deteriorating influence upon the man on the physical plane. It is absolutely the only thing, so far as I know, that a gentleman will deliberately do when he knows it to be offensive to others. But the hold which this noxious habit gains upon its slaves appears to be so great that they are utterly incapable of resisting it, and all their gentlemanly instincts are forgotten in this mad and horrible selfishness. The effect on the astral body after death is also very bad; the man is shut up for a long time as though in prison, and higher vibrations cannot reach him.

The chief objection which is always brought by the more self-indulgent Theosophist against remarks such as these is that our great founder Madame Blavatsky herself smoked. I know this to be true, but it does not in the least alter the facts which I have stated above, which I know just as surely from long-continued personal observation. Madame Blavatsky was in every way so entirely *sui generis*, so emphatically a case apart, that I do not think it reasonable for us to presume that we can safely do what she did. I have often heard her say: "No one but my Master understands my case; do what I tell you, not what I do." Also she once told me that she smoked incessantly "to quiet the vibrations of this old body, and prevent it from shaking itself to pieces." The effects on the physical plane during life and on the astral after death are precisely as I have described them, and it does not seem worth while incurring them for the sake of a petty indulgence.

As for alcohol, there is no doubt whatever that from the point of view of the astral and mental bodies its use is always an evil; and there is also no doubt at all that very undesirable entities are attracted by it. Of course many people who are estimable in other respects have certain most unpleasant habits, such as the drinking of alcohol, the eating of meat or the smoking of tobacco; but the fact that they are otherwise good people does not make these things good and sensible. It is, of course, untrue that any of these things are physical necessities, but a man may accustom his system to the use of almost any kind of drug, until that system, being habituated to it, expects it and misses it if it does not get it. We know that exactly the same habit may be set up with opium or heroin, but that does not make them good things to take. It is, however, generally quite useless to attempt to argue with any man as to his personal habits; he is usually determined to cling to such habits because he likes them, and he cares very little whether they are good in themselves, or even good for him.

You ask my opinion about the regulation of the sale of liquor. In all civilized countries some control is exercised over the sale of poisons, and they are allowed to be supplied only upon a doctor's certificate. The poison of alcohol does many thousands of times more harm than all other poisons put together, so surely the regulations governing its sale ought to be no less strict.

It is perfectly true that every man will have to develop self-control for himself, but I really do not see how that affects our attitude with regard to the making of laws. You surely would not suggest that in order to teach people not to steal, we should continually at every street corner throw in their way special temptations to induce them to steal, and then stand by without any interference to see whether they would develop sufficient strength of mind to resist our temptations.

Yet that is exactly what is now being done with regard to the consumption of alcohol. We allow, encourage and specially license a number of men to make a tempting display in our streets with the avowed object of trying to induce as many people as possible to degrade themselves by the habitual use of this poison. If at last mankind is so far evolving as to develop some sort of conscience with regard to the weaker brethren, it would seem well for us to encourage their advancement rather than to range ourselves against it. If we feel it right to care for and to help the insane, even to the extent of restraining them for their own good and for that of the public, it is surely well for us also to treat the victim of that terrible form of insanity known as drunkenness along exactly the same lines. But it must not be forgotten that the Theosophical Society takes no part whatever in any political movement, although of course its members as private individuals are perfectly free to take any side that they like in political questions.

SECTION SIX

The After-Death
Life

The Theosophist After Death

When a member of the Theosophical Society finds himself upon the astral plane after having permanently laid aside his physical body, it will be well for him to begin by taking stock, as it were—by seeing what is his position, what is the life before him, and how he can make the best use of it. He will do wisely to consult on these matters some friend who has had wider experience than himself, and in practice this is what dead members almost always do. Remember that when the member enters upon the astral plane after death he is not making his first appearance there. Usually he has already done much work there during the sleep of the physical body, and is therefore on familiar ground. As a general rule his first instinct is to make straight for Mrs. Besant, which is probably quite the wisest thing for him to do, as there is no one better qualified to give him sound advice. So many possibilities open out in astral life that one cannot lay down any general rule, though a man cannot go far wrong who tries to make himself useful to those around him. There are plentiful opportunities for learning, as well as for work, and the newcomer will have to decide how he can best apportion his time between them.

The astral world will not be altered for the convenience of

223

members of the Theosophical Society, any more than the physical world is, and they, like every one else, will have to encounter what happens to be there. If a drunken man is walking along a certain road, those who happen to pass along that road will meet him, whether they are members or not, and the astral plane does not, in this respect, differ from the physical. The members, being instructed in regard to the rules governing life on the astral plane, ought to know better than the uninstructed how to deal with such unpleasant beings as happen to come in their way, but they are just as likely as any one else to meet them. They have, however, probably met such beings many times while functioning upon the astral plane during life, and there is no more reason to be afraid of them than before; indeed, meeting them then upon their own level, it will be far easier to come to an understanding with them and to give them such help as they are able to receive.

There is practically no difference between the condition of the ordinary person and the psychic after death, except that the psychic, being somewhat more familiar with astral matters, would feel more at home in his new environment. To be psychic means to be able to bring through into the physical consciousness something of the wider life; it is therefore in the condition of the physical vehicle that there is an inequality between the psychic and the ordinary person, but when the physical is dropped that inequality no longer exists.

The Relation of the Dead to Earth

A dead man is often aware of the feelings of the family that he has left. If you try to think exactly what it is that can be manifested through the astral body, you may easily see how much he is likely to know. He does not necessarily follow in detail all the events of the physical life; he does not necessarily know what his friends are eating, or in what occupations they are engaged. But he knows whether they are glad or sorry, and he is at once aware of such feelings as love or hate, jealousy or envy.

In the astral body there are exact counterparts of the eyes and the nose and the mouth, but we must not therefore think that the astral man sees with those eyes, hears with those ears, or can smell or taste through the nose or mouth. All the matter of the astral body is constantly in rapid motion from one part of it to another, so that it is quite impossible for any astral particles to be specialized in the same way as certain nerve-ends are specialized in the physical body. The senses of the astral body act not through special organs, but through every particle of the body, so that with astral sight a man can see equally well with any part of his body, and can see all around him simultaneously, instead of only in front of him. He could grasp at the astral counterpart of the hand of a living man, but as the two hands would pass through one another without any sense of contact, there would be no object in his doing so. It is, however, perfectly possible for him to materialize a hand which, though invisible, can be felt just as the ordinary physical hand can be, as may often be observed at séances.

There are three subdivisions of the astral plane from which it may be possible (though not desirable) for disembodied men to see and follow events taking place upon the physical plane. On the lowest sub-plane the man is usually occupied in other ways, and concerns himself little with what takes place in the physical world, except, as is explained in our literature, when he haunts vile resorts; but, in the next subdivision, he has very close touch with the physical plane, and may quite probably be conscious of a good many things in connection with it, though what he sees is never the physical matter itself, but always the astral counterpart of it. In rapidly diminishing degree this consciousness is also possible as he ascends through the next two sub-planes; but beyond that, it would be only by the special effort to communicate through a medium that contact with the physical plane could be gained, and from the highest sub-plane even that would be extremely difficult.

The extent of a man's power to see and follow physical events from the astral plane is determined by his character and disposition, as well as by the stage of development to which he has attained. Most of those whom we ordinarily call good people, living out their lives to their natural end, sweep through all these lower stages before awakening to astral consciouness, and they are therefore unlikely to be conscious of anything physical at all. However, some few even of these are drawn back into touch with this world by great anxiety about some one left behind.

Less developed persons have in their composition more of the matter of these lower sub-planes, and are therefore much more likely to be able to follow to some extent what goes on upon earth, especially if they are people whose whole turn of thought is essentially of this world—who have in them little or nothing of spiritual aspiration or of high intellect. This downward tendency grows with the using, and a man who is at first happily unconscious of what lies below him may be so unfortunate as to have his attention attracted to it, frequently by selfish manifestations of the grief of the survivors. He then exerts his will to keep himself from rising out of touch with this life to which he no longer belongs; and in such a case his power of seeing earthly things increases for a time, and then he suffers mentally when he presently finds such power slipping from him. Such suffering is entirely due to the irregularity introduced into the astral life by his own action, for it is absolutely unknown in the ordinary and orderly evolution after death.

If it is complained that in this way the departed does not see the physical world exactly as it really is, we must answer that neither the departed nor we on this plane ever see the physical world as it really is at all, for we (or most of us) see only the solid and liquid portions thereof, and are altogether blind to the far vaster gaseous and etheric parts; while the departed does not see the physical matter at all, nor even the whole astral counterpart of it, but only that portion of the latter which belongs to the particular subplane upon which he is at the time. The only man who gets anything like a comprehensive view of affairs is he who has developed etheric and astral sight while still alive in the physical body.

Another difficulty in the way of the disembodied is that he by no means always recognizes with any certainty the astral counterpart of the physical body even when he sees it. He usually requires considerable experience before he can clearly identify objects, and any attempt which he makes to deal with them is liable to be very vague and uncertain, as is often seen in haunted houses where stone-throwing, trampling, or vague movements of physical matter take place. This power of the identification of objects is thus largely a question of experience and knowledge, but it is little likely to be perfect unless he has known something of such matters before death.

A correspondent writes to ask whether a dead man can enjoy the astral counterpart of a play at a theater, and whether there will be room for him there if the building is already full of people. Certainly a theater full of people has its astral counterpart, which is visible to dead people. The play, however, is not likely to afford them any enjoyment, since they cannot see the costumes and the expressions of the actors at all as we see them, and the emotions of these actors, being only simulated and not real, make no impression upon the astral plane. Astral bodies can and constantly do interpenetrate one another fully, without in the least injuring one another. If you will think for a moment you will see that this must be so. When you sit next to any person in a railway carriage or in a tram-car your astral body and his must necessarily interpenetrate to a very large extent. There is not the slightest difficulty in such interpenetration, since the astral particles are enormously farther apart in proportion to their size even than physical particles are. At the same time they seriously affect one another as far as their rates of vibration are concerned, so that to sit in close proximity to a person of impure, jealous or angry thought is exceedingly prejudicial. A dead friend can, therefore, quite easily enter a theater which is full of people—more especially as the people are seated upon the ground or the platforms, while the astral entity is far more probably floating about in the air.

The man who commits suicide runs away from school before the appointed lesson is learned; he is guilty of the great presumption involved in taking into his own hands a decision which should be left to the working of the Great Law. The consequences of so great a rebellion against nature are always of a momentous character. They are certain to affect the next life, and quite probably more lives than one. The circumstances surrounding a suicide immediately after death are the same as they would be for the victim of an accident, since both of them arrive upon the astral plane with equal suddenness. But there is the enormous difference that the man who dies by accident, not expecting death, is thrown into a condition of unconsciousness, and usually passes through the lowest sub-plane without knowing anything of its varied unpleasantness. The suicide, on the contrary, has acted deliberately, and is generally painfully aware of much that is horrible and repugnant to him. He cannot be saved from the sights and feelings which he has brought upon himself; but he may often be helped to understand them, and may be inspired with patience, perseverance and hope by the good offices of some kind friend.

While fully recognizing that suicide is a mistake, and a most serious one, we are not called upon to judge our brother who commits that mistake. There is a wide difference between different cases, and it is impossible for us to know the various factors which enter into each, although every one of them is duly taken into account in the working of the law of eternal justice.

In trying to estimate the conditions of a man's life on the astral plane after death, there are two prominent factors to be considered—the length of time which he stays upon any particular sub-plane, and the acuteness of his consciousness upon it. The length of a man's stay upon any sub-plane depends, as has been said, upon the amount of matter belonging to that sub-plane he has built into himself during earth-life.

But the degree of consciousness that a person will have upon a given sub-plane does not invariably follow precisely the same law. Let us consider an extreme example of possible variation, in order that we may grasp its method. Suppose a man has brought over from his past incarnation tendencies requiring for their manifestation a large amount of the matter of the lowest sub-plane, and has in his present life been fortunate enough to learn in his earliest years the possibility and the necessity of controlling these tendencies. It is improbable that such a man's efforts at control would be uniformly and entirely successful; but if they were, the substitution of finer for grosser particles would progress steadily though slowly.

This process is at best a gradual one, and it might well happen that the man died before it was half completed. In that case there would undoubtedly be enough matter of the lowest sub-plane left in his astral body to ensure him no inconsiderable residence there; but it would be matter through which in this incarnation his consciousness had never been in the habit of functioning, and, as it could not suddenly acquire this habit, the result would be that the man would rest upon that sub-plane until his share of its matter was disintegrated, but would be all the while in a condition of unconsciousness—that is, he would practically sleep through the period of his sojourn there, and so would be entirely unaffected by its many disagreeables.

It will be seen that both these factors of post-mortem existence—the sub-plane to which the man is carried and the degree of his consciousness there—depend not in the least on the nature of his death, but upon the nature of his life, so that any accident, however sudden or terrible, can scarcely affect them. Nevertheless, there is reason behind the familiar old prayer: "From sudden death, good Lord, deliver us;" for though a sudden death does not necessarily affect the man's position upon the astral plane in any way for the worse, at least it does nothing to improve it, whereas the slow wasting away of the aged or the ravages of any kind of long-continued disease are almost invariably accompanied by a considerable loosening and breaking up of the astral particles, so that when the man recovers consciousness upon the astral plane, he finds some at any rate of his chief work there already done for him.

The great mental terror and disturbance which sometimes accompany accidental death are in themselves a very unfavorable preparation for the astral life; indeed, cases have been known in which such agitation and terror persisted after death, though that is happily rare. Still, the popular desire to have some time in which to prepare for death is not a mere superstition, but has a certain amount of reason at the back of it. Naturally, to anyone who is leading the Theosophical life it will make but little difference whether the transition from the physical plane to the astral comes slowly or quickly, since he is all the time doing his best to make as much progress as possible, and the object before him will remain the same in either case.

To sum up then: it seems clear that death by accident does not necessarily involve any lengthy residence on the lowest level of the astral plane, though it may in one sense be said slightly to prolong such residence, since it deprives the victim of the opportunity of burning out the particles belonging to that level during the sufferings of a lingering disease. In the case of young children it is exceedingly unlikely that in their short and comparatively blameless young lives they will have developed much affinity for the lowest subdivisions of astral life; indeed, as a matter of practical experience they are hardly ever to be found in connection with that sub-plane at all. In any case, whether they die by accident or disease, their life on the astral plane is a comparatively short one; the heaven-life, though much longer, is still in reasonable proportion to it, and their early reincarnation follows as soon as the forces which they have been able to set in motion during their short earth-lives work themselves out, precisely as we might expect from our observation of the action of the same great law in the case of adults.

Nothing that is likely to be done in *ordinary* life to his physical corpse *need* make any difference whatever to the man living on the astral plane. I am obliged to make these two reservations because, in the first case, outside of ordinary life there are certain horrible magical rites which would very seriously affect the condition of the man on the other plane, and in the second, although the state of the physical corpse *need* not make any difference to the real man, it nevertheless sometimes does, by reason of his ignorance or foolishness. Let me endeavor to explain.

The length of a man's astral life after he has put off his physical body depends mainly upon two factors—the nature of his past physical life, and his attitude of mind after what we call death. During his earth-life he is constantly influencing the building of matter into his astral body. He affects it directly by the passions, emotions and desires which he allows to hold sway over him; he affects it indirectly by the action upon it of his thoughts from above, and of all the details of his physical life (his continence or his debauchery, his cleanliness or his uncleanliness, his food and his drink) from below. If, by persistence in perversity along any of these lines, he is so stupid as to build for himself a coarse and gross astral vehicle, habituated to responding only to the lower vibrations of the plane, he will find himself after death bound to that plane during the long and slow process of that body's disintegration. On the other hand if, by decent and careful living, he gives himself a vehicle mainly composed of finer material, he will have very much less post-mortem trouble and discomfort, and his evolution will proceed much more rapidly and easily.

This much is generally understood, but the second great factor—his attitude of mind after death—seems often to be forgotten. The desirable thing is for him to realize his position on this little arc of his evolution—to learn that he is at this stage withdrawing steadily inward towards the plane of the true ego, and that consequently it is his business to disengage his thought as far as may be from things physical, and fix his attention more and more upon those spiritual matters which will occupy him during his life in the heaven-world. By doing this he will greatly facilitate the natural astral disintegration, and will avoid the sadly common mistake of unnecessarily delaying himself upon the lower levels of what should be so temporary a residence.

Many people, however, simply will not turn their thoughts upwards, but spend their time in struggling with all their might to keep in touch with the physical plane which they have left, thus causing great trouble to anyone who may be trying to help them. Earthly matters are the only ones in which they have ever had any living interest, and they cling to them with desperate tenacity even after death. Naturally, as time passes on, they find it increasingly difficult to keep hold of things down here, but instead of welcoming and encouraging this process of gradual refinement and spiritualization they resist it vigorously by every means in their power. The mighty force of evolution is eventually too strong for them, and they are swept on in its beneficent current, yet they fight every step of the way, thereby not only causing themselves a vast amount of entirely unnecessary pain and sorrow, but also seriously delaying their upward progress.

Now, in this ignorant and disastrous opposition to the cosmic will a man is much assisted by the possession of his physical corpse as a kind of fulcrum on this plane. He is naturally in close rapport with it, and if he is so misguided as to wish to do so, he can use it as an anchor to hold him down firmly to the mud until its decomposition is far advanced. Cremation saves the man from himself in this matter, for, when the physical body has been thus properly disposed of, his boats are literally burned behind him, and his power of holding back is happily greatly diminished.

We see therefore that, while neither the burial nor the embalming of a corpse can in any way force the ego to whom it once belonged to prolong his stay upon the astral plane against his will, either of those causes is a distinct temptation to him to delay, and immensely facilitates his doing so if he should unfortunately wish it. No ego of any advancement would allow himself to be detained upon the astral plane, even by a proceeding so foolish as the embalming of his corpse. Whether his physical vehicle was burned or allowed to decay slowly in the usual loathsome manner, or indefinitely preserved as an Egyptian mummy, his astral body would pursue its own line of quick disintegration entirely unaffected.

Among the many advantages gained by cremation the principal are that it entirely prevents any attempt at partial and unnatural temporary reunion of the principles, or any endeavor to make use of the corpse for the purposes of the lower magic—to say nothing of the many dangers to the living which are avoided by its adoption.

Conditions after Death

Students often ask whether for the ordinary man a subconscious or an active existence is more desirable on the astral plane. This depends upon the nature of the active existence, and upon the stage of development of the ego concerned. The ordinary man dies with a certain amount of unexhausted desire still in his composition, and this force must work itself out before it is possible for him to sink into a subconscious condition. If the only activity possible for him is that of the lower desires, it is obviously better for him that nothing should be allowed to interfere with his sinking into comparative unconsciousness as soon as possible, since any new karma that he makes is little likely to be of an advantageous kind.

If, on the other hand, he is sufficiently developed to be able to be of use to others on the astral plane, and especially if he has already been in the habit of working there during sleep, there is no reason why he should not usefully employ the time of his enforced sojourn there, though it would be inadvisable to set in motion new forces which would lengthen that sojourn. Those who are working under the direction of the pupils of the Masters of Wisdom will naturally avail themselves of their counsel, since they have had much experience along these lines, and can in turn consult others of still wider knowledge.

The astral life may be directed by the will, just as the physical life may be, always within the limits prescribed in each case by karma—that is to say, by our own previous action. The ordinary man has little will-power or initiative, and is very much the creature of the surroundings which he has made for himself, on the astral plane as on the physical; but a determined man can always make the best of his conditions and live his own life in spite of them. What has, after all, been caused by his will can gradually be changed by his will, if time permits.

A man does not rid himself of evil tendencies in the astral world any more than he would in this life, unless he definitely works to that end. Many of the desires which are so strong and persistent in him are such as need a physical body for their satisfaction, and since he has that no longer, they often cause him acute and prolonged suffering; but in process of time they wear themselves out, they become as it were atrophied, and die down because of this impossibility of fulfilment. In the same way the matter of the astral body slowly wears away and disintegrates as the consciousness is gradually withdrawn from it by the half-unconscious effort of the ego, and thus the man by degrees gets rid of what ever holds him back from the heaven-world.

But the worst of his trouble is that the man is generally not alive to the necessity of getting rid of the evil which detains him. It is obvious that if he realizes the facts of the case and gives his mind to the work, he can greatly expedite both the processes referred to above. If he knows that it is his business to kill out earthly desires, and to withdraw into himself as quickly as may be, he will earnestly set himself to do these things; instead of which he usually in his ignorance broods over the desires and so lengthens their life, and clings desperately to the grossest particles of astral matter as long as he possibly can, because the sensation connected with them seems nearest to that physical life for which he is so passionately longing. Thus we see why one of the most important parts of the work of the invisible helpers is to explain facts to the dead, and also why even a merely intellectual knowledge of theosophical truths is of such inestimable value to a man.

The dead man when he first arrives upon the astral plane by no means always realizes that he is dead, and even when that fact comes home to him it does not follow that he at once understands how the astral world differs from the physical. In the physical world man is the slave of a number of imperious necessities; he must have food and clothing and shelter; in order to procure these he must have money; and in most cases in order to obtain money he must do some kind of work. All this is so much a matter of course to us down here that the man who is set free from this slavery finds it difficult for a long time to believe that he is really free, and in many cases he continues unnecessarily to impose upon himself fetters which he has in reality cast aside.

So we sometimes see the newly dead trying to eat—sitting down to or preparing for themselves wholly imaginary meals, or building for themselves houses. I have actually seen a man in the summer-land building a house for himself stone by stone, and even though he made each of these stones for himself by an effort of his thought, he did not yet grasp the fact that he might just as well have made the whole house for himself, with the same amount of trouble, by a single effort of the same kind. He was gradually led to see that, by the discovery that the stones had no weight, which showed him that his present conditions differed from those to which he had been used on earth, and so led him to investigate further.

In the summer-land men surround themselves with landscapes of their own construction, though some avoid that trouble by accepting ready-made the landscapes which have already been constructed by others. Men living on the sixth sub-plane, upon the surface of the earth, find themselves surrounded by the astral counterparts of physically existing mountains, trees and lakes, and consequently are not under the necessity of manufacturing scenery for themselves; but men upon the higher sub-planes, who float at some distance above the surface of the earth, usually provide themselves with whatever scenery they desire, by the method that I have described.

The commonest example of this is that they construct for themselves the weird scenes described in their various scriptures, and therefore in those regions we constantly find ourselves in presence of clumsy and unimaginative attempts to reproduce such ideas as jewels growing upon trees, and seas of glass mingled with fire, and creatures which are full of eyes within, and deities with a hundred heads and arms to correspond. In this way, as a consequence of ignorance and prejudice during their physical life, many men do a great deal of valueless work when they might be employing their time in the helping of their fellows.

To the man who has studied theosophy and therefore understands these higher planes, one of their pleasantest characteristics is the utter restfulness and freedom which comes from the absence of all these imperious necessities which make a misery out of physical life. The dead man is the only absolutely free man, free to do whatever he wills and to spend his time as he chooses, free therefore to devote the whole of his energies to helping his fellows.

Animal Obsession

We are familiar with the idea that an ego on its way down into reincarnation may sometimes be drawn aside from its course and indefinitely delayed at astral levels by the attraction of the group-soul of some kind of animal with whose characteristics it is in too close affinity. We know that the same affinity sometimes seizes upon a soul upon the astral plane after death, and detains it in very intimate association with an animal form, and also that as the result of gross cruelty it is possible to be karmically linked to an animal, and to suffer most horribly with it. All this was described by Mrs. Besant as follows, in a letter to an Indian paper, which was reproduced in *The Theosophic Gleaner*, Vol. XV, page 231:

> The human ego does not reincarnate in an animal, for reincarnation means the entering into a physical vehicle which thereafter belongs to and is controlled by the ego. The penal connection of the human ego with an animal form is not reincarnation; for the animal soul, the proper owner of the vehicle, is not dispossessed, nor can the human ego control the body to which it is temporarily attached. Nor does the human ego become an animal, nor lose its human attributes, while undergoing its punishment. It does not have to evolve up again through the successive lower stages of humanity, but on being set free at once takes the grade of human form to which its previous evolution entitles it. (*See* the cases of Jada Bharata, and of the Rishi's wife set free by the touch of Rama's feet—cases which show that the popular idea that the man *becomes* a stone or an animal is erroneous.)
>
> The facts are these. When an ego, a human soul, by vicious appetite or otherwise, forms a very strong link of attachment to any type of animal, the astral body of such a person shows the corresponding animal characteristics, and in the astral world—where thoughts and passions are visible as forms—may take the animal shapes. Thus, after death, in *Pretaloka* the soul would be embodied in an astral vesture resembling, or approximating to, the animal whose qualities had been encouraged during earth-life. Either at this stage, or when the soul is returning towards reincarnation, and is again in the astral world, it may in extreme cases be linked by magnetic affinity to the astral body of the animal it has approached in character, and will then, through the animal's astral body, be chained as a prisoner to the animal's physical body. Thus chained, it

cannot go onwards to human birth if it be descending
towards physical life. It is truly undergoing penal servitude, chained to an animal; it is conscious in the
astral world, has its human faculties, but it cannot
control the brute body with which it is connected, nor
express itself through that body on the physical plane.
The animal organisation does not possess the mechanism needed by the human ego for self-expression; it
can serve as a jailor, not as a vehicle. Further the
animal soul is not ejected, but is the proper tenant and
controller of its own body. Shri Shankaracharya hints
very clearly at this difference between this penal imprisonment and becoming a stone, a tree or an animal.
Such an imprisonment is not reincarnation, and to call
it by that name is an inaccuracy; hence, while fully
conversant with the above facts, I should always say
that the human ego cannot reincarnate as an animal,
cannot become an animal. This is not the only experience a degraded soul may have in the invisible world,
of which hints may be found in the Hindu Shastras,
for . . . the statements made are partial and very incomplete.

In cases where the ego is not degraded enough for
absolute imprisonment, but in which the astral body is
strongly animalised, it may pass on normally to human
re-birth, but the animal characteristics will be largely
reproduced in the physical body—as witness the
'monsters' who in fact are sometimes repulsively animal, pig-faced, dog-faced, etc. Men, by yielding to the
most bestial vices, entail on themselves penalties more
terrible than they for the most part realise, for nature's
laws work on unbrokenly and bring to every man the
harvest of the seed he sows. The suffering entailed on
the conscious human entity thus cut off for the time
from progress and from self-expression is very great,
and is of course reformatory in its action; it is somewhat similar to that endured by other egos, who are
linked to bodies human in form, but without healthy
brains—those we call idiots, lunatics, etc. Idiocy and
lunacy are the results of vices other in kind from those

that bring about the animal servitude above explained, but the ego in these cases also is attached to a form through which he cannot express himself.

These instances are the explanation (or at least a part of the explanation) of the widely-spread belief that a man may under certain circumstances reincarnate in an animal body. In Oriental books, what we should call three stages of *one* life are quite commonly spoken of as separate lives. It is said that when a man dies to the physical plane he is reborn at once on the astral plane—meaning simply that his specially and wholly astral life begins then; and in the same way what we should describe as the passing into the heaven-life is called a death on the astral plane and a rebirth at the higher level. This being so, it is easy to understand that one of the abnormal cases above mentioned might be described as 'rebirth as an animal,' although it is not at all what we should mean by such a term if we employed it in theosophical literature.

In recent investigations our attention has been drawn to a type of case differing somewhat from either of the above in that the link with the animal is intentionally made by the human being, in order to escape from something which he feels to be far worse. No doubt this type also was known to the ancients, and forms one of the classes referred to in the tradition of animal incarnations. Let me endeavor to explain it.

When a man dies, the etheric part of his physical body is withdrawn from the denser part, and shortly afterwards (usually within a few hours) the astral breaks away from the etheric, and the man's life on the astral plane is begun. Normally the man is unconscious until he has freed himself from the etheric, and so when he awakens to a new life it is that of the astral plane. But there are some people who cling so desperately to material existence that their astral vehicles cannot altogether separate from the etheric, and they awaken still surrounded by etheric matter.

The etheric body is only a part of the physical, and is not in itself a vehicle of consciousness—not a body in which a man can live and function. So these poor people are in a very unpleasant condition, suspended as it were between two planes. They are shut out from the astral world by the shell of etheric matter which surrounds them, and at the same time they have lost the physical sense organs by which alone they can come fully into touch with the world of ordinary earth-life.

The result is that they drift about, lonely, dumb and terrified, in a thick and gloomy fog, unable to hold intercourse with the denizens of either plane, glimpsing sometimes other drifting souls in their own unfortunate positions, yet powerless to communicate even with them, incapable of joining them or of arresting their aimless wandering as they are swept on and engulfed in the rayless night. Now and again the etheric veil may part sufficiently to permit one glance into lower astral scenes, but that is rarely encouraging, and indeed is often mistaken for a glimpse into hell; sometimes for a moment some familiar earthly object may be half-seen—usually from passing contact with a strong thought-image; but such rare and tantalizing liftings of the fog only make its darkness the more soul-shaking and hopeless when it shuts down again.

All the while the poor soul cannot realize that if he would but let go his frenzied grasp on matter he would slip at once (through a few moments of unconsciousness) into the ordinary life of the astral plane. But it is just that feeling that he cannot bear—the feeling of losing even the miserable half-consciousness that he has; he clings even to the horrors of this grey world of all-embracing fog rather than let himself sink into what seems to him a sea of nothingness and complete extinction. Occasionally, as the result of wicked and blasphemous teaching on earth, he fears to let himself go lest he should fall into hell. In either case, his suffering, his hopelessness and utter dreariness are usually extreme.

Out of this unpleasant but self-imposed predicament there are several ways. There are members of our band of invisible helpers who devote themselves specially to seeking out souls who are in this painful condition, and trying to persuade them to let themselves sink out of it; and there are also many kindly people among the dead who take this up as a sort of branch of astral slum work. Sometimes such efforts are successful, but on the whole few of the victims have faith and courage enough to let go their hold on what to them is life, poor apology though it be. In process of time the etheric shell wears out, and the ordinary course of nature reasserts itself in spite of their struggles; and sometimes in sheer despair they anticipate this result, deciding that annihilation is preferable to such a life, and so recklessly letting themselves go—the result being an overwhelming but pleasant surprise to them.

In their earlier struggles, however, there are some who are so unfortunate as to discover unnatural methods of reviving to some extent their touch with the physical plane instead of sinking into the astral. They can do this readily through a medium, but usually the medium's 'spirit-guide' sternly forbids them access. He is quite right to do so, for in their terror and their great need they are often utterly unscrupulous, and they would obsess and even madden the medium, fighting as a drowning man fights for life; and all absolutely uselessly, since the eventual result could only be to prolong their sufferings by strengthening that material part of which most of all they should get rid.

Occasionally they contrive to seize upon some one who is un-consciously a medium—some sensitive young girl, usually; but they can be successful in such an attempt only when the ego of the young girl has a weakened hold on the vehicles by allowing the indulgence of undesirable thoughts or passions. When the ego's relations with the vehicles are normal and healthy they cannot be dispossessed by the frantic efforts of such poor souls as we have been describing.

An animal, however, has no ego behind him, though he has a fragment of a group-soul which may be said to stand for him in the place of an ego. The hold of this fragment upon his vehicles is by no means what that of an ego would be, and so it comes to pass that what for the moment we may call the 'soul' of the animal can be dispossessed much more easily than that of a man. Sometimes, as I have said, the human soul wandering in the grey world is unfortunate enough to discover this, and so in his madness he obsesses the body of an animal, or if he cannot quite drive out the animal soul he contrives to gain partial control, so as to share the tenement to some extent with the rightful owner. In such a case he is once more in touch with the physical plane through the animal; he sees through the animal's eyes (often a very remark-able experience) and he feels any pain inflicted upon the animal; in fact, so far as his own consciousness is concerned, he *is* the animal for the time being.

An old and respected member of one of our English Branches related that he had received a visit from a man who came to ask for advice under peculiar circumstances. The visitor was a man who gave the impression of having seen better days, but he had fallen into such abject poverty that he was compelled to take any work that offered, and thus it happened that he had become a slaughter-man at a huge abattoir. He declared that he was absolutely unable to execute his loathsome task, because when he prepared to slaughter the creatures he was constantly checked by cries of heart-rending anguish, and by voices which said: "Have mercy upon us! Do not strike, for we are human beings entangled with these animals, and we suffer their pain." So, since he had heard that the Theosophical Society occupied itself with unusual and uncanny matters, he came to it to ask for advice. No doubt this man was somewhat clairaudient, or perhaps simply sensitive enough to catch the thoughts of these poor creatures who had associated themselves with the animals, and these thoughts naturally symbolized themselves to him as audible cries for mercy. No wonder he was unable to continue his occupation.

This may well give pause to those who devour flesh, to the man who calls the murder of animals 'sport,' and most of all to the vivisector—the man who kills or tortures an animal may be inflicting unspeakable suffering upon a human being.

I have little doubt that the possibility for a material-minded man of this uncanny blunder is at least part of the rationale of the belief of various tribes that certain creatures must never be killed "lest one should unawares be dispossessing the spirit of an ancestor." For the man who thus entangles himself with an animal cannot abandon that animal's body at will; even if he learned enough to make him desire to withdraw, he could do so only gradually and by considerable effort, extending probably over many days. It is usually only at the death of the animal that he is set free, and even then there remains an astral entanglement to shake off. After the death of the animal such a soul sometimes struggles to obsess another member of the same herd, or indeed any other creature whom he can seize in his desperation.

I have noticed that animals obsessed or semi-obsessed by human beings are often shunned or feared by the rest of the herd, and indeed they are themselves often half-maddened by anger and terror at the strangeness of the thing and at their own helplessness. The animals most commonly seized upon seem to be the less developed ones—cattle, sheep and swine. More intelligent creatures, such as dogs, cats and horses, would presumably not be so easily dispossessed—though my attention was once drawn to a peculiarly horrible instance in which a Catholic priest had in this way attached himself to a cat. Then there is the well-known case of the monkey of Pandharpur, who betrayed so curious a knowledge of Brahmana ceremonies. But in most cases the obsessing soul has to be satisfied with what he can get, for the effort to overpower even the more stupid beasts usually taxes his powers to the utmost.

This obsession of an animal seems to be the modern substitute for the awful life of the vampire. In the time of the fourth root-race, men who had a mad clinging to material life sometimes contrived to maintain a low and unspeakably horrible form of it in their own physical bodies by absorbing living blood from others. In the fifth race that happily seems no longer to be possible, but people of the same type occasionally fall into this snare of animal obsession—bad enough, indubitably, but still not so utterly gruesome and disgusting as vampirism. So even in its very worst and lowest aspects the world is improving!

I have known of isolated cases of two other types of animal connection; one in which a wicked dead person was in the habit of temporarily seizing the body of a certain animal for specific evil purposes, and another in which an Oriental magician had, as an act of revenge for an insult to his religious faith, mesmerically linked his unhappy victim to an animal form after death. This could be done only if there existed in the victim some weakness through which such a magician could seize upon him, and if he had intentionally done something which gave him a karmic hold upon him. Normally neither of these cases would be at all possible.

All obsessions, whether of a human or an animal body, are an evil and a hindrance to the obsessing soul, for they temporarily strengthen his hold upon the material, and so delay his natural progress into the astral life, besides of course making all sorts of undesirable karmic links. This grey life, like almost all other unpleasant possibilities connected with the life after death, can come only as the result of ignorance of the real conditions of that life. The more we learn of life and death, the more emphatic appears the duty of making every effort to spread the knowledge of Theosophy, for it becomes ever clearer and clearer that in that knowledge is life and happiness and progress for all.

Individualized Animals

When an individualized animal dies he has a happy astral life of considerable length, during which he usually remains in the immediate neighborhood of his earthly home and in the closest touch with his especial friend and protector—able to see and enjoy the society of his friend as fully as ever, though himself invisible to the latter, his memory of the past being, of course, just as perfect as it was on earth. This will be followed by a still happier period of what has sometimes been called 'dozing consciousness,' which will last until in some future world the human form is assumed. During all this time he is in a state analogous to that of a human being in the heaven-world, though at a somewhat lower level. He creates his own surroundings, even though he may be but drowsily conscious of them, and they will undoubtedly include the presence of his earth-friend in his very best and most sympathetic mood. For every entity which comes into connection with it, whether only just entering upon human evolution or preparing to pass beyond it, the heaven-world means the highest bliss of which that entity is, at his level, capable.

Localization of States

The idea of location applies to the subplanes of the astral, but only to a limited extent. Matter of all the stages undoubtedly surrounds us here on the surface of the earth, and the living man, employing his astral body during the sleep of the physical, comes into touch with them all simultaneously, and is able to receive impressions from them all. That is, if I, using my astral body during sleep, look at another living man's astral body, I see the whole of it, including of course matter of every sub-plane. But in the case of the average dead man, there has been a rearrangement of the matter of his astral body, consequent upon the proceedings of what is commonly called the desire-elemental,* and broadly speaking only one type of astral matter is available to receive impressions.

What we usually call 'sight' on the astral plane is not really sight at all, for that word implies the use of an organ specialized to receive certain vibrations. Astral cognition is arranged on an

* *See* "The Desire Elemental" in Section Five. Ed.

entirely different scheme. It has often been said that a man can 'see' with any part of his astral body—that is, every particle of that body is capable of receiving impressions from without and transmitting them to the consciousness within. But every particle is not capable of receiving every possible impression.

For example, I became cognizant of the lowest kind of astral matter only by means of matter of the same subdivision existing in my own astral body; and I receive its vibrations through the particles of that lowest type of matter which happen to be at the moment on the surface of my astral body. Since during life all the particles of the astral body are constantly in motion among themselves, much as are the particles of a boiling liquid, it inevitably happens that all the subdivisions of matter are represented upon the surface of the astral body, and that is why I am able to see all the stages simultaneously. The ordinary man after death has for practical purposes only one type of matter outside, because of the concentric shell arrangement; therefore his view of the astral world around him is a very imperfect one.

If he, immured in a shell of matter of the lowest stage, looks at a living man's astral body, he can see only that part of it which consists of that lowest type of matter; but as he has no means of realizing the limitation of his faculties, he inevitably assumes that he sees the whole of the other man's astral body, and therefore that the other man is a person possessing no characteristics but those eminently unsatisfactory ones which alone express themselves through matter of that particular subdivision.

He is living in the midst of all sorts of high influences and beautiful thought-forms, but is almost entirely unconscious of their existence, because those particles of his astral body which could respond to their vibrations are carefully shut in where they cannot be reached. That lowest type of astral matter corresponds to the solid subdivision of physical matter, and the astral counterpart of any solid physical object is composed of that lowest subdivision of astral matter—the seventh class of astral matter, if we number the subplanes from above downwards. The astral counterparts of the floor, walls and furniture of a room are all of the lowest type of astral matter, and consequently the man newly dead usually sees these counterparts vividly, and is almost entirely unconscious of the vast sea of thought forms which encompasses him, because nearly all those forms are built out of combinations of the finer types of astral matter.

In process of time, as the consciousness steadily withdraws inward, the shell of this coarsest type of matter atrophies and begins to disintegrate, and matter of a somewhat higher type is uncovered, and becomes the surface through which impressions can be received. Since this usually happens gradually, it means that the man finds the counterparts of physical objects growing dimmer and dimmer, while the thought forms become more and more vivid to him, so that without necessarily moving at all in space, he finds himself living in a different world. If while this process is going on he should encounter you at intervals he will be sensible of what will appear to him as a great improvement in your character—not that you have necessarily changed, but that he is becoming able to appreciate the higher vibrations of that character, and is losing the power to receive the lower ones. Your disposition may remain just what it was, but the dead man, having commenced by seeing only its worst features, will pass it all slowly in review until presently he reaches a condition in which only the best and highest side of it is within his consciousness.

This then is what is meant by passing from one sub-plane to another—that the man loses sight of one part of the wonderful complexity which is the astral world, and that another part of it comes into his view. It is after all only a repetition on a smaller scale of what happens to each one of us as we pass from plane to plane. The whole astral world and the whole mental world are both around us here and now, yet so long as our consciousness is focussed in the physical brain we are blankly unconscious of them. At death the consciousness is transferred to the astral body, and at once we find ourselves seeing the astral part of our world, having lost sight of the physical. When later on we lose the astral body in turn, and live in the mental body, we are then conscious (though only partially) of the mental part of our world, and have altogether lost for the time both the astral and the physical. Just as it is possible for the man living on the astral plane to defy the desire-elemental and insist upon keeping the particles of his astral body in constant motion, just as they were during his physical life, so it is possible for the man still in physical life to train himself to have at his command the physical and astral and mental consciousness practically simultaneously; but this means considerable advancement.

A Theosophist, who comprehends the conditions of the astral plane, altogether declines to permit the rearrangement of his astral body by the desire-elemental in the first place; or if that should happen during the momentary unconsciousness which immediately succeeds death, those of us who are trying to help the man immediately break up the elemental's arrangement and restore the astral body to exactly the condition in which it was during life, with all its varieties of matter mingled in the natural way, so that the dead man can perceive the whole of the astral plane, instead of only one subdivision of it. In this way his astral life is perfect from the first, and he can be a much more useful person than if he were confined to the consciousness of one subdivision only.

Heaven-Life Conditions

The principal difficulty in understanding the conditions of the heaven-world comes from our inveterate habit of thinking of the personality as the man. If two friends are bound by ties of affection, we must try to remember that the bond is between the souls and not the bodies—that they are friends now on earth because in quite different bodies they have known and loved each other perhaps for thousands of years. That fact draws their physical bodies together on this plane, but it does not enable them to understand more of one another than their physical capabilities permit; and further, each wears three heavy veils, in the shape of the mental, astral and physical bodies, to conceal his real self from the other.

When one of them dies he passes on to the astral plane, and there he meets his living friend face to face during the sleep of the latter. Even already he can see somewhat more of his friend than before, because for each of them, during those hours of sleep, the heaviest of the three veils has been withdrawn. The dead man is still dealing with the personality of his friend only, and therefore if some great sorrow should fall upon the waking life of that friend, it would inevitably be reflected in his astral life, and the dead man would perceive it. For our sleeping and waking lives are in reality but one, and during our sleep we are aware of that fact, and have the continuous memory of both open before us. You will see, therefore, that the astral body of his living friend (with which the dead man is dealing) is the astral body of the personality, and he is therefore fully conscious of what is happening to that personality.

When the heaven-world is reached all this is changed. The dead man is then functioning in his mental body—the same mental body which he has used during his past earth-life; but he does not meet there the mental body which his friend is using during life. On the contrary, the dead man himself by his thought builds for his friend an entirely separate mental body, and it is the ego of his friend which ensouls it, working from its own level and from the causal body. This is an additional opportunity for mental plane activity for the friend, and is entirely separate in every way from the personality of his physical life.

It is not possible for one man to ensoul more than one physical body at one time, but it is quite possible for him to ensoul simultaneously any number of the thought forms which other people may make of him on the mental plane in the course of their heaven-life. I think it is a misunderstanding of this fact which had led some to think that several physical bodies may be incarnations of one man.

You will see, therefore, that any sorrow or trouble which may fall upon the personality of the living man, and may conceivably influence his mental body, will not in the least affect his other thought-form which his ego is using as an additional mental body. If in that manifestation he knows at all of such sorrow or trouble, he will regard it as he would from the causal body—that is to say, it will not be to him a sorrow or trouble at all, but only a lesson, or the working out of some karma. There is no delusion at all in this view of his, because he is seeing the matter as it really is, from the point of view of the ego on his own plane. It is our lower personal view that is the delusion, because we see sorrow and trouble where in reality there are only the steps on our upward way.

The two friends may know far more of each other at that level, because each has now only one veil, that of the mental body, cast over his individuality; but there is still that veil. If the dead man has known only one side of his friend during life, it will be only through that side that the friend can express himself in the heaven-world. He can express that side of himself much more fully and satisfactorily than ever before; but he is largely confined to that side. Still, it is a fuller expression than the dead man has ever been able to see upon the lower planes. He by no means forgets that there is such a thing as suffering, because he remembers clearly his past life; but he now understands many things that were not clear when he was on the physical plane, and the delight of the present is for him so great that sorrow seems to him almost like a dream.

It is asked how we who still live on earth converse with our friends in heaven; if by 'we' you mean our personality, that does not converse with friends in heaven. The real does do so, as has been said, but in the veil of this personality we know nothing of that.

Suppose that a good Catholic mother died, who dearly loved her daughter, and that after the mother had reached the heaven-world, her daughter embraced theosophy. The mother would go on imagining her daughter as merely orthodox; would she not in this be under a delusion? Yes, she would, for this is an instance of one of the possible limitations to which I have previously referred. If the mother could see only such of her daughter's thought as could be expressed by orthodox ideas, there would naturally be points in the new revelation which had come to the daughter which the mother would be little able to grasp. But in so far as the ego of the daughter profited by what the personality had learned, there would be a tendency on her part gradually to widen out and perfect the conception of the mother, but always along the lines to which the mother was accustomed. There would be no sense of difference of opinion, and no avoidance of subjects of religion.

You will understand that I am speaking here of the ordinary person; in the case of a more advanced man who was already fully conscious in the causal body, he would put himself down consciously into the thought form provided for him by a friend in the heaven-world, as into an additional mental body, and work through it with definite intention; so that if such a man should acquire additional knowledge he could directly and intentionally communicate it to that friend. In this way the Masters work on such of their pupils as take the heaven-life, and alter their characters immensely.

A man's condition in the heaven-life depends upon the amount of spiritual force in him. Of two people of the same class or type the more spiritual would naturally remain a longer time; but it must be borne in mind that the force may be used up quickly or slowly according to the necessities of each man's evolution. Those who have devoted themselves especially to the work of serving the Great Ones, and through them humanity, are likely in this respect to have experiences differing somewhat from the ordinary. It is evident that our Masters have already, many millennia ago, formed a special band of servers and helpers from those who have offered themselves for such work, and They use this body of men as a kind of regiment of pioneers to be sent wherever special work of that kind is needed.

Those who have read the lives of Alcyone, as published in *The Theosophist*, will realize that the hero of that remarkable story is a member of that band—or perhaps we should rather say of one of those bands; and for that reason it will be found that over and over again the same set of people come together in all sorts of different places, in their successive incarnations. It is obvious that in a group of a hundred people there must be many divergences; some of them will assuredly generate more spiritual force than others, and their karma would naturally be such as to take them into differing surroundings, yet the one great fact that they are devoted to service overpowers all these considerations, and they are brought together in order that they may be utilized as a whole.

Be sure that in this there is no injustice, and that no one of them, for this or any other reason, escapes one jot of the karma which is legitimately due to him. Indeed, those who offer themselves for service not infrequently suffer considerably in the course of that service—sometimes because it is necessary that their past karma should be cleared up quickly, in order that they may be free to do higher work without any hindrance from it, and in other cases because their work may have made it impossible for them to reap life after life the karma that would otherwise have come to them, and so a considerable accumulation may descend upon them at once in some gigantic catastrophe. Instances of the working of both these methods may be found in the lives of Alcyone.

In the case of the great bulk of humanity there is no special interference from without, and the heaven-life of each works itself out at whatever may be its ordinary rate. Naturally this difference in the time of working out involves also a difference of intensity which is shown by a greater or less brilliancy in the light of the mental body. The more developed man, especially if he has before him the idea of service, usually generates karma during his heaven-life, and thus he may modify it even while it is in progress.

It is true that Madame Blavatsky states in *The Key to Theosophy* that it is impossible for a materialist to have any heaven-life, as he had not while on earth believed in any such condition; but it seems probably that she was employing the word materialist in a more restricted sense than that in which it is generally used, for in the same volume she also asserts that for them no conscious life after death is possible at all, whereas it is a matter of common knowledge among those whose nightly work lies upon the astral plane that many of those whom we usually call materialists are to be met with there, and are certainly not unconscious.

For example, a prominent materialist intimately known to one of our members was not long ago discovered by his friend in the highest subdivision of the astral world, where he had surrounded himself with his books and was continuing his studies almost as he might have done on earth. On being questioned by his friend he readily admitted that the theories which he had held while on earth were confuted by the irresistible logic of facts, but his own agnostic tendencies were still strong enough to make him unwilling to accept what his friend told him as to the existence of the still higher spiritual state of the heaven-world. Yet there was certainly much in this man's character which could find its full result only in the heaven-world, and since his entire disbelief in any life after death has not prevented his astral experience, there seems no reason to suppose that it can check the due working out of the higher forces in him upon the mental plane.

We constantly find down here that nature makes no allowance for our ignorance of her laws; if, under an impression that fire does not burn, a man puts his hand into a flame, he is speedily convinced of his error. In the same way a man's disbelief in a future existence does not affect the facts of nature, and in some cases at least he simply finds out after death that he was under a mistake. The kind of materialism referred to by Madame Blavatsky was probably something much coarser and more aggressive than ordinary agnosticism—something which would render it exceedingly unlikely that a man who held it would have any qualities requiring a heaven-life in which to work themselves out; but no such case as that has yet come under our observation.

Karma in the Heaven Life

In the earlier days of our study of theosophy we were led to look upon all other worlds but the physical as almost exclusively the theater of results and not of causes. It was supposed that man spent his physical life to a large extent in generating karma, and his existence on the astral and mental planes in working it out, and the suggestion that a man could by any means make any more karma, even on the astral plane, was regarded as almost heretical.

As the years rolled on and some of us became able to study astral conditions at first-hand, it became obvious that this idea had been an error, since it was manifestly possible for us in working on that plane to perform actions of various sorts which produced far-reaching results. We soon saw also that not only the man still attached to a physical body could produce these results, but that they were equally within the power of one who had cast off that vehicle. We found that any developed man is in every way quite as active during his astral life after physical death as during his physical life before it; that he can unquestionably help or hinder not only his own progress but that of others quite as much after death as before, and consequently that he is all the time generating karma of the greatest importance.

This modified view of after-death conditions gradually found its way into our literature, and may be considered now as universally accepted by all Theosophists. But for many years after we had corrected our misconceptions upon this important point, we still held to the idea that in the heaven-world at least man could do practically nothing but enjoy the conditions which he had made for himself during the previous stages of his existence. Broadly speaking, this is true for the ordinary man, though we do not always realize that even in the course of that enjoyment the inhabitant of the heaven-world is affecting others, and therefore producing results.

One who has succeeded in raising his consciousness to the level of the causal body has already unified the higher and lower selves (to use the older terminology), and to him the statements made as to average humanity naturally do not apply. Such a one has the consciousness of the ego at his disposal during the whole of his physical life, and that is not at all affected by the death of the physical body, nor even by the second and third deaths in which he leaves behind him the astral and the mental bodies respectively. For him the whole of that series of incarnations is only one long life, and what we call an incarnation is to him a day in that life. All through his human evolution his consciousness is fully active, and it naturally follows that he is making karma just as much at one period of it as at another; and while his condition at any one moment is the result of the causes which he has set in motion in the past, there is no instant at which he is not modifying his conditions by the exercise of thought and will.

Men who have reached that level are at present rare; but there are others who possess a similar power in a minor degree. Every human being, after he has passed through his life on the astral and lower mental planes, has a momentary flash of the consciousness of the ego, in which he sees his last life as a whole, and gathers from it the impression of success or failure in the work which it was meant to do; and along with this he has also a forecast of the life before him, with the knowledge of the general lesson which that is to teach, or the specific progress which he is intended to make in it. Only very slowly does the ego awaken to the value of these glimpses, but when he comes to understand them he naturally begins to make use of them.

Thus by imperceptible degrees he arrives at a stage in his evolution when this glimpse is no longer momentary—when he is able to consider the question much more fully, and to devote some time to his plans for the life which lies before him. His consciousness gradually increases, and he comes to have an appreciable life on the higher levels of the mental plane each time that he touches them. When he arrives at this stage he soon finds that he is one among a vast number of other egos, and that he can do something else with his life among them besides making plans for his own future. He may and does live a conscious life among his peers, in the course of which he influences them in many ways, and is himself influenced in turn. Here therefore is a possibility of making karma, and of making it on a scale which is entirely out of his reach on these lower planes, for every thought on those higher mental levels has a force quite out of proportion to that of our limited thought during physical life.

This of which I am speaking is quite distinct from the consciousness which comes with the unifying of the higher and lower selves. When that feat has been performed the man's consciousness resides in the ego all the time, and from that ego it plays through whatever vehicle he may happen to be using. But in the case of a man who has not yet achieved that union the consciousness of the ego on his own plane comes into activity only when he is no longer hampered by any lower vehicles, and exists only until he puts himself down again into incarnation; for as soon as he takes up a lower body his consciousness can manifest for the time only through that body.

Short of that perfect consciousness of the ego, there are stages of development which it is necessary to note. The ordinary 'man in the street' has usually no definite and reliable consciousness outside of the physical plane. His astral body may be fully developed and quite capable of being used as a vehicle in any and every way; yet he is probably not in the habit of so using it, and therefore his experiences of the astral world are of a vague and uncertain character. He may sometimes remember one of them vividly, but on the whole the time of the sleep of the physical body is for him a blank.

The next stage beyond this is that of the gradual development of the habit of using the astral body, accompanied as time goes on by some recollection of what is done in it. The end of this is the opening of the astral consciousness, though usually that comes only as the result of definite efforts along the line of meditation. When this opening is attained the man's consciousness is continuous through night and day, and up to the end of the astral life, so that he avoids the usual temporary suspension of consciousness at the death of the physical body.

The next stage beyond this—a long stage usually—is the development of the consciousness of the mental body, and when that is achieved, each personality remains conscious from physical birth until the end of its life in the heaven-world. But even then it is only the consciousness of the personality, and not yet of the ego, and still another step must be taken before complete unification is attained.

It is clear that men who have reached any of these stages are making karma as far as their consciousness reaches; but what as to the ordinary man, who has not yet quite succeeded in linking even the astral consciousness to the physical? In so far as he has any activities on the astral plane during sleep, he must be producing results. If he feels, even blindly, love and affection towards certain persons, and goes out towards them during sleep with vague thoughts of goodwill, he must inevitably affect them to a certain extent, and the effect must be a good one. Therefore there is no possibility of avoiding a reaction upon himself which will also be good. The same is true, unfortunately, if the feeling be one of dislike or of active hatred, and the result for him in that case cannot but be painful.

When, after death, he lives entirely in the astral world, his consciousness is usually much more definite than it has been during the sleep of his physical body, and he is correspondingly better able to think and act with determination in regard to other men, and so his opportunities of making good or bad karma are the greater. But when such a man ends his astral life and passes into the heaven-world he reaches a condition where activity is no longer possible for him. He has encouraged activities in his mental body, during life, in certain directions only, and now that he comes to live entirely in that mental body he finds himself enclosed within it as in a tower, shut off from the world around him and able to look out upon it only through the windows in it which he has opened by means of those activities.

Through those windows the mighty forces of the plane play upon him; he responds to them and leads a life of vivid joy—which is, however, confined to those particular lines. But, though he is thus shut away from the full enjoyment of the possibilities of the mental world, it must not be supposed that he is in the slightest degree conscious of any curtailment of his activities or his feelings. He is, on the contrary, filled with bliss to the very utmost of which he is capable, and it is to him incredible that there can be any greater joy than that which he is himself experiencing. True, he has shut himself in within certain limits; but he is quite unconscious of those limits, and he has all that he can possibly desire or think of within them. He has surrounded himself with images of his friends, so that through these images he is actually in closer connection with them than he has ever been on any other plane.

Let us see then what are his possibilities for making karma in this curiously limited life—limited, we must remember, from the point of view of the mental world only, for along the lines of its special directions its possibilities are far greater than those of physical life. A man under such conditions cannot originate a fresh line of affection or devotion, but his affection and devotion along the lines which he has already decided will be distinctly much more powerful than they ever could have been while he was laboring under the heavy limitations of the physical body.

An ordinary man such as we have described is, quite unintentionally and unconsciously to himself, producing three separate results, during the whole of his heaven-life. Let us take as an example the emotion of affection. He feels this strongly for certain friends, and it is probable that even after his death those friends still think of him with kindly remembrance, and thus his memory is not without its effect even upon their personalities. But entirely apart from this is the effect to which I have above referred—that he makes an image of each friend and, in so doing, draws forth a strong response from the ego of that friend. The affection which he pours upon that ego (manifesting through the thought form which he has made for it) is a mighty power for good, which bears no inconsiderable part in the evolution of that ego. It evokes from him an amount of affection which would not otherwise be stirred up in him; and the steady intensification of that most admirable quality throughout the centuries of the heaven-life raises the friend considerably in the scale of evolution. To do this for another ego is unquestionably an act which generates karma, even though the man who has set all this machinery in motion has done so uncomprehendingly.

Occasionally the action of such a force upon the ego of a surviving friend may manifest itself even in the personality of that friend upon the physical plane. The action is upon the ego through the special thought form; but the personality of the surviving friend in this world is a manifestation of the same ego, and if the ego be considerably modified, it is at least possible that that modification may show itself in the physical manifestation on this lower plane. It may be asked why the thought of the man in the heaven-world should not act upon his friend precisely as does the thought of a living man—why not the vibrations sent forth from his mental body cannot strike directly upon the mental body of his friend, and why it should not generate a thought form which would travel through space and attach itself to his friend in the ordinary way. If he were moving freely and consciously about the mental plane that is precisely what would happen, but the reason that it does not lies in the peculiar condition of the man in the heaven-world.

The man in the heaven-life has shut himself out absolutely from the rest of the world—from the mental plane as much as from the lower levels, and he is living inside the shell of his own thoughts. If his thoughts could reach us in the ordinary way, ours could reach him in precisely the same way, but we know that that is not so. The thought form which he makes of his friend is within his own shell, and therefore he can act upon it; and since the ego of the friend has poured himself down into that thought form, the force reaches the ego of the friend in that way, and from that ego it may, as we have said, to some extent manifest itself even in the personality of the friend down here. The shell is as regards the mental plane much like the shell of an egg on the physical plane. The only way to get anything into the shell of an egg, without breaking it, would be to pour it in from the fourth dimension, or to find a force whose vibrations are sufficiently fine to penetrate between the particles of the shell without disturbing them. This is true also of this mental shell; it cannot be penetrated by any vibrations of matter of its own level, but the finer vibrations which belong to the ego can pass through it without disturbing it in the least; so that it can be acted upon freely from above, but not from below.

The thought form made by the dead man may be considered as a kind of additional artificial mental body, made for, and presented to, the friend upon whom the love is being poured forth. The personality down here knows nothing of this, but the ego is fully conscious of it and plunges down into it with delight and avidity, realizing incidentally that this affords him an additional opportunity of manifestation, and therefore of evolution. From this it follows that the man who has made himself generally beloved—the man who has many real friends—will evolve with far greater rapidity than a more ordinary man; and this again is obviously the karma of his development within himself of the qualities which make him so lovable.

So much for the direct result of his action upon individuals; but there are also two aspects of its general action which must not be ignored. A man who thus pours out a great flood of affection, and evokes in response other floods from his friends, is distinctly improving the mental atmosphere in his neighborhood. It is good for the world and for the humanity evolving in it that its mental atmosphere should thus be charged with such feelings, for they play upon all its inhabitants—devas, men, animals, plants—and on every one of these widely different forms of life they have their influence, and always an influence for good.

The second and more important of the results produced for the world at large will be readily comprehensible to those who have studied the book on *Thought-Forms*, as an attempt is there made to indicate the outpouring which flows down from the Logos in response to a thought of unselfish devotion. It has often been explained that such response comes not only to the individual who originated the thought, but that it also helps to fill the reservoir of spiritual force, which is held by the Nirmanakaya at the disposal of the Masters of Wisdom and their pupils, to be used for the helping of mankind.* What is true of devotion is true also of unselfish affection, and if every outrush of such affection or devotion during the comparatively limited physical life produces so magnificent a result, it is easy to see that a far stronger outrush, sustained through a period of perhaps a thousand years, will make to that reservoir a really considerable contribution, and this will bring to the world a benefit which is not calculable in any terms that we can use upon the physical plane.

So it is clear that while a man's power for good augments as his consciousness in these higher worlds increases, even the quite ordinary man, who has as yet no special development of consciousness, is nevertheless capable of doing an enormous amount of good during his sojourn upon the higher planes. During his long stay in the heaven-world he may benefit his fellow-men, and so make a large amount of good karma for himself; but, in order to do that, he must be a man of unselfish love or unselfish devotion. It is this quality of unselfishness, of self-forgetfulness, which puts the power into his hands; and that, therefore, is the virtue which every man must cultivate now in full consciousness, in order that after death he may use to the best advantage those far longer periods whose conditions it is now so impossible for him to realize.

---

*Nirmanakaya—highly evolved being who chooses to remain in touch with earth in order to generate streams of spiritual force to help in evolution.

SECTION SEVEN

Astral Work

Invisible Helpers

People often write to us, applying to be admitted to the band of invisible helpers, and asking what preparation is necessary. Those who desire to take up this work should familiarize themselves thoroughly with the book written under that title, and should especially take care to develop within themselves the qualifications which are there described. I have little to add to what I have there written, except that I should advise every one who wishes to take up work on the astral plane to learn as much as he can beforehand of the conditions of life on that plane.

In the astral life we are absolutely the same persons as we are down here, but with certain limitations removed. Our interests and activities on that plane resemble those on the physical; a student is still studious; an idle person is still idle; an active helper on the physical plane is still a helper there. Some people still gossip there just as venomously as ever, and are still continuing to make just the same bad karma by doing so. Most dead people haunt, for a long time, the places to which they have been accustomed in life. Many a man hovers round his ancestral home, and continues daily to visit the astral counterpart of the temple which he used to support. Others drift round and make pilgrimages, without trouble or expense, to all the great shrines which during life they have in vain wished to visit.

And yet, ordinary people usually do very little in the way of real work on the astral plane. They do not know, in fact, that they can work, and even if they did know they would probably see no particular reason why they should. A man may spend a very enjoyable time in the astral world, just drifting about and experiencing various pleasurable emotions. That seems to most people the only thing to do, and it needs a powerful motive to rouse them out of that, and make them take the trouble of devoting their time to the helping of others. We must admit that for the ordinary man this motive does not exist; but when we have begun to study theosophy, and in that way learn the course of evolution and the purpose of things, there arises within us an earnest desire to help forward that evolution, to accomplish that purpose, and to put our fellow-men in the way of understanding it also, in order that thereby their troubles may be lightened and the path of their progress made easier.

Now, when a man thus awakens to his duty, how is he to set about it? We are, all of us, capable of such work to a greater or lesser extent, though probably not in the habit of doing it. All people of ordinary culture and development have their astral bodies in working order, just as all reasonably healthy people possess the necessary muscles and the necessary strength to enable them to swim; but if they have not learned how to use them they will need a certain amount of instruction before they can usefully or even safely take to the water. The difficulty with the ordinary person is not that the astral body cannot act, but that for thousands of years that body has been accustomed to being set in motion only by impressions received from below through the physical vehicle, so that men do not realize that the astral body can work on its own plane and on its own account, and that the will can act upon it directly. People remain 'unawake' astrally because they get into the habit of waiting for the familiar physical vibrations to call out their astral activity.

There are several ways in which a man may begin to help. Suppose, for example, that a relation or friend dies. In order to reach and to help him during sleep, all that is necessary is to think of him before retiring to rest, with the resolve to give him whatever assistance he most needs. We do not need any help in order to find him, or to communicate with him. We must try to understand that as soon as we leave the physical body at night we stand side by side with a departed friend, exactly as we did when he was with us on the physical plane. One great thing to remember is the necessity of curbing all sorrow for the so-called dead, because it cannot but react upon him.

If a man allows himself to despair about the dead, the feeling of despair will affect them very strongly, for emotions play through the astral body, and consequently those who are living in their astral vehicles are much more readily and deeply influenced by them than people who have a physical body to deaden their perceptions. The dead can see us, but it is our astral body that they see; consequently they are at once aware of our emotions, but not necessarily of the details of our physical condition. They know whether we are happy or miserable, but not what book we are reading for example. The emotion is obvious to them, but not necessarily the thought which causes it. The dead man carries with him his affections and hatreds; he knows his old friends when he meets them, and he also often forms new friendships among new companions whom he meets for the first time on the astral plane.

Not only must we avoid sorrow, but also excitement of any kind. The invisible helper must, above all, keep perfectly calm. I have known a worthy lady who was full of the most earnest desire to help, and in her eagerness to do so keyed herself up into a tremendous state of excitement. Now, excitement shows itself in the astral body in great increase of size, violent vibration and the flashing forth of fiery colors. So the newly-dead person, who was quite unused to astral surroundings, and consequently in a state of timidity and nervousness, was horrified to see a huge flaming, flashing sphere come rushing at him with evident intention. Naturally he took this for the theological devil *in propria persona*, and fled shrieking before it to the ends of the earth, though for a long time it increased his terror by persistently following him.

One case in which it is often possible for even a beginner to make himself useful is that of some friend or neighbor who is known to be about to die. If one has access to him physically, and if his illness is of a nature which makes it possible to discuss with him the conditions of death and of its after-states, a little rational explanation of these will often very greatly relieve his mind and lighten his burdens. Indeed, the mere meeting with a person who speaks confidently and cheerfully about the life beyond the grave is frequently the greatest consolation to one who finds himself approaching it.

If, however, for any reason this physical communication is impossible, much may be done during sleep by acting upon the dying man from the astral plane. An untrained person seeking to give such help should follow the rules laid down in our books; he should fix the intention of aiding that particular person in his mind before going to sleep, and he should even decide as far as possible upon the arguments which should be presented and even the very words which should be used, for the more precise and definite the resolution is made while awake, the more certain it is to be faithfully and accurately carried out in the astral body during sleep.

The explanation to be given to the sick man is necessarily the same in both cases. The main object of the helper is to calm and encourage the sufferer, to induce him to realize that death is a perfectly natural and usually an easy process, and in no case a formidable or terrible leap into an unknown abyss. The nature of the astral world, the way in which a man ought to order his life in it if he wishes to make the best of it, and the preparation necessary for progress toward the heaven-world which lies beyond; all these should be gradually explained by the helper to the dying man. The helper should always remember that his own attitude and state of mind produces even more effect than his argument or his advice, and consequently he must be exceedingly careful to approach his task with the greatest calmness and confidence. If the helper himself is in a condition of nervous excitement he is quite likely to do more harm than good, as did the poor lady whom I have just mentioned.

The assistance offered should be continued after death. There will be a certain period of unconsciousness then, but it may last only for a moment, though often the moment expands into a few minutes, or several hours, and sometimes even into many days or weeks. A trained pupil naturally observes for himself the condition of the 'dead' person's consciousness and regulates his assistance accordingly; the untrained man will do well to offer such assistance immediately after death, and also to hold himself in readiness to give it for several succeeding nights, in order that he may not fail to be at hand when his services are needed. So many diverse circumstances affect the duration of this period of unconsciousness that it is scarcely possible to lay down any general rule in the matter.

We should at least determine each night to comfort someone who is in trouble, and if we know the exact nature of the trouble we must do our best to adapt our measures to the needs of the case. If the sufferer be weak and exhausted, the helper should use his will to pour into him physical strength. If, on the other hand, he is excited or hysterical, the helper should endeavor to enfold him in a special aura of calm and gentleness—wrap him up, as it were in a strong thought form of peace and harmony, just as one would wrap a person in a blanket.

It is often difficult for one who tries to help to believe that he can have been successful, when he wakes in the morning and remembers nothing whatever of what has taken place. As a matter of fact some measure of success is absolutely certain, and as the helper goes on with his work he will often receive cheering little indications that he is producing definite results in spite of his lack of memory.

Many a member has set himself to try this, and for a long time has known nothing as to results, until one day it has happened to him to meet physically the person whom he has been trying to assist, and to be much comforted to see the improvement in him. Sometimes it happens that the friend dates the commencement of his recovery from a particular night on which he had a pleasant or a remarkable dream; and the helper is startled when he remembers that it was on that very night that he made a specially determined effort to help that man. The first time that this happens, the helper probably persuades himself that it is a mere accident; but when a sufficient number of coincidences have accumulated he begins to see that there is something more in it than that. The beginner, therefore, should do his best and be content to wait as far as results are concerned.

There is another simple experiment which has greatly helped some beginners in gaining confidence. Let a man resolve to visit

astrally some room which is well known to him—one, let us say, in
a friend's house; and let him note carefully the arrangement of
the furniture and books. Or if, without previously intending it,
the experimenter finds himself during sleep in a spot which he
recognizes (that is, in ordinary parlance, if he dreams of a certain
place) he should set himself to observe it with great care. If when
he remembers this in the morning it seems to him that everything
in that room was exactly as when he last saw it physically, there is
nothing to prove that it was not really a mere dream or memory;
but if he recollects some decided change in the arrangements, or
if there is something new and unexpected, it is distinctly worth his
while to go physically in the morning to visit that room, in order to
test whether his nocturnal vision has been correct.

All those of us who are definitely engaged in astral work have
necessarily, at one time or another, taken in hand a number of
cases which needed help. Such help may occasionally be of the
nature of a surgical operation—something which can be done
once for all, and then put aside; but far more often what is needed
is comfort, reassurance and strengthening which must be repeated day after day in order that it may gradually sink into the
texture of some wounded nature and transmute it into something
braver and nobler. Or sometimes it is knowledge which must be
given little by little as the mind opens to it and is able to bear it.
Thus it comes that each worker has a number of chronic cases,
clients, patients—call them what you will—whom he visits every
night, as a doctor upon earth makes a regular round among his
patients.

It often happens also that those who have been thus helped are
filled with gratitude towards the worker, and attach themselves to
him in order to second his efforts, and to pass on to others the
benefits which they have thus received. So it evolves that each
worker is usually the center of a small group, the leader of a little
bank of helpers for whom he is always able to find constant
employment. For example, a large number of people who die are
much in the position of children afraid of the dark. One may
reason with them, and argue patiently and convincingly that
there is nothing whatever to fear; but a hand that the child can
hold is of more practical use to him than a whole chapter of
arguments.

The astral worker, with a score of other cases needing immediate attention, cannot possibly spend the whole night stand-

ing by and comforting one nervous or doubting patient; but he can detach for that purpose one of his earnest followers who is not so busily occupied, and is therefore able to devote himself to that charitable work. For to comfort the child in the dark no brilliant scientific knowledge is needed; what he wants is a kindly hand and the sense of companionship. So that work can be found in the astral world for any number of workers, and everyone who wishes, man, woman or child, may be one of them. For the larger and more comprehensive varieties of work, and for the direction of the work, much knowledge is of course required; but a heart full of love and the earnest desire to help is equipment enough to enable any one to become one of the minor comforters, and even that humble effort brings in its train a blessing beyond all calculation.

When the astral worker finally lays aside the physical body for this incarnation, he finds himself among an army of grateful friends who rejoice unreservedly that he is now able to spend the whole of his life with them instead of only a third of it. For such a worker there will be no sense of strangeness or newness in the condition of the life after death. The change for him means only that he will then be able to devote the whole of his time to what is even now by far the happiest and most effective part of his work —a part which he takes up every night with joy and lays aside every morning with regret—the real life, in which our days of physical existence are but dull and featureless interludes.

There are one or two other points with regard to the astral life which it is desirable for the worker to try to understand. One of these is the method of what I suppose we must call speech—the communication of ideas on the astral plane.

It is not always easy to understand down here the substitute for language which is used in the astral world. Sound in the ordinary sense of the word is not possible there—indeed it is not possible even in the etheric part of the purely physical plane. As soon as one rises above the air into the etheric regions there is no more possibility of sound as we understand the word. Yet the symbol of sound is used very much higher, for we constantly find references to the spoken word of the Logos, which calls the worlds into manifestation.

If in the morning we remember an experience of the previous night, such as the meeting with a friend or the attendance at a lecture, it will always seem to us that we heard a voice in the usual terrestrial way, and that we ourselves replied to it, also audibly. In reality this is not so; it is merely that when we bring through a recollection to the physical brain we instinctively express it in terms of the ordinary senses. Yet it would not be correct to say that the language of the astral world is thought-transference; the most that could be said is that it is the transference of a thought formulated in a particular way.

In the mental world one formulates a thought and it is instantly transmitted to the mind of another without any expression in the form of words. Therefore on that plane language does not matter in the least; but helpers working in the astral world, who have not yet the power to use the mental vehicle, must depend on the facilities offered by the astral plane itself. These lie as it were half way between the thought-transference of the mental world and the concrete speech of the physical, but it is still necessary to formulate the thought in words. It is as though one showed such formulation to the other party in the dialogue, and he replied (almost simultaneously, but not quite) by showing in the same way his formulated reply. For this exchange it is necessary that the two parties should have a language in common; therefore the more languages an astral plane helper knows, the more useful he is.

The pupils of the Masters, however, have been taught to form a special kind of temporary vehicle, in order to meet these difficulties. They habitually leave their astral bodies with the physical; they travel about in their mental bodies, and they materialize a temporary astral body from surrounding matter when they need it for astral work. All who have been taught to do this have the advantage of the mental plane method of thought-transference, so far as understanding another man is concerned, though their power to convey a thought in that way is limited by the degree of development of that other man's astral body.

Apart from definitely trained pupils, there are very few people who consciously work in the mental body—for to do so means years of practice in meditation and special effort. We know that a man in the heaven-world shuts himself up within a shell of his own thoughts, and that these thoughts then act as channels through which the life of the mental world can affect him. But we cannot call this functioning on the mental plane, for that involves the free moving about on that plane, and the observation of what exists there.

Fortunately, the mental elemental does not rearrange the mental body after death, so that we have not the same kind of trouble with it as with the desire-elemental on the astral plane. Indeed, the elemental essence of the mental plane differs greatly from that of the astral. It is a whole chain behind the other, and therefore it has not the same force.* It is difficult to deal with, for it is largely responsible for our wandering thoughts, as it darts constantly from one thing to another; but at least it does not make a shell of any sort, although certain portions of the mental body may become hardened, as I have explained when dealing with that subject.

When a man functions in the mental vehicle he leaves the astral body behind him in a condition of suspended animation, along with the physical. If he finds it necessary he can easily surround that torpid astral body with a shell, or he can set up in it vibrations which render it impervious to all evil influences. It is unquestionably possible for any man in process of time, by meditation upon the Logos or the Master, to raise himself first to the astral and then to the mental levels; but none can say how long it will take, as that depends entirely upon the past of the student.

It is quite possible for any person when upon the astral plane after death to set himself to study, and to acquire entirely new ideas. I have known people who learned theosophy for the first time in the astral world. I have even heard of a case in which a lady learned music there, but that is unusual. Probably some dead person gave her lessons, or it may be that the teacher was a living musician who was on the astral plane at the same time as the lady. In astral life people often think that they are playing on astral instruments, but in reality they are only making vibrations by their thought, which produce the effect of sound. There is a special class of devas who respond to music and express themselves through it, and sometimes they are willing to teach people to whom music is the first and only thing in life.

There is no such thing as sleep in the astral world. The need of sleep on the physical plane is that it calms the physical centers and allows them time to rebuild themselves chemically, so that the astral body can work more freely, through a better vehicle; but on the astral plane there is no fatigue, unless we may call by that

*Chain—a scheme of evolution in which the life-wave inhabits each of the seven globes seven times. Ed.

name the gradual slackening down of all the energies when the end of the astral life is approaching.

It is possible to forget upon the astral plane, just as it is upon the physical. I mean in this case not the loss of memory between two planes, which is so common, but the actually being unable to remember on the astral plane tonight some of the details of what one did last night or last year. Indeed, perhaps it is even easier to forget on the astral plane than on the physical, because that world is so busy and so populous.

Knowledge of a person in the astral world does not necessarily mean knowledge of the physical life of that person. For example, many of us know Madame Blavatsky in her new body exceedingly well on the astral plane, yet none of us have yet seen that body physically. She often uses her old form, though generally she is in the new astral body now.

Remembering Astral Experience

There is perfect continuity in the astral life. That life is in many ways much more real than this, or at least much nearer to reality, and this physical existence is only a series of breaks in it during which our activity is greatly limited and our consciousness but partially operative. To most of us in this lower life the night seems a blank, and in the morning we remember nothing of what we have done; but we must not therefore suppose that we are equally dense on the astral plane. That wider consciousness fully includes this, and every night we remember vividly not only what we did on all previous nights, but also all that we have done on the intermediate days. It is the physical brain which is dull and clogged, and it is upon return to it that we lose our memory of all except that with which it has been directly concerned. The astral life is much more vivid and its emotions are far stronger than any that we know down here. What we ordinarily call an emotion is only the comparatively small fragment of one which remains after the greater part of it has been exhausted in setting in motion the clumsy physical particles, so it is not difficult to see how far more intense and real that other life must be.

A special link must be made, or rather an obstacle must be removed, in order to bring the memory of astral life through into the physical brain. In the slow course of evolution the power of perfect memory will come to every one, so that there will no longer be any veil between the two planes. Apart from this full development sometimes something occurs which the man feels that he ought to remember on the physical plane, and in that case he makes a special effort to impress it upon the brain, in order that it may be remembered in the morning. There are some events, too, which make such a vivid impression upon the astral body that they become impressed upon the physical brain by a kind of repercussion.

It is comparatively rarely, however, that such an impression is perfect, and there may be many stages of imperfection. This is one source of what we call dreams, and we know how confused and incomplete and even ridiculous they may often be. One form of distortion which frequently occurs in the case of the unpracticed helper is that he confuses himself with the person to whom he has been giving assistance.

I remember a case of a member of our band who was deputed to assist the victim of an explosion. He was warned a few minutes beforehand, and had time enough to make an effort to calm and steady the man's mind, and then immediately after the outburst had taken place he was still on hand to continue the same process; but in the morning, when he described the event to me, he declared that it seemed exactly as though he himself had been the victim of the explosion. He had identified himself so closely with his patient that he felt the shock and the sensation of flying upwards exactly as, we must presume, the victim felt them. In another case the same member was called upon to assist a soldier who was driving an ammunition wagon down an execrable mountain road, and was thrown off and killed by the wheels passing over his body. In this case also our member entirely identified himself with the soldier, and his memory of the event was that he had dreamed of driving such a wagon and being thrown from it and killed, just as the real driver had been.

In other cases what is remembered is not at all what really happened, but rather a sort of symbolic description of it, sometimes quite elaborate and poetical. This comes evidently from the image-making characteristic of the ego—his faculty of instantaneous dramatization—and it sometimes happens that the symbol is recollected without its key; it comes through untranslated, as it were, so that unless the helper has a more experienced friend at hand to explain matters, he may have only a vague idea of what he has really done. A good instance of this came before my notice many years ago—so many that, as I made no record of it at the time, I am not now quite certain of one or two of its points, and am therefore obliged to omit some of it, and make it a little less interesting than I think it really was.

The helper came to me one morning to relate an exceedingly vivid dream which he felt sure was in reality something more than a dream. He remembered having seen a certain young lady drowning in the sea. I believe that he had the impression that she had been intentionally thrown in, though I do not think that he had any vision of the person who was supposed to have done this. He himself could not directly assist her, as he was present only in the astral body, and did not know how to materialize himself; but his keen sense of the imminence of the peril gave him strength to impress the idea of danger upon the young lady's lover, and to bring him to the scene, where he at once plunged in and brought her ashore, delivering her into the arms of her father. The helper remembered the faces of all these three characters quite clearly, and was able so to describe them that they were afterwards readily recognizable. The helper begged me to look into this case, so that he might know how far his clear remembrance was reliable.

On doing so, I found to my surprise that the whole story was symbolic, and that the facts which had really occurred were of a different nature. The young lady was motherless, and lived practically alone with her father. She seems to have been rich as well as beautiful, and no doubt there were various aspirants to her hand. Our story, however, has to do only with two of these; one, a most estimable but bashful young fellow of the neighborhood, who had adored her since childhood, had grown up in friendly relations with her, and had in fact the usual half-understood, half-implied engagement which belongs to a boy-and-girl love affair. The other was a person distinctly of the adventurer type, handsome and dashing and captivating on the surface, but in reality a fortune-hunter of false and unreliable type. She was dazzled by his superficial brilliancy, and easily persuaded herself that her attraction for him was real affection, and that her previous feelings of comradeship for her boy friend amounted to nothing.

Her father, however, was much more clear-sighted than she, and when the adventurer was presented to him he seems to have received him with marked coolness, and declined altogether, though kindly enough, to sanction his daughter's marriage with a gentleman of whom he knew nothing. This was a great blow to the young lady, and the adventurer, meeting her in secret, easily persuaded her that she was a terribly ill-used and misunderstood person, that her father was quite unbearably tyrannical and ridiculously old-fashioned, that the only thing left for her to do as a girl of spirit was to show that she meant what she said by eloping with him (the aforesaid adventurer) after which of course the father would come round to a more sensible view of life, and the future would take on the rosiest of hues.

The foolish girl believed him, and he gradually worked upon her feelings until she consented; and the particular night upon which our friend the helper came upon the scene was that which had been chosen for the elopement. In true melodramatic style the adventurer was waiting round the corner with a carriage, and the girl was in her room hurriedly preparing herself to slip out and join him.

Not unnaturally, when it came actually to the point her mind was much disturbed, and she found it very difficult to take the final step. It was this fluttering of the mind, this earnest desire for aid in decision, which attracted the notice of the helper as he was drifting casually by. Reading her thoughts, he quickly grasped the situation, and at once began to try to influence her against the rash step which she contemplated. Her mind, however, was in such a condition that he was unable to impress himself upon her as he wished, and he looked round in great anxiety for someone who should prove more amenable to his influence. He tried to seize upon the father, but he was engaged in his library in some literary work of so engrossing a character that it proved impossible to attract his attention.

Fortunately, however, the half-forgotten lover of her youth happened to be within reach, wandering about in the starlight and looking up at her window in the approved style of young lovers all the world over. The helper pounced upon him, seeing the condition of his sentiments, and to his great delight found him more receptive. His deep love made him anxious, and it was easy enough to influence him to walk far enough to see the carriage and the adventurer in waiting around the corner. His affection quickened his wits, and he instantly grasped the situation, and was filled with horror and dismay. To do him justice, at that supreme moment it was not of himself that he thought, not the fact that he was on the eve of losing her, but that she was on the eve of throwing herself away and ruining the whole of her future life. In his excitement he forgot all about convention; he made his way into the house (for he had known the place since childhood), rushed up the stairs and met her at the door of her room.

The words which he said to her neither he nor she can remember now, but in wild and earnest pleading he besought her to think before doing this terrible thing, to realize clearly into what an abyss she was about to throw herself, to bethink herself well before entering upon the path of destruction, and at least, before doing anything more, to consult openly with the loving father whom she was requiting so ill for his ceaseless care of her.

The shock of his sudden appearance and the fervor of his objurgations awakened her as from a sort of trance; and she offered scarcely any resistance when he dragged her off then and there to her father as he sat working in his library. The astonishment of the father may be imagined, when the story was unfolded before him. He had had not the slightest conception of his daughter's attitude, and she herself, now that the spell was shaken off, could not imagine how she had ever been able really to contemplate such a step. Both she and her father overflowed with gratitude to the loyal young lover, and before he left her that night she had ratified the old childish engagement, and promised to be his wife at no remote date.

This was what had really happened, and one can see that the symbolism chosen by the ego of the helper was by no means inapt, however misleading it may have been as to the actual facts.

Sometimes nothing comes through that can be called an actual memory, but only the effect of something that has been seen or that has happened. A man may wake in the morning with a strong feeling of elation and success, without in the least being able to recall in what he has succeeded. This generally means some good piece of work well done, but it is often impossible for the man to recover the details. At other times he may bring back with him a feeling of reverence, a sense of great holiness. This usually means that he has been in the presence of some one much greater than himself, or has seen some direct evidence of the greater power. Sometimes, on the other hand, a person may wake with a feeling of terrible fear. That is sometimes due only to the alarm of the physical body at some unaccustomed sensation; but it is sometimes also due to having encountered something horrible in the astral world. Or again it may arise merely from sympathy with some astral entity who is in a state of terror, for it is a frequent thing on the astral plane that one person should be strongly influenced by sympathy with another's condition.

Few people, however, when in the astral body, care whether the physical brain remembers or not, and nine out of ten much dislike returning to the body. But if you specially wish to get into the habit of remembering, the procedure which I should recommend is the following:

To make the link, first remember, when you are out of the body, that you wish to do so. Then you must determine to come back into the body slowly, instead of with a rush and a little jerk, as is usually the case. It is this jerk that prevents one from remembering. Stop yourself and say, just before you awake: "There is my body; I am just about to enter it. As soon as I am in it I will make it sit up and write down all it can remember." Then enter it calmly, sit up instantly and write down all you are able to remember *at once*. If you wait a few minutes, usually all will be lost. But each fact that you bring through will serve as a link for other memories. The notes may seem a little incoherent when you read them afterwards, but never mind that; it is because you are trying to give an account in physical words of the experiences of another plane. In this way you will gradually recover the memory, though it may take a long time; great patience is necessary.

You should try to remember when out of the body that you are in the astral world, and that it would be a comfort to the physical consciousness if some memory could be carried through. Be systematic in your efforts. Every time that you succeed in bringing something through, it will make it easier to remember next time, and will bring nearer the period when there will be habitual automatic recollection. At present there is a moment of unconsciousness between sleeping and waking, and this acts as a veil. It is caused by the closely-woven web of matter of the highest subplane through which the vibrations have to pass.

In coming back to the physical body from the astral world there is a feeling of great constraint, as though one were being enveloped in a thick, heavy cloak. The joy of life on the astral plane is so great that physical life in comparison with it seems no life at all. Many men who can function in the astral world during the sleep of the physical body regard the daily return to the physical world as men often do their daily journey to the office. They do not positively dislike it, but they would not do it unless they were compelled.

When the man is free in the mental world, the astral life similarly seems a state of bondage, and so on, until we reach the buddhic world, which is—in its essence—bliss. After once reaching that level, although the man on the physical plane is still cramped and unable to express the bliss, he nevertheless has it all the time, and he knows that all others who are unable to feel it now will feel and know it at some future time. Even if only for a moment you could feel the reality of the higher planes, your life would never again be the same.

Astral pleasures are much greater than those of the physical world, and there is danger of people being turned aside by them from the path of progress. It is quite impossible to realize while one is confined in the physical body the great attractiveness of these pleasures. But even the delights of the astral life do not present a serious danger to those who have realized a little of something higher. After death one should try to pass through the astral levels as speedily as possible, consistently with usefulness, and not yield to its refined pleasures any more than to the physical. One must not only overcome physical desire by knowledge of the astral or the heaven-life, but also go beyond even these, not merely for the sake of the joy of the spiritual life, but in order to replace the fleeting by the everlasting.

The Higher Dimensions

If there are seven dimensions at all, there are seven dimensions always and everywhere, and it makes no difference to that fundamental fact in nature whether the consciousness of any individual happens to be acting through his physical body, his astral body or his nirvanic vehicle. In the last case he has the power to see and understand the whole thing. In any of the other cases his capacities are limited. There is therefore no such thing as a three-dimensional or four-dimensional object or being. If space has seven dimensions, every object must exist within that space, and the difference between us is merely in our power of perception.

Physically we see only three dimensions and therefore we see all objects and beings very partially. One who has the power to see four dimensions still sees objects only partially, although he sees more of them than the other man. We find ourselves in the midst of a vast universe built of matter of varying degrees of tenuity, which exists in a space of (let us suppose) seven dimensions. But we find ourselves in possession of a consciousness which is capable of appreciating only three of those dimensions, and only matter of certain degrees of tenuity. For us, all matter of other and higher degrees is as if it did not exist. All dimensions beyond the three are also to us as though they did not exist.

But our lack of perceptive power does not in any way affect the objects themselves. A man picks up (let us say) a piece of stone. He can see only the physical particles of that stone, but that in no way affects the undoubted fact that that stone at the same time possesses within it particles of matter of the astral and mental and other higher planes. In just the same way, that stone must theoretically possess some sort of extension, however small, in all the seven dimensions; but that fact is in no way affected by the other fact that the man's consciousness can appreciate only three of those dimensions.

To examine that object the man is using a physical organ (the eye) which is capable of appreciating only certain rates of undulation radiated by certain types of matter. If he should develop what we call astral consciousness he would then be employing an organ which is capable of responding only to the vibrations radiated by another and finer part of that piece of stone. If in developing the astral consciousness he had lost the physical—that is, if he had left his physical body—he would be able to see only the astral and not the physical. But of course the object itself is not affected in any way, and the physical part of it has not ceased to exist because the man has, for the time, lost the power to see it. If he developed his astral consciousness so that he could use it simultaneously with the physical, he would then be able to see both the physical and astral parts of the object at the same time, though probably not both with equal clearness at absolutely the same moment.

Now, just as all the higher forms of matter exist in every object, although untrained people cannot see them, so all the dimensions of space must appertain to every object, although the number of those dimensions that we can observe depends upon the condition of our consciousness. In physical life we can normally conceive only three, though by careful special training the brain may be educated into grasping some of the simpler fourth-dimensional forms. The astral consciousness has the power of grasping four of these dimensions, but it by no means follows that a man who opens his astral consciousness immediately perceives the extension of every object in four dimensions; on the contrary, it is quite certain that the average man does not perceive this at all when he enters the astral plane. He realizes it only as a certain blurring—a kind of incomprehensible difference in the things that he used to see; and most men go through their astral lives without discovering more than that of the qualities of the matter which surrounds them.

We should say, then, not that the possession of astral vision at once causes the man to appreciate the fourth dimension, but rather that it gives him the power to develop that faculty by long, careful and patient practice, if he knows anything about the matter and cares to take the trouble. Entities belonging to the astral plane, and presumably ignorant of any other (such as nature-spirits, for example) have by nature the faculty of seeing the fourth-dimensional aspect of all objects. But we must not therefore suppose that they see them perfectly, since they perceive only the astral matter in them and not the physical, just as we with our different kind of limitation perceive only the physical and not the astral.

It has never been taught, so far as I am aware, that the entities of the astral plane are conscious of us upon the physical plane. They quite clearly and definitely are *not* conscious of physical matter of any kind. But they are conscious of the astral counterpart of that physical matter, which for all practical purposes comes to very nearly the same thing, though not quite.

I should not expect the higher dimensions to manifest themselves as qualities of matter to our physical consciousness, though it is conceivable that some of them might do so in certain special cases. The density of a gas, for example, might be a measure of its extent in the fourth dimension.

If an object passes through a wall, the question of the fourth dimension is not raised, nor are the properties connected with it employed at all. But in order that the object may so pass through, either it or a portion of the wall corresponding in size to it must be disintegrated—that is, reduced either to the highest or to one of the etheric conditions, so that the particles may pass freely among one another without hindrance. That is entirely a three-dimensional method. Another and quite different feat is not to disintegrate at all either the object or the wall, but to bring the entire object in by another direction altogether, where there is no wall. But that direction is unknown to us in our physical consciousness.

If one had a cup made of porous earthenware, one could no doubt fill it with water by the process of reducing the water to steam and forcing it through the sides of the cup; that would be equivalent to the ordinary process of disintegration and reintegration, for the water, reduced to a higher state for the purpose of being forced through the pores of the cup, would resume its natural condition when it had passed through. But it would also be possible to fill the cup by the simpler process of taking off the lid and pouring in the water from above, and in this case the water need not be changed in any way, because it is introduced into the cup from a direction in which there is no wall to penetrate. These are simply two ways of producing the same result, and they do not mutually exclude each other.

SECTION EIGHT

The Mental Body
and the
Power of Thought

The Mental Body

After reading *Man Visible and Invisible* students have sometimes remarked that the list of qualities there given seems incomplete,* and that nothing is said as to some others which are at least equally common—such for example as courage, dignity, cheerfulness, truthfulness, loyalty. The reason that these were not included in that first account is that unlike other qualities, they do not have readily distinguishable colors; but it must not therefore be supposed that their presence or absence would be indistinguishable by clairvoyant vision. Such qualities are indicated by differences in the structure of the mental body, or by changes in its surface; but it might be said, broadly speaking, that they are represented rather by form than by color.

It will be remembered that, in the drawings of the mental body given in the book above-mentioned, the colors which indicate some of the principal qualities are shown, and something is said as to their general arrangement in the vehicle. In a general way, all

Man Visible and Invisible contains colored illustrations of the astral and mental bodies of various people. In it C. W. Leadbeater explains the correspondence between the colors in these and qualities of character. Ed.

the colors denoting good qualities are to be found in the upper half, and those denoting unpleasant qualities are mostly in the lower half. The violet of high aspiration, the blue of devotion, the rose color of affection, the yellow which indicates intellect, and even the orange of pride or ambition—all these belong to the upper part, while thoughts prompted by anger, selfishness or jealousy gravitate towards the bottom of the ovoid. While the illustrations given there fairly indicate what would be the appearance of the mental body if it ever were really at rest, there is considerable variation from those types when the man is in the act of thinking strongly or definitely.

The mental unit may be regarded as the heart and center of the mental body,* and upon the relative activity of the different parts of that unit the appearance of the body as a whole to a great extent depends. The various activities of the mind fall naturally into certain classes or divisions, and these divisions are expressed through different parts of the mental unit. Mental units are by no means all the same. They differ greatly according to the type and the development of their owners. If such a mental unit lay at rest the force radiating from it would make a number of funnels in the mental body, just as the light shining through the slide in a magic lantern (or a film projector) makes a large radiating funnel of light in the air between the lantern and the sheet.

In this case the surface of the mental body may be likened to the sheet, because it is only at the surface that the effect becomes visible to one who is looking at the mental body from the outside; so that, if the mental unit were at rest, we should see on the surface of the mental body a number of pictures in color, representing the various types of thought common to the person, with presumably dark spaces between them. But the mental unit is rotating rapidly on its axis, and the effect of this in the mental body is a series of bands, not always quite clearly defined, nor always of the same width, but still readily distinguishable, and usually in about the same relative positions.

Where aspirational thought exists, it invariably shows itself in a beautiful little violet circle at the top of the ovoid of the mental body. As the aspirant draws near to the gateway of the Path this circle increases in size and radiancy, and in the initiate it is a splendid glowing cap of the most lovely color imaginable. Below it

*Mental Unit—A single molecule or unit of the fourth mental subplane which remains with the man as a stable core during the whole of his incarnation. Ed.

there is often the blue ring of devotional thought, usually rather than a narrow one, except in the case of the few whose religion is really deep and genuine. Next to that we may have the much broader zone of affectionate thought, which may be of any shade of crimson or rose color, according to the type of affection which it indicates. Near the zone of affection, and frequently closely connected with it, we have the orange band which expresses proud and ambitious thought; and again in intimate relation with pride comes the yellow belt of intellect, commonly divided into two bands, denoting respectively the philosophical and the scientific types of thought. The place of this yellow color varies much in different men; sometimes it fills the whole of the upper part of the egg, rising above devotion and affection, and in such a case pride is generally excessive.

Below the group already described, and occupying the middle section of the ovoid, is the broad belt devoted to concrete shapes—the part of the mental body from which all ordinary thought forms issue. The principal color here is green, shaded often with brown or yellow according to the disposition of the person.

There is no part of the mental body which varies more widely than this. Some people have their mental bodies crowded with a vast number of concrete images, whereas others have only few. In some they are clear and well-outlined, in others they are vague and hazy to the last degree; in some they are classified and labelled and arranged in the most orderly fashion, in others they are not arranged at all, but are left in hopeless confusion.

In the lower part of the ovoid come the belts expressing all kinds of undesirable thoughts. A kind of muddy precipitate of selfishness too often fills the lower third or even the half of the mental body, and above this is sometimes a ring portraying hatred, cunning or fear. Naturally, as men develop, this lower part vanishes, and the upper gradually expands until it fills the whole body, as shown in the illustrations in *Man Visible and Invisible*.

Degrees in the feeling which prompts thought are expressed by brilliance of color. In devotional feeling, for example, we may have the three stages of respect, reverence and worship; in affection we may have the stages of good will, friendship and love. The stronger the thought the *larger* is the vibration; the more spiritual and unselfish the thought the *higher* is the vibration. The first produces brilliancy, the second delicacy of color.

Within these different rings or zones we usually see more or less clearly marked striations, and many qualities of the man can be judged by an examination of these striations. The possession of a strong will, for example, brings the whole mental body into far more level definite lines. All the striations and radiations are steady, firm and clearly distinguishable, whereas in the case of a weak and vacillating person this firmness and strength of line would be conspicuously absent; the lines separating the different qualites would be indeterminate, and the striations and radiations would be small, weak and wavy. Courage is shown by firm and very strongly-marked lines, especially in the orange band connected with pride. Dignity also expresses itself principally in the same part of the mental body, but by a calm steadiness and assuredness which is quite different from the lines of courage.

Truthfulness and accuracy are portrayed very clearly by regularity in the striations of the part of the mental body devoted to concrete forms, and by the clearness and correctness of the images which appear there. Loyalty shows itself by an intensification both of affection and of devotion, and by the constant formation, in that part of the ovoid, of figures of the person to whom the loyalty is felt. In many cases of loyalty, affection and devotion, a very strong permanent image is made of the objects of these feelings, and that remains floating in the aura of the thinker, so that, when his thought turns towards the loved or adored one, the force which he pours out strengthens that already existing image, instead of forming a new one, as it would normally do.

Joy shows itself in a general brightening and radiancy of both the mental and the astral bodies, as also in a peculiar rippling of the surface of the body. General cheerfulness shows itself in a modified bubbling form of this, and also in a steady serenity which is pleasant to see. Surprise, on the other hand, is shown by a sharp constriction of the mental body, accompanied by an increased glow in the bands of affection if the surprise is a pleasant one, and by a change of color usually involving the display of a good deal of brown and grey in the lower part of the ovoid when the surprise is an unpleasant one. This constriction is usually communicated to both the astral and the physical bodies, and often causes singularly unpleasant feelings, which affect sometimes the solar plexus (resulting in sinking and sickness) and sometimes the heart center, in which case it brings palpitation or even death; so that a sudden surprise may occasionally kill one who has a weak heart. Awe is the same as wonder, except that it is accompanied by a profound change in the devotional part of the mental body, which usually swells out under this influence, and has its striations more strongly marked.

At the moment when a person's thought is strongly directed into one or another of these channels, the part of the mental body which corresponds to that thought usually bulges outwards in form in addition to brightening in color, and so disturbs for the time the symmetry of the ovoid. In many people such bulging is permanent, and that always means that the amount of thought of that type is steadily increasing. If, for example, a person takes up some scientific study, and therefore suddenly turns his thoughts in that direction much more than before, the first effect will be such protuberance as I have described; but if he keeps the amount of his thought on scientific subjects steadily at the same level which he has now adopted, the protruding portion will gradually sink back into the general outline of the void, but the band of its color will have become wider than before.

If however the man's interest in scientific subjects steadily increases in force, the protrusion will still remain in evidence even though the band has widened. The general effect of this is that in the undeveloped man the lower portion of the ovoid tends always to be larger than the upper, so that the mental and astral bodies have the appearance of an egg with the small end uppermost; while in the more developed man the qualities expressing themselves in the higher part are always tending to increase, and consequently we have for the time the effect of an egg with its smaller end pointing downwards. But the tendency always is for the symmetry of the ovoid to re-assert itself by degrees, so that such appearances are only temporary.

Reference has frequently been made to the ceaseless motion of the matter in both the mental and astral bodies. When the astral body, for example, is disturbed by any sudden emotion, all its matter is swept about as if by a violent hurricane, so that for the time being the colors become very much mixed. Presently, however, by the specific gravity of the different types of matter which reflect or emit these various colors, the whole arrangement will sort itself once more into its usual zones. Even then the matter is by no means at rest, as the particles are all the time rushing round these zones, though comparatively rarely leaving their own belt and intruding on another. But this movement within its own zone is entirely a healthy one; one in whom there is no such circulation is a mental crustacean, incapable of growth until he bursts his shell. The activity of the matter in any particular zone increases in proportion to the amount of thought devoted to the subject of which it is an expression.

If the man should permit his thought upon any given subject to stagnate, that stagnation will be faithfully reproduced in the matter appropriate to the subject. If a prejudice should grow up in the man, thought on that particular subject ceases altogether, and a small eddy forms in which the mental matter runs round and round until it coagulates and becomes a kind of wart. Unless and until this wart is worn away or forcibly rooted out, the man cannot use that particular part of his mental body, and is incapable of rational thought on that subject. This foul thickened mass blocks all free movement either outward or inward; it prevents him on the one hand from seeing accurately, or from receiving any reliable new impressions on the matter in question, and on the other from sending out any clear thought with regard to it.

These diseased spots in the mental body are unfortunately also centers of infection; the inability to see clearly increases and spreads. If part of the man's mental body is already stagnant, the other parts are likely to be affected; if a man allows himself to have a prejudice on one subject he will probably soon develop prejudices on others, because the healthy flow of mental matter has been checked and the habit of untruth has been formed. Religious prejudice is the commonest and the most serious of all, and it completely prevents any approach to rational thought with regard to the subject. Unfortunately a very large number of people have the whole of that part of their mental bodies which should be occupied with religious matters inactive, ossified and covered with warts, so that even the most rudimentary conception of what religion really is remains utterly impossible for them until a catastrophic change has taken place.

In *Man Visible and Invisible* drawings are given of the astral bodies of men of the devotional and scientific types. Variants of these with which we frequently meet are the intuitional person and the matter-of-fact person. The latter has generally much of yellow in his mental body, and his various bands of color are usually regular and in order. He has far less emotion and less imagination than the intuitional man, and therefore often in certain ways less power and enthusiasm; but on the other hand he is far less likely to make mistakes, and what he does will generally be well and carefully done. In the vehicle of the intuitional man we find much more of blue, but the colors are generally vague and the whole body ill-regulated. He suffers much more than the steadier type, but sometimes through that suffering he is able to make rapid progress. Of course, both the glow and enthusiasm and the steadiness and regularity have their place in the perfect man; it is only a question of which is acquired first.

Mystical thought and the presence of psychic faculties are indicated by colors of which we have no equivalents on the physical plane. When a man begins to develop along occult lines, the whole of his mental body must be rapidly purified and brought into thorough working order, for every part of it will be needed, and every part must be absolutely at its best if he is to make any real progress. It is eminently necessary that he should be able to make strong and clear thought forms, and in addition to this it is a great help and comfort to him if he is able to visualize them clearly. The two acts must not be confused; one man may be able to make a stronger and clearer thought form than another, and yet not be able to visualize it so well. The formation of a thought is a direct act of the will, working through the mental body; the visualization is simply the power to see clairvoyantly the thought form which he has made. Let him think strongly of any object, and the image of it is there in the mental body—just as much there whether he can visualize it or not.

It must be remembered that all mental work done on the physical plane must be done through the physical brain, so that in order to succeed it is necessary not only to develop the mental body, but to get the physical brain into order, so that the mental body may readily work through it. It is well-known that certain parts of the brain are connected with certain qualities in the man and with his power to think along certain lines, and all these must be brought into order and duly correlated with the zones in the mental body.

Another point, the greatest of all, is that there is another connection to be made and kept active—the connection between the ego and his mental body; for he is the force of all these qualities and powers which makes use of them. In order that we may think of anything we must first remember it; in order that we may remember it we must have paid attention to it; and the paying of attention is the descent of the ego into his vehicles in order to look out through them. Many a man with a fine mental body and a good brain makes little use of them because he pays little attention to life—that is to say, because the ego is putting but little of himself down into these lower planes, and so the vehicles are left to run riot at their own will. I have written elsewhere of the cure for this state of affairs; put very briefly it comes to this: Give the ego the conditions which he desires, and he will promptly put himself down more fully, to take advantage of them. If he desires to develop affection, give him the opportunity by cultivating affection to the fullest extent on these lower planes, and at once the ego will respond. If he desires principally wisdom, then endeavor by study to make yourself wise upon the physical plane, and once more the ego will appreciate your effort and be delighted to cooperate. Find out what he wants and give it to him, and you will have no reason to complain of his response.

A Neglected Power

People who have not made a special study of the matter never understand what a tremendous power there is in thought. Steam-power, water-power, these are real to them, because they can see them at work; but thought-power is vague and shadowy and intangible to them. Yet those who have taken the trouble to look into the subject know very well that one is just as real as the other.

This is true in two senses—directly and indirectly. Everybody, when it occurs to him, recognizes the indirect action of thought, for it is obvious that a man must think before he can do anything, and the thought is the motive power of his act just as the water is the motive power of the mill. But people do not generally know that thought has also a direct action on matter—that whether or not a man translates his thought into a deed, the thought itself has already produced an effect.

Our readers are already aware that there are many kinds of matter finer than those which are visible to physical sight, and that the force of man's thought acts directly upon some of these and sets them in motion. A thought shows itself as a vibration in the mental body of man; that vibration is communicated to external matter, and an effect is produced. Thought therefore is itself a real and definite power; and the point of vivid interest about it is that everyone of us possesses this power. A comparatively small number of rich men have concentrated in their hands the steam-power and the electric power of the world; money is needed to buy its use, and therefore for many it is unattainable. But here is a power which is already in the hands of everyone, poor and rich, young and old alike; all we have to do is to learn to use it. Indeed, we are all of us using it to some extent even now, but because we do not understand it we often unconsciously do harm with it instead of good, both to ourselves and to others.

In the book *Thought Forms* it is explained that a thought pro-duces two principal external effects—a radiating vibration and a floating form. Let us see how these affect the thinker himself, and how they affect others.

The first point to remember is the force of habit. If we accus-tom our mental bodies to a certain type of vibration they learn to reproduce it easily and readily. If we let ourselves think a certain kind of thought today, it will be appreciably easier to think that same thought tomorrow. If a man allows himself to begin to think evil of others, it soon becomes easy to think more evil of them and difficult to think any good of them. Hence arises a ridiculous prejudice which absolutely blinds the man to the good points in his neighbors, and enormously magnifies the evil in them.

Then his thoughts begin to stir up his emotions; because he sees only the evil in others he begins to hate them. The vibrations of mental matter excite those of the denser astral matter just as the wind disturbs the surface of the sea. We all know that by thinking over what he considers his wrongs a man can easily make himself angry, though we often seem to forget the inevitable corollary that by thinking calmly and reasonably a man can prevent or dismiss anger.

Still another reaction upon the thinker is produced by the thought form which he generates. If the thought be aimed at someone else, the form flies like a missile towards that person, but if the thought be (as is so often the case) connected chiefly with the thinker himself, the form remains floating near him, ever ready to react upon him and reproduce itself—that is to say, to stir up in his mind the same thought once more. The man will feel as though it were put into his mind from without, whereas the experience is nothing but the mechanical result of his own previ-ous thought.

Now see how this fragment of knowledge can be utilized. Obvi-ously every thought or emotion produces a long-lasting effect, for it strengthens or weakens a tendency; furthermore, it is constantly reacting upon the thinker. It is clear, therefore, that we must exercise the greatest care as to what thought or emotion we permit to arise within ourselves. We must not excuse ourselves, as so many do, by saying that undesirable feelings are natural under certain conditions; we must assert our prerogative as rulers of this kingdom of our mind and emotions. If we can get into the habit of evil thought, it must be equally possible to get into the habit of good thought. We can accustom ourselves to look for the desirable rather than the undesirable qualities in the people whom we meet; and it will surprise us to find how numerous and how important those desirable qualities are. Thus we shall come to like these people instead of disliking them, and there will be at least a possibility that we may do them something approaching to justice in our estimate of them.

We may set ourselves definitely as a useful exercise to think good and kindly thoughts, and if we do we shall very soon begin to perceive the result of this practice. Our minds will begin to work more easily along the grooves of admiration and appreciation instead of along those of suspicion and disparagement; and when for the moment our brains are unoccupied, the thoughts which present themselves will be good instead of bad, because they will be the reaction of the gracious forms with which we have labored to surround ourselves. "As a man thinketh in his heart, so is he;" and it is obvious that the systematic use of thought-power will make life much easier and pleasanter for us.

Now let us see how our thought affects others. The radiating undulation, like many other vibrations in nature, tends to reproduce itself. Put an object in front of a fire, and presently that object becomes hot; why? Because the radiations of rapid vibration coming from the incandescent matter in the grate have stirred the molecules of the object into more rapid oscillation also. In the same way, if we persistently pour the undulation of kindly thought upon another, it must in time awaken a similar vibration of kindly thought in him. Thought forms directed towards him will hover about him and act upon him for good when opportunity offers. Just as a bad thought may be a tempting demon either to the thinker or to another, so a good thought may be a veritable guardian angel, encouraging virtue and repelling vice.

A grumbling and fault-finding attitude towards others is unfortunately sadly common at the present day, and those who adopt it never seem to realize the harm that they are doing. If we study its result we shall see that the prevalent habit of malicious gossip is nothing short of wicked. It does not matter whether there is or is not any foundation for scandal; in either case it cannot but cause harm. Here we have a number of people fixing their minds upon some supposed evil quality in another, and drawing to it the attention of scores of others to whom such an idea would never otherwise have occurred.

Suppose they accuse their victim of jealousy. Some hundreds of people at once begin to pour upon this unhappy sufferer streams of thought suggesting the idea of jealousy. Is it not obvious that if the poor man has any tendency towards that unpleasant quality, it cannot but be greatly intensified by such a cataract? And if, as is commonly the case, there is no reason whatever for the spiteful rumor, those who so eagerly spread it are at any rate doing their best to create in the man the very vice over the imagined presence of which they gloat so savagely.

Think of your friends by all means, but think of their good points, not only because that is a much healthier occupation for you, but because by doing so you strengthen them. When you are reluctantly compelled to recognize the presence of some evil quality in a friend, take especial care *not* to think of *it*, but think instead of the opposite virtue which you wish him to develop. If he happens to be parsimonious or lacking in affection, carefully avoid gossiping about this defect or even fixing your thought upon it, because if you do, the vibration which you will send him will simply make matters worse. Instead of that, think with all your strength of the quality which he needs, flood him with the undulations of generosity and love, for in that way you will really help your brother.

Use your thought-power in ways such as these, and you will become a veritable center of blessing in your corner of the world. But remember that you have only a limited amount of this force, and if you want to have enough to be useful you must not waste it.

The average man is simply a center of agitated vibration; he is constantly in a condition of worry, of trouble about something, or in a condition of deep depression, or else he is unduly excited in the endeavor to grasp something. For one reason or another he is always in a state of unnecessary agitation, usually about the merest trifle. This means that he is all the time wasting force, frittering away vainly that for the profitable use of which he is definitely responsible—that which might make him healthier and happier.

Another way in which he wastes a vast amount of energy is by unnecessary argument; he is always trying to make somebody else agree with his opinions. He forgets that there are always several sides to any question, whether it be of religion, of politics, or of expediency, that the other man has a perfect right to his own point of view, and that anyhow it does not matter, since the facts of the case will remain the same, whatever either of them may think. The great majority of the subjects about which men argue are not in the least worth the trouble of discussion, and those who talk most loudly and most confidently about them are usually precisely those who know least.

The man who wishes to do useful work, either for himself or for others, by means of thought-power, must conserve his energies; he must be calm and philosophic; he must consider carefully before he speaks or acts. But let no one doubt that the power is a mighty one, that any one who will take the trouble may learn how to use it, and that by its use each one of us may make much progress and may do much good to the world around him.

You should understand this power of thought, and the duty of repressing evil, unkind or selfish thoughts. Thoughts will produce their effect, whether we wish it or not. A wise man produces his results intentionally. Each time you control your thoughts it makes control easier. Sending out of thoughts to others is as real as giving money; and it is a form of charity which is possible for the poorest of men. To radiate depression is wrong, and it prevents higher thoughts from coming in. It causes much suffering to sensitive people, and is responsible for much of the terror of children at night. It is not right to cloud a young life, as so many do, by allowing bad and miserable thoughts to fall upon it. Forget your depression, and send strengthening thoughts to sick people instead.

Your thoughts are not (as you might suppose) exclusively your own business, for your vibrations affect others. Evil thoughts reach much farther than evil words, but they cannot affect a man who is entirely free from the quality which they carry. For example, the thought of the desire for drink could not enter the body of a purely temperate man. It would strike upon his astral body, but it could not penetrate, and it would then return to the sender.

The will can be trained to act directly upon physical matter.

The example most likely to be within your own experience is that of a picture much used for purposes of meditation which may often be observed to change in expression; the actual physical particles are unquestionably affected by the power of the strong sustained thought. Madame Blavatsky used to make her pupils practice this, telling them to suspend a needle by a silk thread, and then learn to move it by the force of the will. A sculptor also uses this power of thought in an entirely different way. When he sees a block of marble he makes a strong thought form of the statue which he can carve out of it. Then he plants this thought form inside the block of marble, and proceeds to chip away the marble which lies outside the thought form, leaving only that portion of it which is interpenetrated by it.

Make it a practice to set apart a little time each day devoted to formulating good thoughts about other people, and sending them to those people. It is capital practice for you, and it will unquestionably do good to your patients also.

Intuition and Impulse

You ask how you are to distinguish impulse from intuition. I fully appreciate your dilemma. At first it is difficult for the student to do this, but take comfort from the thought that the difficulty of decision is only a temporary matter. As you grow you will reach a stage at which you will be absolutely certain with regard to intuition, for the distinction between that and impulse will be so clear that mistake will be impossible.

But since both come to the brain from within, they seem at first exactly alike, and therefore great care is necessary, and it is hard to arrive at a decision. One or two considerations may perhaps help you. I have heard Mrs. Besant say that it is well always to wait awhile whenever the circumstances permit such a course, because if we wait a little an impulse usually grows weaker, while an intuition is unaffected by the passage of time. Then an impulse is almost always accompanied by excitement; there is always something personal about it, so that if it is not at once obeyed—if anything crosses it—there arises a feeling of resentment; whereas a true intuition, though decided, is surrounded by a sense of calm strength. The impulse is a surging of the astral body; the intuition is a scrap of knowledge from the ego impressed upon the personality.

Sometimes the sudden impression is not really from within at all, but from without; a message or suggestion from some one on a higher plane—most commonly some passing dead person, or perhaps a departed relation. It is well to treat such advice precisely as though it were given on the physical plane—to take it if it commends itself to our reason, and ignore it if it does not; for a person is not necessarily wiser than we merely because he happens to be dead. In this matter, as in all others, we must regulate our actions by strong, sturdy commonsense, and not rush off wildly after imaginations and dreams.

At this stage I should advise you always to follow reason when you are certain of the premises from which you reason. You will learn in time and by experience whether your intuitions can invariably be trusted. The mere impulse has its birth in the astral body, while the true intuition comes directly from the higher mental plane, or sometimes even from the buddhic. Of course the latter, if you could only be sure of it, might be followed without the slightest hesitation, but in this transition stage through which you are passing one is compelled to take a certain amount of risk—either that of sometimes missing a gleam of higher truth through clinging too closely to the reason, or that of being occasionally misled by mistaking an impulse from an intuition. Myself, I have so deep-rooted a horror of this last possibility that I have again and again followed reason as against intuition, and it was only after repeatedly finding that a certain type of intuition was always correct that I allowed myself to depend fully upon it. You too will no doubt pass through these successive stages, and you need not be in the least troubled about it.

Thought-Centers

In the higher levels of the mental plane our thoughts act with greater force because we have the field almost to ourselves. We have not many other thoughts to contend with in that region. All people when thinking of the same thing tend to come to some extent into rapport with one another. Any strong thought anywhere in the world may be attracted to you, and you may be influenced by the thinker of it. Strong thought acts fairly constantly, and is more likely to act in connection with those subjects about which comparatively few are thinking, because in those cases the vibrations are more distinctive, and have freer play. Any sudden idea or vision which comes to you may be simply the thought form of some person who is keenly interested in the subject in hand. The person may be at any distance from you, though it is true that physical proximity makes such transference easier.

There is such a thing as a kind of psychometrization of a thought form. Masses of thought on a given subject are very definite things, which have a place in space. Thoughts on the same subject and of the same character tend to aggregate. For many subjects there is a thought-center, a definite space in the atmosphere; and thoughts on one of these subjects tend to gravitate to its center, which absorbs any amount of ideas, coherent and incoherent, right and wrong. In this definite center you would find all the thought about a given subject drawn to a focus, and might then psychometrize the different thought forms, follow them to their thinkers, and acquire other information from them.

It is easy to see that when one thinks of something a little difficult, one may attract the thought of another person who has studied the same subject, and even the person himself if he be on the astral plane. In the latter case the person may be either conscious or unconscious. Plenty of people, either dead or asleep, do try to help others along their particular lines; any one of such, seeing another struggling with some kind of conception, would be likely to go and try to suggest the way in which he thinks that other man ought to think of it. It does not follow, of course, that his ideas would be correct. If you think you will see that this is perfectly natural. You would help people on this physical plane simply from pure good nature. So also after death. You feel the same sympathies without a physical body; and though your idea may be wrong or right, you give it.

Sometimes such an idea may come in symbolic form; the serpent and elephant, for example, are often used to signify wisdom. There are many sets of symbolisms. Each ego has his own system, though some forms seem general in dreams. It is said that to dream of water signifies trouble of some sort, though I do not see any connection. But even though there be no real connection, an ego (or for that matter some other entity who desires to communicate) may use the symbol if he knows that it is understood by the personality. Water has no necessary relation to trouble, but an ego who could not convey a clear message to his personality, and knew that it held that peculiar belief about water, might very likely impress such a dream on its brain when he wished to warn it of some impending misfortune. When a passing thought crosses the mind, it is usually caused by suggestion. The power or thought and the multiplicity of thought forms are tremendously great, and yet they are but little understood and taken into account.

In the case of a particular idea coming into the mind, any one of half-a-dozen things may have happened. I do not know of any method that is open to the ordinary student for ascertaining the exact source of an idea which strikes him. One has to develop the astral and mental sight in order to see the thought form, and trace from whom it comes. It is connected by vibration with its creator.

It is only speculation to offer suggestions in any particular case without actual knowledge of what took place. One is quite likely to be affected by one's own thought forms. You may make thought forms about a subject which will hover about you and persist proportionately to the energy put into them; and these often react upon you just as though they were new suggestions from outside. In a place like Adyar any newcomer will find a mass of thought forms already floating about, and probably he may accept some of these ready-made rather than set to work to produce new ones for himself. One should take up thought forms with caution. I have seen a man take up thought forms and be converted by them when they were quite wrong, and he himself had before been perfectly accurate in his opinion. Sometimes, however, it is advantageous to try to put oneself in touch with a thought form at the beginning of study.

There are vast numbers of thought forms of a comparatively permanent nature upon the astral plane, often the result of the accumulative work of many generations of people. Many such thought forms refer to alleged religious history, and the seeing of them by sensitive people is responsible for a great many quite genuine accounts given by untrained seers and seeresses—such for example as Anne Catherine Emmerich. She had visions in the most perfect detail of the events of the passion of Jesus exactly as it is recorded in the Gospels, including many events which we know never really occurred. Yet I have no doubt that the statements of that seeress were perfectly genuine; she was not laboring under an hallucination, but only under a mistake as to the nature of what she saw.

To read the akashic records clearly and correctly needs special training; it is not a matter of faith or of goodness, but of a special kind of knowledge.* There is nothing whatever to show that the saint in question had this particular form of knowledge; on the contrary, she probably never heard of such records at all. She would therefore most likely be quite incapable of reading an akashic record clearly, and certainly, if she did happen to see one, she would be unable to distinguish it from any other kind of vision.

In all probability what she saw was a set of such collective thought forms as we have described. It is well-known to all investigators that any great historical event upon which much is supposed to depend has been constantly thought of and vividly imaged to themselves by successive generations of people. Such scenes would be, for the English, the signing of Magna Charta by King John, and for the Americans the signing of the Declaration of Independence.

Now these vivid images which people make are real things, and are clearly to be seen by anyone who possesses a little psychic development. They are definite forms existing upon the mental plane, and wherever there is any strong emotion connected with them they are brought down to the astral plane and materialized there in astral matter. They are also perpetually strengthened by all the new thoughts which are ever being turned upon them. Naturally, different people imagine these scenes differently, and the eventual result is often something like a composite photograph; but the form in which such an imagination was originally cast largely influences the thought of all sensitives upon the subject, and tends to make them image it as others have done.

This product of thought (often, be it observed, of quite ignorant thought) is much easier to see than the true record, for while, as we have said, the latter feat requires training, the former needs nothing but a glimpse of the mental plane, such as frequently comes to almost all pure and high-minded ecsta-

---

*Akashic records—the divine memory; a sort of living photographic representation on a high plane, of everything that has ever happened. Ed.

tics. Indeed in many cases it does not need even this, because the thought forms exist upon the astral levels as well.

Another point to be borne in mind is that it is not in the least necessary for the creation of such a thought form that the scenes should ever have had any real existence. Few scenes from real history have been so strongly depicted by popular fancy in England as have some of the situations from Shakespeare's plays, from Bunyan's *Pilgrim's Progress*, and from various fairy stories, such as Cinderella or Aladdin's Lamp. A clairvoyant obtaining a glimpse of one of these collective thought forms might very easily suppose that he had come across the real foundation of the story; but since he knows these tales to be fictions he would be more likely to think that he had simply dreamed of them.

Now, ever since the Christian religion materialized the glorious conceptions originally committed to its charge, and tried to represent them as a series of events in a human life, devout souls in all countries under its sway have been striving as a pious exercise to picture the supposed events as vividly as possible. Consequently we are here provided with a set of thought forms of quite exceptional strength and prominence—a set which can hardly fail to attract the attention of any ecstatic the bent of whose mind is at all in their direction. No doubt they *were* seen by Anne Catherine Emmerich, and by many another. But when such clairvoyants come, in the course of their progress, to deal with the realities of life, they will be taught, as are those who have the inestimable privilege of the guidance of the Masters of Wisdom, how to distinguish between the result of devout but ignorant thought and the imperishable record which is the true memory of nature; and then they will find that these scenes, to which they have devoted so much attention, were but symbols of truths higher and wider and far grander than they had ever dreamed, even in the highest flights which were made possible for them by their splendid purity and piety.

Thought and Elemental Essence

Elemental essence when molded by thought adopts a certain color—a color which is expressive of the nature of the thought or feeling.* Of course all that this really means is that the es-

---

*Elemental essence—the life of astral or mental matter which is at an earlier stage of manifestation even than the minerals. Ed.

sence composing the thought form is for the time compelled to vibrate at a certain definite rate by the thought which is ensouling it. The evolution of the elemental essence is to learn to respond to all possible rates of undulation. Therefore when a thought holds it for a time vibrating at a certain rate, the elemental essence is helped to the extent, that it becomes habituated to that particular rate of oscillation, so that next time it comes within reach of a similar rate, it will respond much more readily than before.

Presently those atoms of essence, having passed back again into the general mass, will be caught up again by some other thought, and will then have to swing at some totally different rate, and so will evolve a little further by acquiring the capacity to respond to the second type of undulation. So by slow degrees the thoughts, not only of man, but also of nature-spirits and devas, and even of animals so far as they do think, are evolving the elemental essence which surrounds them—slowing teaching here a few atoms, and there a few atoms, to respond to this or that different rate of oscillation, until at last a stage will be reached when all the particles of the essence shall be ready to answer at any moment to any possible rate of vibration, and that will be the completion of their evolution.

It is for this reason that the occultist avoids when possible the destruction of an artificial elemental,* even when it is of evil character, preferring rather to defend himself or others against it by using the protection of a shell. It is possible to dissipate an artificial elemental instantly by an exertion of will-power, just as it is possible on the physical plane to kill a poisonous snake in order that it may do no further harm; but neither course of action would commend itself to an occultist, except in very unusual circumstances.

Whether the thought ensouling it is evil or good makes no difference whatever to the essence; all that is required for its development is to be used by thought of some kind. The difference between the good and the evil would be shown by the quality of essence which it affected, the evil thought or desire needing for its appropriate expression the coarser or denser matter, while the higher thought would require correspondingly finer and more rapidly vibrating matter for its covering. There are plenty of

*An artificial elemental is a thought form of astral and/or mental matter which has a life of its own for a time. Ed.

undeveloped people always thinking the coarser lower thoughts, and their very ignorance and grossness are made use of by the great Law as evolutionary forces to help on a certain stage of the work that is to be done. It is for us, who have learned a little more than they, to strive ever to think the high and holy thoughts which cause the evolution of a finer kind of elemental matter, and so to work in a field where at present the laborers are far too few.

SECTION NINE

Psychic Faculties

Psychic Powers

The possession of psychic powers does not necessarily involve high moral character, any more than does the possession of great physical strength. It is quite true that the man who enters the Path of Holiness will presently find such powers developing in him, but it is quite possible to gain many of the powers without the holiness. Powers can be developed by any one who will take the trouble, and a man may learn clairvoyance just as he may learn to play the piano, if he is willing to go through the necessary hard work. It is far better and safer for the vast majority of people to work at the development of character, to try to fit themselves for the Path, and to leave the powers to unfold in due course, as they certainly will. Some people are in too much of a hurry to do this, and set themselves to force the powers sooner. Well, if they are quite certain that they desire them only for the sake of helping others, and that they are wise enough to use them rightly, it may be that no harm will come of it; but it is not easy to be quite certain on these points, and the slightest deflection from the right line will mean disaster.

If a man must try to obtain the powers, there are two ways open to him; of course there are many more than two methods, but I mean that they all fall under two heads—the temporary and the permanent. The temporary method is to deaden the physical senses in some way—actively by drugs, by self-hypnotization, or by inducing giddiness, for example, or passively by being mesmerized—so that the astral senses may come to the surface. The permanent way is to work at the development of the ego, so that he may be able to control the lower vehicles and use them as he wishes.

It is somewhat like controlling a troublesome horse. A man who knows nothing of riding may so stupefy a horse with drugs that he can somehow keep on his back, but that will not in the least enable him to control any other horse. So a man who stupefies his physical body may use his astral senses to some extent, but that will in no way help him to manage another physical body in his next birth. The man who will take the far greater trouble of learning to ride properly can then manage any horse, and the man who develops his ego until it can manage one set of vehicles will be able to control any others that are given to him in future lives. This latter course means real evolution; the other does not necessarily involve anything of the sort. It does not follow that everyone who is on the Path must have psychic powers; they are not absolutely necessary until a certain stage is reached.

Short of the real psychic powers, there are various other methods by which men endeavor to obtain some of the same results. One of these, for example, is the repetition of invocations. Charms and ceremonies may sometimes produce an effect; it depends upon the way in which they are performed. I have seen a man who was able to answer questions in rather a curious way; he first entranced himself by repeating charms over and over again, and his invocations not only influenced himself, but also attracted nature-spirits who went for the desired information, obtained it and put it into his mind.

Lord Tennyson, by repeating his own name over and over again and drawing his consciousness further and further within himself, raised himself into touch with the ego, and then all this life seemed to him child's play, and death nothing but the entrance into a greater life.

The result of many repetitions may often be to throw oneself into the trance condition; but this is not a training of the ego. Its effects last at most only for one life, whereas the powers which result from real spiritual development reappear in subsequent bodies. The man who entrances himself by the repetition of words or charms may probably return as a medium or at least a mediumistic person in his next life, and it must be remembered that mediumship is not a power, but a condition.

Such repetitions may easily lead on to the coarser physical mediumship (by which I mean the sitting for materialization and sensational phenomena of all sorts) which is frequently injurious to health. I do not know that mere trance-speaking injures the body quite so much, though considering the feebleness of the platitudes which are usually the staple of the communications it might certainly be thought likely to weaken the mind!

Let us consider what it is that is required from a physical medium. When an entity on the astral plane, whether it be a dead man or a nature-spirit, wants to produce any result on dense physical matter—to play on a piano for example, to cause raps, or to hold a pencil in order to write—he needs an etheric body through which to work, because astral matter cannot act directly on the lower forms of physical matter, but requires the etheric matter as an intermediary to convey the vibrations from the one to the other—much in the same way as a fire cannot be lighted with paper and coals alone; the wood is needed as an intermediary, otherwise the paper will all burn away without affecting the coal.

A physical medium lacks cohesion between the etheric and the dense parts of the physical vehicle, so that an astral entity can easily withdraw a good deal of the man's etheric body and use it for his own purposes. Of course he returns it—in fact its constant tendency is to flow back to the medium, as may be seen from the action of the materialized form—but still the frequent withdrawal of part of the man's body in this way cannot but cause great disturbance and danger to his health.

The etheric double is the vehicle of vitality, the life-principle, which is perpetually circulating through our bodies; and when any part of our etheric double is withdrawn that life-circulation is checked and its current broken. A terrible drain on vitality is then set up, and that is why the medium is so often in a state of collapse after a séance, and also why so many mediums in the long run become drunkards, having first taken to stimulants in order to satisfy the dreadful craving for support which is caused by this sudden loss of strength.

It can never under any circumstances be a good thing for the health to be constantly subjected to such a drain as this, even though in some cases the more intelligent and careful "spirits" try to pour strength into their medium after a séance, in order to make up for the loss, and thus support him without absolute breakdown for a much longer period than would otherwise be possible.

In cases of materialization, dense physical matter, probably chiefly in the form of gases or liquids, is frequently borrowed from the body of the medium, who actually decreases temporarily in size and weight; and when it takes place, naturally that is a further source of serious disturbance to all the functions.

Of the mediums with whom I used to have sittings thirty years ago one is now blind, another died a confirmed drunkard, and a third, finding himself menaced by apoplexy and paralysis, escaped with his life only by giving up séances altogether.

Another form of materialization is that in which the astral body is temporarily solidified. The ordinary materializing "spirit" takes his material from the medium, because that, being already specialized, is more easily arranged into human form, and more readily condensed and molded than free ether would be. No one connected with any school of white magic would think it right to interfere with the etheric double of any man in order to produce a materialization, nor would he disturb his own if he wished to make himself visible at a distance. He would simply condense, and build into and around his astral body a sufficient quantity of the surrounding etheric matter to materialize it, and hold it in that form by an effort of will as long as he needed it.

When part of the etheric double is removed from the physical, as in the case of materialization of the ordinary kind, a connecting current is visible to any one capable of seeing matter in the etheric condition; but the method of connection with the astral body is entirely different, for nothing in the nature of a cord or current of astral matter joins the two forms. Yet it is difficult to express in terms of this plane the exact nature of the exceeding closeness of the sympathy between them; perhaps the nearest approximation we can get to the idea is that of two instruments tuned to exactly the same pitch, so that whatever note is struck upon one of them instantly evokes a precisely corresponding sound from the other.

There is no harm in using will-power to cure diseases, so long as no money or other consideration is taken for what is done. There are several methods; the simplest is the pouring in of vitality. Nature will cure most diseases if the man can be strengthened and supported while nature is left to do her work. This is especially true of the various nervous diseases which are so painfully common at the present day. The rest cure, which is often advised for them, is quite the best thing that can be suggested, but recovery might often be greatly hastened if vitality were poured into the patient in addition. Any man who has surplus vitality may direct it by his will to a particular person; when he is not doing that, it simply radiates from him in all directions, flowing out principally through the hands. If a man is depleted of strength so that his spleen does not do its work properly, the pouring in of specialized vitality is often of the greatest help to him in keeping the machinery of the body going until he is able to manufacture it for himself.

Many minor diseases can be cured merely by increasing the circulation of the vitality. A headache, for example, is generally due either to a slight congestion of blood, or to a similar congestion of the vital fluid; in either case a clairvoyant who can see the obstruction may deal with it by sending a strong current through the head, and washing away the congested matter. A man who cannot see clairvoyantly can also produce this result, but since he does not know exactly where to direct this force he generally wastes a great deal of it.

Sometimes people perform cures by imposing their own magnetic conditions upon others. This is based on the theory (which is quite correct) that all disease is in harmony of some sort, and that if perfect harmony can be restored the disease will disappear. So in this case the person who wishes to effect a cure first raises his own vibrations to the highest degree which is possible for him, fills himself with thoughts of love and health and harmony, and then proceeds to enfold the patient within his aura, the idea being that his own powerful vibrations will overbear those of the patient, and gradually bring him into the same harmonious and healthy condition. This method is often effective, but we must remember that it involves imposing the whole of the personality of the magnetizer upon the patient, which may not always be desirable for either of the persons concerned.

One should take care not to be caught or entangled on the astral plane, either through his virtues or his vices, as a man may easily do if he is not exceedingly cautious. For example, it is possible to affect others by thought, and thus obtain whatever is wanted from them, and the temptation of this power to an ordinary man would be overwhelming. Again, you could easily *force* those whom you love out of a wrong path into a right one if you wished, but this you must not do; you may only persuade and argue. Here again is a temptation. You may by force prevent your friend from doing wrong, but often the weakening effect of the compulsion on his mind will do him more harm than the wrong-doing from which you save him. Drunkenness can be cured by mesmerizing the man, but it is far better to persuade him gradually to conquer the weakness for himself, since this is a thing which he will have to do in some life. It is said that in some cases the man has yielded himself to this awful habit for so long that his will-power is entirely in abeyance, and he actually has not the strength to refrain; and it is claimed that for such a man mesmerism is necessary, for it is the only method of giving him an opportunity to reassert himself as a human being, and to regain some sort of control of his vehicles. This may be so, and I can well understand the desire to save, by any lawful means, the soul which has come to so dire a pass; yet even then I would counsel the greatest care in the use of mesmerism, and in the choice of the mesmerist.

A man can use the faculties of his astral body without moving away from his physical vehicle. That is called the possession of astral powers in the waking state, and is a definite stage in development. But it is more usual for the astral body to leave the physical in order to operate or observe at a distance from the physical body.

The Indian term "sky-walker" generally refers only to one who is able thus to travel in his astral body. But sometimes also it means levitation, in which the physical body is lifted and floats in the air. In India this happens to some ascetics, and some of the greatest of Christian saints have in deep meditation been thus raised from the ground. It involves, however, the expenditure of a good deal of force. When a disciple is commissioned to undertake some special work for humanity, the adepts may give to him, for the purpose, some extra force but though he is left free to use it as he pleases he must not fritter it away uselessly. So it happens that even those who can produce these strange effects at will do not do so to amuse themselves or others, but only for real work. It would be quite possible for some disciple to use this force for the purpose of carrying his physical body through the air to a distant place; but as that would mean a tremendous expenditure of force, it is not likely that he would so use it unless definitely directed to do so.

On the other hand there have been cases in which such powers were used—for example, to save a man from undeserved suffering. There was once a case in which a young man was accused of the forgery of an important document. He was to a certain extent technically guilty, although quite innocent of any evil intention. He had very foolishly imitated a certain signature upon a blank sheet of paper, and then some one who was unfriendly to him has obtained possession of the sheet of paper, written in certain instructions above the signature, and then cleverly cut the paper so as to make it appear to be a letter conveying orders. The accused had to admit that the signature was in his writing, but his account of the circumstances under which it was written was not unnaturally disbelieved, and it seemed impossible for him to escape the most terrible consequences. But it happened that one of our Masters was called as a witness to testify to the handwriting of the prisoner. The sheet was handed to Him with the question:

"Do you recognize that handwriting as that of the prisoner?"

The Master just glanced at it, and instantly returned it, saying: "Is this the sheet which you intended to give me?"

In that instant the sheet had become an absolute blank! The counsel for the prosecution of course supposed that in some utterly incomprehensible way he had mislaid the paper; but for want of it the prosecution fell through, and so the young man was saved.

Clairvoyance

The possession of clairvoyant power is a very great privilege and a very great advantage, and if properly and sensibly used it may be a blessing and a help to its fortunate holder, just as surely as, if it is misused, it may often be a hindrance and a curse. The principal dangers attendant upon it arise from pride, ignorance, and impurity, and if these be avoided, as they easily may be, nothing but good can come from it.

Pride is the first great danger. The possession of a faculty which, though it is the heritage of the whole human race, is as yet manifested only very occasionally, often causes the ignorant clairvoyant to feel himself (or still more frequently herself) exalted above his fellows, chosen by the Almighty for some mission of worldwide importance, dowered with a discernment that can never err, selected under angelic guidance to be the founder of a new dispensation, and so on. It should be remembered that there are always plenty of sportive and mischievous entities on the other side of the veil who are ready and even anxious to foster all such delusions, to reflect and embody all such thoughts, and to fill whatever *role* of archangel or spirit-guide may happen to be suggested to them. Unfortunately it is so easy to persuade the average man that he really is a very fine fellow at bottom, and quite worthy to be the recipient of a special revelation, even though his friends have through blindness or prejudice somehow failed hitherto to appreciate him.

Another danger, perhaps the greatest of all because it is the mother of all others, is ignorance. If the clairvoyant knows anything of the history of his subject, if he at all understands the conditions of those other planes into which his vision is penetrating, he cannot of course suppose himself the only person who was ever so highly favored, nor can he feel with self-complacent certainty that it is impossible for him to mistake. But when he is, as so many are, in the densest ignorance as to history, conditions and everything else, he is liable in the first place to make all kinds of mistakes as to what he sees, and secondly to be the easy prey of all sorts of designing and deceptive entities from the astral plane. He has no criterion by which to judge what he sees, or thinks he sees, no test to apply to his visions or communications, and so he has no sense of relative proportion or the fitness of things, and he magnifies a copy-book maxim into a fragment of divine wisdom, a platitude of the most ordinary type into an angelic message. Then again, for want of common knowledge on scientific subjects he will often utterly misunderstand what his faculties enable him to perceive, and he will, consequently, gravely promulgate the grossest absurdities.

The third danger is that of impurity. The man who is pure in thought and life, pure in intention and free from the taint of selfishness, is by that very fact guarded from the influence of undesirable entities from other planes. There is in him nothing upon which they can play; he is no fit medium for them. On the other hand all good influences naturally surround such a man, and hasten to use him as a channel through which they may act, and thus a still further barrier is erected about him against all which is mean and low and evil. The man of impure life or motive, on the contrary, inevitably attracts to himself all that is worst in the invisible world which so closely surrounds us; he responds readily to it, while it will be hardly possible for the forces of good to make any impression upon him.

But a clairvoyant who will bear in mind all these dangers, and strive to avoid them, who will take the trouble to study the history and the rationale of clairvoyance, who will see to it that his heart is humble and his motives are pure—such a man may assuredly learn very much from these powers of which he finds himself in possession, and may make them of the greatest use to him in the work which he has to do.

Having first taken good heed to the training of his character, let him observe and note down carefully any visions which come to him; let him patiently endeavor to disentangle the core of truth in them from the various accretions and exaggerations which are sure at first to be almost inextricably confused with them; let him in every possible way test and check them and endeavor to ascertain which of them are reliable, and in what way these reliable ones differ from others which have proved less trustworthy—and he will very soon find himself evolving order out of chaos, and learning to distinguish what he can trust and what he must for the present put aside as incomprehensible.

He will probably find in course of time that he gets impressions, whether by direct sight or only by feeling, in reference to the various people with whom he comes into contact. Once more the careful noting down of every such impression as soon as it occurs, and the impartial testing and checking of it as opportunity offers, will soon show our friend how far these feelings or visions are to be relied on; and as soon as he finds that they are correct and dependable he has made a very great advance, for he is in possession of a power which enables him to be of far more use to those among whom his work lies than he could be if he knew only as much about them as can be seen by the ordinary eye.

If, for example, his sight includes the auras of those around him, he can judge from what it shows him how best to deal with them, how to bring out their latent good qualities, how to strengthen their weaknesses, how to repress what is undesirable in their characters. Again, his power may often enable him to observe something of the processes of nature, to see something of the working of the non-human evolutions which surround us, and thus to acquire most valuable knowledge on all kinds of recondite subjects. If he happens to be personally acquainted with some clairvoyant who has been put under regular training he has of course a great advantage, in that he can without difficulty get his visions examined and tested by one upon whom he can rely.

Generally speaking, then, the course to be recommended to the untrained clairvoyant is that of exceeding patience and much

watchfulness; but with this hope ever before his eyes, that assuredly if he makes use of the talent entrusted to him it cannot but
attract the favorable notice of those who are ever watching for
instruments which can be employed in the great work of evolution, and that when the right time comes he will receive the
training which he so earnestly desires, and will thus be enabled
definitely to become one of those who help the world.

Special training should be arranged from early childhood for
clairvoyant children. The modern system of education tends to
suppress all psychic faculties, and most young people are over-
strained by their studies. In Greece and Rome these psychic
children were promptly isolated as vestal virgins or postulants for
the priesthood, and specially trained. There is a natural tendency
in the present day, apart from education, to repress these faculties. The best way to prevent the loss of these to the world is to put
the boys into some sort of monastery where the monks know
about the higher life and try to live it, for family life is not suitable
for this development. Where such clairvoyance appears it ought
to be encouraged, for many additional investigators are wanted
for the Society's work, and those who begin young are likely to
adapt themselves to it most readily.

People who are psychic by birth generally use the etheric double a great deal. People who possess what has sometimes been
called "etheric sight"—that is, sight capable of observing physical
matter in a state of exceedingly fine subdivision, though not yet
capable of discerning the subtler matter of the astral plane—
frequently see, when they look keenly at any exposed portion of
the human body, such as the face or the hand, multitudes of tiny
forms, such as dice, stars, and double pyramids. These belong
neither to the thought-plane nor to the astral, but to the etheric
part of the physical. They are simply the exceedingly minute
physical emanations from the body—the waste matter, consisting
largely of finely-divided salts, which is constantly being thrown
out in this manner. The character of these tiny particles varies
from many causes. Naturally loss of health often alters them
entirely, but any wave of emotion will affect them to a greater or
lesser extent, and they even respond to the influence of any
definite train of thought.

Professor Gates is reported as saying (a) that the material emanations of the living body differ according to the states of the
mind as well as the conditions of the physical health; (b) that these
emanations can be tested by the chemical reactions of some salts

of selenium; (c) that these reactions are characterized by various tints or colors according to the nature of the mental impressions; (d) that forty different emotion-products, as he calls them, have already been obtained.

People sometimes see animated particles quivering with intense rapidity, and dashing about in the air before them. This again shows the possession of much increased etheric vision, not of mental. It is unfortunately only too common for the person who gains for the first time a glimpse of astral or even of etheric matter to jump at once to the conclusion that he is at least upon the mental level, if not upon the nirvânic, and holds in his hand the key to all the mysteries of the entire solar system. All that will come in good time, and these grander vistas will assuredly open before him one day; but he will hasten the coming of that desirable consummation if he makes sure of each step as he takes it, and tries fully to understand and make the best of what he has, before desiring more. Those who begin their experience with nirvânic vision are few and far between; for most of us, progress must be slow and steady, and the safest motto for us is *festina lente.**

I should not advise anyone to allow himself to be thrown into mesmeric sleep for the purpose of gaining clairvoyant experiences. The domination of the will by that of another produces effects that few people realize. The will of the victim becomes weaker, and is more liable to be acted upon by others. In the scheme of things no man is *forced* to do anything; he is taught by receiving always the result of his actions; and it is better to allow clairvoyant powers to come gradually in the natural course of evolution, rather than to try to force them in any way.

We must not always assume that a man who sees something pertaining to higher planes is necessarily becoming clairvoyant. By clairvoyance, for example, we may undoubtedly see an apparition, but on the other hand there are various other ways in which a man may see or suppose himself to see something which to him would be exactly the same as an apparition.

The apparition of a dead person may be (a) one's own imagination, (b) a thought form produced by another person, (c) or by the person seen, (d) an impersonation, (e) the etheric double of the person, or (f) the real person actually there. In the last case one of three things must have happened—that is, supposing that the apparition is dead or sleeping and in his astral body, and that the

---

*Festina lente—make haste slowly.

man who sees him is himself in his physical body and wide awake. Either (a) the dead man has materialized himself, and is for the time a physical object, which may be seen by any number of people with ordinary physical sight; (b) the dead man is in his astral body, in which case only those possessing astral sight can perceive him; he has probably succeeded by some special effort in temporarily opening that sight for the person to whom he wishes to show himself, and is therefore most likely visible to that one person only, and not to any others who may happen to be present; or, (c) the dead man has mesmerized the living, so as to impose upon him the idea that he sees a figure which is not really visible to him, though it may be really present.

If the apparition be an etheric double, it will not stray far away from the dense body to which it belongs or used to belong. An unpracticed apparition—one who is new to the astral plane—often shows traces of the habits of his earth-life. He will enter and depart by a door or a window, not yet realizing that he can pass through the wall just as easily. I have even seen one squeeze through the crack of a locked door; he might as well have tried the keyhole! But he moves as he has been accustomed to move—as he *thinks* of himself as moving. For the same reason an apparition often walks upon the earth, when he might just as well float through the air.

It is a mistake to think that if you see a vision, it must necessarily mean something for you, or be specially sent to you. If you for the moment become sensitive, you see whatever happens to be there: Suppose I am sitting in a room, and a curtain is drawn across the window, so that the street outside is invisible to me. Suppose the wind lifts the curtain for a moment, so that I get a glimpse of the street, I shall then see whatever happens to be passing at that moment. Let us imagine that I see a little girl in a red cloak, carrying a basket. That little girl is probably going about her own business, or perhaps her mother's; should I not be very foolish if I chose to fancy that she had been *sent* there especially for me to see, and began to worry myself as to what could be symbolized by the red cloak and the basket? A flash of clairvoyance is usually just the accidental lifting of a curtain, and generally what is seen has no special relation to the seer. There may occasionally be instances in which the curtain is intentionally lifted by a friend because something of personal interest is passing; but we must not be too ready to assume that that is the case.

Among the real psychic powers, however, which are attained by slow and careful self-development, there are some which are of very great interest. For example, for one who can function freely in the mental body there are methods of getting at the meaning of a book, quite apart from the ordinary process of reading it. The simplest is to read from the mind of one who has studied it; but this is open to the objection that one gets not the real meaning of the work but that student's conception of the meaning, which may be by no means the same thing. A second plan is to examine the aura of the book—a phrase which needs a little explanation for those not practically acquainted with the hidden side of things.

An ancient manuscript stands in this respect in a somewhat different position from a modern book. If it is not the original work of the author himself, it has at any rate been copied word by word by some person of a certain education and understanding, who knew the subject of the book, and had his own opinions about it. It must be remembered that copying (done usually with a stylus) is almost as slow and emphatic as engraving; so that the writer inevitably impresses his thought strongly on his handiwork. Any manuscript, therefore, even a new one, has always some sort of thought-aura about it which conveys its general meaning, or rather one man's idea of its meaning and his estimate of its value. Every time it is read by anyone an addition is made to that thought-aura, and if it be carefully studied the addition is naturally large and valuable.

This is equally true of a printed volume. A book which has passed through many hands has an aura which is usually better balanced than that of a new one, because it is rounded off and completed by the divergent views brought to it by its many readers; consequently the psychometrization of such a book generally yields a fairly full comprehension of its contents, though with a considerable fringe of opinions *not* expressed in the book, but held by its various readers.

On the other hand, a book used in a public library is not infrequently as unpleasant psychically as it usually is physically, for it becomes loaded with all kinds of mixed magnetisms, many of them of a most unsavory character. The sensitive person will do well to avoid such books, or if necessity compels him to use them he will be wise to touch them as little as may be, and rather to let them lie upon a table than to hold them in his hand.

Another factor to be remembered with regard to such books is that a volume written upon a special subject is most likely to be read by a particular type of person, and these readers leave their impress upon the aura of the volume. Thus a book violently advocating some sectarian religious views is not read except by persons who sympathize with its narrowness, and so it soon develops a decidedly unpleasant aura; and in the same way a book of an indecent or prurient nature quickly becomes loathsome beyond description. Old books containing magical formulae are often for this reason most uncomfortable neighbors. Even the language in which a book is printed indirectly affects its aura, by limiting its readers largely to men of a certain nationality, and so by degrees endowing it with the more prominent characteristics of that nationality.

In the case of a printed book there is no original copyist, so that at the beginning of its career it usually carries nothing but disjointed fragments of the thought of the binder and bookseller. Few readers at the present day seem to study so thoughtfully and thoroughly as did the men of old, and for that reason the thought forms connected with a modern book are rarely so precise and clear cut as those which surround the manuscripts of the past.

The third method of reading requires some higher powers, in order to go behind the book or manuscript altogether and get at the mind of its author. If the book is in some foreign language, its subject entirely unknown, and there is no aura around it to give any helpful suggestion, the only way is to follow back its history to see from what it was copied (or set up in type, as the case may be) and so to trace out the line of its descent until one reaches its author. If the subject of the work be known, a less tedious method is to psychometrize that subject, get into the general current of thought about it, and so find the particular writer required, and see what he thinks. There is a sense in which all the ideas connected with a given subject may be said to be local—to be concentrated round a certain point in space—so that by mentally visiting that point one can come into touch with all the converging streams of thought about that subject, though these are linked by millions of lines with all sorts of other subjects.

Another interesting power is that of magnification. There are two methods of magnification which may be used in connection with the clairvoyant faculty. One is simply an intensification of ordinary sight. It is obvious that when in common life we see anything, an impact of some sort is made upon the retina—upon its physical rods and cones. The effects there produced, or the vibrations set up, are transmitted, in some way by no means thoroughly understood, by the optic nerve to the grey matter of the brain. Clearly, before the true man within can become conscious of what is seen, these impressions made upon the physical brain-matter must be transmitted from that to the etheric matter, from that in turn to the astral, and from that to the mental—these different degrees of matter being, as it were, stations on a telegraph wire.

One method of magnification is to tap this telegraph wire at an intermediate station—to receive the impression upon the etheric matter of the retina instead of upon the physical rods and cones, and to transfer the impression received directly to the etheric part of the brain. By an effort of will the attention can be focussed in only a few of the etheric particles, or even in one of them, and in that way a similarity of size can be attained between the organ employed and some minute object which is to be observed.

A method more commonly used, but requiring somewhat higher development, is to employ the special faculty of the center between the eyebrows. From the central portion of that can be projected what we may call a tiny microscope at the etheric level, having for its lens only one atom. In this way again we produce an organ commensurate in size with the minute objects to be observed. The atom employed may be either physical, astral or mental, but whichever it is it needs a special preparation. It must be opened up and brought into full working order, so that it is just as developed as it will be in the seventh round of our chain.

This power belongs to the causal body, so if an atom of lower level be used as an eye-piece a system of reflecting counterparts must be introduced. The atom can be adjusted to any subplane, so that any required degree of magnification can be applied in order to suit the object which is being examined. A further extension of the same power enables the operator to focus his own consciousness in that lens through which he looks, and then to project it to distant points. The same power, by a different arrangement, can be used for diminishing purposes when one wishes to view as a whole something far too large to be taken in at once by ordinary vision.

The Mystic Chord

Questions have often been asked as to the method by which a person at a distance of some thousands of miles can be instantly found by a trained clairvoyant. Apparently this remains somewhat of a mystery to many, so I will endeavor to give an explanation of the plan commonly adopted, though it is not easy to put it quite plainly. A clear expression of super-physical facts cannot be achieved in physical words, for the latter are always to some extent misleading even when they seem most illuminative.

Man's various forces and qualities, manifesting in his bodies as vibrations, send out for each vehicle what may be called a keynote. Take his astral body as an example. From the number of different vibrations which are habitual to that astral body there emerges a sort of average tone, which we may call the keynote of the man on the astral plane. It is obviously conceivable that there may be a considerable number of ordinary men whose astral keynote is practically the same, so that this alone would not suffice to distinguish them with certainty. But there is a similar average tone for each man's mental body, for his causal body, and even for the etheric part of his physical body; and there have never yet been found two persons whose keynotes were identical at all these levels, so as to make exactly the same chord when struck simultaneously.

Thus the chord of each man is unique, and it furnishes a means by which he can always be distinguished from the rest of the world. Among millions of unevolved souls there may possibly be cases where development is as yet so slight that the chords are scarcely clear enough for the differences between them to be observed, but with any of the higher types there is never the least difficulty, nor is there any risk of confusion.

Whether the man be sleeping or waking, living or dead, his chord remains the same, and he can always be found by it. How can this be so, it may be asked, when he is resting in the heaven-world, and has therefore no astral or etheric body to emit the characteristic sounds? So long as the causal body itself remains, it has always attached to it its permanent atoms, one belonging to each of the planes, and therefore, wherever he goes, the man in his causal body carries his chord with him, for the single atom is quite sufficient to give out the distinctive sound.

The trained seer, who is able to sense the chord, attunes his own vehicles for the moment exactly to its notes, and then by an effort of will sends forth its sound. Wherever in the three worlds that man who is sought may be, this evokes an instantaneous response from him. If he be living in the physical body, it is quite possible that he may be conscious only of a slight shock in that lower vehicle, and may not in the least know what has caused it. But his causal body lights up instantly; it leaps up like a great flame, and this response is at once visible to the seer, so that by that one action the man is found, and a magnetic line of communication is established. The seer can use that line as a kind of telescope, or if he prefers he can send his consciousness flashing along it with the speed of light, and see from the other end of it, as it were.

The combination of sounds which will produce a man's chord is his true occult name; and it is in this sense that it has been said that when a man's true name is called he instantly replies, wherever he may be. Some vague tradition of this is probably at the back of the idea so widely spread among primitive cultures that a man's real name is a part of him, and must be carefully concealed, because one who knows it has a certain power over him, and can work magic upon him. Thus it is also said that the man's true name is changed at each initiation, since each such ceremony is at once the official recognition and the fulfilment of a progress by which he has, as it were, raised himself into a higher key, putting an additional strain upon the strings of his instrument, and evoking from it far grander music, so that thenceforward his chord must be sounded differently. This name of the man must not be confused with the hidden name of the Augoeides, for that is the chord produced by the vibrations of the âtmic, buddhic and mental atoms, the three principles of the ego, and the monad behind them.

In order to avoid such confusion we must keep clearly in mind the distinction between two manifestations of the man at different levels. The correspondence between these two manifestations is so close that we may almost consider the lower as the repetition of the higher. The ego is triple, consisting of âtmâ, buddhi, manas, three constituents each existing on its own plane—the âtmâ on the nirvânic, the buddhi on the buddhic, and the manas on the highest level of the mental. This ego inhabits a causal body, a vehicle built of the matter of the lowest of the three planes to which he belongs. He then puts himself further down into manifestation, and takes three lower vehicles, the mental, astral and physical bodies. His chord in this lower manifestation is that which we have been describing, and consists of his own note and those of the three lower vehicles.

Just as the ego is triple, so is the monad, and this also has its three constituents, each existing on its own plane; but in this case the three planes are the first, second and third of our system, and the nirvânic is the lowest of them instead of the highest. But on that nirvânic level it takes to itself a manifestation, and we call it the monad in its âtmic vehicle, or sometimes the triple âtmâ or triple spirit; and this is for it what the causal body is for the ego. Just as the ego takes on three lower bodies (mental, astral, physical), the first of which (the mental) is on the lower part of his own plane, and the lowest (the physical) two planes below, so the monad takes on three lower manifestations (which we commonly call âtmâ, buddhi, manas), the first of which is on the lower part of his plane, and the lowest two planes below that. It will thus be seen that the causal body is to the monad what the physical body is to the ego. If we think of the ego as the soul of the physical body, we may consider the monad as the soul of the ego in turn. Thus the chord of the Augoeides (the glorified ego in his causal body) consists of the note of the monad, with those of its three manifestations âtmâ, buddhi, manas.

It must be understood that the chord cannot be accurately considered as sound in the sense in which we use that word on this plane. It has been suggested to me that an analogy which is in some respects better is that of the combination of lines in a spectrum. Each of the elements whose spectrum is known to us is instantly recognizable by it, in whatever star it may appear, no matter how great the distance may be—so long as the lines are bright enough to be seen at all. But the chord of which we have been speaking is not actually either heard or seen; it is received by a complex perception which requires the practically simultaneous activity of the consciousness in the causal body and in all the lower vehicles.

Even with regard to ordinary astral perception it is misleading (though practically unavoidable) to speak of "hearing" and "seeing." These terms connote for us the idea of certain sense-organs which receive impressions of a well-defined type. To see implies the possession of an eye, to hear implies the existence of an ear. But no such sense-organs are to be found on the astral plane. It is true that the astral body is an exact counterpart of the physical, and that it consequently shows eyes and ears, nose and mouth, hands and feet, just as the latter does. But when functioning in the astral body we do not walk upon the astral counterparts of our physical feet, nor do we see and hear with the counterparts of our physical eyes and ears.

Each particle in an astral body is capable of receiving a certain set of vibrations—those belonging to its own level, and those only. If we divide all astral vibrations into seven sets, just like seven octaves in music, each octave will correspond to a subplane, and only a particle in the astral body which is built of matter belonging to that subplane can respond to the vibrations of that octave. So "to be upon a certain subplane in the astral" is to have developed the sensitiveness of only those particles in one's astral body which belong to that subplane, so that one can perceive the matter and the inhabitants of that subplane only. To have perfect vision upon the astral plane means to have developed sensitiveness in all particles of the astral body, so that all the subplanes are simultaneously visible.

Even though a man has developed the particles of one subplane only, if those are fully developed he will have on that subplane a power of perception equivalent to all of our physical senses. If he perceives an object at all, he will in that one act of perception receive from it an impression which conveys all that we learn down here through those various channels which we call the senses; he will simultaneously see, hear and feel it. The instantaneous perception which belongs to higher planes is still further removed from the clumsy and partial action of the physical senses.

In order to see how the chord helps the clairvoyant to find any given person, it must also be understood that the vibrations which cause it are communicated by the man to any object which is for some time in close contact with him, and therefore permeated by his magnetism. A lock of his hair, an article of clothing which he has worn, a letter which he has written—any of these is sufficient to give the chord to one who knows how to perceive it. It can also be obtained very readily from a photograph, which seems more curious, since the photograph need not have been in direct contact with the person whom it represents. Even untrained clairvoyants, who have no scientific knowledge of the subject, instinctively recognize the necessity of bringing themselves *en rapport* with those whom they seek by means of some such objects.

It is not necessary for the seer to hold the letter in his hand while examining the case, or even to have it near him. Having once held the letter and sensed the chord, he is able to remember it and reproduce it, just as any one with a good memory might remember a face after seeing it once. Some such link as this is always necessary to find a person previously unknown. We had recently a case of a man who had died somewhere in the Congo district, but as no photograph of him was sent by the friend who wrote about him, it was necessary first to seek that friend (somewhere in Scandinavia, I think) and make a contact in a roundabout way through him.

There are, however, other methods of finding people at a distance. One which is most effective requires higher development than that just described. A man who is able to raise his consciousness to the atomic level of the buddhic plane there finds himself absolutely in union with all his fellowmen—and therefore of course among the rest with the person whom he seeks. He draws his consciousness up into this unity along his own line, and he has only to put himself out again along the line of that other person in order to find him. There are always various ways of exercising clairvoyance, and each student employs that which comes most naturally to him. If he has not fully studied his subject, he often thinks his own method the only one possible, but wider knowledge soon disabuses him of that idea.

How Past Lives Are Seen

As a series of past lives of enthralling interest has recently been published in *The Lives of Alcyone*, many enquiries have been received as to the exact method by which the record of such lives is read by the investigators. It is not easy to explain the matter satisfactorily to those who have not themselves the power to see them, but some attempt at a description of the process may at least help students on the way towards comprehension.

To begin with, it is by no means easy to explain what the akashic record is which is to be read. A suggestion leading towards an idea of it may perhaps be obtained by imagining a room with a huge pier-glass at one end. Everything which took place in that room would be reflected in that mirror. If we further suppose that mirror to be endowed with the properties of a kind of perpetual cinematograph, so that it records all which it reflects, and can afterwards under certain circumstances be made to reproduce it, we have advanced one stage towards understanding how the record presents itself. But we must add to our conception qualities which no mirror ever possessed—the power to reproduce all sounds as a phonograph does, and also to reflect and reproduce thoughts and feelings.*

Then we must further try to understand what the reflection in a mirror really is. If two persons stand in relation to a mirror so that each sees in it not himself but the other, it is obvious that the same area of glass is reflecting the two images. Therefore if we suppose the glass to retain permanently every image which has ever been cast upon it (perhaps it actually does!) it is again clear that the same part of the glass must be simultaneously recording those two images. Move up and down and from side to side, and you will soon convince yourself that *every* particle of glass must be simultaneously recording every part of every object in the room, and that what you happen to see in it depends upon the position of your eye. Hence it also follows that no two people can ever see at the same moment exactly the same reflection in a mirror, any more than two people can see the same rainbow, because two physical eyes cannot simultaneously occupy exactly the same point in space.

What we have supposed to happen with regard to the particles of our mirror does really happen with regard to every particle of every substance. Every stone by the roadside contains an indelible record of everything that has ever passed it, but this record cannot (so far as we yet know) be recovered from it so as to be visible to the ordinary physical senses, though the more developed sense of the psychometrist perceives it without difficulty.

The records must not be thought of as originally inhering in matter of any kind, though they are connected with it. In order

*At the time of this writing motion pictures were not available for Leadbeater to use as an analogy. E(

to read them it is not necessary to come into direct contact with any particular material object, since they can be read from any distance, when a connection has once been made.

Nevertheless it is also true that each atom retains the record, or perhaps only possesses the power to put a clairvoyant *en rapport* with the record, of all that has ever happened within sight of it. It is by means of this quality that psychometry is possible. But there is this very curious limitation attached to it, that the normal psychometrist sees by means of it only what he would have seen if he had been standing at the spot from which the object psychometrized has been taken. For example, if a man psychometrizes a pebble which has been lying for ages in a valley, he will see only what has passed during those ages in that valley; his views will be limited by the surrounding hills, just as if he had stood for all those ages where the stone lay, and had witnessed all those things.

True, there is an extension of the psychometric power, by which a man may see the thoughts and feelings of the actors in his drama as well as their physical bodies, and there is also another extension by which, having first established himself in that valley, he may make it the basis of further operations, and so pass over the surrounding hills and see what lies beyond them, and also what has happened there since the stone was removed, and even what occurred before it in some manner arrived there. But the man who can do that will soon be able to dispense with the stone altogether. When we use the senses of the causal body on the counterparts of physical things, we see that every object is thus throwing off pictures of the past.

How is it possible, men ask, for an inanimate particle to register and reproduce impressions? The answer is that the particle is *not* inanimate, and that the life which ensouls it is part of the Divine Life. Indeed, another way in which one may attempt to describe the record is to say that it is the memory of the Logos Himself, and that each particle is somehow in touch with that part of His memory which includes the events which have taken place in its neighborhood, or what we may call within sight of it. It is probable that what we call *our* memory is nothing but a similar power of coming into touch (though often very imperfectly) with that part of *His* memory which refers to events which we happen to have seen or known.

So we might say that every man carries about with him on

the physical plane two memories of anything which he has seen—his brain-memory, which is often imperfect or inaccurate, and the memory enshrined in any unchanged particles of his body or of the clothes that he wears, which is always perfect and accurate, but is available only for those who have learned how to read it. Remember also that the brain-memory may be inaccurate, not only because it is itself imperfect, but because the original observation may have been defective. Also, it may have been colored by prejudice: we see, to a large extent, what we wish to see, and we can remember an event only *as it appeared to us*, though we may have seen it partially or wrongly. But from all these defects the record is entirely free.

It is obvious that a man's physical body can have neither a memory nor a record of a past incarnation in which it did not participate; and the same is true of his astral and mental bodies, since all these vehicles are new for each new incarnation. This at once shows us that the lowest level at which we can hope to get really reliable information about past lives is that of the causal body, for nothing below that can give us firsthand evidence. In those previous lives the ego in his causal body was present—at least a certain small part of him was—and so he is an actual witness; whereas all lower vehicles were *not* witnesses, and can only report what they have received from him. When we recollect how imperfect is the communication between the ego and the personality in the ordinary man, we shall at once see how entirely unreliable such second, third, or fourth-hand testimony is likely to be. One may sometimes obtain from the astral or mental bodies isolated pictures of events in a man's past life, but not a sequential and coherent account of it; and even those pictures are but reflections from the causal body, and probably very dim and blurred reflections.

Therefore to read past lives with accuracy the first thing necessary is to develop the faculties of the causal body. Turning those faculties upon the causal body of the man to be examined, we have before us the same two possibilities as in the case of the physical man. We can take the ego's own memory of what happened, or we can as it were psychometrize him and see for ourselves the experiences through which he has passed. The latter method is the safer, for even the ego, since he has seen these things through a past personality, may have imperfect or prejudiced impressions of them.

This then is the mechanism of the ordinary method of investigating past lives—to use the faculties of one's own causal body, and by its means to psychometrize the causal body of the subject. The thing could be done at lower levels by psychometrization of the permanent atoms, but as this would be a much more difficult feat than the unfolding of the senses of the causal body it is not at all likely ever to be attempted successfully. Another method (which, however, requires much higher development) is to use the buddhic faculties—to become absolutely one with the ego under investigation, and read his experiences as though they were one's own—from within instead of from without. Both of these methods have been employed by those who prepared the series of lives which appear in *The Lives of Alcyone*, and the investigators have also had the advantage of the intelligent cooperation of the ego whose incarnations are described.

The physical presence of the subject whose lives are being read is an advantage, but not a necessity; he is useful if he can keep his vehicles perfectly calm, but if he becomes excited he spoils everything.

The surroundings are not specially important, but quiet is essential, as the physical brain must be calm if impressions are to be brought through clearly. Everything which comes down to the physical level from the causal body *must* pass through the mental and the astral vehicles, and if either of these is disturbed it reflects imperfectly, just as the least rippling of the surface of a lake will break up or distort the images of the trees or houses upon its banks. It is necessary also to eradicate absolutely all prejudices, otherwise they will produce the effect of stained glass; they will color everything which is seen through them, and so give a false impression.

In looking at past lives it has always been our custom to retain full physical consciousness, so as to be able to make a note of everything while it is being observed. This is found to be a much safer method than to leave the physical body during the observations, and then trust to memory for their reproduction. There is, however, a stage at which this latter plan is the only one available, when the student, though able to use the causal body, can do so only while the physical vehicle is asleep.

The identification of the various characters encountered in these glimpses of the past sometimes presents a little difficulty, for naturally egos change considerably in the course of twenty thousand years or so. Fortunately, with a little practice it is possible to pass the record in review as rapidly or as slowly as may be desired; so when there is any doubt as to an identification we always adopt the plan of running quickly along the line of lives of the ego under observation, until we trace him to the present day. Some investigators, when they see an ego in some remote life, at once feel an intuition as to his present personality; but though such a flash of intuition may often be right, it may certainly also sometimes be wrong, and the more laborious method is the only one which is thoroughly reliable.

There are cases in which, even after many thousands of years, the egos of ordinary people are instantly recognizable; but that does not speak particularly well for them, because it means that during all that time they have made but little progress. To try to recognize twenty thousand years ago some one whom one knows at the present day is rather like meeting as an adult some one whom one knew long ago as a little child. In some cases recognition is possible; in other cases the change has been too great. Those who have since become Masters of the Wisdom are often instantly recognizable, even thousands of years ago, but that is for a very different reason. When the lower vehicles are already fully in harmony with the ego, they form themselves in the likeness of the Augoeides, and so change very little from life to life. In the same way when the ego himself is becoming a perfect reflection of the monad, he also changes but little, but gradually grows; and so he is readily recognizable.

In examining a past life the easiest way of all would be to let the record drift past us at its natural rate, but that would mean a day's work to look up the events of each day, and a lifetime spent upon each incarnation. As has been said, it is possible to accelerate or retard the passage of events, so that a period of thousands of years may be run through rapidly, or on the other hand any particular picture may be held as long as is desired, so that it may be examined in detail. The acceleration or retardation may perhaps be compared to the hastening or slackening of the movement of a panorama; a little practice gives the power to do this at will, but as in the case of the panorama, the whole record is really there all the time.

What I have described as the unrolling of the record rapidly or slowly at will is in reality a movement not of the record, but of the consciousness of the seer. But the impression which it gives is exactly as I have stated it. The records may be said to lie upon one another in layers, the more recent on the top and the older ones behind. Yet even this simile is misleading, because it inevitably suggests the idea of thickness, whereas these records occupy no more space than does the reflection on the surface of a mirror. When the consciousness passes through them, it does not really move in space at all; it rather puts on itself, as a kind of cloak, one or other of the layers of the record, and in doing so it finds itself in the midst of the action of the story.

One of the most tiresome tasks connected with this branch of enquiry is the determination of exact dates. In fact, some investigators frankly decline to undertake it, saying that it is not worth the trouble, and that a round number is sufficient for all practical purposes. Probably it is; yet there is a feeling of satisfaction in getting even details as accurate as possible, even at the cost of tedious counting up to very high numbers. Our plan is of course to establish certain fixed points and then use those as a basis for further calculation.

One such fixed point is the date 9,564 B.C., when the sinking of Poseidonis took place. Another is the date 75,025 B.C., for the commencement of the great previous catastrophe.* In the course of the investigation of the lives of Alcyone we have thus established a number of points, up to the date of 22,662 B.C., and as those lives were worked backwards, and the intervals were therefore counted one by one and not all at once, the scheme was not too insufferably tedious, as it certainly would be with very large numbers. In certain cases astronomical means are also employed. A description of these different methods will be found in my book *Clairvoyance.*

It is on the whole somewhat easier to read lives forwards than backwards, because in that case we are working with the natural flow of time instead of against it. So the usual plan is to run rapidly to some selected point in the past, and then work slowly forwards from that. It must be remembered that at first

*The huge islands of Ruta and Daitya, remnants of the continent of Atlantis, were destroyed in 75,025 B.C. Poseidonis, the last Atlantean remnant, sank in 9,564 B.C. Ed.

sight it is rarely possible to estimate accurately the relative importance of the minor events of a life, so we often skim over it first, to see from what actions or occurrences the really important changes flow, and then go back and describe those more in detail. If the investigator himself happens to be one of the characters in the life which he is examining, there opens before him the interesting alternative of actually putting himself back into that old personality, and feeling over again just what he felt in that ancient time. But in that case he sees everything exactly as he saw it then, and knows no more than he knew then.

Few of those who read the life-stories, which are often somewhat meager outlines, will have any conception of the amount of labor which has been bestowed upon them—of the hours of work which have sometimes been given to the full comprehension of some trifling detail, so that the picture finally presented may be as nearly a true one as is possible. At least our readers may be sure that no pains have been spared to ensure accuracy, though this is often no easy task when we are dealing with conditions and modes of thought as entirely different from our own as though they belonged to another planet.

The languages employed are almost always unintelligible to the investigator, but as the thoughts behind the words lie open before him that matters little. On several occasions those who were doing the work have copied down public inscriptions which they could not understand, and have afterwards had them translated on the physical plane by someone to whom the ancient language was familiar.

A vast amount of work is represented by the sets of lives which are now appearing; may that labor bring its fruit in a more vivid realization of the mighty civilizations of the past and a clearer comprehension of the working of the laws of karma and reincarnation. Since the first set of lives which appeared have culminated in the initiation of the hero in his present incarnation,* they are surely a valuable study for those whose aspiration is to become the pupils of a Master of the Wisdom, for their own progress should be the more rapid when they have learned how a brother has attained the goal towards which they are striving. This progress has been made the more

---

*Krishnamurti.

easy for them because that brother has taken the trouble to record for us in that most admirable little book *At the Feet of the Master* the teachings which led him to that goal.

About a hundred and fifty of those who are at present members of the Theosophical Society are the prominent characters in the drama which lies before the readers of *The Lives*; and it is deeply interesting to note how those who in the past have often been linked by the ties of blood relationship, though born this time in countries thousands of miles apart, are yet brought together by their common interest in theosophical study, and bound to one another more closely by their love for the Masters than they could ever have been by any mere earthly connection.

There are two sources of possible error in examining the records clairvoyantly; first, personal bias, and secondly, limited views. There are fundamental differences of temperament, and these cannot but color the views taken of other planes. The adept has a perfect perception of life, but below that level we are sure to have some prejudices. The man of the world magnifies unimportant details and omits all the important things, because he is in the habit of doing that in daily life; but on the other hand a man starting on the Path, may in his enthusiasm, lose for a time his touch with the ordinary human life from which he has emerged. Even then he has made a great advance, for those who see the inside of things are nearer to the truth than those who see only the outside.

The statements of clairvoyants may and must be colored by opinions already formed, as was clearly the case with Swedenborg, who used a very Christian terminology to describe the facts of the astral plane, and unquestionably saw many things through strong thought forms which he had made in previous years. He started with certain definite preconceptions, and he made everything which he saw fit into those preconceptions. You know how it is possible down here on the physical plane to start with some preconception about a man and distort his most innocent words and actions to fit that preconception—to read into them ideas of which the unfortunate man never even dreamed. The same thing is possible on the astral plane if one is careless.

Theosophical investigators try to be always on their guard against this danger of personal bias, and use constant checks of all kinds to avoid it. To minimize the chance of error from this source the Masters usually select people of radically different types to work together.

Secondly, there is the danger of a limited view—of taking a part for the whole. For example, there has been much said of the corruption and black magic of later days in Poseidonis, but there existed there, at that very time, a secret society that was quite pure and had high aims. If it had happened that we had seen only this society, we might easily have thought of Poseidonis as a most spiritual country. It is possible, you see, that such limited views may be taken as applying to a whole region or community. Generalizations must be checked and verified. There is, however, a general aura of a time or a country, which usually prevents any great mistakes of this sort. A psychic who has not been trained to sense this general aura is often unconscious of it, and thus the untrained man falls into many errors. In fact, long-continued observation shows that all untrained psychics are sometimes reliable and sometimes unreliable, and those who consult them always run a risk of being misled.

As we develop our inner consciousness and faculties, life becomes continuous; we reach the consciousness of the ego, and then we can travel back even as far as the group-soul in which we lived the animal stage, and look through animal eyes at the human beings of that period and the different world that flourished then. But there are no words to tell what is seen in that way, for the difference of outlook is beyond all expression.

Short of that continuous consciousness, however, there is no detailed memory—not even of the most important facts. For example, a person who knows the truth of reincarnation in one life does not necessarily carry his certainty over to the next. I forgot it myself, and so did Mrs. Besant. I did not know anything of it in this life, until I heard of it from outside, and then I instantly recognized its truth. Whatever we have known in the past will spring up in the mind in this way as a certainty when it is next presented before us.

As a child I used constantly to dream of a certain house, which I afterwards learned was a house in which I had lived in a previous life. It was quite unlike any with which I was at that time familiar on the physical plane, for it was built round a central courtyard (with a fountain and statues and shrubs) into which all the rooms looked. I used to dream of it perhaps three times a week, and I knew every room of it and all the people who lived in it, and used constantly to describe it to my mother, and draw ground-plans of it. We called it my dream-house. As I grew older I dreamed of it less and less frequently, until at last it faded from my memory altogether. But one day to illustrate some point my Master showed me a picture of the house in which I had lived in my last incarnation, and I recognized it immediately.

Any one may intellectually appreciate the necessity of rein-carnation; but actually to prove it one must become, in the causal body, cognizant of the past and future. The only way of casting off the fetter of doubt is by knowledge and intelligent comprehension. Blind belief is a barrier to progress, but this does not mean that we are wrong in accepting intelligently the statements of those who know more than ourselves. There are no authoritative dogmas which must be accepted in the Theosophical Society. There are only statements of the results of investigation, which are offered in the belief that they will be as helpful to other minds as they have been to the investigators.

Foreseeing the Future

It is very difficult to explain how the future is foreseen, but there is no doubt whatever as to the fact. Apart from appa-rently accidental pictures and flashes of intuition, often effec-tive but not under control, there are two ways in which the future may definitely be foreseen by means of the higher clair-voyance. One is quite readily explicable and comprehensible; the other is not explicable at all.

Even with only physical senses we may see enough to foretell certain things. If, for instance, we see a man leading an extra-vagant life of debauchery, we may safely predict that, unless he changes, he will presently lose both health and fortune. What we cannot tell by physical means is whether he will change or not. But a man who has the sight of the causal body could often tell this, because to him the reserve forces of the other would be visible; he could see what the ego thought of it all, and whether he was strong enough to interfere. No merely physical prediction is certain, because so many of the causes which in-fluence life cannot be seen on this lower plane. But when we raise our consciousness to higher planes we can see more of the causes, and so can come much nearer to calculating the effects.

Obviously if *all* the causes could be perfectly seen and

judged, all their results would be readily calculable. Perhaps none but the Logos can see *all* causes in His system, but an adept would surely be able to see all that could affect an ordinary man! So it is probable that by this method an adept could foretell the life of that man quite accurately. For the ordinary man has little will power; karma assigns to him certain surroundings, and he is the creature of those surroundings; he accepts the fate marked out for him, because he does not know that he can alter it. A more developed man takes hold of his destiny and molds it; he makes his future what he wills it to be, counteracting the karma of the past by setting fresh forces in motion. So his future is not so easily predictable; but no doubt even in this case an adept, who could see the latent will, could also calculate how he would use it.

That method of foretelling the future is entirely comprehensible, and it is clear that the chief events of any life could be prophesied along that line. But there is another way for which we cannot so easily account. One has only to raise the consciousness to a plane sufficiently high, to find the limitation which we call time disappearing and the past, present and future spread out before us like an open book. How that can be reconciled with our freedom of action I am not prepared to say, but I can testify that the fact is so; when this sight is employed the future is simply *there*, down to the minutest detail. I believe myself that we *are* free to choose, though only within certain limits; yet a power, far higher than we, may well know how we *shall* choose. You know what your dog will do under certain conditions, but that does not in the least *make* him do it; so a power as much higher than man, as man is than the dog, may know quite well how man will use his fragment of free will.

For it *is* only a fragment; the plan of the Logos is to trust us with a little freedom, and see how we use it. If we use it well and wisely, a little more is given to us; and so long as we continue to use it in harmony with His great intention of evolution, we shall find more and more freedom of choice coming to us. But if we are so foolish as to use it selfishly, so as to bring harm to ourselves and hinder His plan, we shall find ourselves cramped in our action and forced back into line. A child must have freedom to walk, even though that involves a risk of falling, or else he will never learn; but no one would let him make his experiment on the edge of a precipice. So we have freedom enough to do ourselves a little harm if we use it wrongly, but not freedom enough to destroy ourselves altogether.

Times of choice certainly come to us, but between those times we have often little option. When we have made our choice we must abide by its consequences. Looked at from above, human destiny seems rather like a network of railway lines. A man starts out on a locomotive, and chooses his line or rail; but when he has chosen it he must run along it, and cannot swerve to the right hand or the left until he reaches the first set of points. Then he may descend and set the points as he will, but having once set them and started on his way he must accept the consequences of his decision; he has no power to turn aside until the next point of choice comes in his way. We must not confuse free will with freedom of action.

Now to possess fully the power of forecasting the future by either of the methods described means considerable development; but isolated pictures reflected from both of them may often be had at very much lower levels. What is called in Scotland second-sight appears to be an example; by that, a future event is often seen with quite a wealth of detail.

I remember reading of a case where a seer told a skeptic that a certain man known to them both would die at a given time, and furthermore gave a detailed description of his funeral, mentioning the pallbearers by name. The skeptic ridiculed the whole prediction, but when the appointed time came the man indicated did die as had been prophesied. The skeptic was astonished, but still more annoyed, and he determined that the rest of the story should *not* come true, for he himself would interfere to falsify it. He therefore got himself appointed as one of the pallbearers! But when the day came and the party was just about to start, he was called aside for a moment, and when he returned he found that the procession had already moved away, and that the pallbearers were those who had been seen in the vision.

I have myself had similar pictures of scenes in the future—scenes of no interest to myself, and of no use so far as I could see; but they have always happened exactly as I had seen them, in every case where I have had the opportunity of verifying them.

The Logos had thought out the whole life of His system, not

only as it is now, but as it has been at every moment in the past, and as it will be at every moment in the future. And His thought calls into existence that of which He thinks. These thought forms are said to be on the cosmic mental plane—two whole sets of seven planes above our set of seven. He thinks out what He intends each of the planetary chains to do; He comes down to smaller details, for He thinks of the type of man for every root-race and sub-race, from the beginning of all, through the Lemurian, the Atlantean, the Aryan and the succeeding races. Thus we may say that on that cosmic mental plane the whole of the system was called into existence simultaneously by that thought—an act of special creation; and it must all be now simultaneously present to Him. So that it may well be that His mighty consciousness to some extent reflects itself even on very much lower levels, and somehow we sometimes catch faint glimpses of those reflections.

Devas
and
Nature-Spirits

The Aura of the Deva

The devas are a mighty kingdom of spirits. You may think of them as great and glorious angels, but of course they are of many different kinds, and different degrees of evolution. None of them has physical bodies such as we have. The lowest kind are called *kamadevas*, and they have astral bodies, while the next higher variety have bodies made of lower mental matter, and so on. They will never be human, because most of them are already beyond that stage, but there are some of them who have been human beings in the past. When men come to the end of their evolution as men, and become something greater than human, several paths open before them, and one of these is to join this beautiful deva evolution.

Devas and men differ in appearance. For one thing devas are more fluidic—capable of far greater expansion and contraction. Secondly, they have a certain fiery quality which is clearly distinguishable from that of any ordinary human being. The only kind of human being with whom it might be possible to confound them would be the highly-developed—an arhat, for example, who had a large and well-arranged aura;* but even then one who had seen both would not be likely to mistake them. The aura of the ordinary man is capable of a certain amount of temporary expansion. It has a definite size, which is the same as that of a section of the causal body, and as the causal body grows, that section becomes larger, and the man has a larger aura; but such increase comes only gradually.

The plates in *Man Visible and Invisible* show that the ordinary man, as far as the causal body is concerned, is far from being fully developed. When you look at the causal body of the developed man, you will see that it is full of color, so the first stages of improvement in the case of the ordinary man consists in its filling up, not its enlargement. He must get the ovoid filled with different colors, and then expansion begins.

If any sudden rush of feeling comes over the ordinary man, it shows itself, as depicted in the book, by the flashing in the aura, and out from it, of the color of the quality expressed— rose for affection, blue for devotion or green for sympathy; and also in the pulsating bands of that color, and in the general intensification of everything connected with that emotion. It does not do more than that for the ordinary man; an exceedingly vivid rush of affection, for example, fills the aura with rose and sends out thought forms of that color in the direction of its object; but it does not usually appreciably increase, even temporarily, the size of the aura.

The developed man, however, has already filled the causal body with color, so in his case the effect produced by such a rush of affection or devotion or sympathy is not only to suffuse the body with color and cause a great outrush of thought forms, but also to produce a considerable temporary expansion, though the aura afterwards contracts to its normal size. Each such outrush of feeling makes the aura permanently just a little larger than before. The more it increases, the more power the man has to feel. Intellectual development also increases the aura, but in that case yellow is the predominant color.

Remember that utterly unselfish affection or devotion belongs not to the astral but to the buddhic plane, and that is why when a wave of such feeling rushes over a man it causes great

*An arhat is one who has passed the fourth initiation, the one preceding adeptship.

temporary expansion of his aura; yet it never increases to the same tremendous extent as with a deva. The fluctuations in the aura of a deva are so great as to be startling to those who are not used to them. One who recently did us the honor to pay us a visit at Adyar, to give us information about the foundation of the sixth root-race, had normally an aura of about one hundred and fifty yards in diameter; but when he became interested in the teaching which he was giving to us, that aura increased until it reached the sea, which is about a mile away from us.

No human being could feel sufficient emotion to produce such an increase as this. Even in the case of a Master the proportionate temporary enlargement would never be so great. I do not mean anything derogatory to the deva, when I say that the Master is steadier, and that the permanent growth of His aura would be as great as that of the deva, but the temporary expansion less in proportion. The texture of the deva's aura is, as it were, looser. The same extent of aura in a human being contains more matter, because it is more condensed or concentrated. The deva in question was no further advanced than an arhat, whose aura might probably extend a third of the distance. But it might easily happen that a clairvoyant who had not seen either before might realize only that he was surrounded by a cloud of glory in either case, and he probably would not know the difference.

Expansion and growth take place in the astral and mental bodies as well as in the causal. These three bodies are all of the same extent, although you must remember one is dealing with only sections, and even sections of sections. There used to be a theory that the causal body of the ordinary man was about the size of a pea, and that it gradually increased; but that is not correct. The undeveloped causal body is the same size as any other, until the expansion begins.

As I have said, the aura of a deva has fiery characteristics which are not easy to describe, though very readily recognizable. All of the colors are more fluidic, and of the nature of flame rather than of cloud. A man looks like an exceedingly brilliant, yet delicate cloud of glowing gas, but a deva looks like a mass of fire.

The human form inside the aura of a deva is very much less defined than in a man. He lives more in the circumference, more all over his aura than a man does. Ninety-nine per cent of the matter of a man's aura is within the periphery of the physical body, but the proportion is far less in the case of a deva. Devas usually appear as human beings of gigantic size. Somebody has suggested that there are devas who look as though they were feathered. There is some justification for this idea; I know exactly the appearance that the man was trying to describe, but it is not easy to put it into words. The great green devas whom I saw in Ireland have a very striking appearance, being enormous in size and most majestic. One cannot describe them accurately; in words it is only possible to approximate. The painters usually represent angels with wings and feathers, but I think where these are mentioned in the Christian scriptures they are always symbolical, for when real angels appear they are sometimes mistaken for human beings (as by Abraham, for example); so obviously they could not have had wings.

In many cases a deva may be distinguished by the form which he happens to be taking inside his ovoid. It is nearly always a human form. Nature-spirits take human form almost invariably, but with a peculiarity of some sort—always a little odd. I should be disposed to say the same of the devas; but it would be wrong to think of their forms as in any way distorted, for they have a great dignity and majesty.

The devas produce thought forms as we do, but theirs are not usually so concrete as ours until they reach a high level. They have a wide generalizing nature, and are constantly making gorgeous plans. They have a color-language, which is probably not as definite as our speech, though in certain ways it may express more.

As regards the size of the aura, that of an ordinary man extends about eighteen inches on each side of the body. If he puts his elbow against his side and stretches out his arm and hand, his finger-tips will be near the circumference. The average Theosophist may be a trifle larger than the quite uninterested person; but there are fine, large auras outside the Society as well. Intense feeling means a larger aura.

We may have a distortion of the aura—it may be a little out of shape. As I have explained before, most people have the small end of the egg upwards, but we who are students tend to grow larger at the top, because the characteristics which we are developing express themselves in matter which naturally floats in the upper part of the aura because of its specific gravity.

The increased size of the aura is a prerequisite for initiation, and the qualifications should be visible in it. The aura of a Buddha is said in the books to be three miles in radius; at one stage below His, I have myself seen one which extends about two miles. It naturally increases with each initiation.

The devas do not come along our line of development, and do not take such initiations as we do, for the two kingdoms converge at a point higher than the adept. There are ways in which a man can enter the deva evolution, even at our own stage, or lower.

You ask if the devas are often near at hand and willing to teach men. They are usually quite willing to expound and exemplify subjects along their own line to any human being who is sufficiently developed to appreciate them. Much instruction is being given in this way; but most people have not prepared themselves for it yet, and so are unable to profit by it. We know nothing of any rule or limit for the work of the devas; they have more lines of activity than we can imagine.

There are usually plenty of them here at Adyar. We have many great advantages here, where the Masters come so frequently. In order to see them, all that is required is a little clairvoyance at the right moment. There is a stimulus from these Beings, which some feel in one way and some in others. Perhaps in the earlier incarnation of the Lord Gautama as the first Zoroaster, the fire which is one of the signs of His development may have been one of the reasons why He was mistaken for a deva. It is said that during meditation flames leapt from the aura of the Lord Buddha; but we must remember that an ordinary thought form would often appear flame-like to a person who was not used to such things. The shining of the Christ at the transfiguration is a similar case.

There are plenty of glorious influences all around us here, but their effect upon each one of us can be only in proportion to his receptivity. We can take from all this just what we make ourselves fit to take, and no more. A person who is thinking of himself all the while may bathe in this glowing magnetism for a year, and not one iota the better for it. He may even be the worse; for these tremendously strong vibrations tend to intensify a man's qualities, and sometimes the undesirable are strengthened as well as the desirable; or he may be altogether upset, and become unbalanced and hysterical. To a man who is wise enough to take it, a stay at Adyar is an opportunity such as few men have ever had during history; but what we make of it depends entirely upon ourselves.

The Spirit of a Tree

The spirit of a great tree, such as a banyan, not infrequently externalizes itself, and when it does so it usually takes on a gigantic human form. I have noticed one near here, for example, whose form is about twelve feet high, and looked like a woman the last time I saw it. Its features were quite clear, but its form was misty. There are also nature-spirits which cling round a tree, and do not at all like to be disturbed. I have heard it said that nature-spirits do not cling round the trees which man fells for timber; but such observations as I have been able to make do not bear out this contention, and it seems to me that it must have been invented by men who wished to destroy the tree without feeling any unpleasant twinges of conscience.

Although it takes so fine a form, the spirit of a tree is not individualized, nor even within measurable distance of individualization. Nevertheless, it is already much higher than the lower forms of animal life. It has its likes and dislikes, and these show in its aura, though the color and definition are naturally altogether vaguer and dimmer than in the case of an animal. Indeed, in animals who glow with affection its color is often remarkably strong; stronger in the case of some animals than that which is shown by some human beings, because it is so much more concentrated and one-pointed.

The strong attraction which some people feel for particular kinds of trees or animals depends often upon the line of animal and vegetable evolution through which those people have risen.

Reincarnation

Three Laws of Human Life

The ordinary ego is by no means yet in a position to choose a body for himself. The place of his birth is usually determined by three factors, or perhaps it would be better to say by the combined action of three forces. First comes the law of evolution, which causes an ego to be born under conditions which will give him an opportunity of developing exactly those qualities of which he stands most in need. But the action of this force is limited by the second factor, the law of karma. The ego may not have deserved the best possible opportunity, and so he has to put up with the second or third best. He may not even have deserved any great opportunity at all, and so a tumultuous life of small progress may be his fate.

A third factor also comes into play—the force of any personal ties of love or hate that the ego may have previously formed. This may modify the action of the first and second forces, for by it a man may sometimes be drawn into a position which he cannot be said to have deserved in any other way than by the strong personal love which he has felt for some one higher in evolution than himself.

A man who has worked much beyond the ordinary—a man who has already entered the Path which leads to adeptship—

may be able to exercise a certain amount of choice as to the country and family of his birth; but such an one will be the first to put aside entirely any wish of his own in the matter, and resign himself absolutely into the hands of the great eternal law, confident that whatever it brings to him must be far better for him than any selection of his own.

Parents cannot choose the soul who shall inhabit the body to which they give birth, but by so living as to offer an unusually good opportunity for the progress of an advanced ego they can make it exceedingly probable that such an ego will come to them.

The Return to Birth

The whole of our solar system is a manifestation of its Logos, and every particle in it is definitely part of His vehicles. All the physical matter of the solar system taken as a totality constitutes His physical body; all the astral matter within it constitutes His astral body; all the mental matter, His mental body, and so on. Entirely above and beyond His system He has a far wider and greater existence of His own, but that does not in the least affect the truth of the statement which we have just made.

This solar Logos contains within Himself seven planetary Logoi, who are as it were centers of force within Him, channels through which His force pours out. Yet at the same time there is a sense in which they may be said to constitute Him. The matter which we have just described as composing His vehicles also composes theirs, for there is no particle of matter anywhere in the system which is not part of one or other of them. All this is true of every plane; but let us for a moment take the astral plane as an example, because its matter is fluid enough to answer the purposes of our inquiry, and at the same time it is near enough to the physical to be not entirely beyond the limits of our physical comprehension.

Every particle of the astral matter of the system is part of the astral body of the solar Logos, but it is also part of the astral body of one or other of the seven planetary Logoi. Remember that this includes the astral matter of which your astral body and mine are composed. We have no particle which is exclusively our own. In every astral body there are particles belonging to each one of the seven planetary Logoi, but the propor-

tions vary infinitely. The bodies of those Monads which originally came forth through a planetary Logos will continue all
through their evolution to have *more* of the particles of that
Logos than of any other, and in this way people may be distinguished as primarily belonging to one or other of these seven
great Powers.

In these seven planetary Logoi certain psychic changes
periodically occur; perhaps they correspond to in-breathing
and out-breathing, or to the beating of the heart with us down
here on the physical plane.

However that may be, there seem to be an infinite number of
possible permutations and combinations of them. Now since
our astral bodies are built of the very matter of their astral
bodies, it is obvious that no one of these planetary Logoi can
change astrally in any way without thereby affecting the astral
body of every man in the world, though of course more especially those in whom there is a preponderance of the matter
expressing that particular Logos; and if it be remembered that
we are taking the astral plane merely as an example, and that
exactly the same thing is true on all the other planes, we shall
then begin to have an idea how important to use the motions of
these planetary Spirits are.

Madame Blavatsky writes of a certain order of supernal Beings whom she calls the Lipika, or Lords of Karma. We are told
that their agents in the administration of karma are the four
(really seven) great rulers who are known as the Devarajas or
Regents of the Earth. Each one of them is at the head of a
certain vast group of devas and nature-spirits, and even of
elemental essence. Once more for purposes of explanation let
us confine ourselves to the astral plane, but always with the
memory at the back of our minds that the same thing applies to
all the other planes as well. Astral matter as a whole is specially
under the control of one of these Great Ones, but the second
sub-plane of *every* plane is also to a certain extent under the
direction of the same Great One, because that sub-plane holds
the same relation to the plane of which it is a part as the astral
plane does to the whole set of planes. Therefore for every
sub-plane there are two influences—the influence of the ruler
of the plane as a whole, and the sub-influence of the ruler of
the sub-plane.

Now out of this astral matter, every particle of which belongs to the garment of one or other of the seven planetary Logoi, and is at the same time under the predominating influence of the Devaraja of the astral plane, and also under the subordinate influence of another Devaraja who indirectly rules its sub-plane, our astral bodies have to be built. In order to help us to grasp this, let us think of the sub-planes of the astral plane as horizontal divisions, and of the types of matter belonging to the seven great planetary Logoi as perpendicular divisions crossing these others at right angles.* (There are still further subdivisions, but we will take no account of them for the present, in order that the broad idea may stand out clearly). This, then, already gives us forty-nine distinctly marked varieties of astral matter, because on each of its sub-planes we have matter belonging to each of the planetary Logoi.

Even taking no account of the further subdivisions, we see that we have already the possibility of an almost infinite number of combinations; so that whatever may be the characteristics of the ego he is able to find an adequate expression for himself.

Let us consider the case of an ego who is about to descend into incarnation. We must think of him as resting upon the higher part of the mental plane in his causal body, and having no vehicle lower than that. Since the death of his last physical body he has been drawing steadily inwards, first into his astral and then into his mental vehicle, and at the end of the heaven-life he has cast off even the latter. He then rests for a certain period on his own plane—a period which varies, according to the stage of his development, from two or three days of unconsciousness in the case of an ordinary undeveloped man to a long period of years of conscious and glorious life in that of exceptionally advanced people. Then he begins once more to turn his attention downwards and outwards. As in the course of his upward movement he has withdrawn his attention from the physical and the astral planes respectively, the permanent atoms have passed into a dormant condition, and have ceased the vigorous vibration which is their usual characteristic. The same thing happens to the mental unit at the end of the heaven-life, and during his rest on his own plane the ego has these three appendages within himself in a quiescent condition.

*As explained earlier, planes and sub-planes are not actually divided into horizontal and vertical layers but interpenetrate. CWL depicts divisions here for purposes of explanation. Ed.

When he turns his attention once more to the mental plane, the mental unit immediately resumes its activity, and because of that it at once gathers round it such matter as is required to express that activity. Precisely the same thing happens when he turns his attention to the astral atom, and puts his will into that. It attracts to itself material capable of providing him with an astral body of exactly the same type as that which he had at the end of his last astral life. It is necessary to have this fact clearly in mind, that what he thus acquires as he descends is not a ready-made astral body, but simply the material out of which he is to build an astral body in the course of the life which is to follow.

In the case of lower class monads with unusually strong astral bodies, who reincarnate after a very short interval, it sometimes happens that the shade or shell left over from the last astral life still persists, and in that case it is likely to be attracted to the new personality. When that happens it brings with it strongly the old habits and modes of thought, and sometimes even the actual memory of that past life.

The astral matter is at first evenly distributed throughout the ovoid; it is only when the little physical form comes into existence in the middle of the ovoid that the astral and mental matter are attracted to it, and begin to mold themselves into its shape, and thereafter steadily grow along with it. At the same time with this change in arrangement the mental and astral matter are called into activity, and emotion and thought appear.

The aura of the little baby is comparatively colorless, and it is only as the qualities develop that the colors begin to show. This is the material which is given to him out of which to fashion his astral vehicle, the material which he has earned by the desires and emotions which he allowed to play through him in his previou life; but he is by no means compelled to utilize all this material in building for himself his new vehicle. If he is left entirely to himself, the automatic action of the permanent atom will tend to produce for him, from the materials given, an astral body precisely similar to that which he had in the last life; but there is no reason whatever why all these materials should be used, and if the child is wisely treated and reasonably guided he will be encouraged to develop to the fullest all the germs of good which he has brought over from his previous life, while the evil germs will be allowed to slumber. If that is done these latter will gradually atrophy and drop away from him, and the ego will unfold within himself the opposite virtues, and then he will be free for all his future lives from the evil qualities which those germs indicated. Parents and teachers may help him towards this desirable consummation, not so much by any definite facts which they teach him as by the encouragement which they give to him, by the rational and kindly treatment uniformly accorded to him, and above all by the amount of affection lavished upon him.

We must remember that while the higher vehicles, the mental and the astral body, are expressions of the man at his present stage of evolution (as far as that can be expressed in the matter of their respective planes), the physical body is a vehicle or a limitation imposed upon him from without, and is therefore pre-eminently the instrument of karma. The evolutionary force comes into play in the selection of its materials, but even in this it is at every turn limited and hampered by the karma of the past. The parents have been chosen because they are fitted to give such a body as will be suitable for the development of the ego committed to them, but with every pair of parents there are manifold possibilities. Each of them represents a long line of ancestry, and often a particular parent may be chosen, not for anything that he is or has in himself, but because of some quality which appeared to an unusual degree in one of his ancestors—because he possesses a power which he has not used, though it is latent in his physical body because it is physically descended from that ancestor. In that parent, and in many preceding generations, the faculty to express that quality may have slept entirely without effect, but when there comes into the line an ego which possesses the quality, the faculty to express it leaps out from the dormant into the active condition, and we have a case of what is called reversion to a remote type.

In the formation of the physical body there are three principal forces at work: first, the influence of the ego who is intending to take up the new form; secondly, the work of the building elemental formed by the Lords of Karma; and thirdly, the thought of the mother. Now suppose that an etheric body is about to be formed for an ego in the process of his descent into incarnation. He is himself an ego of a certain type and subtype, and these characteristics of his are impressed upon his physical permanent atom, and this in turn determines which of the perpendicular divisions of etheric matter shall enter into the composition of that etheric body and in what proportion they shall be used. This quality of his, however, does not determine which of the horizontal divisions shall be employed, and in what proportion; that matter is in the hands of the four Devarajas, and will be determined according to the past karma of the man. Each of these Devarajas has vast hosts of assistants at his command, so that no one of the births which are momentarily taking place upon earth is ever overlooked. The Devarajas make a thought form, the building elemental mentioned above, which is charged exclusively with the production of the most suitable physical body that can be arranged for the man. For his evolution he requires a body which has within it certain possibilities; for that purpose he may be born of a parent who himself possesses these qualities, and therefore can directly hand them on, or he may be born of a parent whose ancestors, on one side or the other, possessed them, so that the unawakened germs which can respond to them may be handed on by that parent to his offspring.

Remember that this elemental, which is put in charge of the development of the physical body, is the joint thought form of the four Devarajas, and that its primary business is to build the etheric mold into which the physical particles of the new baby-body are to be built. In building this new etheric body it has four varieties of etheric matter which it can use (the four over which its creators respectively preside) and the type of the etheric body which is produced depends upon the proportion in which these constituents are employed. Remember that the elemental has no power of choice with regard to the perpendicular subdivisions, but it has every freedom with regard to the horizontal kinds of matter.

It is quite impossible for us at our present level to understand the working of so mighty a consciousness as that of a Devaraja, so we can only chronicle the fact, without pretending to explain it, that the elemental in doing its work appears somehow not to be entirely separated from the minds which projected it. In some way inexplicable to us it still remains to some modified extent within their consciousness, and in rare cases, where a developed ego is (even at an early age) beginning to take active possession of his body, it would seem that he may come into direct contact with them, and call down upon himself by their consent more karma than they had originally apportioned to him.

One who can do that while the elemental is still at its work can also retain during later life this touch with the karmic deities, and therefore his power to appeal to them for further modifications. So far as we have seen, however, this possible modification may be only in the direction of the increase of the karma to be worked out, not in that of its decrease. The awakening of consciousness, which enables an ego thus to come into touch with the Devarajas and to cooperate willingly with them so far as their work with himself is concerned, may commence at any time; so that an ego who was not in touch with them during the working of the elemental which built his physical body may yet, by stupendous efforts along the line of self-development and usefulness, attract their attention later in life and evoke from them a definite response.

The germ which is to expand into the physical body of the man has within itself two constituents, with two sets of potentialities. (The student must be careful not to confound this physical germ which comes from the parents with the physical permanent atom which the ego brings with him). It is essentially an ovum, which has within itself all the possibilities of the maternal ancestry, but it has been pierced by a spermatozoon which brings with it all the potentialities of the paternal ancestry.

These two sets of possibilities are wide, as may easily be seen if we reflect upon the number of ancestors which any one of us must have had, say a thousand years ago. But wide though they be, they have their limitations. For example, take the case of one of our gardeners here at Adyar—a man of what is called the coolie or unskilled laborer class. Going back a thousand years that man's ancestors must have been counted by millions; yet all those millions must have been of the coolie class. They must have included all possible varieties of coolie, good and bad, clever and stupid, kind and cruel; but they were all coolies.

From among these potentialities the elemental has to make its selection. For that purpose it has two questions to consider, quality and form. Of these the former is infinitely more important. The latter is concerned chiefly with the matter of the lower sub-planes. But the quality of the etheric matter selected for the building of that higher part of the physical body will to a large extent determine the capacities of that body during that incarnation—whether it will be naturally clever or stupid, placid or irritable, energetic or lethargic, sensitive or unresponsive.

So the first work of the thought form or elemental of the Devarajas is to select which of these possibilities shall be brought into prominence in the building of the new physical body—especially in the building of its brain. The mere outer form is a minor consideration, though also an important one, but this too is part of the work of the elemental. If the man has deserved the limitation of deformity in his physical body or of weakness in some of its organs—the heart, the lungs, the stomach—it is through the elemental that his karma is adjusted. Its instructions (if we may use such a term) are to build a body of a certain kind and degree of strength, and with certain characteristics brought into prominence. But these are not instructions given to it to carry in its mind, for it has no mind; they are rather itself, its very life, for when those instructions have finally been carried out it ceases to be, because the work for which it was created is done.

It is a well-known fact to students of embryology that in their earlier stages the embryos of a fish, a dog and a man are practically indistinguishable. They all grow in the same manner, but the difference between them is that one of them stops at one stage of that growth, while the others go on further. The reason for this obvious fact is not clear to those who adopt the materialistic view.

The compulsory force is not an inherent quality in the matter, but the divine life pressing forward to ensoul this matter, and molding it into the form suited to itself at that particular stage of its development. As soon as the entity becomes individualized, and therefore commences to make individual karma, this additional factor of the molding thought form of the karmic deities comes into play, and takes possession of the growing embryo, even before its own ego can grasp it.

The form and color of this elemental vary in different cases. At first it accurately expresses in shape and size the baby body which it has to build, as that body should look (as far as the elemental's work is concerned) at the time of its birth. Clairvoyants, seeing this doll-like little figure hovering about (and afterwards within) the body of the mother, have sometimes mistaken it for the soul of the coming baby, instead of the mold of its physical body. When the foetus has grown to the size of the mold, that much of its task is successfully achieved, and it sheds that outer husk of itself and unfolds the form of the next stage at which it has to aim—the size, shape and condition of the body as it ought to be (taking only the elemental's work into account) at the time when the elemental will leave it. All further growth of the body after the elemental has retired is under the control of the ego himself.

In both of these cases the elemental uses itself as the mold. Its colors represent to a large extent the qualities which it is calculated to evoke in the body which it has to build, and its form is also usually that which is destined for the body. It exists only for its work, and when the amount of force with which it has originally been supplied is exhausted, there is no longer any power left to hold together the particles, and it simply disintegrates.

This elemental takes charge of the body from the first, but some time before physical birth takes place the ego also comes into contact with his future habitation, and from that time onwards the two forces are working side by side. Sometimes the characteristics which the elemental is directed to impose are but few in number, and consequently it is able to retire at a comparatively early age, and to leave the ego in full control of the body. In other cases, where the limitations are of such a character that a good deal of time is necessary for their development, it may retain its position until the body is seven years old. Egos differ greatly in the interest which they take in their physical vehicles, for some hover over them anxiously from the first and take a good deal of trouble about them, while others are almost entirely careless with regard to the whole matter.

When a child is stillborn, there has usually been no ego behind it, and consequently no elemental. There are vast hosts of souls seeking reincarnation, and many of them are still at so early a stage of their evolution that almost any ordinary surroundings would be equally suitable for them; they have so many lessons to learn that it matters little with which one they begin, and almost any conceivable set of surroundings will teach them something which they sorely need. Nevertheless it does sometimes happen that there is not at a given time any ego able to take advantage of a particular opportunity, and in that case, though the body may be formed to a certain extent by the thought of the mother, as there is no ego to occupy it, it is never really alive.

In building the form the elemental takes the etheric matter which it needs from that which it finds ready within the body of the mother. That is one reason for the necessity of the greatest care on the part of that mother during the time the child's body is being formed. If she supplies nothing but the best and purest materials, the elemental will find itself compelled to choose from those. Another factor which has an exceedingly powerful influence is the thought of the mother during this period, for that also molds the shape which is slowly growing within her. Again this shows us why the mother's thought must at that time be especially pure and high, she must be kept away altogether from all coarse or agitating influences, why only the most beautiful forms and colors should surround her, and the most harmonious conditions should prevail in her neighborhood.

If the elemental's instructions do not include some special development in the way of features, such as unusual beauty or unusual ugliness, that part of the shaping of the new body will most likely be done by the thought of the mother—and by the thought forms which are constantly floating round her. If she thinks often with devoted love of her husband there is a strong probability that the child will resemble its father; if on the contrary she looks often at her reflection in the mirror and thinks much about herself, it is probable that the child will bear considerable resemblance to her. Equally, if it happens that she is constantly thinking with devoted affection or admiration of some third person, the child is likely to resemble that person—always supposing that the elemental has no definite instructions in this matter. When the children grow older their physical bodies are influenced largely by their own thoughts, and as these differ from those of the mother, we often see that considerable changes in physical appearance take place, the child in some cases growing more beautiful and in other cases less so as the years roll by. "As a man thinks, so is he" is true on the physical plane as well as on others; and if the thought is always calm and serene, the face will surely reflect it.

To an advanced ego all the earlier stages of childhood are

naturally exceedingly wearisome. I remember that the late Mr.
T. Subba Rao complained quite bitterly about it when he first
took his new body. He declared that, do what he would, he
could not make that baby body sleep more than twenty hours
out of the day, and the rest of the time he actually had to wait
near it and watch it squirming about, and listen to its plaintive
ululations, and endure to be fed through it with tasteless and
nauseous varieties of pap! Sometimes a really advanced person
decides to avoid all this by asking someone else to give him an
adult body, a sacrifice which any of his disciples would always
be delighted to make for him.

But this method also has its drawbacks. However wearisome
it may be to pass through childhood, at least in that way a man
grows a body for himself, which is as nearly as may be an expression of him, and agrees with all his little peculiarities; but
one who takes an adult body finds it already full of peculiarities
of its own, which have worn in it deep grooves of habit that
cannot readily be changed. It cannot but be to some extent a
misfit, and it takes a long time to make its vibrations synchronize with his own. An ego coming into incarnation has always to adapt himself to a new set of conditions, but when he
comes to birth in the ordinary way this can at least be done
gradually, as the child grows up; but one who takes an adult
body has instantly to adapt himself to all these fresh surroundings, which is often a very difficult business. In this case he has
retained his old astral and mental bodies; but they are naturally
counterparts of his previous vehicle, and they have to be
adapted to the new form. Once more, if that form be a baby
this can be done gradually, but if it is an adult form it must be
done immediately, which means an amount of strain that is distinctly unpleasant.

Personal Characteristics

I have looked up many cases, and I find that for the ordinary
man there seems to be but little continuity of personal appearance life after life; but I have known cases of strong similarity
as well as great unlikeness. As the physical body is to some extent an expression of the ego, and that remains the same, there
must be some cases where it expresses itself in similar forms;
but racial, family and other characteristics usually override this

tendency. When an individual is so advanced that the personality and ego are unified, the personality tends to have impressed upon it the characteristics of the glorified form in the causal body, which is relatively permanent.

When the man is an adept and all his karma is worked out, the physical body is the nearest possible presentment of that glorified form. The Masters will therefore remain recognizable through any number of incarnations. I have noticed that one of the Masters who comparatively recently attained adeptship is as yet not quite like the others, having somewhat ruffed features. I am sure that will be different in the next incarnation. I should not expect to see much difference in the bodies of our Masters, even if they should choose to take others, and even though they might be of another race. I have seen prototypes of what bodies are to be like in the seventh Race; they will be transcendently beautiful.

The glorified form in the causal body is an approach to the archetype, and comes nearer to it as man develops. The human form appears to be the model for the highest evolution in this particular solar system. In other solar systems forms may possibly be quite unlike it; we have no information on that point.

Bringing Over Past Knowledge

We do not yet know with any certainty the laws which govern the power to impress the detailed knowledge of one life upon the physical brain of the next. Such evidence as is presently before us seems to show that details are usually forgotten, but that broad principles appear to the new mind as self-evident. Many of us have exclaimed when for the first time in this incarnation we read a theosophical book: "This is exactly what I have always felt, but I did not know how to put it into words!" In some cases there seems scarcely that much of memory, yet as soon as the teaching is presented it is instantly recognized as true. Mrs. Besant as Hypatia must unquestionably have known a great deal of this philosophy which was not clearly formulated in her present brain during the orthodox or free-thought periods of this incarnation.

If any reliance at all is to be placed upon exoteric tradition, even the Buddha himself, who descended from higher planes with the definite intention of taking birth to help the world, knew nothing clearly of his mission after he had entered his new body, and regained full knowledge only after years of searching for it. Undoubtedly he could have known from the first had he chosen, but he did not choose; he submitted himself to what seems to be the common lot.

It is possible that in his case there may be another explanation. The body which was born of King Suddhodana and Queen Maya may not in its earlier years have been inhabited by the Lord Buddha. He may have acted as the Christ did; he may have asked one of his disciples to take care of that vehicle for him until he needed it, and he may have entered it himself only at the moment when it fainted after the long austerities of the six years of searching for truth. If this be so, then the reason that Prince Siddartha did not remember all that the Lord Buddha previously knew was because he was not the same person. But in any case we may be sure that the ego, who is the true man, always knows what he has once learned; but he is not always able to impress it upon his new brain without the help of a suggestion from without.

Fortunately for our students it seems to be an invariable rule that one who has accepted occult truth in one life always comes into contact with it in the next, and so revives his dormant memory. I suppose we may say that the opportunity of thus recovering the truth is the karma of having accepted it, and of having earnestly tried to live according to it in the previous incarnation. There is, however, every probability that much of what we now call distinctively theosophical belief will be the ordinary accepted knowledge of the day by the time that we return to take up again our work on the physical plane, so it may be that we shall all be educated in it as a matter of course. If that be so, the difference between those who have studied it this time and those who have not will be that the former will take it up with enthusiasm and make rapid progress, while to the latter it will mean no more than does the science of today to the entirely unscientific mind. In any case, let no one for a moment suppose that the benefit of our study and hard work can ever be lost.

SECTION TWELVE

Karma

The Law of Equilibrium

When we are considering the life of man we have three principal forces to take into account, all interacting and limiting one another: the steady pressure of evolution, the rule of cause and effect which we call karma, and the free will of man. The action of the evolutionary force has, so far as we can see, no reference whatever to the man's pleasure or pain, but only to his progress, or rather his opportunities for progress. One would say that it was absolutely indifferent as to whether the man was happy or unhappy, and that it might press him sometimes into one of these conditions and sometimes into the other, according to what was best calculated to afford opportunity for the development of the particular virtue on the formation of which he is for the moment engaged. Karma appears as the manifestation of the action of the man's free will in the past. He has accumulated energies which either afford opportunities for the evolutionary force, or limit it in its operation. Then the man's present use of such free will as he possesses is a third factor.

The doctrine of karma explains that advancement and well-being are the results of well-doing; but there should be no mistake as to exactly what is meant by well-doing and well-being respectively. The object of the entire scheme is, so far as we are concerned, the evolution of humanity; and consequently the man who does best is he who does most to help forward the evolution of others as well as his own. The man who does this to the utmost extent of his power and opportunity in one life will certainly find himself in the next in possession of greater power and wider opportunities. These are likely to be accompanied by worldly wealth and power, because the very possession of these usually gives the opportunity required, but they are by no means a necessary part of the karma; and it is important for us to bear in mind that the result of usefulness is always the opportunity for further and wider usefulness, and we must not consider the occasional concomitants of that opportunity as themselves the reward of the work done in the last incarnation.

One instinctively shrinks from the use of such words as reward and punishment, because they seem to imply the existence, somewhere in the background, of an irresponsible being who deals out both at will. We shall get a truer idea of the way in which karma works if we think of it as a necessary readjustment of equilibrium disturbed by our action—as a kind of illustration of the law that action and reaction are always equal. It will also help us much in our thinking if we try to take a broader view of it—to regard it from the point of view of those who administer its laws rather than from our own.

Though the inevitable law *must* sooner or later bring to each man unerringly the result of his own work, there is no immediate hurry about it; in the counsels of the eternal there is always time enough, and the first object is the evolution of humanity. Therefore it is that one who shows himself a willing and useful instrument in forwarding that evolution always receives as his "reward" the opportunity of helping it still further, and thus, in doing good to others, to do best of all for himself. Of course if the thought of self-advancement were his *motive* for thus acting, the selfishness of the idea would vitiate the action and narrow its results; but if, forgetting himself altogether, he devotes his energies to the single aim of helping in the great work, the effect upon his own future will undoubtedly be as stated.

A definite protest ought once and for all to be entered

against the theory that suffering is the necessary condition of spiritual progress. Exercise is the condition of attaining physical strength, but it need not be painful exercise; if a man is willing to take a walk every day, there is no need to torture him on the treadmill in order to develop the muscles of his legs. For spiritual progress a man must develop virtue, unselfishness, helpfulness—that is to say, he must learn to move in harmony with the great cosmic law; and if he does this willingly there is no suffering for him but that which comes from sympathy with others.

Granted that at the present time most men refuse to do this, that when they set themselves in opposition to the great law suffering invariably follows, and that the eventual result of many such experiences is to convince them that the path of wickedness and selfishness is also the path of folly; in *this* sense it is true that suffering conduces to progress in those particular cases. But because we wilfully elect to offend against the law, and thereby bring down suffering upon ourselves, we have surely no right so to blaspheme the great law of the universe as to say that *it* has ordered matters so badly that without suffering no progress can be made. As a matter of fact if a man only will, he can make far more rapid progress without suffering at all.

It must, however, be remembered that any man who has once realized the glorious goal which lies before us can never be perfectly happy until he has attained that goal, and that he finds an ever-present source of dissatisfaction in his own failings. Even dissatisfaction is a modified form of suffering; and from that no man can hope to be free until the imperfection has been outgrown. "God, Thou hast made us for Thyself, and our hearts are ever restless till they find their rest in Thee."

Whether it is comforting or the reverse to know that one's sufferings are deserved may be a matter of opinion; but that in no way alters the undoubted fact that unless they had been so deserved they could not possibly come to us. It is lamentable that so many people should adopt the unphilosophical (and indeed childish) attitude which leads them to assume that any idea which does not fall in with their particular sectarian preconceptions cannot possibly be true. Unintelligent people constantly say: "The Theosophical teaching about karma does not

seem to me so comfortable as the Christian idea of forgiveness
of sins," or "The Theosophical heaven-world does not seem so
real and beautiful as the Christian, and so I will not believe in
it."

They evidently think, poor creatures, that their likes and dislikes are powerful enough to alter the laws of the universe, and
that nothing of which they do not approve can possibly *be* on
any plane. We, however, are engaged in studying the facts of
existence, which after all are not modified because Mr. and
Mrs. So-and-so would rather believe them to be otherwise than
they are. If it were possible for anyone to be an innocent victim
there would be no certainty of the operation of the great law of
cause and effect anywhere in the universe, which would be a
far more terrible thing for us than having to work out the results of any amount of sin committed in former lives. It can
never be too strongly emphasized that the law of karma is not
the vindictive vengeance of some angry deity but simply an *effect*, naturally and inevitably following upon its cause in obedience to the action of universal law.

Every individual will have to pay to the utmost every debt
that he contracts, and to every individual the most perfect justice will be done; but for this purpose it is not always necessary
that a vast crowd of egos should be perpetually meeting one
another in successive lives. If one man so acts towards another
as seriously to hasten or retard his evolution, if he does anything which produces upon the other a marked or permanent
effect, it is fairly certain that the two must meet again in order
that the debt may be adjusted. It is obvious that that may be
done in various ways.

A man who murders another may conceivably sometimes
himself be murdered in another incarnation; but he can cancel
the karma much more satisfactorily if he happens to have an
opportunity in that next incarnation of saving the life of his
former victim at the cost of his own. It would seem that sometimes he may cancel it without losing his own at all; for among
the many lines of lives which have been examined we found at
least one case in which a murderer apparently fully expiated
his fault by patiently devoting the whole of a later life to the
service of the person whom he had previously slain.

There is a vast amount of minor karma which appears to go
into what may be described as a kind of general fund. The

schoolboy who mischievously pinches a classmate will certainly not have to meet that classmate a thousand years hence under other skies in order to be pinched by him in return, though it is unquestionable that even in so small a matter as this perfect justice will be done to both the parties. Constantly as we pass on through life we shower small kindnesses upon those whom we meet; carelessly and often unconsciously we do them small injuries in thought and word and deed. Every one of these brings its corresponding result of good or evil to ourselves, and we too, though we knew it not, were the agents of karma in those very actions. The small kindness which we attempt will prove a failure if the recipient does not deserve even that much of help; the careless slight will pass unnoticed by its victim if there has been nothing in his past for which it is a fitting retribution.

It is not easy to draw the line between these two classes of karma—that which necessitates personal adjustment and that which goes into the general fund. It is certain that whatever influences a person seriously belongs to the first category, and small everyday troubles belong to the second; but at present we have no means of knowing exactly how much influence must be exerted in order that an action may rank in the first class.

We must remember that some of the greatest and most important of all karma can never be personally repaid. In all our line of lives, past and future, no benefit can be greater than that which the Masters have conferred upon us in giving us access to the theosophical teaching; yet to them as individuals we can make absolutely no return, since they are far beyond the need of anything that we can do. Yet even this stupendous debt must be discharged like all the rest; but the only way in which we can ever repay it is by handing on the knowledge to others. So we see that here is another kind of karma which may be said to go into the general fund, though not quite in the same sense as before.

A querent asks, "If it is a man's karma to have scarlet fever, by what mechanism is the result brought about?"

I do not think that, in the sense in which the questioner means it, it ever is a man's karma to have scarlet fever. It is his karma in a given incarnation to have as the result of his actions in past lives a certain amount of physical suffering, and if a scarlet fever germ happens to be at hand when he is in a sensitive condition, it may be permitted to fasten upon him, and part of that debt of suffering may be discharged in that way. But if such a germ does not happen to be there at the moment, one of cholera or tuberculosis will do just as well, or instead of a disease there may be a broken limb caused by a bit of orange peel on the pavement or by a passing motor car.

I am aware that there are books which lay down with great precision the exact type of karma which follows upon certain actions—as, for example, that if a man is rude to his father in one incarnation he will be born lame of the right leg in the next, whereas if it is with his mother that he has a difference of opinion it will be the left leg which is affected, and so on. But in the many lines of lives which we have examined in order to study the working of karma we have found no such rigidity. On the contrary, we were especially struck no less by the wonderful flexibility of karma than by its unerring certainty. By no possible effort can the man escape a single featherweight of the suffering destined for him, but he may often avoid it in one shape only to find it inexorably descending upon him in a different form, from some unsuspected quarter.

Just as a debt of ten pounds can be paid in a single note, in two smaller notes, in gold or silver, or even in a bagfull of copper, so a certain amount of karma may come in one terrible blow, in a number of successive but less severe blows of various kinds, or even in a long series of comparatively petty annoyances; but in any and every case the full debt must be paid.

The same sin, committed under the same circumstances by two exactly similar people, must result in the same *amount* of suffering, yet the *kind* of suffering might be almost infinitely varied, according to the requirements of the case. Take as an example one of the very commonest of failings, and let us think what would be the probable result of selfishness. This is primarily a mental attitude or condition, so we must look for its immediate result on the mental plane. It is undoubtedly an intensification of the lower personality at the expense of the individuality, and one of its results will therefore certainly be the accentuation of that lower personality, so that selfishness tends to reproduce itself in aggravated form, and to grow steadily stronger.

Thus more and more of the higher would be lost in each life through entanglement with the lower, and persistence in this fault would be a fatal bar to progress; for nature's severest penalty is always deprivation of the opportunity for progress, just as her highest reward is the offering of such opportunity. So here we have already a glimpse of the way in which selfishness may itself bring about its own worst result, in so hardening the man as to make him insensible to all good influences, and to render his further progress impossible until he had conquered it.

There would also be the karma on the physical plane of all the unjust or unkind *acts* which the man's selfishness might lead him to commit; but the worst penalty that those could bring upon him would be trivial and evanescent beside the effect upon his own mental condition. It is possible that one result might be that he would be drawn by affinity into the society of selfish people, and so through suffering from this vice in others he would learn how heinous it is in himself. But the resources of the law are endless, and we mistake if we imagine it as cramped down to the line of action on which we in our ignorance think it ought to be administered.

A large proportion of the man's suffering is what Mr. Sinnett calls "ready-money karma"—that is to say, it is not due to the result of actions in past lives, and not in any real sense necessary at all. But his actions, in spite of examples put before him and advice freely given to him, are so foolish, and his ignorance is so invincible, so apparently perverse, that he is constantly involving himself in suffering the causes of which are transparently obvious and readily evitable. I do not think that I exaggerate when I say that nine-tenths of the suffering of the ordinary man is utterly unnecessary, for it is not the result of the distant past, but is simply the outcome of the mistaken action or foolish attitude of this present life.

Another point to be taken into account is that man in his calculations so often fails to discriminate between good and evil effects. The average man regards death as the greatest of all evils, either for himself or for his friends; yet in many cases karma grants it as a reward. It is, indeed, hardly ever an evil or a punishment, but simply an incident—a kind of move in the game, inevitable at certain intervals, but at all times available as a temporary solution of a difficult position when it is seen to be desirable. It is rarely a matter of anything approaching the importance which is commonly attributed to it.

We have behind us a great mass of accumulated energy of

both kinds, desirable and undesirable, and I can hardly imagine any conceivable "accident" that would not suit as an expression for some part of its infinite variety. Therefore shipwreck or financial ruin does not discriminate, because it need not; there is always something which can work itself out in that way in the whole mass of karma which lies behind an ordinary man. In the rare cases where there is nothing remaining which can so work itself out, the man cannot be injured, and is therefore what is commonly called miraculously saved.

Nothing could be more wildly absurd than the idea that anything we can do can prevent the working out of karma. For example, if a child is born under circumstances which lead to its being cruelly treated, no doubt such treatment is in accordance with its previous karma; but if kindly intervention delivers it from the demons in human form who torment it, then that intervention also is in accordance with its karma. If it were not, then the well-intentioned effort to rescue it would fail, as we know it sometimes does. Our obvious duty is to do all the good we can, and to render all the help within our power in every direction; and we need have no haunting fear that in doing so we are interfering with the work of the great karmic deities, who are assuredly perfectly capable of managing their business with absolute exactitude, whatever we do or do not do.

Does karma seem merciless? If that adjective can be correctly applied to the working of Nature's laws, I suppose we must admit that it is so, just as the law of gravitation is. If a child slips over the edge of a precipice, no matter how sad may be the circumstances surrounding the slip, he usually falls to the bottom of that precipice just as effectually as would an older and more responsible person; if a man seizes a red-hot iron bar, he is equally burnt whatever may have been his object in seizing it, or whether he knew that it was hot or not. Yet it would hardly occur to us to think of the bar or the precipice as merciless, or to blame the law of gravitation or the law of the radiation of heat. Does not exactly the same thought apply in the case of karma?

The Method of Karma

It is scarcely possible to put into words the appearance presented to clairvoyant vision on the higher planes by the working of this law of karma. It seems as though the man's action built cells or channels stored with energy, through the reactions of which he can be reached by the law of evolution. The appearance is as though all sorts of forces are playing round him, but they are able to influence him only by acting through these energies which he has himself set in motion. He is continually adding to the number of these cells or channels of energy, and so is continually modifying the possibilities of reaching him. The marvellous and all but incredible adaptability and versatility of karma is exhibited in meeting and dealing with all these kaleidoscopic changes, and yet in spite of them all getting in its work and accurately performing its task.

There is another aspect of karma the consideration of which I have found helpful in the effort to understand its working; but it belongs to a plane so high that it is unfortunately impossible to put it clearly into words. Imagine that we see each man as though he were absolutely alone in the universe, the center of an incredibly vast series of concentric spheres. Every thought, or word, or action of his sends out a stream of force which rushes towards the surfaces of the spheres. This force strikes the interior surface of one of the spheres, and, being at right angles to it, is necessarily reflected back unerringly to the point from which it came.

From which sphere it is reflected seems to depend upon the character of the force, and this also naturally regulates the time of its return. The force which is generated by some actions strikes a sphere comparatively near at hand, and is reflected back very quickly, while other forces rush on almost to infinity, and return only after many lives. But in any case they inevitably return, and they can return nowhere but to the center from which they came forth. Each man makes his own spheres, and the play of his forces is in no way affected by the action of those sent up by his neighbor, for they cross one another without interfering, just as do the rays of light from two lamps. And the medium through which they move is frictionless, so that the amount of force which returns is precisely that which the man himself has generated.

There are three great types of karma which the Indians call *sanchita*, *prarabdha* and *kriyamana*. The first—sanchita—is the whole vast mass of unexhausted karma, good or bad, which still waits to be worked out; let us call it mass-karma. The second—prarabdha—is that particular part of the first which has been selected to be worked out in this incarnation; let us call it the man's destiny for this life. The third—kriyamana—is the new karma which we are constantly making by our present actions.

It is the karma of the second type that the astrologer or palmist tries to read; and his calculations are often invalidated by intrusions from the other two varieties. It is quite certain that nothing can happen to a man which is not in the great mass of his karma, but unquestionably something may happen which was not originally included in his destiny for this life.

The *prarabdha* karma of an individual, that is, the karma selected by the authorities for him to discharge in his present life, divides itself into two parts. That which is to express itself in his physical body is made by the Devarajas into the thought form or elemental which builds the body, of which we have spoken in a previous section; but the other and far larger block which is to indicate his fate through life, the good or evil fortune which is to come to him—this is made into another thought form which does not descend; hovering over the embryo, it remains upon the mental plane. From that level it broods over the man and takes or makes opportunities to discharge itself by sections, sending down from itself a flash like lightning to strike, or a finger to touch, sometimes far down on the physical plane, sometimes a sort of extension which reaches only the astral plane, and sometimes what we may call a horizontal flash or finger upon the mental plane.

This elemental goes on discharging itself until it is quite empty; and then, like the elemental which builds the body, it fades into nothingness, or more correctly is disintegrated and returns to the matter of the plane. The man can modify its action by the new karma which he is constantly making, by the new causes which he is perpetually setting up. The ordinary man has usually scarcely enough will to create any strong new causes, and so the elemental empties itself of its contents according to what may be described as its original program, taking advantage of convenient astrological periods and surrounding circumstances, which make its work easier or more effective; and so the horoscope of the man may work out with considerable exactitude. But if the man be' sufficiently developed to possess a strong will, the elemental's action is likely to be much modified, and the life will by no means follow the lines laid down in the horoscope. Sometimes the modifications introduced are such that the elemental is unable fully to discharge himself before the time of the man's death; and in that case whatever is left of it is again absorbed into the great mass of the *sanchita* karma—that which has not yet been worked out; and out of that another, and more or less similar, elemental is made ready for the beginning of the next physical life.

The great mass of the accumulated karma can also be seen hovering over the ego. Usually it is not a pleasant sight, because by the nature of things it contains more evil than good result. In the earlier days of their development in the remote past, most men have done many things that they should not have done, and thereby have laid up for themselves as a physical result a good deal of suffering on this lowest plane. In the present day all civilized beings have risen at least to the level of good intention, and consequently there is much less of directly evil karma being made by such people. We all do foolish things at'times; we all make mistakes; but still on the whole the average civilized being is trying to do good and not harm, and therefore on the whole is likely to be making more good karma than bad. But by no means all of the good karma goes into that great accumulated mass, and so we get the impression in that of a preponderance of evil over good.

The result of most good thoughts or good actions is to improve the man himself, to make one or other of his bodies vibrate in response to higher forces, or to bring out in him qualities of courage, determination, affection, devotion, which he did not possess in so full a measure before. All this effect then shows in the man himself and in his vehicles, but not in the mass of piled up karma which is waiting for him. If, however, he does some good action definitely with the thought of its reward in his mind, good karma for that good action will come to him, and will store itself up with the rest of the accumulation until such time as it may be brought forward and materialized into activity. This good karma naturally binds the man to earth just as effectually as evil karma, and consequently the man who is aiming at real progress learns to do all actions absolutely without thought of self or of the result of his action, because if there is no thought of self, results of the ordinary kind cannot touch him.

Not that the man can escape the benefit of a good deed, any more than he can escape the result of an evil deed; but if the man thinks of the reward that will come to him he will receive the benefit in the shape of that reward, whereas if he forgets himself entirely and does this thing out of the fullness of his heart, because it is the right thing to do and therefore he can do no other, then the whole force of the result is spent in the building of his own character, and nothing of it remains to bind him to the lower planes. The fact is that in each case the man gets what he wants. As the Christ said Himself: "Verily I say unto you, they have their reward." The man who thinks of good result to himself obtains that good result; the man who is not thinking of himself at all, or thinking only of making himself a channel for the forces of the Logos, is made into a better channel as the result of the action which that thought prompted.

Another complication is introduced by the fact that many people do good deeds in the name of and for the sake of some other, and in that way they make that other a partaker with them of the results. Many a man does a good deed in the name of the Christ, or if he be a Theosophist, in that of the Master, and justice demands that in such a case, since it is the thought of the Christ or the Master which has produced this result, something of the effect must go to the great person in question. In this way vast stores of helpful magnetism are constantly at the disposal of those Great Ones to whom many send thoughts of affection and devotion, in whose name many kindly deeds are done. Naturally it would be utterly impossible that the result of such action should in any way bind the Great One. It simply provides him with additional spiritual force for the work which he has in hand.

The Karma of Death

It is by no means certain that in the majority of cases a time for death is definitely appointed by the Lords of Karma at all. The whole arrangement is far more elastic and adaptable than most students suppose. The clue to its comprehension lies in never forgetting the three types of karma.

Suppose the case of a man on board a vessel which is about to be wrecked, or in the first car of a train which is about to have a collision. It may or may not be in the destiny appointed for this particular life that that man should die about this time. If it is, he will no doubt be killed; if it is not, he may be saved, if such saving does not involve too great an interference with the ordinary laws of nature. I think we may say that he probably *will* be saved if the prolongation of his physical life would appreciably hasten his evolution. It is intended that in each life some lesson should be learned, some quality developed. If that life-work is already done—or if, on the other hand, it is obvious that the man will not succeed in doing it this time, no matter how long he lives—he has nothing to gain by continued physical life, and he may just as well be delivered from it.

Also, if there be in the vast mass of his previous karma some debt that can be adequately cancelled by whatever of physical or mental suffering may be involved in such a death, the opportunity of that cancellation may very well be taken when it thus offers itself, even though it may not have been included in the original plan for this particular life. But if in the whole of the mass-karma there is nothing that will fit in with such a death, the man simply *cannot* die that way, and he will inevitably be saved, even though it be by means which seem miraculous. We hear of such cases—cases in which a huge beam has fallen so as just to save a man from being crushed by the superincumbent weight of the wreckage, or in which an ocean steamer has gone down with all hands, one man has somehow floated ashore on a hen-coop.

We must not forget the influence on our destiny of that third variety of karma which we are making for ourselves every day. A man may be doing such good work that for the moment he cannot be spared; he may or he may not have acted so as to deserve release from the physical plane at that particular period. Our tendency is to attach an altogether exaggerated importance to the time and the manner of our death. If for a moment we try to imagine how the matter must present itself to the Great Beings in charge of our evolution, we shall gain a much truer appreciation of relative values. To them the progress of the egos in their charge is the one matter of importance. They know the lessons to be learned, the qualities to be developed.

They must regard it much as a schoolmaster regards the amount of work which a boy has to do before qualifying himself for entrance to the university. The schoolmaster divides that work according to the time at his disposal; so much must be done in each year, and the year's work in turn must be subdivided into terms and even into days. But he will allow himself a considerable amount of latitude with regard to these minor divisions; he may decide to devote two days instead of one to some specially difficult point, or he may close a lesson earlier than he intended if its object is clearly achieved.

Our lives are exactly these days of school life, and the lesson may be lengthened or shortened as the teacher sees to be best. Death is merely the release from school at the end of one day's lesson. We need not trouble ourselves about it in the least; we should thankfully accept it whenever karma permits it to us. We must realize that the one important thing is that the appointed lesson should be learned. The sections into which that lesson shall be divided, the length of the various lesson-hours, and exactly when they shall begin or end—all these are details which we may well leave to the agents of the Great Law.

From this point of view no death can be described as premature, for we may always be absolutely certain that what comes to us from without is what is best for us. Our business is to do our very best with each life, and to make every effort to retain it as long as possible. If we ourselves cut it short by recklessness or improper living, we are responsible, and the effect will assuredly be prejudicial; but if it is cut short by something entirely beyond our control, we may be sure that the curtailment is for our good.

Nevertheless what has been written in some of our books about "premature" death is quite true. In extreme old age desire fades away, and so something of the work of the astral life is already done before the man leaves the physical plane. A similar result is achieved by long sickness, and so in either of these cases the astral life is likely to be comparatively short and without serious suffering. This may be called the ordinary course of nature, and it is only by comparison with it that an earlier death may be spoken of as "premature." If a person dies in youth, desire is still strong, and therefore a stronger and more strenuous astral life may be expected—a condition on the whole less desirable. But if the powers behind decided that an earlier death is best, we may feel sure that they know of other considerations which outweigh the prolongation of the astral life.

It seems probable, therefore, that in the majority of cases the exact time and manner of a man's death is *not* decided before or at his birth. Astrologers tell us that in many instances they cannot actually foretell the death of the subject whose horoscope they are examining. They say that at a certain time malefic influences are strong, and the man *may* die then, but if he does not, his life will continue until a certain other occasion when evil aspects threaten him, and so on. In the same way a palmist will tell us that at such and such points there are serious breaks or markings upon the life-line; they may indicate death, or it may be only serious illness. It is likely that these uncertainties represent points which were left open for later decisions, depending largely upon the modifications introduced by the action of the man during his life, and by the use which he makes of his opportunities. At any rate we may be well assured that whatever decision is made it will be a wise one, and that, whether in death or in life, all things are working together for our good.

Karma as an Educator

No man can ever receive what he has not earned, and all things come to us as the result of causes which we ourselves have set in motion. If we have caused anything we have also caused its result, for the cause and the effect are like the two sides of a coin—we cannot have one without the other; indeed, the result comes upon us as part of our original action, which may be said in this case to be still continuing. Everything which comes to us is our own doing, good and bad alike; but it is also being employed definitely for our good. The payment of the debt is being utilized to develop the man who owes it, and in paying it he may show patience, courage, and endurance in the face of adverse circumstances.

People constantly grumble against their circumstances. A man will say: "I cannot do anything, situated as I am, with so many cares, with so much business, with so large a family. If only I had the liberty which so-and-so has!"

The man does not realize that these very hindrances are part of his training, and that they are put in his way just in order to teach him how to deal with them. He would like no doubt to have some opportunity of showing off the powers which he has already developed, but what is needed is that he should develop the powers which he has not, and this means hard work and suffering, but also rapid progress. There is assuredly no such thing as punishment and reward, but there *is* the result of our actions, which may be pleasant or unpleasant. If we upset the equilibrium of nature in any way it inevitably readjusts itself at our expense.

An ego sometimes chooses whether he will or will not take certain karma in the present life, though often the brain-mind may know nothing of this choice, so that the very adverse circumstances at which a man is grumbling may be exactly what he has deliberately chosen for himself in order to forward his evolution. When he is becoming a disciple, and is therefore somewhat out of the stage of evolution which is normal at present, he often dominates and largely changes his karma—not that he can escape his share, or any least portion of it, but that he gains much new knowledge and therefore sets in motion new forces in many directions, which naturally modify the working of the old ones. He plays off one law against another, thus neutralizing forces whose results might hinder his progress.

It has often been said that the disciple who takes steps to hasten his own progress thereby calls down suffering upon himself. That is not perhaps quite the best way to put it. All that he does is to take his own evolution earnestly in hand, and to endeavor, as rapidly as may be, to eradicate the evil and develop the good within himself, in order that he may become ever a more and more perfect living channel of the divine love. It is true that such action will assuredly attract the attention of the great Lords of Karma, and while Their response will be to give him greater opportunity, it may (and often does) involve a considerable increase of suffering in various ways.

But if we think carefully we shall see that this is exactly what might be expected. All of us have more or less evil karma behind us, and until that is disposed of, it will be a perpetual hindrance to us in our higher work. One of the earliest steps in the direction of serious progress is therefore the working out of whatever of this evil still remains to us, and so the first response of the Great Ones to our upward striving is frequently to give us the opportunity of paying off a little more of this debt (since we have now made ourselves strong enough to do it) in order that it may be cleared out of the way of our future work. The manner in which this debt shall be paid is a matter which is entirely in their hands and not in ours; and we can trust them to manage it without inflicting additional suffering upon others—unless of course those others have also some outstanding karmic debt which can be discharged in this way. In any case the great karmic deities cannot act otherwise than with absolute justice to every person concerned, whether directly or remotely.

Varieties of Karma

The karma of service done is always the opportunity for more service. This is one of the rules which emerge with the greatest certainty from our study of the working of karma in the many past lives which have been examined. When a man leads a particularly good life it by no means follows that in the next one he will be rich or powerful or even comfortable; but it does absolutely follow that he will have wider opportunities for work. Clearly the Logos wants His work done, and if we wish for opportunities of progress we must show that we are willing to work.

Knowledge brings responsibility, along with opportunity. To yield to what you know to be wrong, or to go back a step in order to gain force for a greater spring forward, is to miss your opportunity. Many lives may pass before you gain the same opportunity again. If you neglect the knowledge or vision which points out to you a fault, you will certainly be born in the next life without that knowledge or vision. Knowledge should always be used; it is a mistake to think that you can postpone your activity and retain the knowledge.

There are certain kinds of action which bring unusually horrible karma as their results. For example, the karma of cruelty of any kind, whether to men or to animals, is always especially awful in character; it often brings with it chronic physical ailments, accompanied by most acute sufferings, and also often it produces insanity—this last more especially when the cruelty is of a refined and intentional character. We have found, for example, that many members of the ignorant mob who tortured Hypatia in Alexandria have been reborn in Armenia, and have themselves suffered all sorts of cruelties at the hands of the Turks. People who are now, apparently by accident, burned to death with awful sufferings are often those who have burned others in the middle ages, or looked on with glee at those ghastly scenes of martyrdom.

Any injury done to a highly developed person reacts terribly upon the doer. We should indeed be careful about our attitude towards any Great One who may come, for he, being far in advance of us, is likely to be misunderstood—to be different from what we have expected, and therefore not to be appreciated. One reason why the Great Ones do not more often come amongst men is that the karma of misjudging and ill-using them is dreadful, and the fools among mankind are sure to incur it. I have myself seen a case in which a great soul, born where he was not understood, fell when young into the hands of a brutal and incompetent pedagogue who shamefully abused him. I have also been allowed to see the karma which will follow upon that cruelty, and I shudder when I think of it. Truly may it be said of that miserable wretch, in the words attributed to the Christ, that before he had "offended one of these little ones, it had been better for him that a millstone had been hanged about his neck, and he had been drowned in the depths of the sea."

Closely associated with this is the subject of the karma of ingratitude, which is always exceptionally heavy—most of all when the ingratitude is shown to an occult teacher. People are constantly pressing forward, desiring to come into touch with the Masters, to attract their attention; and they sometimes think that the pupils of those Masters try to hold them back, or at any rate decline to assist them in their efforts to approach. The pupil of the Masters exists only to help others, and nothing pleases him more than to draw another to the Feet where he has learned so much himself. But when he sees from the type of the aspirant that he does not yet understand those Great Ones, that his attitude towards them is captious, irreverent, presumptuous, he will take no responsibility in the matter, for he knows that serious disaster is certain to result. A man of such temperament is sure to make bad karma anywhere; it would be foolish to put him into a position where he can multiply it a hundredfold.

The fact that a man has a large amount of bad karma behind him makes anything like occult advancement impossible for him until it is worked off. No one could become an adept if he had evil karma behind him, because he must be free from any necessity for rebirth. A man who can function freely in his buddhic or rational vehicle, and so drop the causal body, need never again take up the latter; but naturally this cannot be done until all the karma of the lower planes is exhausted. The Master sends out all of his forces in open curves; but any lower thought of self causes the force sent out to travel in a closed curve, so that, whether it be good or bad, it has to return to its source and the man must come back to receive it.

A man is not free from the binding results on lower planes until he is perfectly selfless on those planes. A man who when helping another feels perfectly the unity with him, obtains the result of his action on the mental plane only, and not lower down. Do not forget also that we are making karma on the astral plane, for a man can make karma wherever his consciousness is developed, or wherever he can act or choose. I have seen cases where actions done on the astral plane have borne karmic fruit in the next physical life. Another point to remember is that there is always a general karma belonging to an order or a nation, and that each individual in that order or that nation is, to a certain extent, responsible for the action of the whole. For instance, a priest has a certain responsibility for all that the collective priesthood does, even though he may not personally approve of it.

Animal Karma

Students often ask questions upon the working of karma in connection with the animal kingdom, saying that since it is scarcely conceivable that animals can have made much karma of any kind, it is difficult to account for the extreme differences to be observed in their conditions—one being well and kindly treated, while another is subjected to all kinds of brutalities, one always protected and well-fed, while another is left to starve and to fight for the bare right of living.

There are two points to be borne in mind in this connection: first, an animal often *does* make a good deal of karma; second, the well-treated animal has not always so much advantage as he appears to have, for association with man does not always improve the animal or tend to evolve it in the right direction. The sporting dog is taught by the hunter to be far more savage and brutal than it could ever become in any form of life that could come to it by nature; for the wild animal kills only to satisfy his hunger, and it is only man who introduces into animal life the wickedness of killing for the lust of destruction. However much his intelligence may be developed, it would have been far better for this unfortunate creature if he had never come into contact with humanity; for through him this group-soul *has* now made karma—karma of the most evil kind, for which other dogs which are expressions of that group-soul will have to suffer later in order that gradually the savagery may be weeded out.

The same may be said of the lap dog who is pampered by some foolish mistress so that he gradually loses all the canine virtues, and becomes an embodiment of selfishness and love of ease. In both these cases man is abusing his trust with regard to the animal kingdom, and is deliberately developing the lower instead of the higher instincts in the creatures committed to his care, thereby making bad karma himself, and leading a group-soul to make bad karma also. Man's duty towards the dog is clearly to evolve in him devotion, affection, intelligence and usefulness, and kindly but firmly to repress every manifestation of the savage and cruel side of his nature, which a brutalized humanity has for ages so sedulously fostered.

Questioners sometimes speak as though they thought that a dog or a cat receives a certain incarnation as a reward of merit. We are not as yet dealing with a separated individuality, and therefore there is for that particular animal no past in which individual karma in the ordinary sense of the word can have been generated—nothing either to merit or to receive a re-ward. When a particular block of that life of the Logos which is evolving along the line of animal incarnation which culminates in (let us say) the dog, has reached a fairly high level, the sepa-rate animals which form its manifestation down here are brought into contact with man, in order that its evolution may receive the stimulus which that contact alone can supply.

The block of elemental essence ensouling that group of dogs has as much of karma as is involved reaching the level where such association is possible; and each dog belonging to that group-soul has his share of the result. So that when people ask what an individual dog can have done to merit a life of ease or the reverse, they are allowing themselves to be deceived by the illusion of mere outward appearance, and forgetting that there is no such thing as an individual dog, except during the latter part of that final incarnation in which the definite breaking away of a fresh soul from the block has occurred.

Some of our friends do not realize that there may be such a thing as the commencement of an entirely new piece of karma. When an injury is done by A to B, they always fall back on the theory that at some previous time B must have injured A, and is now simply reaping what he has sown. That may be so in many cases, but such a chain of causation must begin somewhere, and it is quite as likely that this may be a spontaneous act of injustice on A's part, for which karma will assuredly have to repay him in the future, while B's suffering, though undeserved as far as A is concerned, is the payment for some other act or acts which he has committed in the past in connection with some one else.

If we can conceive two newly-formed egos standing side by side, absolutely primitive and karmaless, and one of them should kill the other, or, indeed, act in any way with regard to the other, a result would be produced which would be, strictly speaking, undeserved. I doubt whether any such condition ever exists, for I think that the individualized animal brings over something of karma into his first human birth.

Many animals have a sense of right and wrong, or at least a knowledge that some things ought to be done and that others ought not to be done; and they are capable of feeling ashamed when they have done what they think to be wrong. They have in many cases a power of choice; they can exercise (*or not* exercise) patience and forbearance; and where there is a power of choice there must be responsibility, and consequently karma. The savage animal becomes a savage and cruel man; the gentle and patient animal becomes a gentle and kindly man, however primitive he may be. This serious difference is clearly the consequence of karma made in the animal kingdom. Such karma must inhere in the group-soul, but must be equally distributed through it, so that when a portion breaks off as an individual, it will carry within it its share of that karma.

It may be said that this only pushes our difficulty a little farther back, for there must be a first step sometime, and we must technically consider the result of that first step as unjust.

Not necessarily. Let us suppose the first step to be a fight between two animals. The wish to kill or wound would be equally present in both; the karma of that wish would in the case of the vanquished be worked out at once by death, whereas the victor would still owe a debt which would probably be discharged later by his own death by violence. In considering the case of humanity, however, we need not indulge in any such speculations.

In the case of the ill-treatment of an animal by a man this is certain—that it cannot be the result of previous karma on the part of the particular animal, because if it were an individual capable of carrying over karma it would not have been again incarnated in animal form.

But the group-soul of which it is a part must have acquired karma, or the thing could not happen. Animals do often intentionally cause each other terrible suffering. It is reasonably certain from various considerations that the prey killed by a wild beast for food, in what may be called the natural necessary course of their lives does *not* suffer appreciably; but in the unnecessary and intentional fights which so often occur between animals— bulls, stags, dogs or cats, for example—great pain is wilfully inflicted, and that means bad karma for the group-soul, karma that must, in the future, be paid by it through some of its manifestations.

Not for one moment, however, not by one tittle, does that lessen the guilt of the human who treats the animal cruelly, or causes him to fight or inflict pain on other creatures. Most emphatically there is karma, and exceedingly heavy karma, stored up for himself by the man who thus abuses the power to help which has been placed in his hands, and in many and many a life to come he will suffer the just result of his abominable brutality.

If one takes the trouble necessary to obtain a complete grasp of such knowledge as is already available in theosophical literature on the subjects of karma and of animal reincarnation, the main principles upon which their laws work will be found clear and readily comprehensible. I fully recognize how small and general such knowledge is, and I realize that many cases are constantly occurring in which the details of the method in which the karma works itself out are entirely beyond our ken; but you may see enough to show you that what we have been taught as to the inevitability and the absolute justice of the great law is one of the fundamental truths of nature. Secure in that certainty, you can afford to wait for the more detailed comprehension until you gain those higher faculties which alone will give the power to see the working of the system as a whole.

Assuredly, as we progress, the divine light will illumine for us many corners that as yet remain in shadow, and we shall gradually but surely grow towards a perfect knowledge of the divine truth which even now is enfolding us, guarding and guiding us. All those who have had the privilege of studying these subjects under the guidance and with the help of the great Masters of the Wisdom are so fully persuaded of this that even where at present they do not see fully, they are more than willing and ready to trust to that great Power of which as yet only dim glimpses can be vouchsafed to human eye.

INDEX

A

Accident, astral plane, 195; death by, 227; saved in an, 363
Accumulated *Karma,* 361
Adept, definition of, 12; use of term, 12; future, 138
Adeptship, attainment of, 41
Adi-Buddha, 77
Advanced People, simple in habits, 119
Advantages, of travel, 110; of cremation, 231
Adyar, thought forms in, 160
Affection, double result of, 38; influence of, 255
Agrae, mysteries of, 55
Akoustikoi (hearers), 60
Alcohol, drinking, 120; effect of, 210; use of, 215; evil of, 221; regulation of, 221
Alcyone, seventeenth life of, 156; lives of, 248, 322
Ananda, disciple of Buddha, 79
Angels, 331
Animal, obsession, 234
Animals, attaining individuality, 49; domestic, 133; our duty to, 132; cruelty, 133; carnivorous, 134; in Lemuria, 134; fear of, 135; slaughter of, 135; work of Atlanteans for, 134; entering human kingdom, 182; individualized, 242
Apollonius of Tyana, 8, 14

Apophthegms of the Mysteries, 54
Appearance, of devas, 331
Arhat, 41; the, 331
Arhatship, 42
Aryasangha, 109
Asceticism, 118; meaning of, 118; of black magician, 193
Asekha, achievement of, 2; consciousness of the, 12
Astral, interpenetration, 227; conditions, 228; imprisonment, 236; slum work, 238; cognition, 242; counterparts, 243; help, 258; activity, 261; speech, 263; pleasures, 270
Astral Body, evil qualities, 114; good qualities, 114; colors in, 123; seen clairvoyantly, 122; vibrations in, 123; effect of irritation on, 124; appearance of, 176; after death, 179; during life, 174; working of senses in, 201; result of shock to, 209; effect of tobacco on, 220; senses of the, 224, 242, 314; building of, 230; of ordinary man, 252
Astral Centers, 200
Astral Consciousness, 195
Astral Life, length of, 230; *karma* during, 250; continuity of, 257-258
Astral Matter, corresponds to physical, 157; never solid, 158, 173; luminosity of, 159; attraction of physical, 172; drawn round